Counselling skill

Counselling skill

John McLeod

Open University Press

Open University Press
McGraw-Hill Education
McGraw-Hill House
Shoppenhangers Road
Maidenhead
Berkshire
England
SL6 2QL

email: enquiries@openup.co.uk
world wide web: www.openup.co.uk

and Two Penn Plaza, New York, NY 10121-2289, USA

First published 2007

A catalogue record of this book is available from the British Library

ISBN-10: 0 335 21809 1 (pb)   0 335 21810 5 (hb)
ISBN-13: 978 0 335 21809 7 (pb)   978 0 335 21810 3 (hb)

Library of Congress Cataloguing-in-Publication Data
CIP data applied for

Typeset by RefineCatch Limited, Bungay, Suffolk
Printed in Poland by OZ Graf. S.A.
www.polskabook.pl

The *McGraw-Hill* Companies

Contents

For Julia

Preface

This book is about *doing* counselling. It is about what happens in the meeting between a person who wants to talk through an issue in their life, and another person who is willing to be there to assist them to do this. It is a book about practical things: tasks and methods. It is a book that has been written primarily for people such as doctors, nurses, teachers, clergy, and those who work in social services, human resources, trade unions, community projects, the criminal justice system, advice centres and many other contexts, who are called upon by the people with whom they are dealing to give them some space to deal with pressing personal concerns.

I have found myself drawn towards wanting to write this book for two reasons. First, it seems that even though there has been a massive expansion over the past few decades in the number of counselling agencies and psychotherapy clinics that are available, it is still the case, and probably will always be the case, that the majority of episodes of counselling take place outside of these settings. For example, of the large numbers of people who report in surveys that their lives are visited by depression and hopelessness, it is likely that less than 10 per cent are receiving psychological treatment from a professional counsellor or psychotherapist, or drug treatment from a doctor. Most of these people talk to, or try to talk to, whoever is at hand in their life who seems reliable and competent. There is a great deal of counselling, therefore, that takes place in brief episodes, fitted into consultations with a doctor or nurse, or in the middle of a tutorial with a college teacher. In this book I refer to this type of counselling as *embedded*: the counselling role is embedded within other roles being fulfilled by the practitioner, and the counselling conversation is embedded within other professional tasks (teaching, nursing, career advice) that are being carried out around it. So, the first reason for tackling this book was that the topic seems socially and culturally important. I believe that it would be a good thing if teachers, nurses and other human service workers allowed themselves to respond to the emotional pain of their clients and listened to their personal stories. We live in a world characterized by an all-consuming drive towards efficiency and a bureaucratic approach to people. In this kind of world, a bit of counselling is a humanizing factor.

The second factor that has motivated me to work on this book has been my dissatisfaction with most of the books on this topic that are currently in circulation. I do not think that the existing literature on counselling skills does justice to the reality of embedded counselling. In my view, the counselling profession has sought to distance itself from this domain by its use of the terms such as 'counselling skills' and 'interpersonal skills'. This has happened, I believe, because at a time when counselling profession has struggled to become established as a recognized area of specialist knowledge, it has been in the interest of professional counsellors to emphasize that what they do is special, and can only be done by people who have received lengthy training and can see their clients for hour-long sessions, unencumbered by any complicating factors. I would argue that the battle to gain recognition for counselling as a legitimate profession and occupation has now been won, and that it is time to give some serious attention to the possibilities for doing good counselling work within the fulfilment of other professional roles. One of my worries is that the availability of specialist counsellors and psychotherapists might lead nurses, teachers, doctors and others to believe that they are not capable of responding effectively to emotional needs and personal dilemmas, and to feel that the best they can do for their clients is to refer them on to a counsellor or psychologist. This attitude is reflected in the ambivalence that is often shown towards counselling skills training on professional courses for nurses, doctors, social workers, teachers and the like.

This book challenges the concept of 'counselling skills' and suggests that this idea not only is confused and confusing, but also fails to prepare learners or trainees to deliver what people need, and instead provides them with little more than a friendly and harmless, but ineffectual, way of talking to people. An analogy can be drawn with sports coaching: if I attend a tennis class, I may acquire some skills, but these are by-products – what I really want to be able to do is *play tennis*.

It seems that embedded counselling is a harder and more complex task than is counselling that is carried out within the hourly timetable of a therapy clinic. A person who makes an appointment to see a counsellor at a clinic or agency knows that they will see the counsellor for fifty minutes each week, and will be unlikely to have any contact with the counsellor outside of that time. From the point of view of the counsellor, this is manageable: the person arrives, they talk and then they leave. Between times, the counsellor has plenty of opportunity to think and consult colleagues, about what to do next. Compare this with the situation where an emotionally upset student turns up at their teacher's office door during the morning coffee break. There are many decisions that need to be made around what can be done at that moment, and whether other moments can be found later in the day to follow up the crisis. And in fifteen minutes' time the teacher will be standing in front of another class, performing in teaching mode. This is just one of many challenging scenarios associated with a willingness to build a counselling dimension into other work roles. To be able to respond effectively in such situations requires a framework for practice that goes beyond the parameters of most mainstream counselling theory, which is predicated on an implicit private practice model. This book attempts to begin to build such a framework.

It may be helpful to comment on the way in which this book has been written. I have tried to present what I have had to say in as straightforward and direct a manner as I could, with relatively few references to sources being cited within the main body of the text. For the most part, key sources have been signalled through recommendations for further reading provided at the end of sections and chapters. I have also tried, where possible, to highlight the relevance of research studies by setting them in boxes, so that their interest value is, hopefully, heightened. I have done this because I think that many of the research studies have been written in such a way, and published in such journals, as to make them inaccessible to the majority of practitioners. These research studies can be enormously helpful in terms of understanding the skills of counselling, and I regard one of my roles as a writer as that of finding ways to 'exhibit' those studies effectively. The book includes a number of stories, some of them short case vignettes illustrating aspects of counselling, alongside a longer narrative that links together the different chapters. These stories are based on real people, but disguised and recombined so that individuals cannot be identified.

I would like to record my appreciation to the many friends and colleague whose ideas and conversations have deepened and maintained my interest in counselling: Lynne Angus, Joe Armstrong, Ronen Berger, Tim Bond, Julia Buckroyd, Siobhan Canavan, Anne Chien, Mick Cooper, Edith Cormack, Michaela Cutliffe, Robert Elliott, Stephen Goss, Anjali Goswami, Colin Kirkwood, Elke Lambers, Kate Lanka, Noreen Lillie, Mhairi Macmillan, Dave Mearns, Joanne Regan, David Rennie, Brian Rodgers, Cyndy Rodgers, Dot Weaks, William West and Sue Wheeler. As ever, my greatest debt is to my wife Julia, and my daughters Kate, Emma and Hannah, whose love and support have sustained me throughout some difficult times.

1

Introduction: what this book is about

A brief summary of what this book is about • A narrative approach • Making a space to talk it through • Learning counselling skill • A critical perspective • Conclusions • Questions for reflection and discussion • Suggestions for further reading

A brief summary of what this book is about

This section provides a brief introduction to the key ideas around which the book as a whole is organized. This is a book that is intended for people who are involved in working with people in any kind of helping, managing or facilitative role, for example in teaching, social work, the health professions, clergy, advice work, training, human resources and the justice system. Anyone who does such a job is required to be skilled in many different forms of interpersonal contact, such as communicating information, interviewing to gather information, shared decision making, and counselling. The particular form of interpersonal contact that is known as 'counselling' refers to any interaction where someone seeks to explore, understand or resolve a problematic or troubling *personal* aspect of a practical issue that is being dealt with. Counselling is what happens when a person consults someone else around a *problem in living* – a conflict or dilemma that is getting in the way, that is preventing the person from living their life in the way in which they would wish.

This book offers a framework for making sense of episodes of counselling that are *embedded* in other activities and roles. The book is about counsell*ing*, rather than about being a counsell*or*. It is intended for people who already possess professional knowledge and training in a field such as nursing or teaching, and who recognize the value of developing better strategies for responding constructively and effectively to moments when the person with whom they are working *needs to talk*. The key aim of the book is to make it clear what can be done at such moments and how to do it. It is also to be hoped that the book will be useful to 'specialist' counsellors, people who deliver counselling on a stand-alone basis, typically structured around weekly one-hour meetings with a 'client', and have no other involvement with that person outside the counselling hour, or outwith their counselling role. The value of this book for such specialist counsellors is that it seeks to explain some of the fundamental elements of their craft. However, it needs to be acknowledged that becoming an accredited professional counsellor is about more than learning practical skill: a specialist counsellor is a role that requires several years of training, and the accumulation of an extensive background knowledge.

It is taken for granted in this book that a useful counselling conversation can take place within about eight to ten minutes. This length of time represents the typical window of opportunity that a teacher, doctor or manager has to allow someone to talk through something that is troubling them. Of course, there are many situations in which longer periods of time may be available, or where sequences of separate ten-minute talks may be linked together. But is nevertheless important to recognize that a ten-minute talk can make a difference. Pressure of time should not be used an excuse for avoiding talking things through.

Throughout this book, the terms 'counsellor' and 'person' are used to refer to the one who seeks counselling (the person) and the one who offers it (the counsellor). This use of the term 'counsellor' is *not* intended to imply 'professionally qualified and accredited as a stand-alone counsellor'. Rather, it refers to someone engaged in offering an episode of counselling *at that moment*, someone who is fulfilling the function of counsellor for another person who needs to talk through a matter that is concerning them. On the whole, the term 'person' is employed in preference to 'client' because episodic or embedded counselling rarely involves the kind of formal contracting and role definition ('I am a counsellor with an office and a diploma on my wall') that would justify the use of this word. The examples that are used in this book encompass a wide spectrum of work settings, many of which do not routinely refer to people as clients. For example, users of educational institutions such as schools and colleges are rarely described as clients. However, the terms 'service user', 'patient' and 'client' are used where the context requires.

A narrative approach

This book takes a narrative approach to making sense of how counselling helps people. The idea of a narrative approach refers to a significant movement within the social and health sciences and psychology in recent years (McLeod, 1997a, b; Greenhalgh and Hurwitz, 1998). The enormous success of engineering, technology and the physical sciences in the nineteenth and twentieth centuries led to a situation in which it became commonplace to view human beings as mechanisms, as objects, machines or organisms that might break down and require fixing. It began to be clear to many people that such an attitude, while valuable in some respects, brought with it the danger of dehumanization, of eroding or even losing the essential quality of what makes us human. The concept of narrative provides a succinct and yet powerful means of reminding ourselves of our human qualities, and bringing emphasis to these qualities in our thinking and practice.

Narrative is concerned with the human capacity to tell stories. We use stories to communicate to each other the important or memorable things that happen to us on an everyday basis. Within our heads, and in our own lives, each of us lives out a story or stories, and constructs our identity and sense of self through creating a story of our life, our autobiography. Culturally, the beliefs, value and world-view of a set of people are carried through narrative, in the form of myth, scripture, literature and 'news'.

Narrative simultaneously embraces the individual and the social. Stories are told by individual persons, yet draw in some way on a stock of cultural narratives, and, once told, become a shared product that can be retold. Stories embrace consistency and change in life. Although a story that is told by a person may have a consistent structure and content, every telling is different: the performance of a story always includes some aspect of improvization, in response to a specific listener or audience. Any coherent story conveys information about an event that unfolds over time, involves intention and purpose, reveals the relationship between the protagonist or central figure of the story and other people, and communicates feeling and emotion. Stories also have an evaluative element: events are placed in a moral landscape.

A narrative approach to counselling is therefore one that takes seriously all of the dimensions of humanness (intention, relationship, temporality, feeling and morality) that are involved in a process of storytelling. More specifically, a narrative approach draws attention to the ways in which people use language and talk to construct their lives. A narrative approach to counselling is one that promotes sensitivity to the use of language on the part both of the person seeking help and of the counsellor who supplies that help. A key idea here is that some ways of talking can position the person, in relation to an issue or concern, in such a way that there can seem no possible movement forward. A different way of talking, by contrast, can open up new possibilities for feeling and action. A narrative approach also recognizes the value of the basic human process of storytelling. From such a perspective, it is possible to see that what many people want, when they seek counselling, is merely an opportunity to tell their story, and have it received and affirmed. The conditions of modern life mean that many people are walking around with stories of huge personal significance that they cannot tell because there is no one willing to listen to them. These people are therefore alone with the pain that may be woven through their story, are unable to enlist social support and solidarity from other people, and have limited opportunity to reflect on, and learn from, what has happened for them. This is where counselling fits in.

Making a space to talk it through

At the heart of any form of counselling is *making a space to talk it through*. This phrase is offered as a kind of touchstone throughout the book and operates as a reminder of what the role of counselling actually is in relation to the troubles that people experience. It is a phrase that carries a great deal of meaning, as the following analysis of its constituent parts reveals.

'*Making* a space . . .'. The idea of *making* implies that counselling is an intentional, purposeful activity. It is not something that 'just happens' – it has to be 'made'. This 'making' is an activity that is carried out by both participants, working together. The person cannot make a counselling space in the absence of the willingness and involvement of the counsellor, and vice versa. The notion of making a space also invites consideration of similar concepts, such as creating, building and constructing, all of which are valuable in terms of understanding this process: counselling can be understood as an activity that is 'co-constructed'. The use of these terms in turn introduces the question: what are the materials that are being used in this making or building process? There are several personal 'powers' or abilities that are brought into service in the making of a counselling space: attention, physical posture and proximity, language, the arrangement of seating, control of time and so on. What can be made will depend on the materials that are available in any specific situation.

'Making *a space* to talk . . .'. What is meant by 'a space' in the context of counselling? What kind of space is this? It is a space that exists both in the life of the person who wishes to talk about a problem, and in the relationship between that person and their counsellor. One of the main themes of this book is that it is important to understand people as living their lives within a personal niche that they have made for themselves within their society and culture. This niche, or personal world, can at times be hard to live in – things go wrong. Counselling is a space outside of the person's everyday life, in which they can stand back from their routine and reflect on what they might wish to do to change things to make them better. A counselling space is like a bubble, haven or place of emotional safety into which the person can step for a period of time, and to which they can return when necessary. A counselling space is also a space in the relationship between the person and the counsellor. There are many aspects to the relationship between a person and someone who takes the role of counsellor to them: making arrangements to meet (next week at the same time?), other roles, gender/age/ethnic similarity or difference, shared experiences outside of the counselling room (bumping into each other in the supermarket). However, if counselling is to happen, there needs to be a time when these other facets of the relationship fade into the background, to allow a different kind of conversation to develop. The idea of a space implies boundary: there is an edge to a space. A space is surrounded by other things, but within the space there is nothing: it is a *space*. In counselling, while various structures may be brought in from outside ('let's use this problem-solving format to work through the difficulty you are having in making a decision on your career options . . .'), the basic premise of counselling is that it starts with an empty space, where the person is offered the possibility of talking about (or not talking about) anything they like. The notion of space invites reflection on the nature of other spaces in which meaningful personal and emotional learning can take occur. There are ways in which a counselling space is similar to, as well as different from, the space that a person enters when they read a good novel, the space created on the stage of a theatre, or the space experienced when walking in the hills.

'. . . a space *to talk* it through . . .'. Counselling is in essence about talking. Putting something into words, or bringing it into language, can be a very powerful healing experience. Language incorporates an infinite number of ways of making meaning. Words, phrases and discourses reflect the meaning-making activity of multiple generations of people. There is always another way to talk about something and each way of talking is associated with a different position in relation to the topic, and a different set of things that might be done. Finding the words to say it, naming, differentiating: these accomplishments of talk bring an issue or concern into a space where it can be examined by talker and listener together. It also makes it possible for the talker to hear themselves: talking opens up possibilities for reflection. The talker can observe the impact of their words on the hearer. The shift from monologue – 'this problem has been rattling around in my head' – to dialogue dissolves isolation and social exclusion, and introduces the possibility of sharing and support. Talking invites laughter. Joining together all the separate bits of things that might be said about something, to arrive at the whole story, provides a sense of coherence.

'. . . to talk *it* through . . .'. The idea of 'it' has always been important in counselling, from the concept of the it/id in the writings of psychoanalysts such as Sigmund Freud and George Groddeck, to the formulaic way that many counsellors respond to the person they are helping by prefacing each statement they make with 'it seems that . . .'. The significance of 'it' lies in the fact that the issue or concern that a person wishes to talk about is rarely clearly defined. Usually, there is a vague sense of something being wrong, a painful feeling, a need to talk. The task of counselling typically involves activities that can be described as mapping, exploring or naming the issue, or 'getting a handle on it'. The act of finding the right words to capture the sense of 'it' can lead to a sense of relief ('*that's* what its about'). Mapping the shape and contours of 'it' opens up possibilities for what can be done about 'it'. This process can also be understood in terms of finding a *focus* for a counselling conversation.

'. . . to talk it *through* . . .'. To talk something through implies that a conversation aims to be comprehensive and thorough, encompassing all relevant aspects of an issue. It also implies the possibility of resolution, of talk that reaches a point where nothing more needs to be said. When a person is talking about a significant personal issue, there is a sense of a story unfolding. The person has the experience of being on a 'track', with an awareness of 'nextness' in their talk: there is something else to be said. This something else is rarely pre-planned on the part of the person, but instead arises from being in a situation of being given permission to talk. Talking it through also invokes a sense of movement through a landscape, to arrive at another place.

The idea of 'making a space to talk it through' defines the central purpose of counselling: this is what counselling is in essence about. It represents an understanding of counselling that places an emphasis on the existence of a relationship within which such a space can be created, and the role of language, storytelling and conversation as the medium through which two people can work together to make a difference.

Learning counselling skill

The material included in this book has been used to support the teaching of counselling courses at certificate (introductory) and diploma (advanced) levels. In many ways, this book should be regarded as something akin to a map of the territory covered by a training course. It may be useful, therefore, to give some consideration to what is involved in developing skill in counselling. There are many counselling training courses available and an extensive literature around models of training and on research into training. There are also codes of practice published by professional associations that recommended standards for training programmes. The general consensus is that there are four main areas that should be addressed in this kind of training. First, any person offering a counselling relationship to others should possess an ability to make sense of what they are doing, in the form of a model or theoretical framework. Second, training should involve an extensive period of reflective practice, in which the person develops methods and strategies for face-to-face work. This 'skill' training characteristically involves observing expert counsellors (live or on video), practising methods with and on other members of a training group, and possibly recording and discussing real counselling sessions with people seeking help. Third, training in counselling requires the development of self-awareness. If effective counselling depends on the quality of the relationship between person and counsellor, then it is essential that the counsellor has an understanding of what they bring to that relationship in terms of their own relationship needs and patterns, and their capacity to respond constructively to the type of relationship that is preferred by the person seeking their help. On training courses, the development of self-awareness is typically facilitated through such activities as: reflective group discussion; workshops on difficult relationship issues such as sexuality, difference and control; the experience of being a user or client of counselling; and keeping a personal learning journal. Finally, training courses need to cover professional and ethical issues, such as maintaining confidentiality and using supervision or consultative support.

It is important to be clear that what this book offers is a framework for understanding the skill of counselling, and not the skill itself. Becoming skilful in a counselling role is something that comes about through working with a group of people over a period of time, in a setting that encourages honest support and challenge. While counselling courses are generally experienced by participants as personally rewarding and valuable, this kind of learning can be uncomfortable at times, for example, when other members of a learning group point out one's avoidance and self-protection strategies in interpersonal situations. There is little point engaging in such training unless one is ready to offer a commitment to this type of personal learning.

A critical perspective

This book encourages the adoption of a critical perspective. Issues such as the role of counselling skill in helping people, and the value of different ways of thinking about counselling skill, need to be approached with a questioning and sceptical frame of mind. The idea of a critical perspective is not intended to imply a relentlessly destructive analysis of ideas and practices, in which nothing ends up being good enough. An essential part of a balanced critical approach involves the appreciation and celebration of good practice.

A critical perspective is particularly important in relation to four of the main themes that run through this book:

- *Arguing for the essential value of a personal dimension to relationships between professional helpers and their 'clients'.* We live in a culture in which the activities of practitioners in occupations such as nursing, medicine and teaching are increasingly defined by technical and bureaucratic procedures, leaving little opportunity to listen to the stories and personal experiences of patients, clients and students. A counselling approach represents a challenge to these procedures, by embodying a set of values that runs against the prevailing ethos. It also represents a challenge to individual practitioners.
- *Questioning some of the assumptions that underpin current models of counselling skills.* It is argued in this book that many of the ideas that comprise widely taught models of counselling skills, which reduce the counselling relationship to a set of interpersonal skills, are open to question. For example, it is suggested that the notion of counselling skills is too focused on what the helper does and, as a result, is not sufficiently attuned to what the person/client might need, and that most counselling skills models do not give enough attention to the significance of the relationship between person and counsellor.
- *Questioning the usefulness of the distinction between 'counselling' and 'counselling skills'.* It is argued that the sharp differentiation that is made between the use of counselling skills by practitioners such as nurses and the provision of counselling by independent professional therapists, exists more to serve the interest of the counselling profession than to meet the needs of service users. In this book, the notions of *embedded counselling* and *microcounselling* are introduced as concepts that transcend the old counselling versus counselling skills debate.
- *Emphasizing the role of research and inquiry.* We live in a world of increasing complexity, where the delivery of caring and helping services is influenced by a wide range of technological, cultural and organizational factors. In this context, it is important for any activity or intervention that is undertaken by practitioners to be backed up by appropriate research and inquiry, including research into the experiences, views and preferences of service users. Little research has been carried out on the kind of brief, episodic, embedded counselling that is described within this book. Many of the research studies that have been carried out are described in the book. These studies illustrate the great potential of research for contributing to better understanding and more effective practice in this area of work.

These critical themes are intended to invite reflection on the part of readers about what is involved in creating safe spaces where counselling can occur, and promoting dialogue in wider professional communities about how such moments fit into the flow of other work. The idea is to *problematize* counselling skill. It is only by continuing to think about what is involved in offering this kind of relationship that its value can be kept alive. Counselling that is routinized, or based on ideas that lack resonance and meaning, inevitably fails to engage people.

Conclusions

This introductory chapter has highlighted some of the ideas that thread their way through the book as a whole and are explored in more detail later on. The remaining chapters can be divided into three broad sections. Chapters 2 and 3 examine some basic concepts, beginning with the idea of 'counselling' itself, and then moving in Chapter 4 to an outline of a model of counselling skill. Chapters 5 to 10 break down that model into its various parts and discuss how counselling skill can be applied in practice. Finally, Chapters 11 and 12 stand back from the specifics of actual counselling and consider some broader issues that need to be taken into account in relation to maintaining good practice over a period of time.

Questions for reflection and discussion

1. How important are stories in your own life? Reflect on your relationships with those closest to you. What are the opportunities within these relationships for regularly updating these other people with respect to your story of what has been happening for you on a day-to-day basis (and being updated by them)? How do you react when these opportunities are curtailed in some way? What stories do you 'consume' (for example, from novels, TV soaps and such like)? What significance do these fictional stories have in your life? What would life be like for you if you were denied access to these consumed stories?
2. What assumptions about counselling do you bring to your reading of this book? What are your images of counselling? What is your own critical stance in relation to counselling – what do you believe, at this point, is beneficial or good about counselling, and where are your points of scepticism and reservation?

Suggestions for further reading

There has been little critical debate around the development of counselling skills training and the models that inform it. A powerful chapter by Deborah Cameron in an edited volume by Robb *et al.* argues that current models of communication skills and interpersonal skills have been developed without sufficient attention to the ways in which people in organizations actually relate to each other. (Other chapters in the book present a variety of critical perspectives and are well worth reading.)

Cameron, D. (2004) Communication culture: issues for health and social care. In M. Robb, S. Barrett, C. Komaromy and A. Rogers (eds) *Communication, Relationships and Care: A Reader.* London: Routledge.

There is a huge and ever-expanding literature on the relevance of narrative approaches in health, social care and other fields. Particularly recommended are:

Angus, L. and McLeod, J. (eds) (2004) *The Handbook of Narrative and Psychotherapy: Practice, Theory and Research*. Thousand Oaks, CA: Sage.

Greenhalgh, T. and Hurwitz, B. (eds) (1998) *Narrative-based Medicine: Dialogue and Discourse in Clinical Practice*. London: BMJ Publications.

McLeod, J. (1997) Listening to stories about health and illness: applying the lessons of narrative psychology. In I. Horton *et al.* (eds) *Counselling and Psychology for Health Professionals*. London: Sage.

2

Defining counselling

'See that leaflet that I got from that cancer nurse?'
'Yes.'
'It says she does counselling'
'Counselling? What do you mean?'
'Says here it's about "giving the patient a safe space for talking things through".'
'What sort of things?'
'Says here it's like anything that's bothering you. Like worries.'
'Do you mean, like if you were mental?'
'I don't know?'
'Are you interested then?'
'I don't know. I might be.'

Introduction

The concept of counselling is understood by different people in different ways. It is a concept whose meaning is widely contested. As a result of these competing perspectives, it is difficult to arrive at a single definition of the term that could satisfy everyone. One of the reasons for the complex web of meanings that surround the term 'counselling' is that the activity of counselling has changed and evolved over the years in response to shifting expectations around the kinds of relationships that can take place between people. Another reason for the multifaceted nature of the term is that it refers both to an ordinary, everyday activity and to a professionalized, specialist role. In this respect, the concept of counselling is similar to concepts such as nursing or teaching. All of us are capable, in appropriate circumstances, of nursing or teaching other people. However, at the same time we can acknowledge and respect the special training and expertise possessed by qualified nurses and teachers. In similar fashion, counselling is an activity in which we can all engage, and also a professional role that that requires advanced training and expertise. It is important for anyone who is involved in learning about counselling or providing counselling to be willing to give some attention to the contested meaning of the notion of counselling in order to be able to respond constructively to the kind of confusion and misapprehension that can often occur when talking about counselling with different groups of people.

The concept of 'giving counsel' has a long history. Someone who gives counsel is an independent source of opinion, skill and knowledge, who acts solely on behalf of an individual, to help that individual arrive at the decision or course of action that best fits their personal goals and purposes. Traditionally, the function of giving counsel was restricted to specialist roles within the ruling or dominant social classes within society, for example, legal counsel or counsellors to a monarch. In contemporary society, where almost everyone is faced with difficult life choices, the need for 'counsel' is much more widespread. The role of 'counsellor' has therefore become an integral part of everyday life in modern societies. From the middle of the twentieth century, pro-fessional organizations and training courses began to emerge to qualify people to become full-time counsellors in fields such as education, health and business. At the same time, it began to be recognized that the work function of anyone working in the 'helping' or 'people' professions – nurses, doctors, social workers, personnel officers, teachers and so on – inevitably included some degree of 'counselling' of clients or patients. 'Counselling' then came to be seen as an activity that was embedded, to a greater or lesser extent, in all kinds of human service work, as well as constituting a specialist role with status as an autonomous profession.

All this has taken place in a remarkably short period of time. One way of making sense of the role of culture and society in shaping what we understand as counselling is to imagine what society was like fifty years, one-hundred years and two-hundred years ago. Even fifty years ago there were very few counsellors of any description. One-hundred years ago there were no counsellors, although a few people might have a vague idea of something called 'psychotherapy'. Two-hundred years ago the idea of counselling, or even psychotherapy, would have been quite alien. The demand for counselling has grown as culture and society have become more complex and global-ized. Individuals are saturated with information, detached from traditional sources of meaning, sensitive to risk and lacking in certainty. From a social and historical per-spective, counselling can be understood as a necessary element of the business of main-taining a coherent identity and set of relationships within fragmented and complex industrialized societies. Counselling offers a way of holding a life together.

The aim of this chapter is to clear the ground for what follows by providing an framework for making sense of the multiple uses of the term 'counselling' in con-temporary society. As a means of anchoring the discussion, a user-oriented definition of counselling is offered. The sections which follow explore the different ways that counselling has been understood, with a particular focus on debates around the distinction between 'counselling' and 'counselling skills'.

A definition of counselling

The position taken in this book is that the starting point for a definition of counselling needs to be the perspective of the person who receives or makes use of counselling. The reason for this is that one of the essential elements of any type of counselling is that it can only happen if the person seeking help wants it to happen. Counselling is not something *done to* one person by someone else; counselling is an interaction between two people. Counselling can therefore be defined as 'an activity that takes place when someone who is troubled *invites* and allows another person to enter into a particular kind of relationship with them'. If a person is not ready to extend this invitation, then even though they may be exposed to the best efforts of expert counsellors for long periods of time, what happens will not be counselling. Any episode of counselling therefore begins with the wish or intention of the person seeking help, the 'client'.

A more complete definition of counselling can be summarized in the following terms. Counselling is an activity which takes place when someone who is troubled invites and allows another person to enter into a particular kind of relationship with them. This invitation can be explicit (for example, when someone makes an appointment to see a counsellor, or asks a nurse 'Would it be OK if I took a few minutes to talk about how I feel about . . .?'), or may be implicit (for example, when a person exhibits a signs of emotional distress or confusion).

A person seeks such a relationship when they encountered a 'problem in living' that they have not been able to resolve through their everyday resources and has resulted in their exclusion from some aspect of full participation in social life. The person seeking counselling is looking for the person to provide them with time and space characterized by the presence of a number of elements that may not be readily available in the person's everyday life: permission to speak, respect for difference, trustworthiness and affirmation.

- *Permission to speak.* This is a place where the person can tell their story, where they are given every encouragement to give voice to aspects of their experience that have previously been silenced, in their own time and their own way, including the expression of feeling and emotion.
- *Respect for difference.* The counsellor sets aside, as far as they are able, both their own position on the issues brought by the client and their own needs in the moment, in order to focus as completely as possible on helping the client to articulate and act on his or her personal values and desires.
- *Trustworthiness.* Whatever is discussed is confidential and will be treated with care and respect. The counsellor undertakes to refrain from passing on what they have learned from the person to any others in the person's life.

- *Affirmation.* The counsellor enacts a relationship that is an expression of a set of core values: honesty, integrity, care, belief in the worth and value of individual persons, commitment to dialogue and collaboration, reflexivity, the interdependence of persons, a sense of the common good.

When these elements are in place, an arena is constructed in which support, sharing, reflection and learning can take place. Within this arena, the client and counsellor make use of whatever resources they have (ways of talking, ideas and theories, problem-solving strategies, rituals, altered states of consciousness) to arrive at an enhanced degree of understanding and resolution in relation to the initial problem in living that initiated the decision to seek counselling.

In essence, counselling is a *conversation* in which silenced voices can be expressed, where what needs to be said is said. It is a conversation through which a person can begin to shift from rehearsing over and over again a self-contained monologue of their worries and concerns, or from being locked into emotional knots, to entering into a dialogue with another person. It is through dialogue that other viewpoints and ideas can be taken on board. Whatever the problem in living is that is being faced by a person, there will be someone or some group of people who have developed effective strategies for dealing with it. Conversation and dialogue opens possibilities for making connection with the people or groups who possess this knowledge.

The potential outcomes of counselling can be understood as falling into three broad categories:

- *Resolution of the original problem in living.* Resolution can include: achieving an understanding or perspective on the problem; arriving at a personal acceptance of the problem or dilemma; and taking action to change the situation in which the problem arose. Basically, through counselling the person is able to repair the relationship or pattern of activity that has broken down and to restore a previously satisfying state.
- *Learning.* Counselling may enable the person to acquire new understandings, skills and strategies that make them better able to handle similar problems in future. The person may also learn more about who they are, as a person, or who they want to be – possessing a coherent sense of personal identity can provide the person with a secure base from which to relate more effectively with others.
- *Social engagement and inclusion.* Counselling has the potential to stimulate the energy and capacity of the person as someone who can contribute to the well-being of others and the social good. From being preoccupied with their own personal difficulties, the person is better able to engage more fully in social life as an active participant – they can make their voice heard.

Most of the time, the effect of counselling is to *make a difference* to the person, in the sense of enabling them to move forward in their life. In their most extreme form, these outcomes can be experienced as a *transformation* in the person's sense of self and relationships with others.

By being grounded in a user perspective, this definition of counselling offers a framework that can be used to make sense of the many contrasting types of counselling practice to be found within contemporary society. An example of how this definition can be applied in practice is provided in Box 2.1. Some of the confusion that has existed around the meaning of counselling arises from the fact that counselling always takes place in a social and cultural context, with aspects of the environment shaping and influencing the way that counselling is delivered. The following section examines the role of organizational settings in determining the type of counselling that people receive.

Where counselling takes place: the significance of context

One way to grasp the diverse meanings of counselling is to consider how it has been understood in relation to the various contexts within which counselling is delivered. This section, therefore, explores the question of where counselling takes place. Within any major urban area, a survey of the sites where some kind of activity that could be broadly understood as 'counselling' took place would reveal at least five different types of setting:

- *Private practice.* Some counsellors advertise their services in yellow pages, websites and professional directories, and directly charge a fee to clients. On the whole, these are highly qualified and experienced practitioners. Individuals consult private practice counsellors for help with a wide range of problems. Private practice counselling is largely restricted to those who have sufficient income to pay for it, although there are some charities that will support clients and many counsellors operate a sliding scale of fees. Many private practices are run by solo practitioners, with some partnership and co-operative arrangements. While private practice counselling is in principle highly accessible (the potential client merely needs to phone up and make an appointment), in reality many people are deterred by the potential cost of the service, and may find it hard to make informed choices on the basis of the somewhat confusing and partial information that is available to them concerning the practitioners working in their area. A small but growing sector of private practice counselling is delivered online (Goss and Antony, 2003).
- *Generic voluntary sector counselling agencies.* In most cities there exist counselling agencies that are open to clients with any problems and operate on a charitable or not-for-profit basis. The counsellors working in these agencies may be volunteers or may be paid at sub-professional rates. Many of these agencies began life as church-based projects, and may continue to receive some support from church groups or are linked to mental health charities. Clients are typically asked to make a donation or to pay a fee. Of all the forms of counselling that are on offer, these agencies are probably the most accessible and least stigmatizing. Many of them are located in inner-city offices, where a prospective client can walk in and make an appointment. Because they may be dealing with large numbers of users each year, such agencies tend to be known within a city and may enjoy a good word-of-mouth reputation. On the other

---

Box 2.1   The Hawthorne study and the development of counselling in the workplace

Probably everyone who has studied psychology at any level will have heard of the Hawthorne study. This was a famous psychological experiment, carried out in the Western Electric company in the USA in the 1950s, in which a group of women who assembled electrical equipment were subjected to different working conditions and arrangements, in order to determine the factors associated with increased productivity. To their great surprise, the researchers found that *all* of the interventions they introduced had the effect of increasing productivity. This result seemed to show that being the subject of attention could be sufficient in itself to bring about behaviour change. What is less well known is that the senior managers of Western Electric were so intrigued by these results that they initiated a system of counselling for workers, which involved counsellors being available at all times on the factory floor, to be on hand whenever an employee might wish to talk about a problem. This initiative appeared to have a highly positive impact on morale and productivity (Dickson and Roethlisberger, 1966), although it was clearly expensive to implement. One of the challenges for the company was that it needed to recruit and train a large number of counsellors at a time when the counselling profession in the USA was in its infancy and few training courses existed. The company took a pragmatic, business-like approach to the task of training counsellors, which included writing a job description specifying what they wanted these people to do. What they came up with can still be regarded as capturing something of the essence of what counselling is about:

1. Listen – don't talk.
2. Never argue; never give advice.
3. Listen to:
    (a) what the person wants to say;
    (b) what they do not want to say;
    (c) what they cannot say without help.
4. Become sensitive to the expression of feelings. Learn to recognize and reflect them.
5. Help the person to clarify and accept their own feelings. Do this by summarizing from time to time what has been said (for example, 'Is this the way you are feeling?'). Always do this with great caution, that is, clarify, but do not add or twist.
6. Help the person to make their own decisions; do not make decisions for them.
7. Try to understand the person from their own point of view; do not put yourself in their shoes. Put them in their own shoes.
8. Never forget that you are involved in the situations you are observing. Learn to recognize and accept your own feelings. Don't try to escape from them; learn to accept them and deal with them through skill and understanding.
    (a) Take it easy.
    (b) Stay loose.
    (c) Be flexible.
    (d) Internalize these role prescriptions so that they become congruent with yourself. Don't be a copy cat. Be true to yourself.
    (e) Be natural.

Source: Adapted from Dickson and Roethlisberger, 1966: 42.

hand, some people may assume that voluntary means unprofessional, low quality or less expertise. These perceptions are not founded in reality because the majority of voluntary agencies employ well-established systems for counsellor selection, training and supervision, and quality control.

- *Counselling delivered within the context of specific roles within the mental health system.* Counselling within the healthcare system is provided by clinical psychologists, psychotherapists, counselling psychologists, nurse therapists, art therapists and primary care counsellors. Each of these roles is associated with slightly different training requirements and responsibilities, but all are involved in offering counselling. On the whole, these practitioners are perceived as possessing high levels of expertise and status, and will see clients reporting a broad range of problems. These are also probably the least accessible of all counsellors, because usually a client will need to be referred by a general practitioner (GP) or other health professional – self-referral is unusual. In addition, there are often long waiting lists, particularly to see a clinical psychologist or a psychotherapist. Since these counsellors operate within the mental health system, the counselling may involve some form of diagnostic assessment (although primary care counsellors have tended to be resistant to this practice).

- *Specialist areas of practice.* There are many counselling agencies and services that specialize in specific types of problem (for example, drugs, alcohol, eating disorders), or in working with people at particular points in the life course (for example, at university, in the workplace, at the point of marital breakdown, after a bereavement). Some of these agencies may have charitable/voluntary status, some are funded by the health or social services, and some (such as workplace counselling services) are commercially operated. The characteristics of specialist agencies are therefore similar to those of voluntary, health service or private practice providers, but with the added factor that they need to incorporate specific knowledge of the problem area into their counselling practice. For example, a student counsellor needs to possess knowledge about higher education, adolescent development issues and study skills, in addition to a knowledge of counselling, and to be able to integrate this knowledge into their practice.

- *Counselling embedded within other helping roles.* Despite the existence of all the different counselling agencies discussed above, it is almost certainly the case that the majority of counselling that is offered to people takes place in the context of other helping roles (for example, as teacher, nurse, doctor, social worker, advice worker). For someone who already has a good relationship with their teacher, nurse or social worker, it is a very natural desire to wish to talk to them when a personal issue emerges. It is also unlikely that the teacher, nurse or social worker will have ready access to a counselling or psychotherapy service, and be able to make a referral to a colleague with more training and expertise in counselling. Some nurses and other helpers lack confidence in responding to counselling requests, and will do their best to deflect the person from this pathway. Most professional helpers, however, will do their best to respond to what the person needs and will engage in a counselling conversation to the best of their ability. This form of counselling is, of course, highly accessible, because it is provided by people with whom the person already enjoys contact.

Reflecting on the similarities and differences between the different ways that counselling is delivered reveals a number of important issues. First, with the exception of private practice counselling, all forms of counselling need to take account of organizational factors and other knowledge domains. For example, counsellors working within the health service need to develop strategies for coping with the dominance of the medical model and with resource constraints (waiting lists, limits on the number of sessions that can be offered). Counsellors working within a specialist-focus service, such as a drugs agency, need to know about drug effects, laws and policies, and the roles of other local agencies with which clients might be involved. Second, there are major differences in the extent to which the person's problems are contextualized (understood in terms of a set of specific life circumstances) or decontextualized (understood in terms of individual psychological symptoms). A private practice or health service counsellor has little scope for learning about the specific world in which their client lives, whereas some specialist-focus counsellors, and all embedded nurse counsellors or teacher counsellors have opportunities to see something of the everyday world of the person they are helping, and how that person behaves in that world. Third, services differ a great deal in terms of how accessible they are for people. Within a community, there may be some highly trained, gifted counsellors, but the majority of people who need help will not know that these people exist or how to find them. What this means is that the practical value of advanced expertise may be limited, in terms of its impact on the wider population, while the practical value of a more basic degree of skill may be enhanced because people can tap into it when they need it, and because they have less fear of being labelled or stigmatized as mentally ill. Fourth, there are challenges to confidentiality and trustworthiness in all counselling settings. A client in private practice counselling may find it difficult to know much about the accountability and integrity of their counsellor. A client being seen by a health service counsellor may be reassured by published complaints procedures, but be concerned about the possibility of personal information being recorded in medical files. In either of these settings, the person seeking help will have little or no opportunity to size up the personal integrity of the counsellor in advance of their first session together. By contrast, a person talking to a social worker or nurse may have had plenty of opportunity to make up their mind about how trustworthy that person appears to be.

The key point here is that there is no such thing as an ideal or perfect counselling setting, which is free of influence from outside factors and challenges: it is always essential to take contextual factors into account.

The idea of embedded counselling

This book is mainly concerned with the aim of making sense of counselling that takes place in situations where the helper is not a specialist professional counsellor or psychotherapist, but may be a doctor, nurse, teacher, social worker or in some other work role where counselling is not the primary focus of their job. The concept of *embedded counselling* is used throughout the book to refer to situations where the provision of counselling is incorporated within other roles and tasks.

Box 2.2   Embedded counselling in action: taking advantage of windows of opportunity

Expert practitioners of medicine, nursing and other professionals are able to incorporate powerful moments of counselling within their work with clients or patients. In a study carried out by Branch and Mailk (1993), video recordings were made of twenty doctor–patient consultations conducted by experienced and highly regarded physicians. The length of these consultations ranged from twelve to twenty minutes. Within this series of doctor–patient clinical interviews, the researchers were able to identify five episodes in which patients discussed their concerns about personal, emotional and family issues. These 'windows of opportunity' lasted for between three and seven minutes each. Typically, the doctor would begin the interview by addressing current medical issues. After a few minutes, the doctor would ask an open question, such as 'anything more going on?' or 'what else?' The patient's response to this question would be accompanied by what the researchers described as a 'change of pace' on the part of the doctor: the doctor would listen, speak more slowly and softly, be silent, lean forward. These physicians were skilled in ending these counselling episodes, which they did by expressing understanding, empathically summarizing key themes and making suggestions for further action (for example, making a referral to a specialist counsellor).

Although these doctors did not use a counselling approach throughout their interviews with patients, they were able to do so within the context of focused micro-episodes. Branch and Malik (1993: 1668) concluded that 'the patients seemed satisfied that they had adequately expressed themselves. We think that seasoned clinicians have learned through practice to employ brief but intense windows of opportunity to deal with their patients' concerns, and yet to remain time-efficient.'

This study provides evidence for the potential value of brief counselling conversations that are embedded within other practitioner relationships. It also illustrates the relative infrequency of such encounters – even in this group of expert physicians, such encounters took place in only 25 per cent of consultations, despite psychosocial issues being brought up by patients in the majority of these meetings.

It is important to be clear about the implications of the concept of embedded counselling. First, it views counselling is an *activity* or *process* which can take place in many situations, rather than as a specialist professional role. In other words, counselling is not regarded as 'what counsellors do' but as something that 'everyone should be able to do'. Second, when talking about embedded counselling, the term 'counsellor' is used to refer to the person who provides counselling, even if the counselling they offer comprises a brief conversation of only a few minutes, within a 'window of opportunity' that arises during involvement in other helping, caring or clinical activities (see Box 2.2). While it may be strictly more accurate to use terms such as 'nurse counsellor' or 'teacher responding in a counselling role', such usages are clumsy. Throughout this book, when brief case examples are given, it is always made clear that the counselling being offered is embedded within another primary occupational role.

An essential aspect of embedded counselling is that it emphasizes the needs and goals of the person seeking counselling. From that person's perspective, what they want or need is to talk to someone about an issue that is troubling them. Most of the counselling that people receive does not, in fact, come from specialist counsellors, but from people such as nurses, community workers, clergy and members of many other professional groups, who combine moments or episodes of counselling with other tasks that they perform. If effective and useful counselling is to be made available, it would seem to be essential to develop a framework for understanding counselling skill that addresses the co-existence of the activity alongside other work roles. The provision of embedded counselling is a challenge for those working in professions such as nursing, medicine and teaching because it requires a high level of responsiveness to the needs of service users, and a high level of skill in being able to switch back and forth between primary tasks, such as delivering health care, and counselling tasks, such as working through emotions and relationship issues.

It is essential to acknowledge that there are important differences between counselling that is embedded in other activities and professional or specialist counselling or psychotherapy where counselling is the sole aim. For example, a full-time counsellor can sit in their office and see clients who have made a conscious commitment to be there, will leave at the end of the hour and return the following week (usually) and who are not expecting the counsellor to do anything else but counsel. None of these conditions apply in the case of teachers, social workers and health professionals doing counselling. Embedded and specialist counselling are each associated with distinctive advantages, disadvantages, challenges and opportunities. For example, in embedded counselling the person is starting from a position of trust in the helper, rather than having to develop a relationship of trust, and the broad outline of their life story and family circumstances may already be known to the helper, rather than need to be explained. For these reasons, an embedded counsellor may be able to move much more quickly and confidently to exploration of core issues, compared with a specialist counsellor who is a stranger to the person. On the other hand, a specialist counsellor who has no other contact with the person may be better placed to establish and unequivocal confidentiality boundary, and will almost certainly be able to talk with the person for more extended periods of time.

Microcounselling: making a difference in a short space of time

A basic assumption that underpins the approach taken in this book is that helpful and effective counselling episodes can take place within brief time periods. This is an idea that is hard for many specialist counsellors and psychotherapists to accept. Training in specialist counselling and psychotherapy is generally organized around the belief that therapy requires one-hour (or fifty-minute) sessions, and that for the majority of people who seek help a significant number of such meetings will be required. There is no doubt that extended counselling, which takes place over months or years, can be helpful to people. However, there is also strong evidence that brief counselling conversations, and single meetings, can be helpful too. Not everyone who is trying to cope with a distressing problem wishes or is in a position to commit themselves to regular sessions with a counsellor or psychotherapist, even if they are convinced that such a course of action would be effective. Other people find that a single conversation is sufficient to put them on the right track in terms of seeing what they need to do to sort out their current difficulties.

The study by Branch and Mailk (1993) described in Box 2.2 provides an example of the kind of valuable counselling process that can occur within brief (ten- or twenty-minute) health consultations. An important book by Moshe Talmon (1990) demonstrates that, even in situations where people with emotional and relationship difficulties are offered long-term therapy, around 30 per cent of them do not return after the first session because they feel that they have got what they need from that single meeting. Talmon, working in clinics in the USA and Israel, carried out follow-up interviews with clients who did not return after a single therapy session. He found that the majority of these individuals reported that talking about their problem to someone who was external to their life situation helped them to identify the pivotal choice points and become empowered to use the resources that were available to them (such as friends and family members) to go back home and implement desired changes. On the basis of his research, Talmon has drawn up a set of useful guidelines for enhancing the impact of single-session counselling encounters. In a controlled study of the role of brief counselling with people suffering from depression, the British psychologists Michael Barkham and David Shapiro found that two counselling meetings, with a planned follow-up meeting a few months later, proved to be just as effective as long-term therapy for many clients (Barkham, 1989; Barkham and Shapiro, 1989, 1990).

The term 'microcounselling' refers to brief, one-off counselling sessions where the aim is to enable the person to talk through an issue or engage in a counselling task without any expectation that there will necessarily be any further sessions. Micro-counselling can be understood as a kind of self-contained counselling episode. For practitioners whose counselling function is embedded in another role, such as that of nurse or physician, there may of course be many future meetings with the person who is seeking help, and further opportunities to return to emotional and interpersonal issues that call for a counselling response. However, because of pressure of other professional tasks, such a practitioner is unlikely to be in a position to plan for further counselling meetings or to initiate an ongoing or formal counselling 'contract'. The best they can do, most of the time, is to be ready to respond to the person's counselling needs as and when these are expressed.

Counselling is not the same as other, apparently similar activities

Any definition of counselling opens up the question of the similarities and differences between counselling and other activities that fulfil the same kind of purpose. The activity that overlaps most with counselling is *psychotherapy*. Many papers and books, and much debate, has been devoted to arguing the differences between counselling and psychotherapy, or whether there are indeed any differences. Most commentators would agree that there is a high degree of similarity between these two practices in terms of the types of problems that are dealt with, the theories and methods that are used, and the type of training that is required. Sometimes, the difference between the two is organizational – for instance, services for college students are called student *counselling*, whereas health service provision for young people is more likely to be called *psychotherapy*. Sometimes the difference is due to culture and language – for example, in many European countries the term 'psychotherapy' is used to refer to services that would be described in the USA, Canada or Britain as 'counselling'. In addition, there are some distinguishing features between counselling and psychotherapy that most (but not all) observers would agree on: (i) psychotherapy is generally longer term – certainly it would be unusual to describe a brief, one-off conversation as 'psychotherapy'; (ii) psychotherapy training tends to be more extensive than counselling training; (iii) counselling is often a response to life events and transitions (for example, bereavement), whereas many psychotherapists are more interested in 'deeper' psychological problems, such as depression, and (iv) users tend to see 'counselling' as less threatening and stigmatizing than 'psychotherapy', which may hold connotations of mental illness.

Despite these contrasts, the convergence of counselling and psychotherapy in the minds of many practitioners and members of the public is an undeniable fact. Many people use the term 'therapy' to refer to both activities. Some practitioners use the term 'therapeutic counselling' to imply a fusion of the two traditions.

There are a number of occupational terms that can be confused with counselling. Clinical psychologists, arts therapists, psychiatric/mental health nurses, psychiatrists, psychiatric social workers, spiritual directors and life coaches may be trained in counselling, and may offer counselling within their work roles. However, each of these job titles covers other activities in addition to counselling. For example, a clinical psychologist might be expected to carry out research, psychological assessments, supervision and training, in addition to counselling or psychotherapy.

There are some activities that are mistakenly equated with counselling. In the past, within some organizations, 'counselling' has been used to describe a disciplinary interview, where a student or employee is sent to see a manager or supervisor to receive admonishment for wrong doing. This usage of the term, which is in decline, does not correspond at all with the meaning of counselling used in this book. Other activities that are popularly confused with counselling are *advice giving* and *guidance*. Counselling is not about giving advice. Rather, counselling is about working collaboratively with a person to understand and resolve issues: it is a process that depends on the active involvement with the person, rather than viewing the person as a passive recipient of information or guidance. Advice and guidance are valuable activities in their own right, but they are not counselling. For example, a student leaving university may be uncertain about the best choice of career. He consults various tutors, guidance workers and websites, and assembles a large amount of information and advice. At this point, he may find it useful to meet with a career counsellor to talk through his appraisal of the guidance he has received, and arrive at a choice that is best for him in the context of his goals for his life as a whole. In this case, the counsellor is working with advice, but as a listener and facilitator, rather than primarily as an advisor.

Other activities that may mistakenly be considered as forms of counselling include hypnotherapy, persuasive/influencing interventions, such as some forms of religious 'counselling', and highly structured programmes (for example, stress management, exercise or diet regimes). While each of these activities may be quite effective in helping people to deal with troubling problems, they do not embrace essential elements of counselling, such as the importance of the relationship, the emphasis on client control and choice in the process, and a commitment to client-defined outcomes. It is therefore confusing to regard these interventions as forms of counselling.

A final area of activity around which there has been some debate concerns the nature of *counselling skills* and a *counselling approach*. The idea of a counselling approach refers to the application in work situations of values and attitudes from counselling, such as believing in the worth of the individual, and in the person's capacity to develop and grow. The idea of counselling skills has been used to refer to the use of counselling methods in non-counselling roles, such as nursing or teaching. The implication has been that 'counselling' or being a 'counsellor' is fundamentally different from being a 'user of counselling skills'. The question of the distinction between counselling skills and counselling is central to the approach taken in this book, and is therefore addressed in some detail in the following sections.

Counselling as a specialist professional role

There has been a powerful movement in the direction of the professionalization of counselling. One of the consequences of professionalization is that there has been a tendency in recent years to regard counselling as 'something that is done by professional counsellors', with any counselling-type activity that is carried out by anyone else (for example nurses and teachers) to be defined as the use of *counselling skills*, or informed by a *counselling approach*. The distinction between *counselling* and *counselling skills* has become embodied in the professional statutes of organizations such as the British Association for Counselling and Psychotherapy, and is widely reflected in the titles of training courses. Despite the widespread acceptance of the counselling/ counselling skills distinction, there are some significant problems associated with this formulation:

- Comparison of recordings of a 'counsellor' working with a client and of a nurse using 'counselling skills' with a patient will often show that the same helping and learning process is taking place in both cases.
- The central activity of counselling – a relationship within which problems in living are understood and resolved – can occur in a wide variety of settings. From the point of view of the person seeking help, episodes of 'counselling' may take place in many different relationships.
- The concept of 'counselling skills' reflects an attempt by the counselling professional to appropriate activities that are better understood as basic human competences and which are used for many different purposes – there is nothing unique to counselling about 'active listening' or 'summarizing'.

- An emphasis on 'using counselling skills' highlights the practical or behavioural dimension of counselling and can lead to a lack of attention to the relational and moral dimensions of counselling.

Within the counselling profession, the argument that counselling can be carried out only by qualified counsellors and that anyone else involved in a counselling role is deemed as using 'counselling skills', has been a necessary and important strategy within the struggle for official state recognition of counselling as an occupation. It is also a position that supports the safety of users of counselling services, by seeking to ensure that counselling is delivered by people who have been properly trained, in settings where there is a strong boundary of confidentiality and an absence of role conflict. The counselling versus counselling skills dichotomy served the profession well at a time when the main priority was to establish counselling as a valued and legitimate activity within the health and social care system.

In my view, however, defining counselling in terms of a specialist professional role is drawing the circle too tight, at the cost of excluding many activities and relationships that embody the spirit of counselling. I also believe that this tight definition has restricted innovation in the types of services that are provided for people, by making counsellors fearful of working with people in need outside of a tightly delimited and contracted environment, and making members of other professions reluctant to explore personal and emotional issues with their clients or patients for fear of being regarded as illegitimate 'counsellors'. We are now at a point where there is a good level of public and inter-professional understanding of the role of specialist counsellors and of the difference between the type of ongoing, intensive therapy that would be on offer from someone designated a counsellor, and the more episodic, focused and limited counselling assistance that would be on offer from a nurse or social worker.

Throughout this book, the term 'counselling' is used in a broad sense, to refer to an activity and relationship that is possible within many different settings. The safety and confidentiality of the person seeking help, and the impact of work role and setting on the counselling, are treated as issues that need to be understood by anyone offering a counselling relationship, in any situation. The phrase 'counselling skill' refers to a collection of competences and values that is associated with the activity of doing counselling well. The term 'counselling *skills*', in the plural, is a form of terminology that arises from an approach which attempts, unhelpfully, to reduce the skill of counselling to a set of sub-routines, and which thereby loses sight of what a counselling relationship is trying to achieve. The limitations of the *skills* perspective is explored in the following section.

The limitations of reductionism

In recent years much of the writing and thinking around counselling that is provided by people who are not specialist, full-time counsellors, has analysed the activity in terms of the use of counselling skills. The idea that psychological processes and inter-personal behaviour can be viewed as skills can be traced back to the 1950s. During the

Second World War, psychologists employed by the British armed forces were required to analyse the tasks performed by soldiers and aircrew, such as assembling and firing a weapon, with the aim of making suggestions regarding how these tasks could be performed more effectively and accurately, and the best ways in which training could be provided for people carrying them out. These psychologists came up with the idea of breaking down each task or function into a set of component skills, which could be learned separately and then built up into the final complete task sequence. The model of skill that emerged emphasized the sequence of actions that the operator needed to go through, and the operator's attention to feedback around whether each operation had been effective in achieving its intended goals. In the immediate post-war years, the concept of skill proved to be valuable as a means of analysing task performance in a variety of areas. In particular, the concept of skill was embraced by social psychologists, such as Michael Argyle, who were interested in understanding the way that people interacted with each other (Argyle and and Kendon, 1967). Interesting and important advances in applied social psychology were made in respect of interpersonal and social skills, which established the idea that the concept of skill could be usefully applied to the analysis of social interaction and performance. By the 1970s, under the leadership of the British clinical psychologist Peter Trower, the concept of social skill that had been developed by Argyle was being applied in work with people reporting a variety of mental health difficulties (Twentyman and McFall, 1975; Trower et al., 1978). One of the key ideas within this approach was that, instead of viewing intervention for mental health problems as a form of treatment, it was to be regarded as a form of *training*, in which the patient could be guided through a series of learning or skill-acquisition activities.

In the USA, a parallel development was taking place. Within the field of counselling, the late 1940s and early 1950s saw a vast expansion of the psychological therapies in use, largely stimulated by the need to respond to mental health problems in returning service personnel. A great deal of investment at that time was directed into the development of client-centred therapy, an approach to counselling and psychotherapy developed in the 1940s by Carl Rogers. Motivated by the pressure to train counsellors effectively and quickly, some of Rogers' students and colleagues, for example, Charles Truax and Robert Carkhuff, came to the conclusion that it would be sensible to treat the core concepts of client-centred therapy, such as non-directiveness, empathy and unconditional positive regard, as skills. These psychologists then developed training programmes in which students were taught, and practised, a set of counselling skills. This approach became known as the Human Resources Development model (Carkhuff, 1969a, b; Cash, 1984). In the 1960s, a large number of counselling and helping skills programmes were developed by influential figures in the counselling and psychology professions in the USA, such as Gerald Goodman (1984), Thomas Gordon (1984), Bernard Guerney (1984), Allen Ivey (Ivey and Galvin, 1984), and Norman Kagan (1984). The high point of these developments was a book edited by Dale Larson (1984a), which brought together examples of many of the major skills approaches, and in which the editor claimed to observe:

a fundamental shift occurring at the interface of the human services and the larger society. We are witnessing the public's growing interest in and desire for psychological and other human services and a corresponding recognition by professionals that psychological knowledge can be shared with greater and greater numbers of people.

(Larson, 1984b: 1)

All of these skills programmes were inspired by the work by Truax and Carkhuff, and, like their original, broke down the activity of counselling into a series of component skills which were acquired one by one. The assertion that 'psychological knowledge can be shared with greater ... numbers of people' was an echo of a presidential address made by George Miller to the American Psychological Association (Miller, 1969) in which it was argued that the time had come to 'give psychology away'. In other words, scientifically proven principles of therapeutic change, as identified in research originally carried out by Carl Rogers and others, were now to be made available to paraprofessionals, non-psychologists and members of peer support groups (Boukydis, 1984; Gendlin, 1984).

Box 2.3   The microskills model

The microskills model originally developed by Allen Ivey in the 1970s is still widely used as a framework for training in interviewing and counselling (Ivey and Ivey, 1999). The model is constructed around three key ideas. First, the tasks undertaken by a counsellor or interviewer can be broken down into a number of small units of behaviour, or microskills. Second, these skills are hierarchically organized, with more complex skills building on more basic ones. Third, the aim is to produce a counsellor who can respond to a person or client in a way that is not random, or intuitive, or based on common sense, but is *intentional*:

> Intentionality is acting with a sense of capability and deciding from among a range of alternative actions. The intentional individual has more than one action, thought or behavior to choose from in responding to changing life situations. The intentional individual can generate alternatives in a given situation and approach a problem from different vantage points, using a variety of skills and personal qualities, adapting styles to suit different individuals and cultures. The culturally intentional interviewer remembers a basic rule of helping: if something you try doesn't work, don't try more of the same – try something different!
>
> (Ivey and Ivey, 1999: 13)

The aim of skills training, therefore, is to enable the counsellor or helper to be aware of what they are doing, and aware of a repertoire of responses they might make to the person, so that they can select the intervention that is most productive in any particular situation.

A trainee is assisted to become intentional in their helping behaviour by working through a pyramid of microskills. At the foot of the pyramid are the basic skills of attending and listening (using open and enclosed questions, encouraging, paraphrasing, summarizing and reflecting feeling). Further up the hierarchy are more complex skills, such as questioning and client observation, and then advanced skills such as confronting. Having mastered these component skills, a trainee is then ready to learn how to construct a 'well-formed helping interview', which consists of a sequence of skills: building rapport, structuring, defining the problem, defining a goal, exploring alternatives, confronting incongruity and generalizing to daily life. The helper may then acquire more advanced skills (confrontation, focusing and reflection of meaning) and influencing strategies (interpretation, reframe, logical consequences, self-disclosure, feedback, information, advice and giving direction). At the end of this process of learning, the trainee is in a position to consider the value of theoretical perspectives that they might choose in order to provide a framework for further development as a practitioner.

The microskills model has proved highly popular and resilient over four decades by virtue of retaining a solid focus on practical skills while adapting some of the language of the model to accommodate changing circumstances. For example, recent versions of the model reflect Ivey's longstanding commitment to multiculturalism and interest in narrative approaches.

The list of skills included in what became probably the most widely used programme of this type, the Ivey microskills model, can be found in Box 2.3. This kind of framework still forms the basis for the majority of contemporary counselling skills models and training programmes (see, for example, Hill, 2004). The skills approach has generated a technology of counselling training that has been adopted by universities, colleges and training institutions around the world. Typically, students or trainees listen to an explanation of the skill and observe a demonstration, live or on video. They then practise the skill in small groups, and receive feedback. A review of research into the effectiveness of this kind of training model can be found in Baker *et al.* (1990).

The persistence of skills-based approaches to counselling training is a strong testimony to the value of this framework. The success of skills frameworks in counselling training can be attributed to a number of factors. Breaking down the activity of counselling into a set of component skills makes it possible to develop a structured curriculum, with clear learning objectives, thus allowing counselling skills training to be readily incorporated into standard university or college modular structures. Also, the cycle of demonstration–practice–feedback provides an excellent vehicle for systematic reflection on practice.

There are, however, important issues raised by the use of a 'skills' perspective within the field of counselling. The prime difficulty is that the skills that are typically listed as counselling skills, such as listening, attending, paraphrasing and empathic reflection, are not solely used in counselling, but are elements of many – perhaps all – domains of social life. For instance, operatives in call centres and sales staff in many retail outlets are trained in empathic reflection skills, but are certainly not engaged in work that could be considered counselling. These skills are perhaps best regarded as basic human relationship skills, or communication skills, which can be honed and applied to many purposes. The appropriation of these skills by writers and trainers in the counselling profession who have defined them as counselling skills has led to some unhelpful consequences. It can be mystifying for people to be put into a position, on training courses, where they are expected to relearn 'skills' that they already possess. There is a failure to acknowledge that these skills are part of everyday life. This approach reinforces a notion that counselling is somehow special and precious, rather than a routine activity. In some instances, practitioners may hesitate to respond to the counselling needs of their service users because they are afraid that they have not had sufficient counselling skills training to be able to handle the situation. This kind of scenario is an example of what the social critic Ivan Illich (2001) has called deskilling – for example, everyday healthcare skills and knowledge are appropriated by professional groups, with the result that ordinary people begin to believe that the only way that they can be helped is by consulting a professional doctor or nurse, rather than using their own resources.

The way in which the idea of skill has been applied to counselling reveals a lack of understanding of theory and research into the psychology of skill acquisition and use, and the more recent developments in this field. The concept of skill has proved to be most useful as a means of analysing relatively simple sequences of motor performance, that lead to a clear-cut, observable outcome, for example, assembling a weapon, hitting a golf ball or giving an injection. In fields in which more complex sequences of work performance have been analysed and evaluated, the concept of *competence* has proved to have more utility than has the concept of skill. The notion of competence refers to broader domains of activity, in which the person has a greater degree of discretion, flexibility and choice in terms of how they complete a task. For example, in the field of counselling, formulating a verbal response that accurately and succinctly summarizes the main themes in the person's narrative (empathic reflection) could be regarded as a skill, whereas engaging in a therapeutic conversation in which the person is able to explore the meaning of events and experience, is a competence. From the perspective of the service user, what is wanted is a person who is competent in 'facilitating the exploration of meaning'. Within this competence, the narrower skill of empathic reflection may or may not be useful, depending on the style of conversation that the person finds most useful.

The basic underlying problem with a skills perspective is that it is open to the dangers of *reductionism*. Modern science and academic disciplines have created a vast structure of knowledge that is ultimately based on a strategy of reducing complexity to the smallest possible units of analysis. A philosophy of reductionism lies behind microskills models and also taxonomies of counsellor interventions (see, for example, the taxonomy presented in Hill, 2004). This philosophy can be contrasted with a holistic approach, which places any activity or event in context, and seeks to understand the whole picture, including purpose. Moreover, a holistic approach questions the wisdom of the reductionist attempt to analyse processes in terms of cause-and-effect sequences. For example, does the skill of active listening result in an enhanced level of client exploration of feelings? Well, sometimes it does, but there will be times when exploration of feelings helps the counsellor to listen better, by offering the counsellor a vivid narrative that is easy to engage with. In other words, there is a reciprocal causal link, or mutual influence, existing between active listening by the counsellor and exploration of feeling on the part of the client – they are both aspects of a complex *relationship*.

The most significant limitation of a skills perspective in counselling is that it focuses attention on the wrong things. Any book or training course on counselling skills is inevitably organized around learning about action sequences – bits of behaviour such as summarizing, paraphrasing, questioning and so on. However, when users of counselling are asked what they found helpful, or when experienced practitioners are asked about what they have learned about their craft, they rarely mention anything that could be understood as the delivery of skills. In fact, they mention three things. They talk about the importance of a relationship of trust, a person with whom they feel safe and to whom they can talk freely and openly. They talk about the experience of being taken seriously, of being valued and affirmed as a person. And they mention the critical importance of being given permission to express their feelings and emotions. Underlying these themes is a sense that what matters is the willingness of the counsellor to meet the person, to be a witness and companion to them. Although the majority of writers and trainers who employ a skills framework certainly acknowledge the importance of relationship, values and emotion, the effect of a skills model is always to foreground technical activities such as skills, and to relegate the human relationship to the background.

For these reasons, despite the important contribution that skills frameworks have made to counselling theory, research and practice, the term 'skills' (plural) is not used within this book. Instead, throughout the book, the term 'counselling skill' (singular) is used to refer to the skilful accomplishment of the practicalities of doing counselling.

Conclusions

The intention of this chapter has been to define counselling as a joint activity. It is an activity that requires two or more participants working and interacting together: it is a type of relationship. Counselling is an activity that is brought into being by the person seeking help, and by the willingness of another person (the counsellor) to respond to this initiative. One of the aims of the chapter has been to establish that this activity can take place in many different settings. It has been argued that any attempt to define counselling as 'what counsellors do' denies the reality of human resourcefulness that enables the activity of counselling to occur whenever people are willing for it to occur. In this chapter, and throughout the book, a *user-oriented* perspective on counselling has been emphasized. In order to offer a counselling relationship, it is necessary to have as clear an idea as possible of what a person might want, and how they might perceive what is being offered to them.

A central theme within this discussion has been the importance of understanding counselling within its social context. In the past, counselling theory and practice have been dominated by a medical private practice model of service delivery, in which an autonomous client met with an autonomous therapist who had no other contact with or knowledge of the service user, and worked towards an ultimate fundamental resolution of the client's problems, typically over an extended period of time. The position taken within this book is that, even if such a model of practice was ever widely applicable, it is certainly lacking in relevance today. A more adequate definition of counselling is one which recognizes that practitioners operate within complex care systems, and that users have access to and information about multiple sources of potential help. Moreover, within a postmodern world, people are less convinced by the possibility of a grand cure, once and for all, but see themselves as episodic consumers of counselling as it is needed. A socially informed definition of counselling is one that incorporates notions of *silencing* and *inclusion*: people need to talk to counsellors because they experience their immediate social environment as not allowing them the chance to talk, as excluding them from participating fully in social and cultural life. What counselling can do is help the person to find their voice and to find their way through whatever it is that is blocking them.

The following chapter takes these principles, and begins to consider the practical steps involved in achieving a helpful counselling relationship.

Questions for reflection and discussion

1. Consider the three potential outcomes of counselling described on page 13: problem resolution, learning and social inclusion. To what extent do the goals of the people with whom you work fit into these categories? Are there other outcomes that seem important?
2. What is the counselling that occurs in your community? List all of the different places that you are aware of where any kind of counselling or psychotherapy takes place. From your knowledge of the people and organizations involved, what are the main contextual factors that shape the type of counselling that is available to the people who seek help from these agencies? In what ways do these factors influence the counselling that is offered (in terms of confidentiality, length of contact, depth of engagement, issues that can be talked about, and so forth)?
3. To what extent is embedded counselling a component of your own work role? How much embedded counselling do you do? What training and support have you received for this aspect of your work? What are your feelings about your counselling role?
4. Identify an occasion where you have personally been the recipient of a piece of 'micro-counselling' (that is, a ten- or twenty-minute focused counselling conversation with a practitioner). How useful (or otherwise) was this episode for you? What did the practitioner do that was helpful or hindering?
5. Have you ever attended a counselling training course or workshop that was based on a 'microskills' approach? What was most useful for you in this course? What did you perceive as the limitations of the course? To what extent do you agree with the criticisms of the microskills model presented in this chapter?

Suggestions for further reading

One of the issues that has been explored in this chapter has been the question of what counselling is, how and why it works, and where it happens. Readers interested in learning more about these questions are advised to consult:

Feltham, C. (1995) *What is Counselling?* London: Sage.
McLeod, J. (2003) *An Introduction to Counselling*, 3rd edn. Buckingham: Open University Press.

What has been described in this chapter as the counselling skills approach has a great deal to offer to anyone involved in an embedded counselling role. Two of the most useful books within this tradition are:

Hill, C. E. (2004) *Helping Skills: Facilitating Exploration, Insight and Action*, 2nd edn. Washington, DC: American Psychological Association.
Tolan, J. (2003) *Skills in Person-centred Counselling and Therapy*. London: Sage.

The debate around the distinction between counselling (as a specialist professional activity) and the use of counselling skills (by people such as nurses and teachers) has been around for a long time. The best analysis of the issues remains:

Bond, T. (1989) Towards defining the role of counselling skills. *Counselling*, 69: 24–6.

3

Basic principles of embedded counselling

Introduction • An overview of key concepts • A case example: counselling embedded in a support worker role • Philosophical principles and underlying assumptions • Conclusions • Questions for reflection and discussion • Suggestions for further reading

On the bus to the hospital. Traffic. The same streets. Bob looks out of the window. Just a couple of weeks to the 70th birthday. The big one. They are planning something, but they won't say what. Months of feeling unwell. Referral to a consultant – worryingly quick. Tests. Diagnosis. Cancer. Medication. Every few weeks, a visit to the cancer nurse, just 'to see how you are getting along'. More tests. It was like a dream. Sleep-walking through it all. 'Isn't he coping well.' Behind the front, a different kind of pain.

Introduction

Offering a counselling relationship to a person who is looking for assistance in talking through a personal issue carries a burden of responsibility. It is not a commitment to be undertaken casually. Being in the role of counsellor often involves learning about and responding to areas of sensitivity, pain and confusion in a person's life. It is essential, therefore, to possess a robust framework for practice, and to be prepared. While it is necessary for anyone offering counselling to be willing to make a genuinely *personal* response, it is also important to be able to refer back to a map or model of the counselling process as a means of reflecting on what is happening, and as a basis for explaining to the person or service user what to expect and why.

The framework that is introduced in this chapter is intended to apply to any occasion when a person asks or invites someone who is reasonably detached from their life situation (in other words, someone in a professional role, rather than a close friend or family member) to help them to talk through a personal issue. Counselling episodes can range from brief (five-minute) microcounselling conversations that are embedded within other roles and relationships (such as when a patient shares his worries with a nurse or doctor), through to ongoing formal counselling and psychotherapy organized around regular one-hour sessions over a period of several months or even years. Because this book is intended mainly for practitioners whose counselling role is embedded within other work functions, such as teaching, caring or nursing, the examples that are used are based on counselling relationships, which are organized around brief, intermittent counselling conversations. However, the framework can equally be applied to ongoing, formal or specialist counselling and psychotherapy settings. The purpose of the chapter is to provide an initial outline of the ideas and assumptions that inform the practice of embedded counselling. Subsequent chapters focus on the application of these principles in practice.

An overview of key concepts

The key concepts that are used in this book to provide a framework for making sense of the counselling process are as follows:

- *Problems in living*. The individual constructs a personal niche in society, within which they seek to live a satisfying and meaningful life. Counselling episodes are triggered when a person experiences a problem in living – a blockage, conflict or absence within their life – that they cannot resolve by using resources that are immediately available to them. One of the main aims of counselling is to help the person to activate the personal, social and cultural resources that they require in order to resolve their current problem in living: effective counselling helps people to become more resourceful.
- *Goals*. The counselling episode is initiated by the person who is seeking help. The person will have some sense of their *goals* or what they wish to achieve, both in relation to their life as a whole and with reference to current problems in living.
- *A collaborative relationship*. In turning to counselling, rather than to other forms of help (for example, reading a self-help manual), the individual experiencing a problem in living is primarily looking through the medium of human companionship and care. The counsellor provides a relationship characterized by a willingness to work together to resolve problems.
- *Values*. Counsellors respond in accordance with a set of values that promote the worth and potential of persons and relationships. These values are reflected in an ethically informed stance in relation to the duty of care towards the person seeking help.

- *Preparation*. The counsellor will put in place all necessary preparations, including an awareness of self-in-role, appreciation of limits, and arrangements for personal support and supervision/consultancy, in advance of offering a counselling relationship.
- *Making a space*. The person and the counsellor collaborate together to organize and create an appropriate safe space, where a frank and meaningful discussion can take place.
- *Tasks*. The person and the counsellor collaborate around the resolution of tasks associated with achieving the person's goals and the maintenance, repair or transformation of the personal niche of the individual seeking help. These tasks include:
  - talking openly and meaningfully about current problems in living;
  - exploring meaning – making sense of a problematic experience;
  - problem solving, planning and decision making;
  - changing behaviour;
  - negotiating life transitions and developmental crises;
  - expressing/letting go of feeling and emotion;
  - finding, analysing and acting on information;
  - enhancing self-care: making use of personal, cultural and social resources.
- *Methods*. Each of these tasks can be completed in a number of ways or using a variety of different methods. Where possible, the counsellor and person agree on the most appropriate method for working on any particular task.
- *Responding to crisis*. The role of counsellor involves monitoring the counselling interaction and closing down the counselling conversation if it is necessary to shift to other forms of help or intervention.

This framework can be characterized as reflecting a *collaborative task* approach to helping. From the point of view of the helper or counsellor, there are two crucial dimensions to the skill of counselling. First, the counsellor works to establish and maintain a relationship and a space within which genuine collaboration can take place. Second, the counsellor and person together identify the goals of counselling and the counselling tasks that need to be carried out to achieve these goals step by step, and then agree on the methods that can be best employed in tackling these tasks. Throughout this process, the counsellor and the person seeking help *work together* around the process of talking things through

As a means of illustrating how the key concepts of the framework can be applied in practice, the following section gives an example of how one voluntary sector worker has integrated the availability of counselling into what is predominantly a practical helping and support role, as a means of meeting the emotional needs of a particular service user.

A case example: counselling embedded in a support worker role

Lorna is a support worker for an organization that assists people who have difficulties in living with epilepsy. Most of her job involves practical help and befriending, ranging from accompanying group members when they go swimming, to gathering information about social benefits and entitlements. Occasionally, Lorna finds herself in situations where group members are upset about some aspect of their lives and want to talk about personal issues. Lorna has learned to be ready for these moments and has carried out a range of preparatory work to enable her to respond sensitively and effectively. For example, she has completed a counselling skills course, and feels reasonably confident about her ability to respond to personal and emotional issues and her capacity to recognize her own limits. She has a mental map of rooms within the project offices, and of quiet coffee shops and public parks, where it is possible to conduct a private conversation in reasonably comfortable surroundings. She has a folder of information about counselling, psychotherapy, self-help and other organizations that might be useful if issues arise that require longer-term, specialist counselling. She has also made contact with some of the workers in these other organizations and is in a position to facilitate referrals. Finally, an essential piece of preparatory work involved arranging regular supervision/consultation with one of the counsellors in another agency and being a member of a regular support group within her own project.

One of the group members for whom Lorna has provided a counselling relationship is Alan. Although successful in his own line of work, Alan sometimes feels disabled by the drugs he needs to take, depressed about the stigmatization that comes with label 'epileptic' and views himself as a 'loser'. An important life goal for Alan is to develop more self-esteem or, in his own words, 'to stand up for myself'. Most of the time, Alan finds it helpful just to talk to Lorna about situations that arose in his day-to-day life, whenever they bumped into each other during his visits to the project office. He has found it supportive to know that there was someone who understood what was happening in his life and how he felt about things, and who could be depended on to listen. Three brief counselling episodes, over a six-month period, illustrate how Alan used his relationship with Lorna to work through some specific emotional/interpersonal *tasks* that contributed to the achievement of his overall life goal.

The first task involved making sense of a problematic experience. Alan had sent off for details of a new job, and had intended to make an application, but when he sat down to fill in the form he realized that he had missed the deadline for sending in his CV. He could not understand how he could have 'forgotten' the cut-off date: 'It was a great job for me, I've been so stupid'. Lorna asked if he had any idea of what would be the best way for him to explore what had happened. He replied that he didn't know where to start. Lorna then asked if he would be willing to look at his feelings about the job. He agreed that this would be valuable. Lorna then invited Alan to slowly talk her through his recollection of receiving the job particulars, opening the envelope and reading what was inside. It soon emerged that, on reading about the new job, he had started to imagine how good it would be to work in this new office, and then what it would be like to be treated as 'different'. The conversation soon moved into a discussion of how threatening it could be for Alan to meet new people and how the prospect of a new job had heightened these fears.

The second task involved planning, problem solving and information processing. Alan was unhappy with his medication regime and had collected a huge amount of information from the Internet about side effects and drug dosages. However, he could not see any way to put across this information to his GP: 'he will just see me as a pest who is never happy with the treatment that's on offer.' Lorna talked through with Alan the different types of scenario that might unfold at his next meeting with his GP, and together they developed a set of plans for engaging the GP in a constructive dialogue.

The third task arose when Alan mentioned that he was under a lot of stress and could not sleep. Lorna asked whether he thought it might be helpful to take a few minutes to look at what was happening. They sat in one of the interview rooms in the project office for several minutes in silence. Lorna asked if it would be all right for her to suggest a way to bring out what he was feeling. Alan indicated that he would find that useful. She invited him to say what he was feeling in his body and to give these feelings a name. Alan quickly went to his abdomen and said 'pain', and then 'hopeless', and then began to weep. After a while, he started to talk about his despair about being 'stuck' in his life and how at some moments he felt that it was 'probably not worth carrying on'. While encouraging Alan to keep talking about all aspects of his feelings, Lorna took some time to check out whether suicidal intentions were implied by the idea of 'not worth carrying on' and to ensure that he knew about other sources of help that might be readily available if the possibility of suicide were to develop further for him.

These three tasks were facilitated by particular methods: re-experiencing a critical moment, working up plans for responding to different scenarios and focusing on a felt sense of a painful inner emotional experience. Other methods could have been used in each instance. The methods that were employed each time were strategies that both Alan and Lorna were comfortable with. Each of these tasks reflected an immediate problem in living that had occurred at that point in Alan's life, but it is possible to see how they also represent steps on the way towards achieving his bigger goal of 'standing up for himself'. Within each of these episodes, Lorna consistently responded to Alan from a position of valuing and accepting him as a person of worth who was capable of developing his own solutions to problems. This value stance was reinforced by Lorna's style of always seeking agreement on how she and Alan could work together around tasks, rather than seeking to take control and be directive. Lorna also monitored her work with Alan, in case risk issues arose that might need to be addressed – for instance, his reference to suicidal thoughts.

The skilful use of counselling by Lorna, within her role as a support worker, shows how the different elements of the collaborative task model fit together in practice. The case of Alan illustrates how problems in living, from this approach, are not viewed as comprising deficits within the individual person, but as tensions and difficulties in the relationship between the person and the world within which they have made their life. The person seeking help, therefore, is regarded as a collaborator or co-worker in doing whatever needs to be done (tasks) to sort things out. Narrative therapists such as White and Epston (1990) vividly capture this sense of the resourcefulness of persons, and the social origins of problems, in their phrase: 'the person is not the problem – *the problem is the problem'*. Some of the thinking behind this way of looking at personal troubles and difficulties is explored in the following section.

Philosophical principles and underlying assumptions

The framework that is presented in this book differs in significant ways from the ideas that inform the majority of counselling textbooks. In the main, current writing about counselling is dominated by an approach that characterizes the problems that people bring to counselling as *psychological* in nature. From a psychological perspective, problems can be viewed in terms of malfunctioning psychological mechanisms or 'deficits' that need to be fixed. For example, from a psychological point of view, a person may be regarded as suffering from low self-esteem, irrational thinking, unprocessed emotions, intrusive memories and so on (Gergen, 1990). In contrast to these ideas, this book takes the view that it is more helpful to understand people as *social* beings who co-construct the human reality within which they live through the way they interact and talk and the stories they tell, and who can work together to resolve problems that arise in the course of everyday life. The advantage of a social perspective is that it highlights the connectedness and solidarity between people, and the cultural traditions within which they live. The key point here is that counselling, as envisaged within this model, is not a matter of addressing deficits that are hypothesized to exist within the individual. Counselling is not a matter of repairing or fixing a faulty mechanism within the 'self' or 'psyche' of a person. The 'problem' is not in the person's mind. Instead, counselling is the business of working with the person to deal with real difficulties in the actual social world in which they live and to locate the resources from within that world that they can use to make a difference. Some of the implications of a social perspective on counselling are outlined below.

Pluralism

The approach to understanding problems that is articulated in this book is informed by postmodern and existentialist (and other) philosophical standpoints that argue that there is no single right way to deal with the difficulties and challenges that life presents to us. The existentialist writer Mick Cooper has described the contemporary world as characterized by a multiplicity of possibilities for living, which in turn calls for an approach to counselling in which the person and the counsellor work together to consider a *plurality* of methods for dealing with life difficulties (Cooper, 2005). An essential aspect of counselling, in a postmodern context, is therefore its *improvisational* quality. Rather than applying a standard problem-solving formula, the person and their counsellor creatively draw on the resources that are available to them to find a way forward. Because we live in a globalized world in which competing belief systems co-exist and huge amounts of information are available to people concerning the advantages and disadvantages of different types of therapeutic methods, it is no longer sufficient for a counsellor to adopt a single method and expect the person seeking help to accept it without question. Effective counsellors need to be responsive and flexible, and able to collaborate with the person seeking help to achieve the best match between what the counsellor can offer and what the person believes will help them.

Problems in living

The collaborative task model of counselling skill emphasizes the importance of viewing the person seeking help as living within a social context, and as actively involved in creating and making a life for themself. On a day-to-day basis, it is inevitable that constant series of problems in living will arise in anyone's life. These problems in living comprise dilemmas and challenges around the negotiation of personal needs and desires, and can take the form of personal issues such as conflicts in relationships with others, uncertainty or confusion around life choices, fear or avoidance of people and situations, and loss of clarity and hope over the future. Most of the time, a person deals with such issues by employing any one of a range of problem-solving resources, for example taking advice from a family member, going for a walk in the hills to think the matter through, praying, reading a book or newspaper article on the topic, and so on. The most frequently used type of informal personal problem solving probably occurs through everyday conversation, storytelling and gossip, where people share their experiences of how they have dealt with the challenges that life has presented them. Occasionally, however, a problem will emerge that cannot be resolved through the use of the resources that are immediately to hand. There can be many reasons why a problem may become intractable. The person may lack people and relationships with whom to share the problem, perhaps because they have moved to a new city or because people with whom they been close have died. Alternatively, the person may have access to a social network, but is reluctant to talk to anyone in that network because of the nature of the problem. This may happen if the person perceives the problem in living as being embarrassing or shameful. For example, a person may find their job stressful, but may work in a high achievement environment where the implicit 'rules' of the organization make it very hard to admit vulnerability to a colleague. Another factor that may contribute to a problem building up and reaching a point where friends and family, and other immediate resources are not enough, is the use by the person of strategies for self-care and coping that are based on avoidance. If a person deals with an issue by 'trying not to think about it' or by self-medicating through drugs and alcohol, they can quite quickly get to a point where the problem is too big to talk about, or it is too embarrassing to admit that they had allowed the problem to get to the point it has reached. An example might be a college student who gets a bad mark for an assignment, worries about failing the course, and deals with these pressures by skipping classes and staying in bed watching television and eating chocolate.

Box 3.1   The social roots of problems in living

It is not helpful, in a counselling role, to view problems in living as psychological problems, that reflect some kind of dysfunction in the individual. Instead, a problem in living perspective makes the assumption that the troubles in a person's life arise from the relationship between a person and their social world. Although psychological theories have generated many valuable ideas for how to help people to change their behaviour, the basic assumption in most psychological models is that there is something wrong with the person. Gergen (1990) has described such approaches as employing a 'language of deficit' – a vast vocabulary for identifying and labelling the inadequacies of the individual. In contrast, one of the main tasks of a counsellor is to position themself on the side of the person who is seeking help. In this respect, the counsellor is standing alongside the person and working with them both to make sense of the social world in which they find themself and to make use of whatever resources are available to create as satisfying a life as possible within that context. In order to support such a stance, it can be valuable for those in counselling roles to make use of some of the ideas developed by contemporary sociologists. The key writer in this area is probably Anthony Giddens, who analyses the ways in which the conditions of modern life make it hard for people to sustain a secure identity or sense of who they are, and argues that the emergence of the counselling profession can be understood as a cultural response to this growing uncertainty. Counselling becomes the place where we can stand back from the details of our everyday life and gain some sense of who we are (Giddens, 1991). These ideas have been further articulated by other sociological writers. For example, Richard Sennett (1998) has studied the ways in which changing patterns of employment, brought about by the global economy, have resulted in the loss of a secure identity as a worker. As people shift from one temporary job to another, are allocated to ever-changing teams within an organization, or work from home, it becomes harder to develop deep relationships with colleagues. More dramatically, Zymunt Bauman (2004) suggests that the global capitalist economy and depletion of planetary resources has been responsible for a vast number of what he calls 'wasted lives': people such as immigrants, refugees, the unemployed, the disabled, who are surplus to the requirements of the economic system, and who therefore cease to matter. A theme that runs through these sociological accounts of modern life is the extent to which people feel *excluded* from full participation in a meaningful social life.

Existential challenges

The idea of 'problems in living' carries with it a number of assumptions about *living*. To live a good life involves at least three major dimensions of existential challenge:

- being in relationships with others and having a sense of mutuality, belonging and involvement in caring
- constructing and maintaining a sense of identity or 'who I am'
- discovering, nourishing and aligning with sources of meaning and purpose that provide a sense of well-being, fulfilment and generativity.

It is never easy to achieve a satisfactory balance between the struggle for everyday survival, in terms of making a living and 'getting by', and the goal of living a 'good life' as defined in terms of the personal and cultural values that inform one's position with respect to relationships with others, personal identity and purposefulness. Divergence between the instrumental (getting by) and expressive (being a person) aspects of every-day life is typically signalled by *emotion*: we feel angry if there is a threat to someone we love; we feel despair if circumstances undermine our hopes. The expression in counselling of emotion and feeling is therefore of critical importance because emotion is an indicator of an existential challenge being experienced by a person.

Agency

In counselling, it is never a good idea to 'objectify' the person, to regard someone seeking help as a passive victim of events or fate. People always make sense of what has happened to them, and devise ways of coping and surviving. We all live in a world that encompasses a rich variety of strategies and ideas about how to deal with problems in living, and we each possess our own repertoire of theories and methods for getting through life. The idea of human *agency*, the capacity of people to be intentional and active in constructing (in concert with others) the reality in which they live, is one of the basic assumptions that informs the counselling framework presented in this book.

Finding a voice

Within the collaborative task model of counselling skill, attention to the social world of a person who is seeking counselling is crucially important because the aim of counsel-ling is to make it possible for the person to re-engage with their social world in ways that are more effective and satisfying for them. A basic proposition of the model is that a person will seek counselling because they have been *silenced* in relation to a significant issue in their life. The person turns to a professional helper for counselling because more readily accessible sources of help or 'counsel' do not exist, will not listen, or will not understand and accept what the person has to say. The main task of a counsellor is to enable the person to give voice to what has been unsaid, first within the counselling space and thereafter within the person's life space.

Promoting life-enhancing values

Behind this kind of social perspective is the view that the social world within which we live can be highly destructive of persons. There is substantial evidence of the highly negative and life-limiting effects on persons of social events such as unemployment, poor working conditions, poor housing, inadequate educational opportunities, sexism, racism, sexual harassment and abuse, military and criminal violence, genocide, death and injury from road traffic accidents, shiftwork, and poisoning from environmental dumping and damage. This list could be extended. Moreover, the effect of these social conditions and events stretches well beyond the people who are immediately affected. It is very clear that the impact can be tracked through to the second or even third generation offspring of, say, a person who has been traumatized by military violence. One of the key aspects of the model of counselling skill that addresses the issue of social oppression is its emphasis on the importance of *values*. A fuller discussion of the values of counselling is provided in Chapter 6. However, the importance of counselling values is that they explicitly challenge, and offer an alternative to, the values that justify social oppression. The common thread running through all forms of social destructiveness such as unemployment and sexual harassment is a sense of individual lives and relationships as essentially worthless, and profits, systems and ideologies as important. The growth of counselling in the twentieth century can be viewed as one of the ways in which people have sought to fight back against some of the dehumanizing trends in modern life. The psychotherapist and social critic Colin Kirkwood makes a powerful case that counselling, for all its imperfections and limitations, can be viewed as a means of nurturing human connection, community and solidarity (Kirkwood, 2003).

The personal niche

A recurring image throughout this book is that of a person engaged in making a space, niche or home for themselves within the social and cultural world in which they live. The global culture within which we, live our lives is immensely complicated and presents us with multiple possibilities and choices. In the distant past, human society was organized around relatively small, highly structured, groups such as clans or tribes, that lived close to nature. In the absence of a written language, knowledge and information were conveyed in the form of songs and stories. Many of the characteristics of that earlier way of life remain with us, for example in the importance that most people place on loyalty, and in the power of narrative. However, the development of written language, mechanized transport, an economic system based on money and capital, and the information technology revolution, have contributed to the existence of a culture of cities. In a city, many separate and different cultural worlds co-exist within the same geographical area.

Building a *personal niche* involves at least three types of interlocking activity. First, there is the task of connecting to other people by maintaining a network of personal relationships. These relationships usually include some mix of family and kinship ties, intimate or partner relationships, friendships, work colleagues and casual acquaintances. Second, a person lives within a set of stories that they tell about themself and which are told about them. These stories reflect and draw upon the stock of stories that are available within a culture, for example, in myths, novels and movies. Third, a personal niche comprises objects, spaces and territories that have meaning for a person, for example, the musical instrument that they play, the food they eat, their bedroom, their garden, a view from the top of a particular hill. A highly significant object and space, always, is the physical body of the person, and how the person creates a home for their self in their body and express their identity through their body.

A sense of well-being, or satisfaction with life, depends on the extent to which the personal niche reflects a sufficient degree of coherence or integration between the story that a person lives within and the relationships and objects through which their story is played out. For example, if someone has constructed their personal world around a story of being 'happily married', and their partner wants to leaves them, then they have a problem. Areas of tension within the life space or niche of a person can be described as 'problems in living'. Often, problems in living can be ignored – the person just carries on with their life as if everything were normal. Sometimes, problems in living resolve themselves (for example, the partner has a change of heart). However, there are also times when a problem in living persists and needs to be dealt with. Purposeful resolution or repair of problems in living requires some means of standing back from the situation, gaining some perspective on it and deciding on a course of action. There are many ways in which this can be achieved. It is possible for someone to work things out for themself during the course of a long walk, or through writing in a journal or allowing themself a period of meditative personal reflection. It is possible to develop new insights and ideas for action through reading or by getting advice from family and friends. Most of the time, these immediate resources provide effective means of dealing with problems in living.

There are occasions, though, when immediate personal and family resources are not sufficient for the challenge of dealing with a problem in living. It may be that the problem is too multifaceted or too frightening. Trusted friends and family members may not be available to talk with. The problem itself may be something that is embarrassing to talk about, or which is threatening to loved ones. In any of these situations, it makes sense to find someone who is knowledgeable, trustworthy and independent of one's immediate circle of family and friends: a counsellor.

Box 3.2   Help is where you find it

Cowen (1982) carried out interviews into the kind of help provided around emotional and interpersonal problems to their clients, by hairdressers, lawyers specializing in family issues, factory supervisors, and bartenders. He found that moderate to serious personal problems were raised with all groups, but particularly with hairdressers and lawyers. A range of different ways of handling these helping conversations were reported, and it was found that some of the strategies used by these informal helpers were much the same as those employed by professional therapists. In this and other research studies, hairdressers have been found to be particularly resourceful in terms of responding to the personal problems of their clients (Cowen et al., 1979; Milne and Mullin, 1987). In a study that looked at the value of informal help from the perspective of the person seeking assistance, McLellan (1991) conducted a survey of university students who reported themselves as having experienced emotional and interpersonal difficulties within the previous six months, to explore their perceptions of the helpfulness of professional counsellors in contrast to informal sources of assistance such as friends. In this sample of students, those who consulted professional counsellors described their problems as more serious, viewed themselves as more emotionally upset, and were more likely to have difficulties around relationships. It appeared, therefore, that those individuals who were more troubled were more likely to seek specialist help. However, when asked about the quality of their relationship with their professional counsellor or informal helper, there was no difference between the two groups in terms of amount of time they received, helper/counsellor availability, or the extent to which they felt understood or accepted. The key differences were that professional counsellors were viewed as offering more *privacy* than informal helpers, were regarded as more competent, and that professional counselling sessions were more emotionally disturbing. Hart (1996) surveyed specialist student counsellors and academic tutors who carried out pastoral work with students, and found that there was a high degree of overlap between the two groups in the use of skills such as listening, understanding feelings and promoting self-esteem. However, some of the tutors were clearly lacking in confidence in relation to their deployment of these skills. The findings of these studies, and many other investigations into the role of non-professional counselling-type help, suggest that a lot of informal and embedded counselling takes place, in a wide variety of community settings. Almost certainly, a much higher proportion of problems in living are handled informally than are ever seen by a professional counsellor or psychologist: whereas around 35 per cent of the population experience mental health problems at any one time, only 3 per cent of the population seek professional help.

Resourcefulness

From a perspective that views the creating and inhabiting of a personal niche as the basis for explaining the origins of problems in living, the aims of counselling can be understood in terms of the concept of resourcefulness. A personal resource can be defined as anything that a person can use to build a life and sense of identity. The way that counselling works is to create a space in which the person can review the resources that are available to them and can look around for other resources that might enable them to build a better life. Much of the time, the resources that people deploy in counselling are very ordinary. For example, a person faced with making a decision may use the everyday resource of *mapping* to draw out the different facets of their problem on a piece of paper. Someone else trying to deal with a difficult relationship may realize, through the process of counselling, that it might be helpful to try *humour* as a means of dealing with a person who is annoying them. Humour and mapping are commonplace resources that are readily available to anyone, but whose relevance in relation to a problem in living may not have been apparent until the point of talking things through with a counsellor. Other resources are more complex. A person struggling to control their diabetic condition may end up seeking out other sufferers or organized self-help groups as resources to enable them to learn new skills. People can find resources in themselves. A person who has moved to a new town and has difficulty in making friends may discover, through counselling, their memories of other times in their life when they had been lonely and had to find new friends, and select from this a specific personal resource such as their memory of *what my grandmother used to say* – 'she always said that you had to be patient and the right person would come along'.

The concept of resource differs in important ways from other concepts that are used in counselling theories to explain what it is the counsellor is supposed to do for people. In recent years, *solution-focused* therapy has become a widely used approach to counselling (O'Connell, 1998). However, a solution merely comprises one answer to a specific current problem, whereas the concept of resource refers to a set of possible solutions, or source of potential solutions, that can be applied to many different problems. Two other concepts that are widely used in the counselling literature are *insight* and *understanding*. These concepts refer to a kind of 'a-ha' experience, where the person makes connections between different parts of their life, in a way that allows them to 'see' things more clearly. Again, the concept of resource is similar to understanding or insight, but is wider in its application: the discovery of a resource involves a moment of 'seeing' that a particular resource can usefully be applied to a set of problems.

The idea of resources is valuable in counselling because it encourages the counsellor to think about whatever resources are available to a person in their current life space or niche (their strengths) and to be on the alert for any reference to resources that the person may mention in passing, but not be using fully. Most important of all, the concept of resource keeps a counsellor grounded in a standpoint that emphasizes the capacity and potential of a person, rather than allowing then to assume that the person is inadequate or lacking in some way. There is an important distinction between resilience and resourcefulness. Resilience assumes that the capacity to respond creatively and flexibly to stress is a personal characteristic, and carries with it the implication that some people may lack resilience (that is, that they are weak). Resourcefulness, on the other hand, assumes that the capacity to respond creatively and flexibly to stress depends on the relationship between the person and the environment (the resources) in which the person finds themself. Working to enhance resourcefulness is a matter of helping the person to search their life space for the resources that can be brought to bear on their problem. Someone who is stuck and not acting in a particularly resourceful way in terms of resolving a problem in living can be regarded not as weak, but as not yet having found the right tools for the job.

The significance of language

Counselling is an activity that takes place in a social and interpersonal space, between two people. The purpose of counselling is to provide a person with an opportunity to reflect on aspects of their life that have been troubling them. The primary tool of counselling is language or talk, which is the main medium within which social and cultural life is constructed and maintained.

Conclusions

The model of counselling skill that has been outlined in this chapter is explored in more detail throughout the rest of the book. The starting point of the model is an analysis of what people want or need. The model proposes that people need:

- to get on with their lives;
- to talk to someone when they get stuck in their lives;
- to have a space where they can safely talk things through, with someone they trust;
- to be treated as resourceful and worthwhile human beings;
- to be in control, and have their ideas about what is helpful (or otherwise) taken seriously;
- to deal with problems step by step.

A skilled counsellor is a person who is able to respond adequately to these needs. The key factor in a counsellor's capacity to respond in a helpful way is not technical expertise and competence, but values and heart. If a counsellor consistently can act on the basis of values that affirm the worth and potential of the person, then there is a good chance that, between them, they will be able to achieve something that is useful. Technical expertise, in the form of knowledge of psychological theories and methods of therapy, that is delivered in the wrong spirit is in the end likely to compound a person's problems.

Questions for reflection and discussion

1. How comfortable are you with the concept of pluralism? Do you accept that different people can view the world in substantially different ways, including diverse ideas about what is helpful? Or do you believe that there is one basic truth or reality that underpins all of human experience?
2. What are the existential challenges in your own life? How do these challenges influence your day-to-day decisions? What opportunities do you have for discussing your existential challenges with other people? If you do have such opportunities, in what ways are they helpful to you?
3. What 'voices' do you use when talking with others? What voices are you aware of, in your head? Where do these voices come from?
4. Get a piece of paper and some coloured pens and draw your personal niche. What have you learned about yourself by doing this? What are the areas of your life space or niche that are most troubling for you? What are the areas that represent your sources of personal strength? Which areas of your niche might you open up to a counsellor, and which might remain hidden?

Suggestions for further reading

The concept of the personal niche is taken for the writings of the Swiss psychotherapist Juerg Willi:

Willi, J. (1999) *Ecological Psychotherapy: Developing by Shaping the Personal Niche.* Seattle, WA: Hogreve & Huber.

The importance of the idea of voices for understanding the complexity of personal experience is explained clearly in:

Honos-Webb, L. and Stiles, W. B. (1998) Reformulation of assimilation analysis in terms of voices. *Psychotherapy,* 35: 23–33.

The ideas that are presented in this chapter are explored, in a somewhat different way, in some of my own writing over the past few years:

McLeod, J. (1999) Counselling as a social process. *Counselling,* 10: 217–22.
McLeod, J. (2004) The significance of narrative and storytelling in postpsychological counseling and psychotherapy. In A. Lieblich, D. McAdams and R. Josselson (eds) *Healing Plots: The Narrative Basis of Psychotherapy.* Washington, DC: American Psychological Association.
McLeod, J. (2005) Counseling and psychotherapy as cultural work. In L. T. Hoshmand (ed.) *Culture, Psychotherapy and Counseling: Critical and Integrative Perspectives.* Thousand Oaks, CA: Sage.

4

The counselling menu: goals, tasks and methods

Introduction • Clarifying the person's goals • Counselling tasks • Methods • Reflecting on methods • The key to using the counselling menu: shared decision making • An example of goals, methods and tasks in practice: Joey's emotional journey • Being on the alert for things going wrong • Conclusions • Questions for reflection and discussion • Suggestions for further reading

You asked me there about what's in the leaflet – about the counselling. Well, basically, it's just a chance for you to talk about anything that might be bothering you. Sometimes people with your condition get worried about what is going to happen to them, or find that the way that people in their family see them has changed, or get worn out by the stress of coming to the hospital every week, or even maybe they get angry with the attitudes of some of the doctors. It could be any of these things or even things that are quite different. Some people don't seem to need to talk to me about what's happening and others do. Everyone is different. What I try to do is to be flexible, in terms of whatever it is you need. Like if it was just to check out a few things or whether you wanted more time to talk things through. One of the things I sometimes do for people who are interested is suggest books and leaflets they can read, and websites, written by people who have had the same illness as you. Some people just use me as a shoulder to cry on – that's all right too. It's whatever will help you get through it. I would never force this on you. It's up to you to use the counselling or not.

Introduction

Throughout this book, people are understood as being actively engaged in responding to the challenges that life presents them. A person seeking help is an active agent, a constructor or creator (in collaboration with others), of their world, someone with choice and responsibility. While it is obvious that events may take place that are outside the control or awareness of a person, the position adopted by a counsellor is always that a person has the capacity to decide what they make of these events, and to shape how they incorporate what happens into their personal niche or life space. People can be understood as carrying out their everyday life within a personal niche assembled from the immense richness and complexity of the culture, society and nature that are known to them. As discussed in earlier chapters, the cultural resources available to both the person seeking help and their counsellor, in the form of ideas, beliefs, practices, rituals, narratives, and tools for thinking and feeling and decision making, form the backdrop to any counselling relationship. An essential element of the skill of counselling therefore involves finding the right approach for each individual. There are huge differences between individuals in terms of what they need or what they find helpful. For example, some people resolve issues by expressing their feelings and emotions, whereas others prefer a more rational approach. Some people look for a helper to take the lead whereas, for other people, the sense of being in personal control may be of paramount importance within a counselling relationship.

A useful way of thinking about how all these possibilities can be incorporated into a counselling relationship is to use the concept of the *counselling menu*. We are all familiar with restaurant menus, which list the various dishes and beverages that are available. However, that kind of menu implies an order or structure – starter, followed by main course, followed by dessert – that is typically associated with the expectation that a diner will partake of a full meal (even though some people may opt for only one course). By contrast, the kind of microcounselling that takes place when counselling is embedded in other work roles is necessarily more flexible, time limited and improvizational, often more like a snack than a full meal. A more appropriate menu image for embedded counselling, therefore, is the kind of drop-down menu that is universally used in PC and Internet applications – a set of options is revealed, which are not in any particular order, and clicking on one of these options may reveal another set of sub-options and so on. Within this chapter, an imaginary counselling drop-down menu is proposed which incorporates three levels of decision making. First, the person seeking help and the counsellor agree on the aims or *goals* of their work together. Second, having agreed the ultimate desired end point or goal, they identify what can be done now to make progress in relation to achieving that goal (the *task*). Finally, they need to decide on the best *method* for tackling that task.

Clarity about goals, tasks and methods is particularly important in embedded counselling situations. A specialist counsellor may have the scope to meet with a client over several weekly sessions, and to allow an agreement over goals, tasks and methods to emerge gradually from their preliminary conversations. Such a counsellor may also have enough time to coach the client in using the methods that are specifically favoured within their theoretical approach. In microcounselling, by contrast, typically there is not enough time to become sidetracked on irrelevant goals, tasks or unproductive methods, and then to renegotiate a more productive way of working. Also, crucially, there are powerful ethical issues associated with deciding which goals and tasks are appropriate to microcounselling, and which may be too risky to attempt within this kind of relationship. Some problems or therapeutic goals require more time, and more specialist expertise, than may be available from a practitioner who is offering counselling alongside another helping role, and would therefore be unlikely to be included in a typical 'menu' offered by a practitioner whose counselling was embedded within another professional role.

The purpose of the counselling menu is to maximize the possibility that a counselling conversation has an appropriate *focus*, so that the person is given every opportunity to talk about what they need to talk about, in a way that is most effective for them. An additional purpose is to make a space for engaging in dialogue around goals, tasks and methods that may *not* be suitable for counselling, or for the actual counselling relationship that is on offer, and the question of where and how these aspirations might be pursued.

Box 4.1   The development of concepts of goal and task within counselling theory and practice

One of the first theorists to highlight the notion that counselling might be understood in terms of goals and tasks was Ed Bordin. In what has become a classic paper, Bordin (1979) was attempting to establish two key points. First, he was arguing that it was possible to make sense of all of the various forms of counselling and psychotherapy that were in use, ranging from psychoanalysis to behaviour therapy, in terms of a common model of the client–therapist relationship. Second, he proposed that, in any counselling or psychotherapy, the quality and effectiveness of the client–therapist relationship could be defined in terms of the level of agreement between the two participants in terms of the goals and tasks of counselling, and the strength of the emotional and personal bond between them. Because the main focus of Bordin's argument was around the significance of the relationship, in this article he did not clearly define what he meant by goals and tasks. The later theoretical and research work carried out by Les Greenberg (Greenberg, 1992; Greenberg *et al.*, 1993) has been invaluable in clarifying the meaning of counselling goals and tasks, and in demonstrating how these concepts can be used to guide practice. For Greenberg, the goals of the person seeking help can be defined simply as 'those problems on which the client wished to work in therapy . . . . [The] therapist seeks to understand the client's view of his or her goals and problems and accepts the client's goals rather than imposing goals on the clien' (Greenberg *et al.*, 1993: 109–10). Influenced by research into the strategies that experts use to carry out problem-solving tasks in fields such as chess playing, Greenberg argued that the same kind of framework could be applied to therapy: the client and therapist carry out problem-solving tasks in relation to the client's therapeutic goals. A major difference between therapy, on the one hand, and activities such as chess on the other, are that in the latter the task is mainly a cognitive or rational one, whereas in the former the task is concerned mainly with the expression and processing of emotions and meanings.

A task, within Greenberg's approach, comprises a sequence of actions with a beginning, middle and end. Greenberg suggested that it was possible for a counsellor to identify markers in what the person was talking about, and the manner of their talking, that would indicate that specific tasks were necessary, and then later on to identify signs that the task had been effectively resolved or completed. Greenberg also believes that it is possible to define, through reflection on practice and systematic research, an optimal sequence of activities for the resolution of any specific tasks: in other words, there is usually a 'best' way to approach a task.

The approach taken within this book has been influenced by the task model developed by Greenberg (1992; Greenberg *et al.*, 1993). However, it differs from Greenberg's model in three main ways. First, the counselling skill model assumes that there are many different ways in which any specific task can be carried out. It is important when reading Greenberg's work to appreciate that he was aiming to establish the validity of his own therapy model, known as process-experiential therapy, rather than trying to formulate a general model that might accommodate all possible approaches. Second, the counselling skill model proposes that it is useful to describe different forms of task resolution as comprising alternative *methods*, and that the range of methods that can be employed is restricted only by the limits of human ingenuity and creativity. Third, the counselling skill model suggests a rather wider set of counselling tasks than those outlined by Greenberg *et al.* (1993). Nevertheless, the task framework developed by Greenberg and his colleagues serves as an essential template for how practitioners can work to help people in ways that avoid the danger, in among the complexity of the person's problems, of 'losing the thread' of what the person seeking help really needs to do to move on.

Some of the ways in which a counselling menu may be applied in practice are illustrated in the following scenarios.

Examples

Sandro is highly fearful of dental treatment. One of the nurses at the surgery has had some training in working with phobic patients, so arranges a consultation a few days before Sandro's scheduled treatment. The nurse begins by asking Sandro what he wants to achieve. He says he is not sure. 'Well,' she replies, 'some people who worry about going to the dentist believe that it's something that is really big for them. For example, they may be afraid of other similar situations, such as going to the doctor, and so they want to look at the whole issue of what is happening for them in these situations. Other people are just looking for a strategy that will help them to cope better with seeing their dentist.' Sandro indicated that he was just looking for a way of dealing with his fear of being in the dentist's chair. The nurse then asked whether he had any idea of what might help. 'Yes, I think I basically need to learn how to relax – I just get myself so wound up.' The nurse then outlined methods that could be used to manage fear and anxiety, including relaxation techniques on tape, cognitive reframing training and a diazepam prescription. Together, they discussed what would be best for him.

Agnes is a social worker who works in a centre that offers support to families. Inez is a single mother, with three young children, who has been struggling with a number of issues around controlling her children's behaviour, as well as ongoing financial problems. Inez comes to trust Agnes and asks if they can have some time together on their own to talk about 'stuff I need to get off my chest'. When they meet and begin to talk, Inez breaks down and begins to talk in a confused way about her experience of being sexually abused as a child, and how seeing her own children 'just brings it all back' and 'paralyses me'. As they talk, Agnes begins to sense that Inez is ready to face these memories and find ways of moving beyond them. She comments, 'I am wondering if what you are talking about has been around for a while but now is something you want to really look at and put behind you.' Inez agrees: 'I want to sort it all out and put my life on a different track.' Agnes explains that she does not think that it would be a good idea for her to offer to do this with Inez: 'I haven't had the right kind of training to feel that I could give you what you need. Also, as you know, with my caseload it would be very hard to guarantee that we could meet like this regularly enough.' They explore the other resources that might be available to Inez in terms of long-term therapy, especially a specialist counselling service and a survivors of sexual abuse group offered by a women's co-operative. They then agreed on the 'bits that I might be able to help you with myself', such as support for making an appointment with one of these services, and 'looking at how the therapy might make a difference to the way you are with the kids'.

What is being described in these examples is not a formal system of assessment and contracting, but an approach to practice in which the counsellor is mindful of the fact that the person seeking help has their own ideas about what they need, and is aware that there are many possible ways of meeting these needs. It is important to recognize that, for anyone involved in offering counselling embedded with another role, facilitating a discussion of goals, tasks and methods does not necessarily require a high degree of training and theoretical knowledge, but can rely on a basic common-sense understanding of life. In the example of Inez, for instance, the social worker had not received much training in counselling or psychotherapy, but was able to make use of her gut response to her client, which was along the lines of 'this would be too much for me to handle'. She was also able to recognize that, within the very broad life goal that Inez had identified ('put my life on a different track'), it was possible to isolate one sub-task ('looking at the effect on the kids') that was clearly within her competence to deliver. In the case of Sandro, by contrast, the nurse responding to his fear of dental treatment had received specific training in relation to this type of problem and was prepared to explore a sophisticated menu of possible sub-tasks and alternative methods with her patient.

The rest of this chapter provides a framework of a counselling menu that may be applicable in many counselling settings. The precise menu that is on offer in any particular counselling situation will depend on the counsellor and the organizational setting in which they are based.

Clarifying the person's goals

It is essential to recognize that a person seeking help always has an aim or goal, in entering a counselling relationship. A counselling goal can be defined as a preferred state of affairs, or outcome, that the person seeking help and their counsellor have agreed to work towards. There is always something that a person *wants* or desires, some area of discomfort with life that they wish to change, that brings a person into a counselling situation. The question 'why now?' is potentially one of the most useful things for a counsellor to keep in mind as a person begins to talk about their troubles. Similarly, when the person has resolved the issue, has received enough of what they want or need, when they have achieved enough of their goals, then they know that they have had enough counselling and that it is time to stop.

The concept of goal can be used to refer to aims and objectives that may be all-encompassing or quite specific. *Life goals* are overarching issues or existential questions that give shape to a person's life. Examples of life goals are:

- Can I move beyond the memory of the abuse I received in childhood, to the point where I can believe in my own value as a person?
- What do I need to do to prove that I am good enough to satisfy my mother and father?
- My Mum and Dad are Sikh through and through, but I grew up in England. How do I define who I am as a person?

Life goals reflect personal issues that permeate all aspects of a person's life or social niche. For instance, 'moving beyond the memory of abuse' may be associated with difficulties and tensions in intimate and work relationships, in the capacity to be alone, and in the capacity to make plans for the future. *Specific* goals, by contrast, refer to more limited situations or scenarios. Examples of such goals might include:

- How can I feel less anxious in interviews?
- What can I do to convey to my doctor that I don't need to take this medication any longer?
- I am caught between wanting to retire and feeling that I should continue to bring home a salary. How can I make a decision?

For practitioners whose counselling function is embedded within other work roles and responsibilities, it is much easier to respond effectively to specific goals than to more global issues. The latter tend to be associated with a massive personal agenda of beliefs, dilemmas and concerns that may need to be explored. To tackle life issues in a satisfactory manner requires plenty of time. Psychotherapists and specialist counselling agencies are in a better position to work with life goals than are counsellors whose practice is embedded in other professional roles. On the other hand, specific or situational goals may be addressed effectively within one or two brief conversations. It is important to keep in mind that not everyone who seeks counselling wants to deal with issues at the 'life goal' level. A person who has identified a specific goal may prefer to focus on that one issue, rather than being expected to open out all aspects of their life, as might happen in psychotherapy. Nevertheless, when working with specific goals it is important to keep in mind that, ultimately, specific goals can always be understood as reflecting broader life goals and as nested within these wider goals. For example, a person who starts off by wanting to talk about 'telling my doctor that I don't want medication' may end up realizing that such a goal represents part of a broader personal agenda that they come to describe as 'moving beyond the memory of the abuse I received in childhood to the point where I can believe in my own value as a person and stand up for what I want with people whom I perceive as powerful and dominant'.

It is important to be clear about the difference between the concept of goal, on the one hand, and the similar concept of problem. A personal goal is always phrased in an *active* and *positive* way, whereas problem-language talks of burdens and inadequacies. A goal can be regarded as similar to a personal quest – a question that the person is trying to explore and answer. It can be useful, therefore, for a counsellor who is talking with a person about their goals to try to use active, positive language which reinforces the person's strengths, so that counselling goals are perceived not as indicators of failure: but as opportunities for development and connection. For instance, Sheila was a participant in a project that was designed to help women return to work after having been carers. She described herself as crippled by fear at interviews, and not able to tell those interviewing her about her relevant experience and qualities. In a consultation session with one of the project tutors, Sheila was asked what she would like to talk about. She replied, 'I have a problem with interviews. I am wracked with nerves. I am just so anxious all the time.' The tutor responded by asking, 'Is this something that we could look at more closely? From what you have told me before about this, I'm thinking that what you want to be able to do is to make sure that you can give these interviewers every chance to know about your experience and qualities, and that the nervousness gets in the way. Would that be a reasonable way to describe what we might aim to work on together?' If the tutor had accepted Sheila's initial formulation of the issue, as 'something that is wrong with me and needs to be fixed', he would have reinforced a way of describing the situation that portrayed Sheila as deficient and passive. By rephrasing the issue in active and positive language, in which Sheila's desired positive outcome is acknowledged ('letting the interviewers know about your good qualities') and the status of anxiety is diminished from a totally incapacitating ('totalizing') entity to being something that merely 'gets in the way'. This use of language on the part of the tutor immediately opened up a space for different kinds of things to happen within the conversation with Sheila.

There is also an important distinction to be made between goals and *symptoms*. Because we live in a culture in which the medicalization of personal and social issues is widespread and pervasive, it is very easy to 'hear' a person's problems as reflecting a set of symptoms. For instance, Sunita was a young woman who had grown up in England, but had lived within a devout Sikh community. She had started to question her sense of cultural identity and was acting in a manner that might be regarded as 'depressed' – low in energy, isolated from others, unable to sleep, lacking in hope. Indeed, Sunita herself used this terminology in her own way of talking, and often described herself as 'depressed'. From a counselling perspective, however, it is not helpful to view problems in symptom terms. There are three reasons for this. First, symptom language tends to be *totalizing*: it suggests that the *whole* of a person can be characterized in terms of an illness such as 'depression'. To think or talk about a person in this way can result in failing to recognize and acknowledge other aspects of the person's life that are not 'depressed'. Second, symptom language portrays a person as a passive object: depression is something you 'have', not something you 'do'. Third, by using a commonplace term such as 'depression', the person is prevented from taking advantage of their capacity for imagination and creativity. For example, Sunita had her own unique phrase – 'that being nowhere feeling' – which effectively conveyed what being 'depressed' meant to her, and was more readily woven into conversations that were anti-totalizing ('yes, there are times when I feel I am somewhere') and positioned her as an active co-constructor of her reality ('How do I get to nowhere? I go through a door marked "leave me alone", for a start . . .').

In some forms of psychotherapy and specialist counselling, the therapist may spend quite a lot of time negotiating a contract with the client, which includes targets or treatment goals. It is seldom either necessary or possible to undertake this kind of formal contracting in embedded microcounselling situations. What is helpful is to invite the person to talk about their goals. It is essential during a counselling conversation to be on the alert for whatever the person might say about what they want – their goals – and to reflect back and check out that what the counsellor has picked up is accurate.

There are many ways of encouraging a conversation about goals. Some potentially useful counsellor statements include:

> 'I can hear from what you are saying that . . . . However, in an ideal scenario, if everything was just as you wanted it to be, how would it be different? How do you want things to be?'

> 'Can you say what it is you would like to gain from talking to me about . . .?'

> 'You have described your problem. Are you able to tell me what you hope will happen if we can sort this problem out? What are you aiming for?'

> (At the end of a counselling session): 'I was wondering – have you got what you needed from our discussion? Is there anything else you need?'

Much of the time, however, the specific goals that a person may have are implicit in the way that they talk about the problem for which they are seeking help. It is up to the counsellor to 'listen for goals' and then to check out what they have heard, rather than paying attention only to problems.

It is essential to acknowledge that people who seek counselling may have enormous difficulties in articulating what their goals are. They may *know*, at a feeling or gut level, what they want, but they may not readily be able to put this into words. There are at least three reasons for this. First, the goal or purpose may be associated with a vague feeling – 'I'm just exhausted all the time and I don't know what its about', or 'there's a big empty space inside me'. In these cases, it is as if the person's body has a sense of purpose and direction, in somehow using tiredness or the sense of an empty space to indicate that something is wrong. In these circumstances, all the person can do is to be willing to follow where their body is leading: the end point is far from clear. A second difficulty that some people have in talking about what they want is that they know what their goal is, but are afraid or ashamed to acknowledge it. For example, Danny knew full well that he needed help to talk about his sexuality and 'come out' as gay, but would not say this until he was fully convinced that his chosen 'counsellor' (for him, a youth worker based at the local community centre) would respond in a non-critical and sympathetic manner. It was only when he felt safe enough with his counsellor that Danny was able to articulate his goals. A third type of difficulty that some people have in expressing their goals for counselling is that they may never have had the opportunity to reflect on what they want, so they can only convey a confusing jumble of reasons. To return to an example used earlier in the chapter, Sunita had a sense that she had never been able to belong or to have a sense of fitting in, but it was only when she attended a counselling skills evening class and took part in personal development exercises that this vague awareness crystallized into a desire to explore and define her cultural identity.

In situations where a person has difficulty being clear about their goals, it is important for a counsellor to be willing to work with the person around the best mutual understanding of their aims that is possible, rather than wait until a fully crystallized goal statement can be formulated. What is important is that both the person seeking help and the person offering counselling should have a sufficient level of agreement over the goals that they are 'on the same wavelength'.

To summarize: the idea of *goal* is important in counselling because it provides a way of structuring and organizing what happens in a counselling session. It is the ultimate reference point for whatever happens in counselling. A person seeking help will gauge whatever is being discussed in counselling against the touchstone of whether it is helping them to move closer to their goals. The concept of goal also provides a way of making a link between the immediate reason the person gives for seeking counselling ('I need to talk to someone about getting into fights with my Dad', 'I feel sad a lot of the time') and the broader direction of the person's life ('can I accept myself as a person in my own terms?'): specific goals are always linked to broader existential questions of meaning, purpose and identity, even if these bigger questions tend to remain firmly in the background in the majority of microcounselling encounters. The notion of the person's goal acts as a reminder that the counselling space exists for a purpose: it is a kind of time out to enable a person to repair their personal niche. It is also a reminder that the person seeking help is an active participant in life, a person who has purposes, rather than problems and symptoms.

Counselling tasks

Although agreement over goals is essential as a way of ensuring that the person and counsellor are working towards the same end, it is difficult to do anything in counselling that will directly impact on a goal. What is necessary instead is to identify specific *tasks* whose completion can allow the person to take a step towards their goal.

The model of counselling skill suggested in this book assumes a process through which a person who is troubled in some way by tensions within their relationships or life space and who has a sense of wanting to do something about it (goals), seeks out a counsellor and negotiates the construction of a safe space within which they can talk through the problem. But what happens next? What does 'talking through' mean in practice? Within the model of counselling skill, the specific business of counselling is understood as being based on the engagement in and completion of a set of distinctive counselling *tasks*. A counselling task can be defined as a sequence of actions carried out by a person, in collaboration with a counsellor, in order to be able to get on with their life. A task is something that the person and the counsellor undertake together. For any specific counselling task, there are a potentially infinite number of different *methods* that can be used to complete it. The safest and most helpful practice occurs when the person and their counsellor *decide together* the task in which they are engaged, and agree on the method that they will use to tackle the task.

The concepts of *task* and *method* are central to the framework for counselling practice that is introduced in this book. In the following chapters, a range of basic counselling tasks are discussed, including:

- talking though an issue in order to understand things better;
- making sense of an event or experience that is puzzling and problematic;
- problem solving, planning and decision making;
- changing behaviour;
- dealing with difficult feelings and emotions;
- finding, analysing and acting on information;
- undoing self-criticism and enhancing self-care;
- negotiating a life transition;
- dealing with difficult or painful relationships.

The precise labels and definitions given to these tasks are inevitably fairly arbitrary. Experienced counsellors evolve their own ways of describing tasks. In practice, a counselling episode may focus on a single facet of one of these tasks (for example, concentrating on understanding barriers to change, rather than working through a whole behaviour change sequence). Sometimes, an episode may encompass two or three interlocking tasks that are pursued at the same time (for example, exploring how I feel in relation to a life transition).

Being able to work with these tasks represents a set of basic competences for anyone involved in offering counselling relationships. These tasks reflect competences that are firmly based in an everyday, common-sense ability to cope with life. We are all able to hold meaningful conversations, make sense of puzzling reactions to situations, solve problems, and so on. Being a good counsellor involves being willing to examine one's individual strengths and weaknesses in relation to being able to carry out these tasks, developing flexibility and sensitivity in relation to engaging with other people around the tasks, and being open to learning new methods and strategies for task resolution. A good counsellor is someone who knows the 'ins and outs' of the kinds of tasks that arise in their practice, and is able to adapt or improvise methods of task completion that are appropriate to the individual with whom they are working.

Box 4.2   An example of a task model: counselling in dementia

Within the past decade, new methods for the early diagnosis of dementia, and the availability of drug treatments that can slow down the development of Alzheimer's disease, mean that there is an increasing number of people who have received a diagnosis of dementia yet may expect to live in their families, at a relatively good level of functioning, for many years. The diagnosis of dementia raises strong feelings and evokes powerful negative images not only in people with dementia, but also within their family and community. In addition, it may be difficult to cope with the gradual memory loss that is associated with the disease. For these reasons, increasing attention is being given to the potential role of counselling at the time of diagnosis as a means of helping people with dementia, and their families, to deal with this event. In research carried out by Weaks *et al.* (2006), people with dementia and their families were interviewed regarding their experience of the diagnosis, and the issues with which they had been confronted in the first six months following the diagnosis. Analysis of these interviews led to the identification of a set of psychotherapeutic tasks that seemed particularly relevant to people in this situation:

- exploring the possibility of life as normal;
- evaluating the usefulness of different sources of information;
- understanding the changing roles within their families and wider social network;
- understanding and dealing with the emotional process;
- addressing deep philosophical questions, such as the possibility of loss of identity;
- embracing and coping with social stigma;
- creating a new and different identity;
- telling and retelling their story;
- finding a way through the health system.

These tasks could be fulfilled using a variety of methods, including from formal/specialist counselling, embedded counselling from doctors, community nurses and clergy, participation in self-help groups and reading. The identification of these tasks makes it possible to design appropriate care systems, and to train and supervise staff, and enables people with dementia and their families to know what to expect.

Methods

Any counselling task can be carried out using a number of different *methods*. People can learn, change or reconstruct their personal niche, in a variety of ways, depending on their upbringing, cultural background, temperament, and their awareness of the change resources and methods that are available within their social world. Theories of counselling, psychotherapy and psychology, religious teachings and practices, and self-help books, as well as common sense, afford a vast repertoire of ways of dealing with problems in living. In any counselling situation, it is up the person and the counsellor to decide together what they can do to complete a task.

Although the range of task-resolution methods that can be employed is potentially limitless, and continually being expanded as a result of human inventiveness and creativity, the toolkit of methods used by most counsellors can be categorized in terms of five broadly defined types:

- *Conversation*. The counsellor and the person seeking help talk about the issue or task, and allow solutions and new understandings to emerge from their dialogue. This method relies on the vast richness of language, and its potential for redescribing and reconceptualizing events. Conversation, or 'just talking', is almost certainly the most frequently used method in any counselling relationship. To return to the metaphor of the software menu employed earlier in this chapter, conversation is the 'default setting' for a counselling relationship;
- *Structured problem-focused activities*. Either the counsellor or the person seeking help may suggest or devise activities or routines that can be applied to resolving the issue. Within the counselling world, cognitive behavioural therapy in particular represents a rich resource of activities, such as relaxation training, homework assignments, initiating rewards for preferred behaviour, identifying and challenging irrational beliefs, and much else.
- *Arts-based creative activities*. There are many counselling tasks that can be resolved by drawing, painting, imaginative writing and enactment. For example, a person struggling to come to terms with difficult and painful emotions may find it helpful to express their feelings in a picture or to write a letter to someone with whom they feel angry.
- *Cultural resources*. A fourth method of task resolution draws on the everyday practices that are used within the person's cultural world to express feelings, maintain connectedness and maintain a sense of personal identity. For instance, many cultural resources can potentially make a difference to someone who may be depressed and lacking in hope and purpose, including physical exercise such as jogging, voluntary work, walking in the countryside, spiritual practices such as meditation and prayer, and attending the cinema or theatre. The role of the counsellor in relation to these methods is not to implement them within a counselling session, but to help the person to explore and find the cultural resources that are personally most meaningful, to provide support and guidance during the stage of starting to get involved, and then, if necessary, to help the person to get maximum value out of the cultural activities they have undertaken, in terms of making an impact on their initial problem in living.
- *The personal resources of the counsellor*. Underpinning all of these other methods is the capacity of the counsellor to apply their experience of life, and their personal accomplishments and learning, to address the needs of the person seeking help.

These methods are discussed in more detail below.

Conversation as method

As mentioned earlier, conducting a therapeutic conversation is the 'default mode' for counselling. 'Talking' can be viewed as a both a task and a method. For example, when a person seeking help first meets with a counsellor, it is almost always necessary to encourage the person to 'just talk' for while, to get their perspective on the problem and to gain some idea of what their goals might be. However, even when some agreement over the goal of counselling is achieved, a key task that may be undertaken to move towards that goal may be to talk about specific aspects of the issue. Talk can have a cathartic and freeing effect: 'it was a relief just to get that off my chest'. Sometimes, people who seek help are holding secrets, and the act of telling another person may be a crucial step in alleviating guilt, embarrassment and shame and in beginning to see oneself as normal or acceptable. Talking and telling are basic elements of the act of seeking social support and are fundamental counselling tasks. However, talk can also be viewed as a method that can be employed in addressing other tasks, such as decision making, dealing with emotions or enhancing self-care. That is because the more a person talks about an issue, the more likelihood there is that they will generate new meanings and possibilities around understanding the issue or doing something different about it. In addition, therapeutic talk involves the participation of a listener, the counsellor, who is skilled in responding in ways that facilitate the creation of meaning and possibility. The role of conversation is so important in counselling that a chapter of this book is devoted to it (see Chapter 8).

Structured problem-focused activities

Structured activities can be viewed as exercises or techniques that are designed to facilitate personal learning. These activities can be effective and helpful in counselling for a number of reasons. First, they provide the person seeking help with clear guidelines for things they can do that will make a difference to their problem. Second, they represent a focus for collaborative activity between the counsellor and the person seeking help, thereby contributing to building a sense of shared purpose and relationship. Third, they bring to the counselling a 'can do' attitude and sense of hope. Even if a structured activity is not entirely successful in allowing a counselling task to be completed, therefore, it can still yield some positive benefits. The disadvantage of structured activities as counselling methods is that an over-reliance by the counsellor on 'techniques' can leave the person seeking help with a sense that all the counsellor is offering is a formulaic set of exercises, from an 'expert role', rather than being willing to meet them in a true person-to-person relationship. The danger, therefore, is that structured activities can be distancing and can threaten the quality of the all-important therapeutic alliance or relationship.

Although structured activities have been developed within many different approaches to counselling, this method is largely associated with the approach known as cognitive behavioural therapy. Cognitive behavioural therapy (CBT) is an approach to psychotherapy that is widely used in the National Health Service, for example, by clinical psychologists and nurse therapists. Its origins are in scientific/academic psychology, initially the behavioural theory of B. F. Skinner, and then more recently in ideas from cognitive psychology. The key figures in the development of CBT have been Donald Meichenbaum, Albert Ellis, Windy Dryden and Aaron Beck. There is an extensive literature on training, research and practice in CBT; useful introductory texts include Trower (1988), Wills (1997), McLeod (2003), and Neenan and Dryden (2005). There are also several many self-help manuals on the market, such as Greenberger and

Padesky (1995), which enable clients to learn and apply CBT techniques in the absence of professional help.

The key ideas within the CBT approach to counselling are:

- Problems that a person has are the result of *learning* – the person has learned to respond to the world in ways that have become dysfunctional. The concept of *reinforcement* is essential for understanding the process of learning: ultimately, a person's behaviour changes because new patterns are rewarded and reinforced, and the reinforcement of old patterns is withdrawn or cut off.
- Awareness of the role that irrational, exaggerated or negative thoughts (cognitions) have in maintaining a problem, and working with the person to challenge and change the way that they think about things.
- The use of simple techniques to facilitate change – for example, systematic desensitization and thought stopping.
- The use of 'homework' assignments to ensure that what is learned in the counselling room is transferred to the real world.
- An image of the role of the counsellor as a teacher or coach, working alongside the person to help to learn and apply new behaviours and skills.

An example of a structured activity that is widely used in CBT is *systematic desensitization*. This activity is employed to help people to overcome reactions of fear and anxiety in specific situations, such as fear of heights. The underlying theory is that, for some reason, the person has learned to associate an anxiety or fear response with a particular stimulus or situation (such as a high place or climbing a ladder). The behaviour of *avoiding* such situations is reinforced through the fact that this avoidance results in feeling calm, whereas any exposure to the fear-inducing situation is stressful or even terrifying. The technique of systematic desensitization aims to eliminate the fear/avoidance response to the target situation by gradually replacing it with an alternative response (in this instance, a relaxation response). The person is therefore first taught a set of systematic relaxation skills, using slow breathing, tensing and relaxing muscles, and attaining a calm mental state. Then, the counsellor invites the person to practise these relaxation skills while encountering the fearful situation. To begin with, the person may be invited to imagine fear-inducing scenes or to look at photographs, all the while using their relaxation skills. Once the person is able to remain relaxed in the presence of imaginary situations, they move on to encountering real-life examples of heights, ladders, stairwells, bridges or whatever it is that they fear, again gradually moving from less frightening to more frightening situations. Throughout this process, the person's feelings of success, satisfaction and achievement, and the praise they receive from others, have the effect of reinforcing the new pattern of behaviour. Systematic desensitization represents a structured activity, devised by cognitive behavioural therapists, that makes a lot of sense to people seeking help for phobic conditions. Although it is a method that can require several sessions of therapy to complete, it nevertheless includes a number of elements that can be used perfectly effectively in microcounselling. For instance, it may be helpful to take a highly anxious person through some relaxation skill exercises, or to talk about how to face up to fears in a graded, step-by-step manner, or to undertake homework activities that involve some of the steps of the systematic desensitization process.

There are many other structured counselling activities that have been developed, both within CBT and in the context of other counselling approaches. Some widely used activities include the following:

- When a person is trying to change their behaviour in relation to a habit such as eating, smoking or drinking alcohol, suggesting to them that they might keep a diary in which they record the frequency of the problem behaviour, the situations that trigger it, and the immediate effects or consequences of engaging in the behaviour. Keeping such a diary is helpful in itself, by making the person more aware of what it is they are doing and also provides invaluable information for later planning around how to change the patterns of behaviour that are unwanted.
- When a person has unresolved emotional 'business' with another person and is unable to confront that person directly (for instance, in a situation where the other person has died), it can be useful to suggest that they write a letter, or series of letters, to the other person, written in as honest and expressive a way as possible. These letters may then be read out in a meeting with the counsellor, and either ritually burned, buried or stored. This kind of letter writing can help a person to arrive at some degree of closure by expressing their deepest thought and feelings, and may allow them to reflect on what they can learn, for themselves, about what happened, as they read the letters they have written.
- When a person is contemplating some kind of transition in their life, such as deciding whether to move to a new city, take a new job, or get married or divorced, it can be useful to keep a record of dream content. From the most remote traditional cultures, through to the work of psychoanalysts such as Freud and Jung, it has been recognized that dreams can convey a degree of personal 'truth' that may be hard for a person to acknowledge during normal, rational discourse. Although there exist many different types of guidelines for dream interpretation, the simplest way to use dreams is to write them down as soon as possible on waking, and then to imagine that the dream is trying to tell you something. Listening closely to the dream is usually sufficient to trigger meaningful self-reflection. The role of the counsellor here is not to be a 'dream expert', but to encourage the person to use their dreams, and to be with them in this process.

These are just a few examples of the many hundreds of structured counselling activities that have been described in the professional literature. Some of these tasks are complex, others are quite simple. Some require a certain degree of training and supervision if they are to be applied effectively, whereas others are self-explanatory and can be put into action on the basis of reading or after hearing them described by a colleague. A valuable source of ideas about structured methods is Seiser and Wastell (2002).

Using expressive arts-based methods

Traditionally, counselling has consisted of a conversation between a person and a counsellor, in which the person talks about issues that concern them, and through dialogue with the counsellor reaches new understandings, makes choices, and so on. In parallel to this mainstream tradition has been a range of approaches to therapy that make use of non-verbal, arts-based methods to assist the person to explore issues in a creative way. These arts-based therapies include art therapy, drama therapy, psychodrama and sociodrama, dance therapy, music therapy and the therapeutic use of photographs. In addition, there is poetry therapy, which draws on verbal creativity. In the main, these therapies have operated as separate specialisms, with distinct professional associations being set up for each area. Also, there has been a tendency for these methods to be used with what have been considered as hard-to-reach clients, such as children, people with long-term mental health issues and people with learning difficulties, on the grounds that these people may be less able or willing to communicate their problems through purely verbal means.

In recent years, however, a different perspective on arts-based methods in counselling has become influential. This perspective takes the view that creative methods are valuable as part of all counselling and psychotherapy and can be integrated into ways of working that may be predominantly conversational in nature. One strand of this movement has been what is known as *expressive therapy*. A key figure in expressive therapy has been Natalie Rogers, the daughter of Carl Rogers (see Rogers, 2000). Counsellors trained in expressive therapy use a variety of creative techniques to help clients to express their feelings. Beyond this specific approach, there are many counsellors who have chosen to integrate arts activities into their style of working with people. A recent survey found that around half of counsellors use arts techniques, such as drawing, on a regular basis in their work despite having had little or no formal training in any of the arts-based therapies. This suggests that many counsellors, and their clients, find that expressive methods are a valuable addition to the usual verbal counselling process.

Some of the arts-based methods that counsellors may use in the context of everyday one-to-one practice are:

- inviting the person to draw a map or a picture that represents their life as a whole, their relationships or their feelings at that moment;
- having objects available – buttons, stones, driftwood, toy figures – that the person can pick up and hold, and can arrange on a table to illustrate their relationships with other people in their life;
- suggesting that the person brings in photographs from significant points in their life, or of significant people (Berman, 1993; Weiser, 1999);
- suggesting that the person brings in an object or image that has particular meaning for them;
- having music or sound-making objects available, or children's modelling clay, that the person can use to express their emotions;
- inviting the person to bring in a tape of a piece of music that has meaning for them.

These methods have a number of potential advantages in counselling:

- when a person is talking about a problem, they are almost always monitoring what they are saying in terms of the impact it will have on the counsellor ('what will she think of me if I say that?'). In contrast, creativity activity has the potential to allow the person to get involved in a task in which they can 'lose themself';
- speaking can sometimes define an issue in a fixed or black-and-white manner, whereas there is always some degree of ambiguity in art – an image can be interpreted in different ways;

- images and other art objects provide a good way of capturing the *whole* of an issue, its complexity or interrelatedness, whereas words restrict the person to saying one thing at a time;
- the act of *doing* something, rather than just talking, can be interesting and energizing for the person;
- arts-based methods make use of a person's imagination and creativity;
- an object such as a picture or sculpture is a permanent reminder of the learning that took place in a counselling session, and may be taken home and kept ('that picture over there was made when I learned how angry I was . . .');
- arts activities introduce the possibility of the person and the counsellor relating in a different way. Rather than one speaking directly to another, they can sit side by side and look together at an object. This can enhance a spirit of co-operation and collaboration.

It is important to be aware that there are also some disadvantages or possible pitfalls associated with use of arts-based methods in counselling. For example, people who say they were 'failures at art in school' may see an art exercise as a test or source of anxiety, and may find it hard to engage. It is always important to address these anxieties, even if they are not immediately apparent. Another disadvantage is that arts-based methods can require time and equipment, and can be difficult to fit into counselling conversations that are unplanned or brief or that take place in a setting where the counsellor has little control over the meeting space (for example, a nurse responding to the emotional distress of a patient in a ward situation).

It is important for a counsellor to introduce an arts-based activity in a way that makes it clear how the activity connects with the counselling conversation at that point ('You have been talking about your family . . . . I was wondering if it might be helpful to use these buttons to show who they all are and the kind of relationship they have with you. It would certainly make it easier for me to get a sense of how they all fit together . . .'). Before using an art activity it is essential to have personal experience of it, both in a client or learner role and in trying it out in practice sessions with colleagues or members of a training course.

Two key principles of using arts methods in counselling are:

- *Ask permission before touching.* The art object belongs to the person and is part of them.
- *Do not interpret.* Sometimes it may be that the person is able to find meaning in an object they have created through silent reflection, and may not wish to talk about it. Usually the process of creating an object will stimulate a wish to talk about it. When this happens, the aim is to work with the person to explore what the object means to them. It can be very tempting for a counsellor to offer their own interpretations, but usually this will get in the way of the person's own process of making sense.

There are several useful books that explore the broad-based use of expressive methods in general counselling situations (Warren, 1993; Silverstone, 1997; Wiener, 2001; Malchiodi, 2004).

Using cultural resources

There is an important sense in which all counselling involves the mobilization, and use of social and cultural resources. Counsellors and counselling agencies can be viewed as resources that are available to people within a community who need to talk through personal problems in living. Theories of counselling and psychotherapy, such as Carl Rogers' person-centred approach or Transactional Analysis are cultural resources that are available to anyone who is able to visit a bookshop or carry out an internet search. However, this section is concerned with a more specific meaning of the idea of cultural resources, referring to the ability of a counsellor to assist a person to find and apply sources of help that are available within their community, in order to resolve a problem in living.

There are several different forms of cultural resource that can be used in counselling. A key cultural resource, for many people, can be found in the area of self-help books and support groups. There is a wealth of written self-help literature that is available, as well as an increasing number of self-help websites. Self-help sources can include manuals that guide a person through a programme of behaviour change, books that describe principles for living a satisfying life, and inspirational novels and films that describe how someone has overcome or lived with a specific problem. At any given time, the non-fiction bestseller lists will include a number of self-help titles – self-help is big business for the publishing industry. One of the difficulties in this area lies in the fact that so many self-help books are available. It can be hard for a counsellor to know what to suggest that a person might read or to comment on the possible value of a book that a person has found for themselves. In this context, it can be worthwhile consulting two publications that serve the useful function of reviewing self-help resources: Norcross et al. (2003) and L'Abate (2004). Online self-help materials are reviewed by Grohol (2004).

Self-help support groups and Internet communities have grown up around every imaginable problem in living. Self-help groups can be defined as supportive or therapeutic groups that are run by and for individuals suffering from a specific problem. Although such groups may draw on professional expertise at times, they are ultimately under the control of members. Some of these networks are local whereas others (such as Alcoholics Anonymous) comprise national or even international organizations. The activities undertaken by self-help groups cover a wide spectrum, from meetings where people can share their experiences through to educational sessions (learning how to cope), practical help, political campaigning and promoting research.

Practitioners whose counselling is embedded in another professional role are in a strong position to engage constructively with people seeking help around the relative merits of different types of self-help resources. This is because nurses, teachers, social workers and other human service professionals generally work with specific client groups, and quickly learn about the self-help groups that are available locally, and the self-help books and websites that have proved to be most beneficial. By contrast, counsellors and psychotherapists working in, for example, private practice are likely to see clients with a wider range of problems and are less likely to get much opportunity to gain an in-depth knowledge of self-help resources that may be relevant for particular problems.

Self-help resources represent only one type of cultural resource. Self-help is always organized around a specific problem. There are many other forms of cultural resource that are potentially applicable to all, or most, problems. For example, there is research evidence to show that the following activities can play a positive role in overcoming problems in living: religious observance, spirituality, sport and exercise, political involvement, voluntary work, enjoyment of nature and pet ownership. There are several reasons why these social and cultural activities can be helpful for people experiencing problems in living:

- access to social support;
- developing a sense of purpose, and the experience of achieving something;
- learning new behaviours, which may be applicable in resolving problems and achieving life goals;
- involvement in new activities gives less time to dwell on problems;
- physical challenges can be energizing and counteract depression.

The importance and potential of social and cultural resources as ways of allowing people to combat problems in living has been a major theme within the emerging academic field of community psychology. The writings of Orford (1992), and Prilleltensky and Nelson (2005) provide excellent introductions to work in this area.

The counsellor's personal resources

There is a final category of counselling methods that is difficult to describe, but is ultimately hugely important. On the whole, when people receive training in counselling they are normally taught about how to facilitate a therapeutic conversation, how to make use of some structured activities, how to maintain appropriate professional boundaries, and how to build a therapeutic alliance or relationship with the person they are trying to help. What is seldom covered in training is the ability and willingness to be able to go *beyond* these professional competences and to find, when necessary, the personal resources that may be required to carry out counselling tasks that cannot be tackled using skills and competences that are based in personal knowledge. There are some counselling tasks that need methods that are derived from idiosyncratic *personal* knowledge.

Each of us has our own personal history, which includes experiences in many different situations and relationships. In the course of our lives, we acquire insights and know-how that are unique to us, and that cannot be incorporated into a professional knowledge base or theoretical model in a straightforward way. In the context of counselling, the personal knowledge that is most significant is that which concerns relationships, life choices and dealing with challenges. There are many other types of personal resource that can be used in counselling.

Examples
Alistair was a social care worker in a residential unit for troubled adolescents. It was very hard to form relationships with many of the young people in the unit, many of whom had been abused by adults and were angry and mistrustful. Alistair grew

up in a traditional fishing community and remembers being taught by one of the older fishermen how to handle a rowing boat in treacherous seas, for example, how to tack diagonally in a head wind and how to hug the shore in a storm. He frequently drew upon these memories when trying to talk through difficult issues with his clients – he *knew* that the best way from one point to the next was seldom a straight line. His method of facilitating a therapeutic conversation, therefore, was structured around a patient readiness to accept the many interactions that appeared to be heading in the wrong direction, while being alert for moments when it was possible to make some headway.

Maria had grown up in a Greek Orthodox family in which great emphasis was placed on every possible reason for celebrating the significance of a day – not only birthdays, but holy days, days for remembering those who had died, and days to mark the change of seasons. As a nurse responsible for looking after a large caseload of patients at different stages of kidney disease, she used her sensitivity to the significance of days to maintain a deeply personal relationship with even those patients whom she was not able to see on a regular basis. Always, at some point during her first assessment of a new patient, she would collect information about their 'dates'. She always sent them a card, phoned or, if she was able to visit, brought some flowers. When a patient talked to her about the impact of their illness on their life, the dates provided her with an initial reference point in relation to the person's world.

The personal resources used by a counsellor help to define their own unique style as a helper. Some counsellors are highly sensitive to language, others are comfortable with reasoned, step-by-step approaches to problem solving, others are attuned to body movement, gesture, voice quality or energy levels. These are all examples of areas of life experience that can make a contribution to the repertoire of methods available to a counsellor.

Box 4.3   Touchstones: a crucial source of personal knowledge

Mearns and Cooper (2005) use the terms 'touchstones' to refer to a kind of personal knowledge that is fundamental to the capacity to offer a counselling relationship. A personal or existential touchstone is a memory that has deep significance for a person, and from which the person has learned something vital about the meaning of being human. Mearns and Cooper define touchstones as 'events and self-experiences from which we draw considerable strength and which help to ground us in relationships as well as making us more open to and comfortable with a diversity of relationships' (p. 137). They provide an example of a counsellor, Lesley, who identified the following touchstones from her own life:

One of my earliest memories is sitting on my grandfather's knee. Every time I met him he had a radiant smile and he would plonk me on his knee. What I get from that is huge – it is the experience of completely *unconditional love*. That is a really secure part of me that helps me to feel 'at ease' even in difficult situations . . . .

In primary school I was frequently ridiculed for being thin. The most distressing event happened each year when we would be ceremonially measured and weighed in front of the whole PE class. In a flamboyant way, demonstrating nothing but her own self-importance, the teacher announced: 'watch that Lesley does not fall through the cracks in the floorboards'. The strength I take from this experience is feeling my own *rage*. At the time it happened I nearly burst into tears but I was determined not to give her the satisfaction so all I felt was the pure rage. It is surprising how often that strong, clean feeling is a source of strength for me with my clients. I can enter that 'angry girl' and get a strong sense of my client's anger. I think it would have been much worse for me then and also now if I had burst into tears.

(Mearns and Cooper, 2005: 138)

Mearns and Cooper suggest that it is by making use of such personal experiences, and what has been learned from them, that counsellors are able to engage with people seeking help at *relational depth*. Alongside concepts and methods developed within psychotherapy theories, and cultural activities such as art, sport or reading, the counsellor's existential touchstones represent a highly significant resource for anyone trying to deal with troubles in their life.

In the theoretical and research literature in counselling and psychotherapy, a great deal of attention and effort has been devoted to analysing the value in therapy of counsellor *self-disclosure*, or occasions when the counsellor shares personal information with their client. The evidence seems to suggest that counsellor self-disclosure can sometimes be highly effective, and sometimes quite unhelpful. It is helpful if it is well timed, cements the bond between the person and their counsellor, and provides the person with information or a message that they find useful. It is unhelpful if it is done as a way of dealing with the discomfort of the counsellor, or results in the person feeling that their counsellor has taken over the session for the purpose of talking about their own difficulties. However, while self-disclosure can be viewed as one way in which a counsellor can use personal resources (in this instance, sharing personal information) as a method, it is essential to recognize that self-disclosure is quite limited as a strategy compared with the other personal resources that have been discussed in this section.

Reflecting on methods

A counselling method is always a *collaboration* between what the counsellor does and what the person does. Some methods may be suggested or initiated by the counsellor, others by the person seeking help. There are methods where the counsellor will take the lead and do most of the talking, and others where the person seeking help will take the lead and talk most. A key issue for a counsellor, when applying any particular method to fulfil a counselling task, is to be aware of what the method requires of them and what it requires of the client. It is usually the job of the counsellor, rather than the person seeking help, to maintain this kind of overview of the interplay between the complementary roles of counsellor and client during the work on a task. For example, if a counsellor suggests a structured activity (such as learning and applying relaxation skills) and this is accepted by the person seeking help as potentially useful, it is up to the counsellor to explain to the person what they will be called upon to do. Conversely, if the person suggests a method, for example using a cultural resource ('I'm going to start going to church again every Sunday, to meet people and make my weekends more meaningful'), the counsellor needs to check what their role would be in relation to this activity – for instance, would it be useful to talk in advance about what to expect from going to church, or to agree to meet another time to look at what had happened and whether the experiment had been a success. Negotiating around using a method therefore involves checking out and discussing the roles and mutual expectations of counsellor and person during the carrying out of the task.

It can be seen that there exists a wide range of methods that can be used in counselling to complete different tasks. The classification of these methods into five domains – conversation, structured activities, expressive activities, cultural resources and the personal resources of the counsellor – is inevitably fairly arbitrary. There are many methods that overlap these boundaries. For example, a person using a self-help book (cultural resource) may find that the book suggests carrying out CBT-type tasks (structured activities) or the use of creative writing (expressive activity). The person using the self-help book may wish to talk with their counsellor about what they have learned from it (conversation) and find that the counsellor is enthusiastic (or otherwise) because they have found benefit (or not) in self-help books in their own life (counsellor's personal resources). The value of separating methods into these domains is mainly to remind counsellors that there are many different strategies that can be helpful for people and that it is important to be creative in exploring all of the possible resources.

One of the key professional development tasks for any counsellor is to make use of training, experience and collegial networks to build up their personal repertoire or toolkit of methods. Clearly, no individual counsellor can ever claim mastery of all the methods that exist. It is not necessary to be able to do everything – but it *is* important for a counsellor to have options around the methods they employ, to allow the person seeking help some space for choice. It is also essential to keep in mind that the best source of methods is the person who is seeking help: what works will be what makes most sense to them.

The key to using the counselling menu: shared decision making

Having described the nature of goals, tasks and methods, and the various possibilities associated with each of these types of counselling activity, it may be worthwhile at this point to review briefly the basic assumptions about counselling and helping that underpin this approach. These are as follows:

- the person who seeks help is already actively engaged in trying to resolve their problems;
- whatever the counsellor does, the person seeking help will modify and adapt what is offered to meet their needs – the person is far from being a passive recipient of 'expert help';
- there is no one process or mechanism of learning and change that is right for everyone – there is a multiplicity of potentially helpful learning/change processes, and each individual who seeks help will have their own preferences among them;
- there is not a counsellor alive who is competent to work with all the possible therapeutic methods and strategies that exist – each practitioner has their own knowledge base, and strengths and weaknesses.

The reality of any counselling situation, therefore, is that there are multiple possibilities on both sides. There are many things that the person seeking help definitely wants, definitely does not want and may be willing to try. There are other things that the counsellor is either able or not able to offer. It is the job of the counsellor to be able to mediate between these two sets of possibilities. The idea of the *counselling menu* represents a way of arriving at a decision, within the shortest possible time, concerning what to do and where to start.

A key competence for any counsellor, therefore, is to be able to create opportunities for discussion about the range of choices that are on offer. This competence is based on two important areas of counsellor self-awareness. The first is awareness of the values that inform their practice (discussed in Chapter 6), and the second is an awareness of the use of language (discussed in Chapter 8 and in other places through this book).

The values dimension of negotiating around goals, tasks and methods is associated with the act of positioning the person as someone who is worthwhile, who knows what is best for them, and whose views are worth knowing. Each opening that the counsellor makes to invite the person to say what they want is affirming these values and at the same time expressing the genuine interest, caring and curiosity that the counsellor holds towards that person. By contrast, every time that the counsellor pre-empts a decision about what is to happen in the counselling session, no matter how sensitively and 'nicely' this is done, they place themself in an 'I know best' position, which negates these values.

At one level, it does not matter what words a counsellor uses, as long as these words reflect the core values and spirit of counselling. At another level, the words matter as well, because it is all too easy to slip into using the language of the 'expert', particularly when the person seeking help may be feeling vulnerable and uncertain. The following are some examples of language use that can contribute to shared decision making:

- Explaining how you work as a counsellor. For example: 'I'd like to say a few words about the way I work as a counsellor. Would it be OK to do that now – I don't want to interrupt anything you might be going to say? The main thing for me is that we are on the same wavelength, that we agree on what you are wanting to get from counselling, and what's the best way to go about achieving what you want. Does that make sense? What I need to do, therefore, is sometimes I need to just check out with you that we both understand what we are doing at that point. Would that be OK?'

- Explaining basic principles. For example: 'In my experience as a counsellor, I have found that different people need different things from me. Some people want me to listen, other people want me to give them feedback, and so on. It's really important for me that this counselling is right for you. At any time, if you feel that what we're doing is not helping, then I would want you to let me know so we can change what we're doing and get things right for you.'
- Asking the person about how they perceive goals, tasks and methods. For example: 'You have told me a bit about your problems. I'd like to ask you, what is it that you want to get from counselling? What's your aim or goal?', or 'I feel I have a pretty good idea of what you want to get from counselling. To get there, we need to take things step by step. At this point, do you have an idea of what you feel you need to do first?', or 'You've talked quite a lot about feeling angry. Would that be something we could spend a bit of time looking at now? I guess that there are different ways we could look at this. Do you want to shout, or hit that cushion, or something else? What do you feel would be the best way for us to approach this right now?'
- Checking out that the person's goal, task or method statement has been understood. For example: 'Can I just check this out, what you are saying is that what you want to do now is . . .'
- Inviting the person to identify what has worked for them in the past. For example: 'When you have felt stuck with an angry feeling before, is there anything that has helped you to deal with it? Is that something that is relevant for what we might do now?'
- Following the completion of a task, checking whether what happened was helpful. For example: 'We have spent a few minutes now talking through that issue about getting closer to people. We seem to have reached an end point of that, at least for the moment. Before we go on to look at some of the other issues you mentioned earlier, I'd just like to ask, was the way we approached that helpful? Is there anything that I could have done, or that you could have done, that would be more helpful?

These strategies serve to punctuate the ongoing flow of the counselling conversation with brief opportunities where the person seeking help and their counsellor can reorient themselves in relation to the person's goals, and remain on track. The sentences and phrases used in the examples given above should not be regarded as a fixed script to be followed by all counsellors: as with everything else in counselling, it is important for the practitioner to develop a style in which principles and competences are integrated with their own personal and cultural identity.

An example of goals, methods and tasks in practice: Joey's emotional journey

Joey is a long-term prisoner nearing the end of a sentence for violent robbery. During his time in prison, Joey has experienced several episodes of what the medical officer has termed depression, and has made several attempts to take his own life. In his current prison there is a well-established peer counselling service in which prisoners can be trained to provide emotional support to others. Joey has formed a good relationship with one of the peer helpers, who has spent many hours listening to Joey's story of a childhood lacking in love, care and consistency. It has been important to Joey to learn that there could be someone who was able to accept him, and like him, even when they knew about some of the things he had done. Although Joey and his peer counsellor had never explicitly agreed on the goals of their work, each of them knew that what Joey wanted was to know that he could be acceptable as a person, particularly in respect of his emotions and feelings. After many of these sessions, the helper observed that Joey seemed to talk in a way that was 'just full of pain'. There was an extended silence, broken eventually by Joey's admission that he felt an emotional pain all the time, but believed that it was not what 'a man' would do to admit this, or even worse to express it: 'I can't afford to lose control – look what can happen when I do.' The helper responded by saying, 'This is where we have got to – I'm wondering whether this pain is the next thing for us to look at.' Over their next meetings, Joey and his helper worked together to find some ways in which Joey could express his pain within their counselling sessions. Once they had made some progress with this, Joey announced that he could see that he needed to figure out how to let his wife know about his pain: 'She knows there is something wrong, but I never tell her what it is. It's keeping us apart. When she visits, sometimes I just sit there in silence because I can't speak. Who knows what she thinks is going on?' This triggered a new focus for the next counselling sessions: how Joey communicated with his wife, and what he could do differently.

Having decided that 'the pain' was something that they would look at together, Joey and his helper talked about how to set about this difficult and demanding task. At first, Joey could not think of anything at all that he could do to express what he felt. His helper made a list of activities that he had personally tried himself and some that he had read about. These included: finding the part of the body where the feeling was located, making a drawing, writing a poem, working through a self-help book about emotions, keeping an emotion diary, and 'just talking about it'. Joey was worried about any activity that involved writing things down on paper because he did not think he had the capacity to keep pieces of paper private. He was worried that any overt expression of emotion could lead to him being sent to the psychiatric unit. He said he would think about the suggestions between sessions. At the next meeting with his helper, he brought a piece of paper and a pencil and began, silently, to write from his pain: 'I am inside. I am crushed . . . .' At the end of their meeting he carefully tore the piece of paper into very small pieces. At the next session he talked about how he had allowed the pain to be in control during a workout in the prison gym. Some weeks later he enrolled for an art class and made clay sculptures of pain. Gradually, he found his own way to do what he needed to do.

This example emphasizes the improvizational nature of counselling. Joey and his peer helper were not operating in an ideal environment, in terms of the level of privacy that was available to them. In addition, the peer helper was aware that he had relatively little training and experience in working with the type of issue that Joey was presenting. Nevertheless, between them they were able to talk about what they could do and to find a way forward. The case, therefore, also exemplifies the basic resourcefulness of people. The counselling that Joey received was life changing for him (and possibly also life saving), in spite of the limited training and experience of his counsellor: he and the counsellor had a relationship that was strong enough to hang in together until they could discover a method that would work for them.

This example illustrates two of the specific counselling tasks that are discussed more fully in later chapters – dealing with feelings and emotion, and changing behaviour – and describes a range of different methods that were used to achieve these tasks. Each of the tasks undertaken by Joey involved using the secure space provided by the relationship with a counsellor to deal with an issue arising from a difficulty within the person's social niche or life space. For instance, the world that Joey lived in had silenced him in relation to a bundle of emotions that he came to describe as his pain. The way that he had learned to communicate with his wife no longer reflected the values that he wished to espouse in his family life. His discussions with his helper-counsellor allowed him an opportunity to reflect on what was happening in his life in relation to these issues and to develop strategies for doing things differently in future.

Being on the alert for things going wrong

In an ideal counselling conversation, which rarely happens, a person will explore an issue, with the help of the counsellor will arrive at a new understanding or plan of action, will learn something useful about themselves, and will leave happy. Alas, there are many things that can happen to disrupt this ideal script. For example, there can be a breakdown, rupture or falling out in the counselling relationship, the person may become suicidal or a risk to others, the person may have a panic attack or other situations may arise that cut across any attempt to make progress around basic counselling tasks. An important competence in any counselling situation, therefore, involves routinely *monitoring* what is happening and knowing what to do if a crisis occurs. At such moments, the counsellor may need to interrupt the flow of the counselling dialogue, for example, to check on issues of client safety. An ongoing task of counselling, therefore, involves monitoring the interaction and conversation in order to become aware of any possible threats to the integrity of the counselling space. If any such threats come to light, it is necessary for the person and the counsellor to review the situation together and to decide what action might be needed to change, strengthen or repair the space, or to look for sources of help outside of the counselling relationship that might be called upon. These issues are discussed further in Chapter 11.

Conclusions

The model of counselling goals, tasks and methods described in this chapter is particularly appropriate to counselling that is embedded in other practitioner roles, where the helper and person may have only a short period of time in which to talk through a problem. If a practitioner is only able to offer ten or twenty minutes to a person, it may still be perfectly possible to complete, or make substantial progress on, a counselling task. Also, if there can only be a brief contact, it is much safer for a person to agree or 'contract' to engage in a specific task ('let's look at what these feelings are telling you', 'would it be useful to try to get a sense of all the information that might be relevant to making a decision about this issue?'), than to attempt to engage in a discussion around major life goals.

The process of identifying and agreeing goals, tasks and methods within a counselling session provides a series of opportunities for dialogue and joint decision making between the counsellor and the person seeking help. It is definitely *not* the intention of this chapter to imply that the counsellor should adopt an expert stance in which they diagnose and then prescribe the goals, tasks and methods that they deem appropriate to an individual client. As far as possible, the person seeking should take the lead. Key skills of any counsellor lie in being able to 'hit the pause button', to suspend the flow of what the client is saying, at the right moments, so that goals, tasks and methods can be discussed and agreed, and in having a sufficiently wide repertoire of methods (and awareness of the how they can be applied to particular counselling tasks) to allow the maximum degree of client choice. It is essential to keep in mind, also, that all this takes place in the context of a relationship between the counsellor and the person with whom they are working. The counselling relationship and the tasks of counselling, need to be viewed as two sides of the same coin. For example, it is possible to define the strength and quality of the relationship between the counsellor and the person in terms of the extent to which they are able to communicate effectively with each other around goals, tasks and methods, their capacity to arrive at a shared agreement over which goals, tasks and methods to pursue, and their joint resourcefulness and creativity in imagining possible methods that might be helpful.

The following chapters explore the nature of some of the most commonly occurring counselling tasks, and suggest some methods that may be applicable to the resolution of these tasks. When reading these chapters it is important to remember that the methods discussed are intended only as examples of what is possible, and certainly do not claim to represent a comprehensive list of all the counselling methods that might be envisaged. The idea of the counselling menu implies flexibility and diversity: there are as many different menus as there are counsellors, and the items on the menu can change according to the ingredients that are available and the requirements of guests.

Questions for reflection and discussion

1. What's on your menu: what can you offer as a counsellor? Make a list of the counselling goals, tasks and methods that you are familiar with and have had experience of at this point in your career as a counsellor. This list can include goals, tasks and methods that you have used in a counselling role, as well as those that you have encountered when seeking help yourself. What are the 'special' items on your menu: with which goals, tasks and methods do you feel most comfortable? What are the gaps on your menu? What are the goals, tasks and methods that you would like to know more about?

2. Within your organization and among the type of people you work with, what are some of the counselling goals that people might present? Devise a list of tasks and methods that might be associated with each of these goals.

3. How have you applied the counselling skill model in practice? Think about *one* person who has come to you for counselling help. What was this person's goal (or goals)? What were the step-by-step tasks that seemed to you to be relevant to the achievement of this person's goal(s)? What were the possible methods that might have been employed to carry out these tasks? What did you do to make it possible for this person to decide which tasks and methods they would pursue?

4. Reflect on people you have helped, in your role as a counsellor. These could be either people in your work setting or fellow students/trainees with whom you have engaged in skill practice. What do you say to the person you are helping, to allow them to decide on the goals, tasks and methods that are right for them? What words and phrases do you use? How effective are these statements in conveying your core values as a counsellor?

Suggestions for further reading

The general approach to counselling that is being recommended in this chapter has been strongly influenced by the writings of the American psychotherapist Art Bohart, around his image of the 'active client'. In a series of important papers, Bohart (Bohart and Tallman, 1996; Bohart, 2000, 2006) has argued that it is essential to recognize that the person seeking help is highly purposeful and active in deciding what they want from a counselling session, to the extent they will often covertly reinterpret suggestions or activities put forward by the counsellor to bring them into line with what they want to happen in counselling. The key source is:

Bohart, A. C. and Tallman, K. (1999) *How Clients Make Therapy Work: The Process of Active Self-healing.* Washington, DC: American Psychological Association.

Another valuable set of ideas about how to practice counselling in a manner that fits into what the person seeking help believes will be most helpful for them, or has found to work for them in the past, lies in the writings of the 'common factors' group of therapy theorists, trainers and researchers such as Scott Miller, Barry Duncan and Mark Hubble. Particularly relevant to this chapter is their way of using the 'client's theory of change' as the basis for collaboratively deciding which methods to use in an individual case. Further information about this approach can be found on their web-site (www.talkingcure.com) or in a series of books authored by these writers, of which the most comprehensive is:

Hubble, M. A., Duncan, B. C. and Miller, S. D. (eds) (1999) *The Heart and Soul of Change: What Works in Therapy.* Washington, DC: American Psychological Association.

A central idea within this chapter is the notion that a counsellor needs to build a toolkit of methods to enable them to make a flexible, client-centred response to what the person seeking help might need. Some highly experienced counsellors have written about their own idiosyncratic toolkits, assembled over many years. Particularly valuable are:

Carrell, S. E. (2001) *The Therapist's Toolbox.* Thousand Oaks, CA: Sage.
King, A. (2001) *Demystifying the Counseling Process: A Self-help Handbook for Counselors.* Needham Heights, MA: Allyn & Bacon.
Yalom, I. (2002) *The Gift of Therapy: Reflections on Being a Therapist.* London: Piatkus.

5

Setting the scene: preparation for offering a counselling relationship

Introduction • Personal readiness • Organizational groundwork • Building a personal and professional support network • Developing a database of resources • Conclusions • Questions for reflection and discussion • Suggestions for further reading

Sitting at the desk in her crowded office, Sally could see the 40th birthday card sent by her teenage son, still there. 'The cancer nurse'. What a job. Always too much to do. The only way to cope was to make lists and cross things off one by one as they got done. The next forty-five minutes was for 'counselling prep'. Check that the stock of leaflets was OK – the unit counsellor, the psychology service, the community mental health team, social services, the Maggie Centre, CRUSE bereavement care, that church place, the websites list, all the different health promotion pamphlets. Diary, email – message to Helen in the stroke clinic with some suggestions for times for a peer supervision session. Quick look at the folder of flyers for training courses. Nothing much there. Ten minutes in the online library. Send away for a couple of articles. Supply of tissues – OK. Still twenty minutes for the worst bit: keeping the journal up to date. Have to do it. The blank page brings the last week flooding back – all these people, all these stories, all that pain. But at least when its written down it somehow looks like its under control.

Introduction

As in many other areas of life, the success of what happens during a counselling session depends to a large extent on the effectiveness of the preparatory work that has taken place. Preparation is particularly important in counselling for two reasons. First, the central task of the counsellor is to devote their attention to the person who is seeking help, to tune in and listen as completely as possible. The more that the counsellor is distractedly thinking about other matters ('how long do I have to my next appointment?', 'is this the best seating arrangement?'), the less space they will have for simply listening. Second, a person who requests counselling usually comes in with a jumble of feelings – worry, anger, loneliness, confusion. What they are looking for in a counsellor is someone who is centred and calm, ready for anything that might come up. The better prepared a counsellor is, the more calm and centred they are likely to be. A counsellor who is worried about 'what happens if . . .' is likely to convey this anxiety to the person seeking help. This is unlikely to be a facilitative thing to do. It can reduce the person's confidence in the counsellor. It can even reinforce the person's sense of demoralization: 'I must be beyond hope – I have only just started to talk about my problem and the counsellor looks worried.' On the other hand, being seen as well prepared communicates a sense of caring and consideration.

To some extent, preparation for offering a counselling relationship is a matter of training. Any good counselling skill training course will provide lots of opportunities for practice and role-play sessions, which allow the trainee to rehearse how they might respond to a person who wanted to talk about a problem. However, preparation is about a lot more than training. For anyone offering a counselling relationship, preparation involves being clear in their own mind about what kind of counsellor they want to be. There are many different styles of counselling, and it is essential for anyone involved in counselling to select and adapt an approach that matches who they are – their personal beliefs and what they have learned about dealing with problems in their own life – and that is consistent with the needs and expectations of the organization in which they work and the people they are working with. Preparation for counselling also involves making sure that the helping or caring *environment* is organized appropriately, for example, that a private space is available.

This chapter highlights two main areas of counsellor preparation. One essential facet of counsellor preparation is for the helper to be clear in their own mind about what they are trying to achieve. This dimension of readiness is discussed below under the theme of personal readiness. Another key aspect of preparation refers to the social and organizational context in which counselling takes place, encompassing issues that range from the image and expectations of counselling that exist within the organization, through to the availability of comfortable seating.

Personal readiness

Most of the time, a counselling conversation takes place in a one-to-one relationship. The counsellor is in there on their own and needs to be ready to handle whatever it is that comes up. What comes up can be difficult for a counsellor to cope with: most of the time, people seek external help for a problem in living only when the issue is something that deeply troubles them. A person seeking help does not want to be met by a counsellor who is muddled, easily shocked by what they hear, or lacks purpose, however well intentioned that counsellor may be. The idea of counsellor *reflexivity* – the capacity to look at oneself and take account of what one finds – represents a critical dimension of what it takes to be a good counsellor. The preparatory activities that are involved in the development of personal readiness and reflexivity include: drawing on personal experience and self-awareness; becoming sensitive to beliefs about helping and change; developing cultural sensitivity and curiosity; understanding the counselling relationship; developing a framework for practice and reflection; values clarification; and nurturing sources of hope.

Drawing on personal experience and self-awareness

Readiness to take on a counselling role requires the development of a sufficient degree of self-awareness. There are three main reasons why self-awareness is important in counselling:

- It contributes to the counsellor's ability to relate to the experiences of the person who is seeking help. The person may be struggling with personal difficulties around such themes as loss, being out of control, hopelessness, despair, powerlessness and confusion. A counsellor is better able to provide a rounded, human response if they have previously explored their own experiences of these issues and are familiar with the contours of the territory that the person is entering.
- Self-awareness gives the counsellor an appreciation of their own areas of vulnerability. When a counsellor allows themself to listen fully to the difficulties of another person, they are inevitably opening themself up to the other person's pain. It is useful for any counsellor to be familiar with the aspects of their life around which they are sensitive or vulnerable, and to work out some strategies for dealing with these areas, rather than discovering these issues during an actual session when they are trying to be there for the other person.
- Self-awareness helps the counsellor to know that the person seeking help is similar to them in some ways, and different in others. It is only by consciously knowing their own reactions and patterns in sufficient detail that a counsellor is able to avoid falling into the trap of assuming that everyone else must think and feel the same as they do.

There are many ways in which this kind of self-awareness can be cultivated, for example, by keeping a journal, writing an autobiography, participating in an experiential learning group or receiving personal counselling. The common thread across all of these activities is that they involve systematic, ongoing *reflection* on personal experience. While it is helpful for a person who is in the role of counsellor to have had a rich experience of life, it is not enough merely to have undergone difficult times. To be able to use these events to inform a counselling response it is necessary to have gone at least some way to putting these experiences into words and making sense of them. A counsellor is not primarily a role model – someone who has survived crises and who therefore acts as an example to be followed – but instead is someone who is better seen as a co-worker. In working with a person seeking help to resolve problems in living through talking about those problems and finding solutions, it is necessary for a counsellor to have reflected upon and explored beforehand some experiences in their own life.

> **Example**
>
> Harbrinder is a teacher whose job involves facilitating an anti-bullying policy that her school has adopted. She has received some basic training in working with groups of young people around bullying issues, but has found it difficult to motivate pupils to remain engaged and committed to the programme. At a residential training workshop for anti-bullying co-ordinators, she is invited to take part in a series of exercises and autobiographical writing tasks that require her to examine her experience of being oppressed by others and of being an oppressor herself. Harbrinder experiences these tasks and activities as very upsetting. However, when she returns to her job the following week, she reports that 'the whole way I approach my role is different – I can relate much better to what it feels like for the kids I'm working with – I am much more open to them now, and when we talk about things we seem to be able to get to a deeper level'.

The concept of self-awareness covers a very wide range of potential topics for self-exploration. Developing an awareness of the central threads of one's life story, or key life events (such as the experience of being bullied at school) are valuable in relation to becoming more sensitive around such themes and issues when they are described by a person seeking help. There is also a useful area of awareness of self around micro-moments of how one responds to another person in terms of simple activities such as smiling, eye contact and proximity.

Sensitivity to a diversity of beliefs about helping and change

Acquiring a sensitivity to the huge range of beliefs that exist about learning, change and 'healing' is an important element in preparation for a counselling role. In any counselling situation, the aim is to provide a person with an opportunity to talk about their problem in living. The core assumption that lies behind this activity is that talking about a problem will be helpful. There are likely to be further assumptions being made by the counsellor about the *how to* talk about the problem. For example, most counsellors believe that it is more helpful to talk about a problem in a way that acknowledges and expresses feelings, and focuses on one's own personal role or responsibility in relation to the problem, rather than in a way that is abstract and distanced, and seeks to blame others for everything that has gone wrong. These assumptions can be understood as reflecting a counsellor's *beliefs about learning and change*. An essential part of the preparatory work that needs to be done before entering a counselling role involves reflecting on the nature and diversity of these beliefs. There are two basic reasons why beliefs about learning and change are important in counselling. The first is that, as a counsellor, it is necessary to develop a style or approach to counselling that is consistent with one's core beliefs. If a counsellor attempts to use counselling methods in which they do not believe, then this lack of conviction will be transmitted to the person seeking help and will undermine the work. For instance, some counsellors believe that problems always have an origin in childhood experience, and therefore assume that a person will only be able to move on in their life once they have made a connection between whatever is troubling them now and relevant events that occurred in childhood. Other counsellors hold an opposite view and believe that a person will only really be able to move on when they stop worrying about past events and set goals to be achieved in the future. Therefore, in a situation where the person wishes to explore their early memories around a problem, a future-oriented counsellor may become impatient on the basis that what is being suggested is a waste of valuable counselling time. Likewise, a counsellor who is sensitive to the person's relationship with their personal history may become impatient when a person with whom they are working wants to discuss future scenarios.

The second reason why beliefs about learning and change are important in counselling is that a person who is seeking help inevitably has their own ideas about how their problem has developed and what needs to be done to sort it out. To continue the example of beliefs about time-orientation, a person who solves problems by action planning and goal setting, and never looks back, is likely to be frustrated and turned off by a counsellor who persistently asks questions such as 'does this remind you of anything?' or 'can you think of the first time this happened?', unless the counsellor can provide a clear and convincing explanation of why examining the past is a necessary precursor to making effective plans for the future.

Beliefs about learning and change are linked in complex ways to demographic factors such as gender, ethnicity and social class. Sensitivity to the person's 'helping belief system' lies at the heart of competence in working effectively with *difference*.

Examples

As a cardiac care health advisor in a primary care clinic, with a key responsibility to work with patients around issues of smoking cessation and obesity, Manjit looks for leverage in relation to long-standing patterns of unhealthy behaviour by mobilizing his patients' beliefs about what will help. After he has met them and come to an agreement about their commitment to change, he says to them, 'I'm wondering about whether you have tried to stop smoking/reduce your weight in the past. Have you? Can you tell me about what has worked for you in the past?' At every subsequent meeting with a patient, he always asks them whether they believe that the approach they are taking is effective, how it can be approved, and what the person thinks that Manjit could do differently that might be more helpful to them.

Ian is a community psychiatric nurse who believes that the people with whom he works have an illness that can best be treated through the administration of drugs, and that his job is to help his clients to understand this, and to work together to find the right dosage and develop strategies for dealing with side effects.

One of his patients, Donald, is a member of a mental health user group, which espouses and promotes a philosophy of survival and recovery based on social solidarity and political action. Ian is frustrated that Donald will take medication only at times of crisis. Donald is frustrated because he does not think that Ian takes his views seriously, and does his utmost to limit the frequency of their meetings.

Eva is a family support worker who is fascinated by the different strategies that the people with whom she works can find in order to resolve their problems. Much of her job involves assisting families with school-age children who have behavioural problems, such as hyperactivity and aggression, are difficult to manage both at home and in school. Eva believes that 'different things work for different people – these families have so much on their plate that they won't commit themselves to anything that doesn't make sense to them'. One of the families that she helps has evolved a routine based on outdoor pursuits such hillwalking and horseriding. Another family has devoted a great deal of time to working out their own methods for consistently rewarding certain types of behaviour in their son. Yet another family places great emphasis on diet.

Beliefs about learning and change inform much of what happens in counselling. However, few people have a very clear idea about what they believe in these areas because there is usually little requirement to think about these questions in the course of everyday life. Preparation for fulfilling a counselling role involves developing a sensitivity to beliefs about problems and how they can be resolved, and devising strategies for inviting people to articulate these assumptions.

Box 5.1 Sometimes men and women benefit from different counselling methods – but what works best may not be what they think they need

Margaret Stroebe, Henk Schut and their colleagues at the University of Utrecht in the Netherlands have carried out important research into the impact of bereavement, and the role of counselling in helping people to cope with loss. One of the findings to emerge is that, on the whole, men and women tend to have different approaches to dealing with bereavement. In general, men attempt to make sense of what happened at a cognitive level, whereas women are more likely to respond to loss by expressing their feelings through conversation and contact with others. In one study, Schut et al. (1997) observed that the people who came for counselling were those for whom their preferred coping strategy had not been effective, for whatever reason. They discovered that, although both men and women benefited from an emotionally oriented form of counselling that encouraged them to express feelings, and a cognitively oriented therapy that focused on making plans for the future and dealing with stress, what was most helpful for people who were stuck in a pattern of grief was to work with them to expand their beliefs about learning and change, by offering them an alternative way of coping. They found that many men were better helped by an emotionally-focused approach to counselling, whereas many women benefited most from a cognitively oriented way of working.

Developing cultural sensitivity and curiosity

All preparatory work around developing personal readiness in relation to offering a counselling relationship should be informed by an appreciation of the importance of cultural difference. The ideas that people have about how life should be lived, and what helps when things are bad, are heavily influenced by their *cultural identity*. We live in a world of staggering cultural multiplicity. Whereas, in the past, people may have been able to live out their lives within a culturally homogeneous group, it is now inevitable that anyone in a practitioner role will be faced by the challenge of understanding the world-view and experience of clients from different cultural and ethnic backgrounds. It is not possible to know about all cultures and lifestyles in detail – the range of diversity is too great. Moreover, within any specific cultural group, there may exist important differences – not all Irish people, or Muslims, or gays hold the same views. In addition, there are many people whose personal and family histories have led them to straddle or embrace different cultures.

When we meet someone else we immediately begin to decode all the cues relating to their cultural position – social class, gender, ethnicity, race, religion, sexual orientation, political affiliation and so on. At the same time, the other person is doing the same with us. In counselling, the counsellor needs to be aware of the various strands of their own cultural identity. This helps the practitioner to:

- be aware of the kind of impact they might be having on the other person;
- appreciate the cultural roots of the assumptions about learning and change that they are using;
- be sensitive to and curious about the other person's cultural identity;
- talk about cultural difference when this becomes relevant within the counselling relationship;
- appreciate the impact of social class, religion and other cultural factors in the life of the client;
- defuse their own fear of the other.

There is plentiful evidence that members of cultural minority groups can lack trust in professionals who are predominantly drawn from mainstream cultural groups, and that they find it hard to talk about their problems to someone whom they may perceive as lacking in understanding. In addition, there are important differences between cultural groups regarding their approach to questions such as power inequalities, gender relationships and time orientation (see, for example, Hofstede, 2003). A useful source of stimulating exercises that focus on awareness of cultural difference is Hofstede *et al.* (2002).

For any counsellor, preparation for offering counselling relationships to people who are culturally different involves actively fostering a sense of cultural curiosity: a willingness to acknowledge cultural difference and to ask questions. Taking the step of talking about potential cultural difference and misunderstanding, with a person seeking help, at least positions the counsellor as being open to finding ways of overcoming the effects of difference. Keeping quiet about these factors, by contrast, either puts the responsibility for addressing issues of cultural difference on to the person seeking help (at a time when they probably have more pressing matters to talk through) or banishes it to the realm of the unsayable and unsaid (Cardemil and Battle, 2003). Inviting and initiating exploration of cultural and racial issues and differences in a counselling session is a key competence for anyone intending to offer counselling relationships.

Understanding the counselling relationship

In much of the published literature on counselling, great emphasis is placed on the idea that the heart of counselling is the *relationship* between the counsellor and the person seeking help. But what does this mean in practice? Surely it is obvious that there is a relationship between the person and their counsellor? It is not as simple as that. The concept of 'relationship' in counselling is used in a particular way, to refer to some key ideas about what counselling is about. When counsellors, and writers on counselling, use the word 'relationship', they are employing it as a shorthand term to refer to a cluster of basic principles. In preparing to enter a counselling role, it is important to have a handle on these ideas, as a prerequisite for working effectively with people.

Any relationship between two people is complex and multifaceted. Within the discourse of counselling, the term therefore operates as a reminder of the potential richness and depth of the interaction between person and counsellor, and the impossibility of reducing this complexity to a single dimension. For many counsellors, this usage has the advantage of acting as a reminder that there are always other aspects of their relationship with a person that may be relevant or deserving of attention. The fact that 'relationship' can never be finally pinned down or fully defined means that any specific relationship must be understood in its own terms. On the other hand, an important disadvantage of the open-ended nature of the concept of relationship is that counsellors can be vague and unfocused about how they understand their relationships with the people who visit them, and unclear about the kinds of relationship they wish to build.

The concept of relationship in counselling is also used as a contrast to notions of technique or method. Many books, research studies and training programmes in counselling are organized around lists of specific methods, skills or interventions, perhaps with some acknowledgement that the effectiveness of these techniques and skills depends on the existence of a good relationship between person and counsellor. In many ways, when thinking or writing about counselling, it is easier to use a language of techniques and methods than it is to use a language of relationship. This is because the actions that are required in order to deliver a technique, such as 'reflecting feelings' or 'challenging irrational beliefs', are fairly easy to describe and observe, whereas relationship factors are complex and implicit. Because it is easier to describe methods and techniques, it can be tempting to allow methods and techniques to dominate training and practice. The more that this occurs, the more the counselling moves away from what people actually want: a safe relationship within which they can talk about their troubles.

Another way of looking at this aspect of the concept of relationship in counselling is to consider that what people are looking for in a counsellor is compassion, sensitivity and humanity. On the whole, people are not looking for psycho-technicians.

The idea of relationship brings with it an understanding that there are two sides to any relationship. Investment and commitment are required from both participants if a relationship is to be meaningful. Conversely, a relationship may be ruptured or undermined by the actions of either person. This understanding underlies a powerful core principle of counselling, that of *collaboration*. The person and the counsellor act together to build their relationship: they co-construct it. The relationship is not something that the counsellor provides, as if taking down a warm pullover from a shelf and handing it over.

By using a language of relationship, a counsellor also opens a space for conversations about the question of responsibility. A person enters a relationship with a counsellor on the basis of trust, and may entrust the counsellor with their secrets and areas of vulnerability. In any relationship there are expectations around honesty and due care, and issues around who is responsible for what, and the duties that each one has to the other. These are important issues in counselling, and are ultimately linked to the idea of the kind of contract or agreement that exists between a person and a counsellor.

It can be seen, therefore, that the concept of relationship in counselling is important because it acts as a reminder of three key principles that underlie this kind of work: the adoption of a human, personal approach, rather than being a distanced technician; a commitment to collaboration; and acknowledgement of moral issues. Preparation for offering a counselling relationship requires attention and planning around all three of these areas: *how* to be personal, *how* to be collaborative, and *how* to address issues of values, ethics and responsibility.

Developing a framework for practice and reflection

Counselling is a complex activity, which may involve responding to other people on several different levels: cognitive, emotional, behavioural and spiritual. In addition, the problems presented by people seeking help can often be chaotic and difficult to understand. As a result, it is important for any practitioner engaged in offering counselling to possess some kind of 'mental map' of what they are trying to do. For the majority of practitioners, the task of constructing this mental map, or framework for practice, is never complete – there is always more that can be learned and new ideas to be assimilated.

Effective and productive reflection on practice involves being able to think clearly about what one is trying to do, in terms of concepts and models. Communicating effectively with colleagues, and using colleagues and supervisors as sounding boards for reflection, also requires the capability to use a conceptual language in which experiences can be categorized.

Many practitioners of counselling find the building blocks of their framework for practice within mainstream theories of counselling and psychotherapy: psychodynamic, cognitive behavioural, person-centred and narrative. However, it is also important to be able to acknowledge and use frameworks from other sources. Practitioners who have training and experience in education, healthcare, management, or other professions, may be able to make use of concepts and models from these domains. Also, each person has their own 'hard-earned truths' that they have gained from personal experience. These can represent particularly valuable elements of a framework for practice because they are highly meaningful and potent for the practitioner.

Values clarification

One of the main ideas introduced in Chapter 2 was the notion that counselling can be understood as an invitation to, or opportunity for, a person to evaluate aspects of their life in a different way. Counselling represents, at its core, a means of promoting and applying a set of values concerning respect for others, acceptance of difference, the worth of human beings and the importance of connectedness and human relationships. In a strict sense, anyone whose helping is not informed by this set of values can be understood as engaged in influencing or persuading, rather than involved in a process of collaborative exploration and decision making. It is important, therefore, for anyone who offers counselling relationships to sort out where they stand in relation to the values of counselling and to the image of the good life that counselling espouses. This topic is explored more fully in the following chapter.

Nurturing sources of hope

A key part of any counselling process can be described as *instillation of hope*. At the point when a person, faced with a problem in living, has exhausted their immediate resources, they can be understood as having reached a point of *demoralization*. The decision to seek help from a professional source can be viewed, in these terms, as an act of hope and the first step on a journey of 'remoralization'. Such a decision invokes hope because it is based on a belief that something can be done, that things may get better. It is then essential for a counsellor to respond to the person in ways that promote hope, and that mobilize the person's energy and motivation to arrive at a satisfactory understanding and resolution of their problem. In order to do this, a counsellor probably needs to be a hopeful person, who is tuned into the sources of hope in their own life. In other words, a counsellor is someone who know what hope is and who appreciates the difference between false hope (for example, reassurance and platitudes) and genuine inspiration or faith.

The various elements of personal readiness to offer a counselling relationship that have been discussed up to this point have ranged from self-awareness to hopefulness. These factors, taken together, map out a substantial 'personal readiness' agenda. It is important to be realistic about how much personal development work of this kind is possible, or necessary, before embarking on providing a counselling role. It would seem reasonable to suppose that an *absence* of readiness in any of these areas represents a barrier to being able to function well as a counsellor. On the other hand, a complete or final readiness in relation to these issues is never achievable – there is always more to be learned. This is one of the reasons why ongoing supervision, consultation, training, and continuing professional and personal development are emphasized so much in the counselling profession.

The discussion now turns to an exploration of areas of preparation beyond the person of the counsellor: setting the scene for counselling in terms of organizational factors and support networks.

Organizational groundwork

For anyone whose counselling work is embedded in another work role, such as nurse or social worker, preparation for counselling requires dealing with organizational factors that may either facilitate the possibility of effective counselling or stand in the way. On the whole, practitioners providing embedded counselling may find that the fact that people seeking help already know them and trust them can be a major advantage, especially when compared with 'stand-alone' specialist counselling where the client does not meet the counsellor until the start of their first session together. Another advantage when counselling is embedded within other roles is that the counsellor may be readily accessible to the person seeking help – for example, a community nurse may routinely visit a patient two or three times a week.

Nevertheless, when counselling is carried out in the midst of other activities, there are a number of organizational or environmental issues that need to be sorted out in advance if a safe and productive counselling relationship is to be possible. These issues include:

- *Time.* How much time is available for counselling and how often might counselling take place?
- *Space.* Can a suitable, comfortable private space be found?
- *Confidentiality.* Who will know about what the person talks about? What are the limits of confidentiality?
- *Freedom to express emotion.* What happens if the person starts to cry or shouts out in an angry voice?
- *Voluntariness.* To what extent is the person an informed user of counselling? Do they know what they are being offered? How do they learn this? Do they feel free to refuse an offer of counselling?
- *Attitudes to counselling.* What do service users, colleagues and managers think and feel about counselling? Do they understand or approve of it or is counselling a furtive activity?

Each of these factors can have a major impact on the ability to offer a counselling relationship. In addition, there are organizational factors that relate to the capacity of the person to be effective in their work on a sustained basis:

- *The level of support that is available to the counsellor.* Are arrangements for supervision, consultation and peer support in place? How acceptable is it to seek out a colleague for support following a demanding counselling session?
- *Procedures for referring people in need to other practitioners and services.* What happens if it emerges during a counselling conversation that the person would be better served by a specialist service or an agency that could offer a greater amount of time or support? Are referral networks in place and is information available for clients about alternative sources of help? What happens if a person mentions suicidal intent during a counselling session?

This list of organizational factors indicates the extent to which careful planning is necessary before offering counselling within other helping roles. Specialist counselling agencies and clinics, which deliver counselling and nothing else, tend to devote a great deal of care and attention to developing protocols that address these issues. In general, practitioners whose counselling is embedded within other work roles tend to be given little time or encouragement to think through these issues, and to carry out this kind of preparatory work. However, the cost to the person seeking help, and to the counsellor, of failing to do the organizational groundwork, can be substantial.

Where counselling is embedded in other practice roles, it is essential to develop mechanisms for signalling to clients and service users both that practitioners are open to talking about problems in living and feelings and that in some instances the practitioner may recommend specialist sources of psychological or other help. There are many ways that this can be done, including written materials such as leaflets, posters and websites, face-to-face contact and using other service users (for example, peer support groups) as intermediaries. The ideal is for the person seeking counselling to be an informed consumer of this kind of service – to know what they want and how to get it.

Building a personal and professional support network

A major limitation of many counselling skills textbooks and training courses is that they fail to give sufficient attention to the *systemic* dimension of providing counselling that is embedded within other organizational roles and responsibilities. Systems theory suggests that, within any social group such as a family or organizational unit, the actions of individuals are mutually interconnected in a state of balance. Any shift within the pattern of connections can unbalance the system as a whole, and to prevent this the system develops mechanisms for counteracting or damping down changes that threaten the status quo. These ideas are important for practitioners involved in offering counselling embedded in other work roles because they act as a reminder that being able to operate effectively as an embedded counsellor is not merely a matter of being able to respond sensitively to the needs of people who seek counselling, but additionally requires setting up a system of emotional care.

Example
Alison was a nurse who had always had an interest in counselling and had completed a substantial amount of counsellor training. She was appointed to a post of senior nurse within a haemodialysis unit for patients who had experienced kidney failure. Knowing that living with renal disease presented individuals with significant problems and stress, she anticipated that she would be able to give expression to her counselling skills in her new job. Over her first few months in post, Alison developed a counselling relationship with several patients and felt satisfaction at being able to help some of them work through difficult life issues. Gradually, other staff on the unit recognized Alison's skills, and directed any patients with emotional and interpersonal difficulties in her direction. She began

to be overloaded. When she made a request for protected time for this area of her work, and funding to pay for access to a counselling supervisor, she was accused of being 'elitist' and 'promising patients a service that we can't deliver'. She felt increasingly isolated in the unit and began to look for another job.

Henry was one of the patients who was helped by Alison. His illness had resulted in loss of his job, bodily changes that made him feel physically unattractive and lethargic, and in time a deteriorating relationship with his wife, who was increasingly required to take on a role as carer. Henry felt that Alison understood what was happening to him and helped him to talk through his problems in a non-judgemental manner, to the point where he was beginning to be able to develop a more hopeful and constructive attitude towards his situation. He was 'devastated' when Alison said that she would not be able to continue with their occasional half-hour 'chats'. Temporarily encouraged by the suggestion that he might be able to see a clinical psychologist, he described himself as 'shattered' by the news that there was a nine-month waiting list for psychology.

This nursing example illustrates some of the issues that can emerge when practitioners begin to respond to the counselling needs of service users, without engaging in sufficient planning and organizational groundwork. In this medical unit, there existed a well-organized system, which prioritized physical care, while giving limited time to the emotional and psychological needs of patients. The introduction of counselling (more attention to emotional and personal issues) unbalanced the system. Colleagues felt both appreciative and envious of the counselling that was taking place. Patients' expectations began to shift, which placed demands on the staff group as a whole. Either the system had to change (to accommodate counselling as an integral part of the nursing service) or the 'experiment' needed to come to an end, to allow the system as a whole to resume its previous state of balance.

The support network that is required for embedded counselling to take place includes three main elements:

- *Managerial.* An understanding on the part of management of the role of counselling, the resources (time, money, space) that are required to be able to offer high quality counselling help, and the nature of confidentiality (for example, not expecting the details of every counselling conversation to be recorded in case notes).
- *Collegial.* Acceptance by co-workers of how counselling operates and what it can achieve, potential demands on time and space, and the limitations of what can be provided (not expecting 'the counsellor' to be able to deal with everything).
- *External.* Suitable arrangements for access to supervision and consultation, and avenues for referral of people who require more specialized services.

It can require a substantial investment of time and resourcefulness in order to build a personal and professional support network. Rather than attempting to achieve such a network through individual effort alone, it may be more effective to find a group of colleagues who share an interest in the development of counselling within an organizational setting and then to work together towards these goals.

Box 5.2   Being prepared: working with women who are victims of domestic violence

Domestic violence is a major social problem in most societies. There is evidence that health professionals in particular are often lacking in effectiveness in terms of detecting domestic violence, and lack competence and confidence regarding how to respond to it. From the point of view of a woman who has been a recipient of domestic violence, there are many barriers to disclosing to doctors and nurses the true reasons for injuries for which they are seeking assistance at accident and emergency departments. Rodriguez *et al.* (1996) conducted focus group interviews with 51 women with histories of domestic violence, concerning their feelings about treatment they had received from health professionals. These women described an 'unspoken agreement' between battered women and other members of society, including medical staff, not to disclose or address the violence to which they had been subjected. One women stated that: 'I was kicked, and cracked two ribs . . . . And the doctor asked me how it happened and I told him I fell down a flight of stairs.' The qualities of health professionals who helped them to 'break the silence' included being supportive and non-judgemental, taking time to listen, and showing compassion and caring through eye contact, facial expression and tone of voice. The majority of these women believed that it was useful for health professionals to ask directly about abuse – they found that many doctors and nurses appeared to prefer to avoid the topic.

In response to the Rodriguez *et al.* (1996) study, and other pieces of research along the same lines, various groups of health professionals have devoted considerable attention to how best they can prepare themselves to offer an effective counselling relationship to both men and women who have received domestic abuse. For example, Glowa *et al.* (2002) have developed a training programme to enable hospital doctors to be more comfortable in responding to patients who may be victims of domestic violence. Dienemann *et al.* (2002) have devised a tool for assessing the needs of women who report intimate partner violence. The tool comprises a one-page checklist of issues (for example, causes of incidents, relationship options, availability of support, medical care for injuries) that may need to be understood and addressed in order to respond comprehensively to the person who is seeking help. The practitioner completes the checklist at the end of their interview with the person. The items on the list act as a reminder to the practitioner of the principles of good practice in front-line embedded counselling with people suffering from this problem. The tool can also serve as the basis for planning supervision, consultation and further training, and as a reminder regarding information (on referral sources, self-help networks and so on) that should be on hand.

Developing a database of resources

Ethical practice in embedded counselling (as in any other area of professional activity) means being aware of the limitations of one's competence. In a situation where a practitioner in a field such as nursing or education may be able to offer only limited or intermittent parcels of time to people seeking counselling, or has received only limited training in responding to problems in living, it is essential to be prepared to refer people seeking help to specialized services when necessary. To be able to do this effectively requires assembling information about the services that are available locally, what they offer and how to access them. In addition, some people who may benefit from engaging in embedded counselling with their nurse or teacher may also benefit from additional help that runs concurrently with this counselling relationship. There is a wide variety of activities that are potentially therapeutic for people seeking help: self-help groups and websites, reading, church groups, community action groups, environmental groups, involvement in learning and education, voluntary work, and so on. It is important to keep in mind that effective counselling does not mean that the person's problem can be resolved only through a conversation or relationship with a counsellor; in many instances, effective counselling can involve supporting the person to find other resources, within their community or personal niche, that may be of assistance. A good embedded counsellor knows what is available for the group of people with whom they work and, when appropriate, will act as a gateway to these resources.

Conclusions

This chapter has discussed some of the tasks and issues involved in being prepared to offer a counselling relationship to a person seeking help. Some of these factors are covered in training courses, but many are not. Being well prepared is a crucial element of effective counselling because it is through careful preparation that a person offering counselling can feel sufficiently emotionally and morally secure. This is important: after all, who wants to share their problems with someone who seems unsure of the ground on which they stand?

Questions for reflection and discussion

1. Take some time to write about the various threads of your personal framework for practice. What have been the main sources of your ideas: counselling theory, professional training in another occupation or personal experience? Are there areas of conflict and tension between these different sets of ideas? For example, are there any ways in which your primary professional training conflicts with what you have learned about counselling? If you are aware of any such conflicts, what can you do to resolve that tension?
2. This chapter has explored a number of factors that need to be taken into account when preparing to offer a counselling relationship. In terms of your own work situation, how well prepared are you in each of these areas? In an ideal world, what would you change to allow yourself to offer more productive counselling relationships to your clients?

Suggestions for further reading

One of the most insightful discussions of what is involved in preparing oneself for the role of counsellor is to be found in:

Mearns, D. and Cooper, M. (2005) *Working at Relational Depth in Counselling and Psychotherapy*. London: Sage, chs 7 and 8.

A useful discussion of the issues that can arise in the delivery of embedded counselling, including legal factors, can be found in:

Stokes, A. (2001) Settings. In S. Aldridge and S. Rigby, S. (eds) *Counselling Skills in Context*. London: Hodder & Stoughton.

There are several books that are based around practitioners' stories of their experience of the organizational settings on the provision of counselling. Particularly recommended are:

Etherington, K. (ed.) (2001) *Counsellors in Health Settings*. London: Jessica Kingsley.
Reid, M. (ed.) (2004) *Counselling in Different Settings: The Reality of Practice*. London: Palgrave.

Further discussion of the context of counselling can be found in a special issue of the *British Journal of Guidance and Counselling* edited by Linda Machin and John McLeod (1998), and in:

McLeod, J. (2003) *An Introduction to Counselling*, 3rd edn. Buckingham: Open University Press, ch. 16.

The Open University Press publishes an invaluable series of books on the use of counselling skills in a wide variety of settings: clergy, emergency services, social work, and so on. These books provide an introduction to the kinds of issues that may arise in different organizational settings.
   Books that discuss the issue of cultural difference in counselling are:

Lago, C. and Thompson, J. (1996) *Race, Culture and Counselling*. Buckingham: Open University Press.
Palmer, S. (ed.) (2001) *Multicultural Counselling: A Reader*. London: Sage.
Pedersen, P. (2000) *A Handbook for Developing Multicultural Awareness*, 3rd edn. Alexandria, VA: American Counseling Association.

A fascinating account of one practitioner's search for her own cultural identity can be found in:

McGoldrick, M. (1998) Belonging and liberation: finding a place called 'home'. In M. McGoldrick (ed.) *Re-visioning Family Therapy: Race, Culture and Gender in Clinical Practice*. New York: Guilford Press.

6

Making a space to meet

Introduction • The counselling space • Values • Trust and confidentiality • Opening a space – responding to empathic opportunities • Setting practical limits to a counselling space: time and space • The issue of dual relationships • Offering a space for counselling: a practitioner checklist • Closing the space • Conclusions • Questions for reflection and discussion • Suggestions for further reading

> What's her room like? Well it's a bit crowded. Its small. There's lots of stuff lying around. Pictures of her family. She has teenage kids. Some birthday cards. We sit in a couple of easy chairs. Usual NHS standard issue. Battered, but comfortable. There's always flowers in a vase. There's always a box of tissues. She's very strict about not answering the phone when I'm there. She's very strict about nobody knocking on the door – one time she gave a student a right scolding for doing that. Its quite nice. Not like being in a hospital at all.

Introduction

It is essential to recognize that a counselling conversation is different from other types of conversational interaction. What makes a counselling relationship helpful is that it allows the person to step back from the action of everyday life, for the purpose of reflecting on that action and possibly deciding to do things differently. In the theatre, sometimes the main character will step to the side of the stage, away from the 'scene', and speak reflectively, honestly and personally to the audience. The main scene is in darkness and the character may be lit by just one spotlight. A good counselling session has some of this quality. It takes place in a bubble or special space, out of the action. Within that space, the person may well talk and act differently from the way they perform elsewhere.

A counselling space requires two key features:

- A boundary – it must be clear when the space has been entered, who can enter it and when it is exited.
- Rules for what can happen inside the space.

In specialist counselling and psychotherapy centres, a great deal of work is done to set the scene, in terms of boundaries and rules, well in advance of a client arriving. The client may receive a leaflet explaining how the agency operates, what to expect from a counselling session and the nature of confidentiality. They will be given appointment information that makes it explicit that the counselling session will begin and end at certain times. When a counselling relationship occurs in a different kind of organizational setting, such as a hospital ward or in the person's own home, boundaries and rules need to be negotiated in such a way as to create the best possible space given the circumstances. To return to the theatre analogy, there are similarities here to street theatre companies, who are able to stage compelling dramas in all kinds of situations. However, even in a formal counselling or psychotherapy agency or clinic, the counsellor can never take it for granted that, at the outset, the client or patient will fully understand the counselling 'contract' – it is always good practice to give the client an opportunity to ask questions or to revisit key points, particularly if the person has not received therapy before.

Some professionally trained counsellors and psychotherapists believe that the therapeutic space or 'frame' is such a important factor in effective work with clients that they are willing to see clients only in a standardized environment, for example, the same therapy room, laid out in the same way, at the same time every week. These counsellors do not think that it is possible to build a sufficiently robust set of boundaries in settings where many factors are out of the therapist's control, for example, in the person's home or in a hospital ward. Their argument is that a counselling relationship should be a place where the person can express strong emotions, and begin to experience patterns of behaviour that had previously been suppressed and are therefore emerging in a somewhat out-of-control way. They suggest that a strong contract and firm boundaries are needed to keep the person (and the counsellor) safe at the point when powerful emotions and 'acting out' take place. The underlying image here is that of a kind but firm parent helping an unruly child or adolescent to gain control of their behaviour.

The position taken in this book is that, while counselling that takes place within a situation of formalized assessment and contracting can be effective, counselling that is carried out in other settings can be effective too. It is important to be sensitive to the needs of individuals. For someone who has found the courage to want to explore, after many years, their experience of sexual abuse in childhood and how it has affected their life, the security of weekly meetings in the counsellor's office provides a predictable structure in which issues and memories can be visited and addressed step-by-step. In contrast, when a patient receiving treatment for kidney disease wishes to talk to their doctor or nurse about the impact of their condition on their role in the family, it is probably a conversation that they want to have there and then, with that specific health professional.

Box 6.1   Counselling spaces can be found in the most unlikely places: the healing fields

---

It is a mistake to think that a nicely decorated room, with two armchairs, is the only, or even necessarily the best, environment for conducting a counselling session. In a profoundly moving and informative book, Sonja Linden and Jenny Grut (2002) describe the psychotherapeutic work carried out in London under the auspices of the Medical Foundation for the Care of Victims of Torture. Over a period of two decades, this group has worked with dozens of families who have been exiled from their home countries and who have been subjected to unbelievable cruelties. For the majority of these people, sitting in a room and being asked to talk about their experiences to a therapist from a different culture would have been a difficult experience for many reasons. Instead, the Medical Foundation secured the use of a set of garden allotments. In these spaces, people who had been exiled worked with their families to clear ground and cultivate plants, some of which came from their home country, and some from England. Together, the participants created a remembrance garden, for all of their friends, colleagues and family members who had not been able to escape. As they worked in their fields, counsellors would work with them, and find moments to begin conversations about their old life that had been destroyed and their new one that was gradually growing. The experience of gardening made possible moments of peace and reflection, as well as a wealth of shared metaphors associated with activities such as clearing the ground, planting seed, keeping fences in good order, seasons, light and darkness, putting down roots, death and much else. This work shows how spaces for counselling can be built into another activity in a way that deepens the possibilities for relationship, connection and meaning-making.

This chapter considers what is involved in creating a space in which counselling can take place. It builds on the discussion in Chapter 5 relating to being prepared – the personal readiness of the counsellor and also the work the counsellor has done within their organizational setting to make counselling relationships possible.

The counselling space

The collaborative task model of counselling skill suggests that, when a person experiences a problem in living that they cannot resolve by using the resources immediately available to them, they look for a space within which they can stand back from the issue and reflect on how best to sort it out. That space can take many forms: walking in the country, entering into the narrative world of a novel or psychology book, finding a place of worship. A counselling relationship represents just one kind of 'healing' or 'reflective' space that is available within modern culture. But what kind of space is this? And how is it created?

There are four aspects that need to be kept in mind when thinking about a counselling space:

- The purpose of the space – what is it for?
- The personal relationship within which the space exists.
- Setting the scene – the physical quality of the space.
- Values – the moral significance of the space.

A counselling space is designed to allow a particular type of conversation to occur, in which the counsellor and the person take up positions from which the 'problem' can be viewed in a different light.

In practice, a counselling space is experienced by a person as time they spend with someone who is in the role of counsellor. The image that a person has of their counselling space is typically an image of the counsellor, the sound of his or her voice, things they say, their look, the room where they meet. Later in their life, when someone looks back on a counselling episode, they are likely to define it jointly in terms of their goal and their relationship with their counsellor: 'that was when I talked to Jack about my bereavement'. The helpfulness of a counselling space therefore depends to a large extent on the strength of the relationship between the person and the counsellor. The topic of the counselling relationship is examined more fully in Chapter 5.

A skilful counsellor is as prepared as they can be for their meeting with the person. This *preparation* is not about the specific characteristics of the individual person seeking help – it is not particularly helpful to have a referral letter, or to be told by a colleague that 'Mr X is depressed', because that information can get in the way of whatever it is the person wants to present of themselves. The preparation of the counsellor is around being ready to receive, in the sense of being able to focus on what the person is saying, and having means of support, consultation and supervision following the counselling episode. Anyone operating in a counselling role needs to be prepared for the fact that the person they are working with may need to express powerful emotions or recount a tragic or harrowing story. Being witness to strong emotions and awful stories inevitably has an impact on a counsellor or helper. It is difficult enough to hear such material at the best of times, but if the hearer knows that they will be left holding the feelings evoked by the material, without support, then they are likely to avoid entering such territory in the first place. The preparation for offering a counselling relationship is bound up with the organizational setting within which the counselling episode takes place. Specialist counselling or psychotherapy agencies are set up to provide as ideal as possible an environment for a counselling relationship to develop: there is time, a quiet comfortable room, support and supervision for the counsellor, clear-cut confidentiality boundaries, acceptance of the expression of emotion, and so on. In other organizational settings, such as hospitals, schools and community centres, a worker who is willing to respond to the counselling needs of clients has to establish in advance the parameters within which they are operating, and almost to create a model of counselling that is appropriate to that setting.

One of the most helpful aspects of any form of counselling is that it provides the person with a space that is safe, where they can say whatever they want, and is separated off from the routines, rules and expectations of everyday life. The counselling space is where the person goes in order to reflect on what has been happening in their everyday life. In counselling relationships that take place outside of specialist counselling agencies, a key task for the counsellor or helper is to set the scene: to assemble a space within which a meaningful counselling conversation can take place. Part of this task involves verbally checking that both participants are agreed that they have moved away from whatever other tasks they have been involved in and are now focusing on exploring the problem in living that the person has brought up. Another aspect of the task is to attend to the physical space within which the conversation is being conducted – for example, can other people overhear? A third part of the task of making a space is to do whatever is necessary to construct a boundary, by agreeing the limits of confidentiality, the length of the session, the possibility of further meetings, and the role of the helper. Competence in making a space also involves knowing how to close the space at the end of the conversation.

Box 6.2   Finding a space to be: creating stillpoints

There is an understandable tendency, when operating in the role of counsellor, to seek to arrive at a resolution or answer to the problem being presented by the person. The idea of counselling as a *space* reflects an assumption that it may be helpful at times for the person to have access to a space in which there is no pressure to do or achieve anything. Ronna Jevne (1987) describes such moments as *stillpoints*, and has written about their importance in her experience of working with people who have cancer. She describes her goal as a counsellor as enabling the person to 'experience a sense of calm and strength in the midst of threat' (p. 1) in which they are aware of their resources, and have the 'strength to handle whatever is necessary' (p. 12). Jevne suggests a number of questions that may help a person to identify their own potential for finding a stillpoint, such as 'can you recall a time when you felt a greater sense of being still inside?' and 'what would be necessary for you to have a stillpoint in the future?' She adds that, in her experience, 'the process is substantially dependent on the helper's capacity to achieve a stillpoint' (p. 8) for themselves. Jevne argues that the creation of a stillpoint is essentially a *non-rational* activity, which draws upon the person's connection with art, literature, spirituality and nature. In a later article, Jevne *et al.* (1998) described stages in cancer counselling where moments of 'calm and strength' may be helpful. However, the image of the stillpoint has implications for all forms of counselling, in revealing an important function of the counselling space. It is likely that most people who make use of counselling have times when all they are looking for, or need, is some assistance to be still.

Values

A crucial dimension of the counselling space concerns the issue of *values*. A fundamental skill of counselling is to be able to create a temporary moral arena in which the person can *evaluate* themselves differently. While the counselling space can be defined in terms of a set of tangible factors such as a particular time and place, and a relationship between a counsellor and person seeking help, it is also essential to recognize that the space needs to possess a less tangible quality: that of a distinctive *ethos*. The basic reason why this is important is that, in most circumstances, the problem for which the person is seeking help has been surrounded by blame and criticism (from self and others). In order to resolve a problem, the person needs to have an opportunity to step outside the negative moral attributions that permeate their discussion of the problem and instead view it in a fresh light. In effect, within the counselling space the counsellor is trying to hold a conversation that is characterized by a core belief in the positive capacity of the person to find and implement solutions, and live a good life, rather than one that is premised on beliefs of personal deficit and weakness.

Some of the core values of counselling are:

- *Deep respect for the person.* Each person is interesting, valuable and lovable. The person is both knowable and worth knowing. This is the kind of moral position that might be expressed in terms such as 'God is in every person', 'every person's life is worth a novel' and 'each person is a hero/heroine'.
- *Affirmation and authentication.* Each person is striving to do the best they can in the situation in which they find themselves. Everything that the person does or talks about is necessary: it was the way they needed to deal with an event or situation in order to preserve their integrity. Behind everything, people are trying to fulfil themselves and to do their best for other people in their life. Everyone is seeking to discover their own 'truth' and 'beauty'.
- *Inclusiveness.* Counselling does not operate from a premise that there is something wrong some deficit, in the person. The person is not seen as an 'other' who is different or dysfunctional; there is always an effort to find the links of common humanity between people. Labelling (for example, the use of psychiatric categories) and stereotyping (the use of social categories) are not consistent with the values of counselling.
- *People are relational beings.* Being a person means living within a network of relationships with other people. Everyone needs to be accepted, valued and loved by others. We cannot get through life without support from others; we are interdependent. Any problem in living has a strong relational element.
- *People develop.* Who we are and what we will become is a developmental process. As we get older, life presents different challenges and tasks. Whether these challenges are viewed as constituting a series of predictable or 'normative' stages, or are seen in more individual terms, they must be addressed and worked through. Any problem in living has a developmental aspect to it: helping people to cope with the process of transition is a key part of the work of counselling. The idea of process operates on a moment-by-moment basis as well: what a person says or feels at one moment is only part of the process – their thoughts and feelings will inevitably shift.
- *People are reflexive.* We are self-interpreting beings, with the capacity to look at ourselves and monitor our actions and intentions.
- *The person is the expert on their own life.* This value statement follows from the idea of deep respect, and is also associated with a position in relation to others which considers the use of interpersonal control, coercion and persuasion to be destructive of the common good.

- *Reality is constructed.* People perceive and understand the same set of events in different ways. In human affairs, there is no 'objective', fixed reality. One of the central tasks for any counsellor is to get 'inside' the reality of the other person, to engage empathically with that person's world as they experience it. Both personal and social realities or worlds are constructed through talk and language. Counsellors therefore need to be sensitive to the way that a person 'construes' their problem in living, in terms of the assumptions that they, the counsellor make about it. There are always different ways of seeing a problem: some of these ways may have the effect of dissolving the problem. To appreciate how someone makes sense of an event, it is necessary to understand the context of the event in terms of the person's life.
- *People are agents.* The external social, economic and physical environment, and our genetic/biological systems, define and constrain the possibilities that are open to us. Nevertheless, at the same time there are always possibilities for choice and agency. Being a person involves making choices and taking responsibility.
- *People are embodied.* Significance is communicated through feeling and emotion. Feelings and emotions are bodily signal systems that tell a person how important people and events in the external world are for them. Emotions signify the direction of action the person is driven to take (for example, love leads to getting closer, fear leads to getting further away). Counselling can never be an entirely rational activity, in the way that problem solving is: it always involves participating in some kind of emotional process.
- *To be a person is to struggle with existential dilemmas.* Underlying all of our problems in living are our attempts to come to terms with the meaning of basic dimensions of human experience such as caring, loving, purpose, authenticity, responsibility, faith, time and death. In other words, we are guided by our engagement with the 'larger meanings' or 'big picture', rather than by material rewards.

The significance of this set of values can be understood more clearly by considering certain aspects of the reality of the everyday world in which people live, and from which problems in living arise. First, it is necessary to recognize that, unlike people in previous periods of history, the majority of people in modern industrial societies do not completely exist within the rules and teachings of a specific belief system or ideology, such as Christianity, Islam or communism. Even if a person locates themself primarily within one of these belief systems, it is almost impossible to avoid being influenced by other moral values and rules. Traditional cultures that operate within a single, all-encompassing belief system provide ways of resolving problems in living that are incorporated into religious ritual and practice, such as prayer, the confessional, spiritual guidance, and so on. By contrast, modern cultures that are characterized by multiple value systems need to provide possibilities for resolving life problems that are not based in a single ideology or belief system. However, living within a pluralistic value system can lead to uncertainty and confusion around moral choices. Counselling provides a space within which at least some of these moral dilemmas can be resolved in relation to everyday personal issues. It does this by using a way of talking about issues that is consistently grounded in some simple assumptions about human goodness and potential. Counselling can be viewed as a kind of 'applied moral philosophy' that is not concerned with eternal truths (for example, does God exist?), but with practical everyday decision making (what is the right thing for me to do in this situation?).

A second aspect underlying the significance of this set of values is that many people find that being exposed to counselling values is a freeing and empowering experience. It is easy to read back through the list of values above and identify alternative value statements that are prevalent within our culture, such as 'some people are not worth knowing', 'our lives are determined by forces beyond our control' and 'people are born evil'. Although these (and other) alternative value positions are part of common currency; they operate as a cage that excludes people from genuine and respectful relationships.

Box 6.3   Expressing affirmatory values in working with people: the language of 'gifts'

One of the very practical ways in which values can inform the practice of counselling within professional roles is through attention to the use of language. The social philosopher Kenneth Gergen (1990) has written about the adoption by many health professionals of a 'language of deficit', a tendency to base their understanding of clients, and conversation with and about these clients, in a language that describes the person as having something wrong with them, as if they were like a broken machine that needs to be fixed. Terminology such as 'borderline', 'dysfunctional' or 'addict' are total descriptions that devalue the person being talked about by characterizing them as lacking in strengths and resources, and implicitly as interesting only in terms of their deficits. A project carried out by a group of public health nurses in British Columbia, Canada, illustrates how a more affirming value position can be maintained through a deliberate attempt to change how language is used. These nurses decided to incorporate a 'language of gifts' into all aspects of their work. Kinman and Finck (2004: 234–5) defined this approach in the following terms:

> [We] enter the each situation with an attitude or spirit that receives the person or group being served as an entity bearing gifts. Even when the discourse surrounding the person or group is permeated with deficit and problems, the practitioner sees her work as one of distinguishing abundance and receiving the fruit of that abundance as gifts offering enrichment and healing . . . . [A]ny form of 'human service' entails collaboration between community and practitioners, and involves the circulation of a series of gift exchanges.

One of the nurses described an example of how adopting a language of gifts had made a significant difference to her approach to working with one young woman whose life had involved a struggle with drug misuse:

> I had gone to see a mom. All her children, up to that point, had been in the care of the government. But she had brought her new baby home, and she was really proud that she had the baby. That was almost a year ago, and now I was reconnected because she has just moved back to this area. However, when I went to see her, while I was in the car, I found myself in deficit thinking. As I got to her house, I realized – no, I needed to just go in there looking to get to know her and hear what her story has been for the last year. After all, I hadn't known her for these last

months. So, instead, I went in just wanting to know her, and then I discovered that she had so many wonderful things to say. When I went to the home, I met this nine-month old who's walking all over the apartment, who was into absolutely every-thing. So I pointed out some of the things I noticed – his curiosity, how stable he was on his feet, and how interested he was in the world. She said, 'Oh yeah, well he's really interested in the world because I never put him in a play pen. I knew that he needed to know his world. I just sensed that'. Here's this mom who for drug-use reasons had lost all her other children, but now she's sensing with this baby that he needs to know his world. I mean – that's beautiful. So then I said, 'Oh that's a wonderful thing you've identified and now look he's nine months old and he's already walking . . . and you did that!'. . . . I know that if I had come in that front door in the same deficit thinking that I had in the car we would never have got there. I would never have heard things like 'I did that' and 'he had to discover his world'. I wouldn't have heard all that. I came away most energized.

(Kinman and Finck, 2004: 235–6)

Kinman and Finck discuss the many ways that a language of deficit is built into the practices of health, education and social services professionals, through legislation, hierarchical forms of organization, the design of forms and accountability procedures, and everyday routines. They argue that a commitment to a language of gifts is no easy matter, and involves critically thinking through basic assumptions that exist within all of these spheres of work.

The values being described here can be understood as being broadly 'humanistic' in nature. Humanistic values have represented a core dimension of moral thinking in western societies for the past two hundred years. It is a mistake to equate humanistic values solely with the field of humanistic psychology, as articulated in the writings of Abraham Maslow, Carl Rogers, Charlotte Buhler and others. Humanism is a much wider philosophical and moral perspective, which finds expression in literature, art and politics. Humanism is essentially based on a respect for the intrinsic value of human beings. It is important to acknowledge that individuals from other cultural backgrounds may not share these values. It is also essential to recognize that other systems of moral values exist within western society itself. For example, the values listed above are in conflict with many aspects of materialist/consumerist values, scientific/rational values, or fundamentalist religious values – all of which are vitally important to some people as guides for living the good life.

The expression of humanist moral principles in counselling leads to the construction of a 'moral arena', which is quite different from everyday life. For many people who use counselling, one of the most powerful aspects of the counselling space arises from the suspension of conventional moral judgements and blaming, which may at other times dominate their lives. Few counsellors seek to engage those who consult them in abstract moral debate. However, most counsellors are highly sensitive to any state-ments that a person might make that include terms such as 'must', 'should' or 'ought', because these phrases articulate a position in which the person defines themself in terms of a fixed set of rules, rather than from a position in which personal conduct is viewed as negotiable and co-constructed. Effective therapeutic conversations provide places in which blame is suspended, thereby allowing the intricacies of what happened, and what the person intended, felt and wished for, to be explored in detail: blame closes down exploration.

The values of counselling are communicated by the ways in which counselling is organized: voluntary, confidential, time to talk, control of the conversation by the person seeking help. These structures give powerful moral messages about the worth of the person's a belief in the person's capacity to develop, and so on. Values are also conveyed in what the counsellor says, for example, the painstaking effort to understand the person and develop a shared language constantly reinforces the idea that 'you are important', 'I respect your capacity to find your own solutions', 'you are the expert' and so forth.

It is probable that people who become comfortable and effective in the role of counsellor are those who find meaning and relevance in the values of humanism in their own lives. From the point of view of the counsellor, one of the key facets of counselling values is a capacity to *accept* the other person. Acceptance can be difficult for a counsellor if they espouse religious beliefs that condemn certain forms of behaviour, such as sex outside marriage, homosexuality or suicide. If a counsellor who holds such beliefs works with a person who is, for example, gay or lesbian, it may be very hard to offer a counselling space that is sufficiently safe and free from blame. Many people who are attracted to the role of counsellor have themselves undergone a process of moral re-evaluation in their own lives, and as a result are sensitive to values issues and strongly believe in the usefulness of relationships that they perceive as blame-free and life enhancing.

Trust and confidentiality

Most of the time, the moral issues discussed in the previous section are far in the background in counselling. People do not (usually) seek counselling in order to talk philosophy; they want to talk things through and sort them out. An awareness of the moral dimension of counselling is therefore largely a matter for the counsellor. For example, in counselling training it can be valuable to record and transcribe a conversation in which one is playing the role of counsellor, and then to read through the transcript to identify the moral positions that are being espoused by each participant. For the person seeking counselling, the moral issues that are of concern centre around *trust* and *confidentiality*. Trust is a quality that can only be built through operating from a position of genuineness and consistency. Confidentiality, however, is a topic that needs to be brought out into the open as soon as a counselling space is created for the first time (or even before, for example, if a practitioner is supplying clients with leaflets or other information about their counselling role). The person seeking help needs to know what will happen to the information that they disclose. They also need to know the limits of confidentiality – for instance, what the counsellor might be obliged to do if there is a crisis.

Opening a space – responding to empathic opportunities

One of the most sensitive issues for practitioners whose counselling role is embedded within other professional responsibilities toward clients or patients, is that of knowing when, and if, the person with whom they are working is at a point of wanting to talk about a problem in living. As suggested in Chapter 5, an essential element of good practice in embedded counselling is thorough preparation, which may include providing the person with information, either verbally or in the form of a leaflet, regarding the possibility of counselling being provided. Doing this can lead to the person taking the initiative and explicitly asking for some time to talk things through. This is the most satisfactory way to negotiate a space for counselling within a professional role, because it maximizes the chance that counselling is what the person really wants, and ensures that participation is entirely voluntary. However, in situations where a person's contact with a practitioner is dominated by practical care or learning tasks, perhaps under pressure of time, there can be many factors that inhibit the person from overtly asking for counselling. In the absence of an explicit request from the person, the counsellor needs to be aware of openings that arise within the routine interaction they have with a person or to deliberately manufacture such openings.

In the course of a discussion between a person seeking help and a practitioner (teacher, nurse, social worker) providing help, there is likely to be a predominant focus on a set of professional tasks such as giving feedback on a student assignment, administering medication or looking at welfare benefit entitlement. Within that discussion, however, there may be moments when the person expresses emotion, verbally or non-verbally, avoids certain topics, or introduces personal information that is not strictly relevant to the task. These moment can be viewed as potential openings for a counselling conversation. It can be useful to regard such events as *empathic opportunities*. In effect, the person has expressed something that allows the practitioner to gain a little more of an entry into the person's private life, or areas of concern. In order to follow up an empathic opportunity, it can be useful to reflect back what has been conveyed in a way that acknowledges its significance for the person ('I'm aware that your eyes are full of tears as you are talking about this. I have a sense of how sad you are about what has happened . . .'). If the empathic reflection is received by the person as a helpful intervention ('yes, it's been awful'), it may then be possible to go further and to enquire about whether the person might wish to talk about their concern a bit more ('would it be helpful to just take a few minutes to stay with how you are feeling?').

Box 6.4   When counselling is embedded in another professional role: using empathic opportunities to indicate whether a counselling response might be appropriate

For practitioners whose counselling function is embedded in another professional role, such as health worker or teacher, it can be difficult to know whether a client or service user is actually looking for a chance to talk about a personal issue, or whether they are happy enough to continue the primary task such as nursing care or learning. In recent years, some researchers in the area of doctor–patient interaction have developed a

---

useful approach to deciding whether a counselling intervention is indicated. These researchers have been exploring the idea that, in a consultation, patients may present their doctors with a series of *empathic opportunities*. Within an interview with a doctor, the main focus of a patient's talk is on reporting relevant medical information, usually in response to questions asked by the physician. From time to time, however, the patient may signal an area of personal concern. The question then is whether the doctor acknowledges this empathic opportunity and is able to follow it up. The following example is provided by Eide *et al.* (2004) from their study of consultations between cancer patients and oncologists.

Patient: I heard quite badly before (*gives medical information*) but now my hearing is much reduced (*gives medical information*), so that I find it hard to function if they say something to me (*potential empathic opportunity*).
Doctor: A lot of sound . . .
Patient: I walk with a watch that supposedly makes a noise (*gives medical information*). And I have boys at home who make a lot of noise, but I can't hear them at all (*gives medical information*).
Doctor: No, I hear that (*laughter*).
Patient: Yes, of course, you hear well, but I don't hear it at all, so that is my biggest handicap (*potential empathic opportunity*).
Doctor: Yes, it may be that it will get a bit better. I don't know if it will return to normal, but I think it's a bit early to say, so soon after the operation . . .
Patient: Yes, I had it before as well, due to the chemo (*gives medical information*).
Doctor: Yes, the chemo, and not the operation, but the chemo . . . . How do you feel . . . something in your feet?
Patient: Yes, I feel as if my feet are tight, that they . . . (*gives medical information*).
Doctor: Well, I think this will improve. It will never be completely as it was, but it can be better.
Patient: That's in my feet and in my hands. I can live with that (*gives psychosocial information*) . . . . But then there's the sound in my ear (*gives medical information*) . . . . If I sit in a meeting, I have to concentrate enormously, and when I come home, then . . . then I am so tired (*empathic opportunity*).

In this excerpt, the researchers have made a distinction between potential empathic opportunities, defined as 'patient statement(s) from which a clinician might infer underlying emotion that has not been explicitly expressed' and actual empathic opportunities, defined as 'direct and explicit expression of emotion by a patient' (Eide *et al.*, 2004: 292). In this case, the doctor has not acknowledged the potential empathic opportunities provided by the patient early in the conversation, choosing to focus only on medical matters. Towards the end of the conversation, the patient returns, in a more explicit manner, to the emotional issue that concerns her.

Bylund and Makoul (2002) explored gender differences in patients' expression of empathic opportunities, and doctors' responses to them. They found that while both male and female patients exhibited the same number of empathic openings, women tended to express their personal concerns with more emotional intensity. They also found that women doctors were significantly more likely to respond to empathic opportunities than were their male colleagues. In addition, this research study showed that, although patients in these medical consultations tended to talk mainly about health matters, in most of the doctor–patient consultations that were observed, there were several clear-cut empathic opportunities where the patient communicated a wish to talk about personal issues and concerns.

It is important that further research is conducted on this topic, particularly to extend our knowledge of the patient/client perspective on what happens during moments when they express emotion during a medical (or other professional) consultation. Nevertheless, it seems likely that the concept of empathic opportunity can be helpful for practitioners as a means of identifying occasions when a person seeking help may appreciate the offer of space to explore feelings and personal concerns.

A different strategy for eliciting openings for the creation of a counselling space is specifically to ask about personal issues and feelings. For example, a doctor breaking bad news to a patient may pause for a few moments and then add, 'I know that what I have said will be a shock to you. I know that if someone had told me I had cancer I would be feeling scared and bewildered, and probably lots of other things as well . . . . I am wondering if any of that is happening for you?' A teacher who is working with a student on a geography project, and who knows that the student has had some problems at home, can routinely ask, 'Before we finish, I just wanted to check how things are at home . . . . I don't want to put you on the spot. It's fine if you don't want to talk about it. It's just that I am concerned, and would like to help if I can in any way.'

A key competence within embedded counselling is to develop a way of opening up spaces for counselling conversations that is appropriate to the client group being worked with, the organizational setting in which the practitioner is based and the personal style of the practitioner themself. There are several strategies that can be employed, as outlined above, but the implementation of these strategies can depend on many factors. For instance, in some situations it may be best to wait until the end of a meeting before inquiring about personal issues, to allow the person an easy exit if they do not wish to enter into a discussion of their concerns. This was the strategy devised by the teacher described in the previous example – he was aware that he was perceived as an authority figure, and did not want to create a situation where the student felt under pressure to talk about his home life. On the other hand, a GP who knows that a patient has been sitting for some time in the waiting room to see her (and becoming more anxious by the minute), and who might think that it would be unfair to prolong the wait for the other people who are in the queue, might wish to pick up on the first empathic opportunity that arises.

Setting practical limits to a counselling space: time and space

Once an opening for counselling has been identified, it is helpful to provide some indication of the length of the space that is available. This may involve a statement such as 'we could talk about this for few minutes now, if you like' or 'I have about fifteen minutes until my next appointment – would that be enough time to begin to look at what's happening for you?' In some circumstances it may be necessary to ask the person how much time they have available: 'would it be possible to keep going for a few minutes so I could hear more about the situation you are in?' What is essential is to avoid a situation where the person in the role of counsellor begins to get distracted by the fact that they are running behind schedule, or they abruptly bring the conversation to an end because they have run out of time. Another useful way of signalling time boundaries is to indicate that 'we only have a couple of minutes left', or to use a phrase such as 'we need to finish soon for today', and then offer a brief summary of what has been said, or the action that has been agreed. An enormous amount can be covered in a few minutes if the person talking knows that the space is there for them. People know that professional helpers such as doctors, nurses, teachers and social workers are operating under time pressures, and will usually accept the realities of what can be offered in terms of time.

Another practical consideration in relation to establishing a workable space for counselling is to be mindful of the physical space. Seating arrangements, proximity, ensuring that the sound of voices does not travel to others, and the availability of drinking water and tissues, all make an important contribution to creating the right kind of space. Counsellors and psychotherapists in private practice go beyond these basic material considerations and give a great deal of thought to developing the right kind of emotional ambience, using lighting, soft furnishing and art. This kind of environmental control is seldom possible in situations where the counsellor is also performing another role, such as that of teacher or nurse. Nevertheless, part of the preparation for being willing to offer a counselling relationship needs to involve identifying the best spaces, within a school or clinic, where private, emotional conversations can safely take place. An issue that confronts many practitioners of embedded counselling is that of seeing a client in their home and finding some way to make an appropriate space in a household where the TV is on, other people are around, and there may be a budgie flying about in the room. In such a situation, the practitioner may need to explain to the person why it is necessary to create a space in which there is some privacy and quiet.

The issue of dual relationships

A topic that receives a great deal of attention within training programmes for specialist counsellors and psychotherapists, and is highlighted in the professional ethical codes for these occupations, is the issue of dual or multiple relationships between counsellors and their clients. A *dual relationship* refers to any situation in which the counsellor has some other role or contact with the client outside of the therapy hour. This contact can range from chance meetings at social events, through working together as colleagues, to being or becoming friends or lovers. On the whole, the received wisdom has been that dual relationships have been regarded as taboo within the counselling and psychotherapy profession (Pope, 1991; Gabriel, 2005). Although this is a complex area, with many different types of dual relationship that can occur, the extreme caution with which most therapists approach the potential for any form of dual relationship can be attributed to three main factors:

- *Risk of exploitation of the client.* The therapy relationship is inevitably one-sided, in that the therapist learns a lot about the client, and is rational and in control at times when the client may be vulnerable. A therapist therefore has a degree of power in relation to a client, and would be in a strong position to manipulate a client into becoming a friend or lover, or into doing favours for them, if they wished to do so. In these situations, a client who may have become emotionally dependent on a therapist may see themself as special – the chosen one who has been adopted as a friend. Placing a ban on dual relationships is an obvious strategy for eliminating, or at least minimizing, this kind of exploitation.
- *Threats to confidentiality.* An essential feature of any counselling space is that it is safe: the person can say whatever they want and (other than times when what they say may invoke risk of harm to self or others) can be sure that their disclosures will go no further. Specifically, people seeking counselling are concerned that what they say to their counsellor will not come back to them, in the sense of being passed on to their family members, friends or colleagues. In this context, any contact between a counsellor or psychotherapist and their client, outside of the therapy hour, raises the danger that the therapist may say something to other people who know the client, that betrays the confidences of the therapy room.
- *The ability to use the client–therapist relationship as a source of insight and learning.* Within the psychodynamic or psychoanalytic tradition in counselling and psychotherapy, one of the primary areas of psychotherapeutic work lies in making sense of the way that the client responds to the therapist (this is known as the client's *transference* on to the therapist). The assumption is that, over time, a client will project patterns of emotion and feeling, and unmet needs, from their formative childhood years, on to their therapist. An example would be if a client consistently feels that the therapist is criticizing them. This kind of pattern could originate in the experience that the person had in being harshly treated by their parents. The value of this perspective is that it allows a therapist to draw the client's attention to dysfunctional patterns as they occur in the actual therapy session. However, this therapeutic strategy works best when the therapist behaves in a neutral way and does not express much of their own personality to the client (recall how Freud's patients lay on a couch, with the great man sitting out of sight behind their head). If the client is able to know the therapist in other situations, the power of this kind of therapeutic process is greatly diluted. For instance, if a client and therapist are colleagues, and the client accuses the therapist of being critical, it becomes very hard for the latter to decide whether the client's statement is based on transference or in fact reflects their knowledge of the therapist in wider settings.

It can be seen, therefore, that there are both ethical (exploitation and confidentiality) and technical (accurate transference interpretation) reasons for striving to keep counsellor–client relationships free from dual or multiple role entanglements. The technical factor (interpretation of transference) is really applicable only to practitioners using a psychodynamic or psychoanalytic approach. However, because of the prestige of psychoanalysis within the therapy world (the earliest form of therapy, the longest training, Freud as a cultural icon), this argument has tended to influence the attitudes of other therapists who do not employ this approach.

In recent years, the taboo around dual relationships has softened (the current debate can be followed in Lazarus and Zur, 2002; Syme, 2003; and Gabriel, 2005). It has become apparent that the position taken by the profession has been overly influenced by a desire to avoid financial and sexual exploitation of clients, and that the resulting blanket ban on dual relationships has made it harder for practitioners and clients to be open about occasions when dual relationships have not harmed clients, and have even been helpful. Within the field of specialist, long-term counselling and psychotherapy, there are some situations in which dual relationships are unavoidable. One of these situations occurs in rural communities, where everyone is known to everyone else. A similar situation arises within gay, lesbian and bisexual communities, where it is impossible for a client to find an 'out' therapist who does not move in the same social circles as they do. For example, the well-known American pioneer of feminist therapy, Laura Brown (2005) has written very sensitively about the ethical challenges involved in being, for a time, the only lesbian therapist in her city. The main theme that has emerged in current writing about dual relationships is that effective counselling can take place in a context of dual or multiple role relationships as long as the practitioner is willing to discuss the advantages and disadvantages of this arrangement with their client, and to use supervision and consultation as a means of checking out the integrity of their practice and to explore any unintended consequences of what they decide to do.

Practitioners whose counselling is embedded in other work roles represent a particular kind of dual relationship that has not been widely discussed in the literature. Any such practitioner will usually be operating within a formal ethical code that is at least as rigorous as the ethical framework espoused by counsellors and psychotherapists, as well as being subjected to powerful informal unwritten rules around conduct in relation to clients, service users and patients. Exploitation of service users, or misuse of confidential information, is strongly condemned in all professional groups. The issue of transference interpretation is unlikely to represent a major consideration for practitioners of embedded counselling because it is unlikely that these practitioners would wish to apply a strictly psychodynamic approach in their work. If they were in a situation of working psychodynamically, this would most likely occur in a setting in which a team of workers had adopted a psychodynamic model – for instance, in a psychiatric rehabilitation day centre, or in a residential group home for disturbed teenagers – and would be supported by colleagues in resolving the intricacies of multiple roles in their work with client transferences.

It is nevertheless important for anyone who offers a counselling relationship to be aware of the potential dangers of dual relationships. At the heart of any counselling relationship is the willingness of the person seeking help to open up and to begin talking about things that are painful, shameful, confusing or distressing. Leakage of what is talked about to a third party is experienced as a very basic kind of betrayal. Turning away from the counselling role and resuming whatever other kind of relationship was in existence ('when I started telling her about the abuse, she became the social worker again') can also be experienced as a betrayal. For those whose counselling practice is embedded in other roles, it is essential to make careful preparations to ensure that such betrayals do not occur, and to discuss with the person seeking help the limitations of what is on offer and how the helper's different roles might best be managed by both participants.

Offering a space for counselling: a practitioner checklist

This book is largely intended for practitioners who are striving to build a counselling dimension into whatever other type of helping or caring role they have in relation to the people with whom they are working. In this type of work role, the activity associated with the practitioner's primary role takes precedence and represents the primary focus of the work that is being carried out. At some point, with some clients or patients, the person seeking help says something that indicates that they want to talk about a personal issue. At this moment, the practitioner has the option of ignoring the person's signal (this is probably what most practitioners do, most of the time), or may choose to accept the invitation to move into a listening and counselling mode. How is this decision made? What are the factors that need to be taken into account when deciding whether it is useful and sensible to offer to provide a counselling relationship? The key issues that call for consideration at such moments can be summed up in the form of a set of questions for the practitioner to ask of themselves:

- Is counselling practicable here and now? Do I have enough time to enter into this kind of discussion? Are we in a sufficiently private place – will anyone interrupt or overhear us?
- Is counselling consistent with the goals and procedures of my team or organization? Is there someone else in the team charged with providing counselling for this person? What might be the implications for me of learning more about the personal problems of this individual – could this information compromise me in other situations?
- Is this something I can handle? Do I have the knowledge, skill and confidence to work with the issue that this person is describing? Does the issue trigger strong feelings in me or feed into my own unresolved dilemmas?
- Do I have the support to enable me to take this further? Is there supervision or consultative support available to me? Do I have sufficient information about referral to specialist services?
- How needy is this person? Are they in a crisis right now or could we return to the issue at a later date? What do they actually want?
- What further information from the person would help me to decide how best to respond right now?

The answers to these questions should determine the kind of response that is made. While it is always important to acknowledge the distress that is expressed by a person, a practitioner needs to recognize that they have a range of options in a situation when a person indicates that they may want to talk through a problem in living. In some situations a practitioner might choose to acknowledge the problem and to explain that this issue is not one that the practitioner feels able to help with, and then lead into further inquiry about whether the person has other sources of help, if necessary advising on what is available and organizing a referral. On other occasions, for example, when time is limited, it may be best to check on the urgency of the issue and to negotiate a more appropriate time when the issue might be explored at greater length.

Closing the space

Once a person has started to talk about an issue for which they are seeking counselling, they may or may not be aware of the time that elapses. It may then be helpful for the counsellor to mention, during a pause in the conversation, that there may be only two or three minutes before they finish. At the point of closing the space, there are a number of things that it may be useful for the counsellor to say:

- Acknowledging the feelings expressed by the person, and the courage they have shown in confronting a troubling or embarrassing issue – by making such a statement, the counsellor is helping to build a solid relationship and demonstrating empathy and caring.
- Summarizing the main theme of themes that have been discussed – this helps the person to know that the counsellor has understood them.
- Inquiring about whether there are other aspects of the issue that have been left unsaid or that require exploration at a future date – this allows the person to feel that, although the time has been limited, there is no sense of premature closure around the difficulties they are facing.
- Reviewing any actions that have been agreed and checking who will be responsible for doing what, by when – the aim here is to reinforce any problem-solving strategies that have arisen during the conversation.
- Asking whether the conversation has been helpful and whether the counsellor could have done anything that might have been more useful – this is a means of reiterating the value of the person's views and of emphasizing the collaborative nature of the counselling relationship.
- If the person has been upset or is in crisis, ensuring that they have somewhere to go or someone who will take care of them.
- Making sure that the person knows the date, time and place of the next meeting and, if necessary what the procedures for 'out of hours' contact or support might be.

It can be seen that the ending of a counselling conversation marks a critical point in any counselling relationship. The closing of the space represents an opportunity to reinforce the relationship and the values upon which counselling depends. It is a point at which the person can be helped to remember important understandings that may have arisen during the conversation. It may also be a moment at which a counsellor may be called upon to demonstrate firmness. Anyone involved in counselling will be familiar with 'doorknob' statements, when the person opens up a new and sometimes dramatic line of conversation just at the point where they are leaving the room. If the lead-up to the closing of the space has been carried out thoroughly enough, it should be possible merely to tell the person that this new topic is something that can be discussed next time. The closing of the space is a necessary part of the need of the counsellor to pace themself rather than risk being overwhelmed by an endless stream of complexity and suffering, and ultimately it is not helpful to allow counselling sessions to go on for longer than the time that the practitioner has available.

Box 6.5   Being prepared for ambivalence on the part of a person who may want help

The majority of people who know that they need help for a personal or emotional life problem find it hard to make the first move. Studies of university students (Grayson *et al.*, 1998), young people (Le Surf and Lynch, 1999) and hospital patients (Schoenberg and Shiloh, 2002) have interviewed people about their attitudes to seeking counselling. All of these studies have found profound levels of ambivalence. The people interviewed were able to generate a host of reasons for not asking for help: the potential helper is too busy; my problem is not serious enough or not relevant; I'm worried about confidentiality; the problem is a part of my character and I cannot do anything about it; I feel ashamed; and so on. Other research (see McLeod, 1990, for a review) has found that even when a person gets as far as sitting down with a counsellor, their experience of the first session is that they were nervous and not able to take in much of what happened. For counsellors, the implications of these research studies are significant. A practitioner offering a counselling relationship is likely to be on their own territory, comfortable with what is happening and in control. For the person seeking help, the situation is completely different: they are in new territory and have little notion of what will happen next. It is essential, at the moment of first contact around a possible counselling contact, for anyone offering a counselling relationship to be willing to make the imaginative leap into the experience of the person seeking help, and to respond sensitively and supportively in a way that minimizes the discomfort, shame and embarrassment felt by the person.

Conclusions

There are many different aspects to be taken into consideration when creating a space for counselling, ranging from practical factors such as chairs and privacy, through to the challenge of implementing an environment in which the person feels safe, taken care of and free from evaluative judgement. A key theme that underpins all of the issues discussed in this chapter is that of managing to allow two people to share a period of time in which neither of them is *distracted* from the task of 'talking things through'. If the person seeking help is worried about being overheard, unsure of whether the practitioner is responding primarily as a nurse, doctor or teacher, rather than as a counsellor, or is fearful of being judged, then they will be distracted from fully telling their story. Similarly, if any of these concerns are present in the awareness of the counsellor, then they, too, are open to distraction. A good counselling conversation is experienced by both participants as being suspended in time and oblivious to the outside world. It is the responsibility of the counsellor to create the conditions for this to happen. At one level, a counsellor may be seen to be merely paying attention and listening. However, to do so in a powerful and focused way, a way that creates a suitable 'stillpoint' for reflection and meeting, requires thought to be given to the issues that have been explored here.

Questions for reflection and discussion

1. What are the values that inform your own work with people who are seeking help? To what extent does the set of counselling values outlined in this chapter reflect the moral basis of your role? What other value positions are relevant for you? In what ways do these other value positions either complement or stand against counselling values?
2. In your own life, what are the spaces in which you find meaning and strength? What are the factors that make these spaces possible?
3. In what ways do you observe potential spaces for counselling in your interactions with people who come to you for help? What do you do to open these spaces?
4. In your work setting, what are the limits to confidentiality in respect of what clients, service users, student or patients say to you? How do the people you are helping learn about how confidentiality is approached in your organization? Under what circumstances would you remind a person about these limits?
5. How satisfactory is the physical setting in which you work, in terms of providing spaces for counselling relationships to occur? What improvements would you like to make to the physical environment in which you see people?
6. Reflect on the nature of the dual (or multiple) relationships you have with people to whom you are offering a service. In your situation, what are the greatest points of tension between the different roles that you perform? In what ways do positive synergies exist between these roles? What do you do to manage potential role conflicts?

Suggestion for further reading

An accessible overview of the idea that counselling is based on a distinctive set of values can be found in:

Christopher, J. C. (1996) Counseling's inescapable moral visions. *Journal of Counseling and Development*, 75: 17–25.

7

Working collaboratively: building a relationship

Its good of you to see me
Regular like this.
You know
I remember
You said at the first time I saw you
That sometimes there are things you can't
Speak
To your family
About.
But I know you will listen.
It's funny, but I can't get it out of my mind.
I don't think there's anyone else knows this.
My grand-dad.
Died the week of his 70th birthday.
The same thing.
They were planning a party.
He was laid out.
In my nan's dining room.

Introduction

Problems in living that lead people to seek counselling can usually be resolved in various ways other than counselling. For example, if a person is experiencing work stress and overload, they can sit down with a piece of paper and make a plan of action, take up yoga and meditation as a means of relaxation, or read a self-help manual. Each of these methods of stress management can be effective. The distinctive feature of counselling, in comparison with these other coping or change strategies, is that counselling operates primarily through the formation of a *relationship*. However, what does this mean? What kind of relationship can exist between a person and their counsellor? How and why does this relationship have a positive impact? After all, if we look at our lives, we can all identify relationships that are at times destructive or limiting, and we may even have difficulty in identifying relationships that have unequivocally been good for us. What is it about a counselling relationship that is different?

At one level, the relationship in counselling is straightforward: it is someone to talk to. If you need to talk something through, then it is essential to have someone who will listen. Beyond this, the relationship in counselling is a relationship with a person who stands outside of the problem, who is independent of one's family, friendship network or work group, and who can respond to the problem in a fresh and unbiased fashion. Beyond this, there is a deeper meaning to the idea of a relationship. A relationship implies an encounter with an *other*, a person who is separate from oneself. At some level, the challenge of making contact with this other evokes a long list of questions that a person may have about how they connect with people in general. For example, can another person be trustworthy? Can I be understood (do I make sense or am I crazy?) and accepted? Can I be really honest with another person? Can I allow someone else to care for me?

When counselling is embedded in other roles and relationships, when it takes place in the context of a nurse–patient relationship, or a teacher–pupil relationship, the significance of the relationship, for the person seeking help, will mainly be at a practical level – someone to talk to who is reasonably detached from the problem, who is accessible, someone that they know and trust. Nevertheless, even in these situations, there is always a deeper resonance to the relationship. In counselling, a person is not seeking help for an 'objective' problem, such as 'how do I fix my washing machine?' Rather, the person is seeking help for a problem in *living*: 'why did I get into an argument with the man who came to fix my washing machine?' Counselling always comes back to questions around 'who am I and how do I relate to other people?' In talking about these questions, a person expresses their subjectivity (this is who I am) in relation to the 'you' or 'other' represented by the counsellor. In turn, the counsellor is trying to find a way to work together ('how can *we* tackle this?'). This core issue, of aloneness and separateness in life, runs through all counselling conversations, sometimes in the background, at other times up front.

The sections that follow discuss some of the main qualities and activities that are involved in building a counselling relationship: listening; being trustworthy; being genuine; caring; and working collaboratively. The chapter concludes by exploring some theoretical frameworks that can be used to make sense of issues that emerge within counselling relationships.

Box 7.1   When the relationship goes wrong

Research carried out by Dianna Kenny (2004) provides a salutary lesson regarding the importance of relationships in health care. Kenny interviewed 20 patients whose treatment for chronic pain had not been successful, and 22 doctors who were chronic pain specialists. Participants were invited to give accounts of their experiences of coping or working with chronic pain. Interviews ranged between 45 minutes and 2 hours in length. Analysis of the transcripts revealed a fundamental breakdown in relationships between these people and their doctors. A key theme was what the researcher categorized as 'a struggle . . . to determine who would assume the role of speaker and who would listen' (p. 300). A typical patient statement in respect of this theme was 'they [the doctors] don't even listen to what you have to say . . . you can tell they are not listening at all – they just write up a script and say see you next month. You have to jump up and down or scream at them to be heard.' A typical doctor statement within this theme was: 'People seem to be very hard to educate. They don't understand. They get fixed ideas about where the pain is coming from. It is hard to change their focus.' Another key theme lay in the different beliefs held by patients and doctors regarding the cause and meaning of the pain. All of the patients made statements along the lines of: 'They [the doctors] don't seem to think that you might really be in pain. They think that it is all in your mind . . . . They all say "take an antidepressant and go home." You start to think – am I mad or stupid?' By contrast, doctors were asserting that: 'It stands to reason. If you have done all the tests possible, and you get nothing, not a hint of a physical problem, what else can you conclude?' These patients wanted, but did not receive, emotional and psychological care from their doctors: 'Doctors can't handle the emotions we present with . . . . You try to talk to them, but you see them watching the clock for the next patient.' Rather than being treated as individuals, patients experienced themselves as being typecast as 'just another chronic pain patient'.

 The results of this study demonstrate vividly the chasm that can open up between practitioners and their clients when relational factors are neglected. For Kenny (2004), the implications of her findings were clear: it is essential that doctors should learn how to treat patients as co-equals, and engage in shared decision making.

The idea of building a relationship

In most professional situations, in teaching, social work and health, the relationship between the person seeking help and the practitioner forms the backdrop to their work together. The focus is largely on what needs to be done, the practical task in hand. The relationship is taken for granted. In counselling situations, the relationship needs to take centre stage, because meaningful counselling depends on the establishment of a bond or alliance that is strong enough for the person to be able to tolerate talking about issues that are emotionally painful, embarrassing and shameful, out of control or confusing. Sometimes, a person who is seeking help, and the practitioner who is in the role of counsellor to that person, may just hit it off from the start, and be able to understand, appreciate and trust each other without difficulty. More usually, however, a relationship needs to be built. This is why counselling can take time: the person seeking help may need to test out the relationship before they can come to rely on it. Good counsellors not only pay attention to the problems and dilemmas presented by the person seeking help, but also continually monitor the quality of the relationship or contact they have with the person, and look for ways to strengthen it.

Building a caring relationship is facilitated by two forms of activity. First, the counsellor can invite the person to talk about what matters most to them, in terms of how they feel that the counsellor needs to be to allow them to make use of the situation. What matters most might include being honest ('don't lie to me'), discussing things in a particular way (for example, by *not* asking questions – 'it's like being interrogated' – or by asking questions – 'your questions help me to talk'), or being open about their own experience of the problem ('do you know what its like to have a habit you can't break?'). Some people in counselling relationships want to know in detail about who will hear about what they say to the counsellor (the limits of confidentiality). Others will want to be reassured about the constancy and availability of the counsellor ('I was just gutted when that other nurse was transferred to a different unit'). Once the person has identified some of their relationship needs, it is important to explore what these needs mean in practice ('what does "not lying" mean to you – what do I have to do to let you know what I'm not lying to you?'). It is not realistic to expect a person to be able to specify all of their desired relationship qualities on first time of asking. On the whole, people are not very aware of what they want or need in relationships, and it may be necessary to return to this issue at regular intervals, to check whether other elements of 'what you need from me in this relationship' might have come to the attention of the person.

A second activity that promotes relationship building is to reflect on the impact of what is happening when the person and counsellor attempt to work together. A counsellor might achieve this by saying something along the lines of 'Would it be OK to pause for a minute to look at what happened there, when I asked you that question? I might be wrong, but I just had a sense that you felt angry with me for asking you about that. Is that right?' Alternatively, the counsellor can open up this topic by disclosing their own intentions, for example, 'I'm wondering what might be the best way to take this forward. I'm aware that there are lots of questions that I have about what you are talking about, but I don't know whether it would be a distraction to you for me to ask them, or whether it would be useful for you . . . or whether you might have some other ideas about what would be best.'

The aim is to work together to build a relationship that makes it possible for the person to use counselling to move forward in their life. If one of the limiting factors in a person's life lies in the area of having difficulties in making relationships, then the very act of being able to experience a caring relationship with a counsellor may allow them to begin to develop a better capability for developing friendships, work relationships and intimate partnership in everyday real-life situations. Some counsellors worry about the danger of their 'clients' becoming over-involved and too dependent on them. This danger exists, but is often overstated. If a person is at a point in their life where they are isolated and distanced from others, then it seems inevitable that once they begin to experience a close relationship (for example, with a counsellor), that many previously suppressed aspects of what is involved in relating to another person, such as depending on them, begin to be expressed. The vast majority of people who use counselling have little interest in being locked into a permanent dependent relationship with their counsellor – they want to get on with their lives, and to use the relationship with the counsellor to that end.

When building a relationship, as when building a house or anything else, it is always important to be prepared for things to go wrong. Part of the art of counselling is to be aware of and skilled in repairing ruptures in the relationship between the counsellor and the person seeking help. A breakdown of relationship can occur because the person seeking help may simply find it hard either to trust anyone or to believe that anyone might care about them. Such a person is likely to dip constantly in and out of being able to collaborate with their counsellor. Alternatively, a rupture can happen when a previously secure relationship between person and counsellor is threatened in some way. In either case, the underlying question that is conveyed by the person to the counsellor is 'can I trust you?', 'is it safe to talk to you?' or 'is it worth speaking to you?' The task of repairing a caring relationship involves suspending any other tasks that might be in progress, and using some time to talk about how both participants experience the relationship. It is futile, and can even be destructively manipulative, to attempt to carry out a one-sided analysis of only difficulties that the help-seeker or client might be experiencing in the relationship: relationship breakdown is always a two-way process. If the counsellor does not acknowledge their feelings and uncertainty about what is happening, the message to the person is that they must have a terrible deficit in respect of forming relationships. If, on the other hand, the counsellor is able to refer to their own worries, strategies, needs and blind spots, then the task of repairing a relationship can be carried out as a genuinely collaborative endeavour.

A final point concerning the building of a relationship is that it is a mistake to view this process as solely focused on what takes place in the counselling conversation. As a counsellor, it is useful to think about other good relationships that you might have and what makes them work well. People with strong relationships remember the facts and stories of each other's lives, celebrate birthdays and achievements, give and receive gifts, anticipate sources of stress and pressure, and much else. Depending on the duration and circumstances of a counselling relationship, some of these behaviours may be relevant. A counselling relationship is different from friendship or a family connection because it is more circumscribed or boundaried, exists for a purpose and is usually fairly temporary. Nevertheless, it is relationship that builds and is strengthened when each of the participants thinks about the other between meetings, and remembers information about the other. In any strong relationship, each person is alive in the life of the other.

The major feature that distinguishes a counselling relationship from most other types of relationship is that a counsellor *listens*. An emphasis on listening is one of the main building blocks of a counselling relationship. There are many other situations in life where a person can tell someone else about a problem that they have been experiencing. However, rarely does the person on the receiving end really listen. For example, telling a friend about a problem will usually elicit reciprocal disclosure from the friend – they will move into describing a similar problem that they have encountered themself. This is a useful response, within a friendship, because it demonstrates solidarity and sharing, and may lead to learning something about the coping and problem-solving strategies that are used by the other person. Telling a professional person, such as a doctor, nurse or social worker, about a problem is likely to lead to an advice-giving response, rather than to listening. This is because the professional helper may not have time to listen, and also because they will probably believe that it is their job to sort out the problem, by offering a concrete, immediate solution.

In counselling, listening is understood as an *active* process. Listening is not a matter of being a passive recipient or recorder of information. In listening, a counsellor is expressing curiosity and interest. It is a form of listening that comes from a position of wanting to know more. There are two senses of wanting to know more. One sense reflects a desire to learn about what happened next or what was the context within which an event took place. The other sense of knowing more is a curiosity about gaps, pauses and significant moments within the person's telling of their story. A counsellor wants to know more about what is being held back in these moments, what is not being said, what is perhaps difficult to say. The psychologist Eugene Gendlin has described this kind of a listening as a curiosity or sensitivity around the *edge* of the person's awareness of what they are talking about. This curiosity, sensitivity and interest marks out the kind of listening that a counsellor does as not merely listening for information (who did what, what their names were, when it happened), but listening for *meaning*. A counsellor is listening for clues about what makes this set of events significant for a person and why they wish to talk about it *now*.

A further aspect of listening within counselling relationships is that a counsellor is characteristically *patient* in their listening. A good counsellor will allow a person to feel as if they have all the time in the world. As an audience, a counsellor rarely interrupts, is willing to allow the person to get to the end of what they want to say, and is curious about how the story ends. A counsellor operates on the basis that there are some things that are very hard to say and require time to emerge, and that eventually the person will find their own way to say what needs to be said.

Finally, counsellors tack back and forward between listening and checking out that what they have heard is accurate. Checking out conveys to a person that they are valued and that understanding what they mean is of paramount importance to the counsellor. Checking out is also a constant reminder to the person that, however they might feel at that moment, there is another person who is doing their best to be 'with' them in their struggle.

A counsellor is always doing their utmost to listen with care and attention to what the person is trying to say, no matter what other counselling tasks they might be working on. The message is: 'this is a relationship within which you are listened to, where you are heard, where what you have to say is important'. This dimension of the relationship can be extremely useful for some people. Even if the counsellor is someone with whom they meet only infrequently, the person carries around with them the knowledge that, in this part of their life space, there is a place where they will be heard.

In recent years, some writers have used the word 'presence' to describe the quality of relationship that can exist when a person in a counselling role is willing to be fully 'there' for someone who is seeking to talk through an issue (see Greenberg and Geller, 2001, for a useful introduction to this topic). The notion of presence implies that the counsellor's attention is focused entirely on the person and what they are saying, rather than on any other matters. The idea also implies that the counsellor is doing more than just listening to the person: they are also physically and sensorily centred, and responding to the whole way of being of the person. There is a co-presence, a being present to each other, that can occur in silence, in the space between words. The idea of presence refers to a kind of deep listening that goes beyond attending merely to the words that the person uses. The concept of presence, or being 'fully present' also acts as a reminder to anyone in the role of counsellor of how important it is to be able to leave aside their own personal business or 'busy-ness', if they are to be able to be there, in the present moment, with the person whom they are seeking to help.

Box 7.2   Nursing Mrs Q: caring presence in action

A case study published by Joan Engebretson (2000), a nurse tutor and supervisor, illustrates some of the ways in which 'presence' may be expressed within a caring relationship. The paper focuses on the role of a student nurse, Brenda, in relation to a patient, Mrs Q, who had given birth the previous day, to a premature baby who was now in intensive care. Mrs Q, we learn, had a history of six pregnancy losses – the current baby was the live birth. Her husband was 'out of town'. Brenda arrived at the post-partum unit at 6.45 am, and was assigned to look after Mrs Q for the day. Within an hour, they were called to the intensive care unit, because the condition of the baby was unstable. Brenda moved Mrs Q's wheelchair close to the isolation unit where her baby had been placed, and after a few minutes drew up a chair and sat beside her. Engebretson described what happened in the following terms:

> The two sat side by side in relative silence against a backdrop of the continual cacophony of human and mechanical noises. In addition to multiple conversations of doctors, nurses and other providers, there was the ceaseless hum of machinery punctuated by the beeps of monitors going off . . . . As the morning advanced, the baby's condition became less stable and increasingly critical. The nurses invited Mrs Q to touch her infant very gently. Brenda sat with her occasionally touching her shoulder . . . it began to be apparent that as the doctors, nurses and various other providers approached Mrs Q and Brenda, there was a noticeable change in their manner. They moved a lot slower and spoke more quietly . . . . After some time, one of the nurses placed the infant in Mrs Q's arms. She gently cradled her newborn, softly caressing his head and stroking his back. Brenda lightly placed her hand on Mrs Q's shoulder, arm or back. Brenda seemed to sense that appropriate touch in this case needed to be very gentle, stable and unobtrusive, almost mirroring the touch Mrs Q used with her infant . . . it felt like time was suspended.

In a discussion with her tutor immediately after her work with Mrs Q,

> Brenda related being really scared at first, but she knew she had to be there for this patient. In order to make this connection to her patient she had first to make a connection with something within herself. The only way she could do that was to sit quietly with Mrs Q to help and heal. She discovered that she could reach an

'internal knowing of what to do' . . . going through that experience was one of the most profound experiences of her life and, although it was sad, it was also extraordinarily rewarding.

Engebretson comments that caring presence of this kind involves connectedness, sharing, loving and 'action beyond the ordinary', in ways that can have an impact not only on the individual recipient of care, but, as in this example, on the whole environment of a clinical unit.

A safe relationship: being trustworthy, reliable and dependable

Another critical characteristic of a counselling relationship is that is *safe*. A counsellor is someone who is unequivocally on the side of the person, whose aim and purpose is to be helpful. By contrast, a counsellor is not someone who has any intention of using, abusing, harming or exploiting the person who comes for help. The counsellor has no axe to grind, no stake in whether the person decides to do one thing or the opposite. The counsellor is a person who can be *trusted*.

Trust has a number of different facets. One aspect of trust centres around dependability. Does the counsellor do what they say that they will do? Do they turn up on time? Do they remember key information? For this aspect of trust to develop, there needs to be consistency between what a counsellor promises and what they deliver. It is for this reason that many people involved in offering counselling roles are careful about checking out expectations with people who come for help, and being clear about what it is that they can and cannot provide. For example, if a person wants or feels they need a counsellor who will be available at the end of a phone in a crisis, it is essential that a counsellor is explicit about whether this level of responsiveness is possible. If a counsellor is unable to respond to crises, it is better to say so and to explore the alternative sources of help that might be accessible during these times. A vague offer to a person to 'phone me if you really need to' runs the risk, if the phone is not answered or the counsellor comes across as irritated at being contacted in the middle of the night, of undermining trust.

Another facet of trust is concerned with how a counsellor responds to a person on a moment-by-moment basis. If there are too many discrepancies between what the counsellor says and how they appear, the person on the receiving end will quickly being to wonder what is going on. For example, if someone who is gay, lesbian or bisexual is told by a counsellor that their sexual orientation is something to be valued and celebrated, but the counsellor looks uncomfortable when they say it, then the person may feel that the counsellor is not allowing themselves to be honest and transparent. In such a situation, the person seeking counselling would be likely to become very cautious about talking about their sexuality or lifestyle to this particular counsellor. Carl Rogers (1961) used the term *congruence* to describe this aspect of the counselling relationship, as a means of drawing attention to the importance for a counsellor of maintaining consistency between what they subjectively thought or felt, and what they said to their clients. Research carried out by Rogers and his colleagues showed that counsellor *incongruence* or falseness or inauthenticity would usually bring any meaningful conversation to a halt. People do not want to talk about their personal issues to someone who is pretending to listen, or pretending to accept their experience, or who seems to be just playing a professional role. What people want is someone who is genuine. For the counsellor, this will involve, sometimes, being truly affected by what a person is saying, and being willing to show the sadness, or anger, or pleasure, that is being felt.

The safety that is associated with a counselling relationship is not only the safety of reassurance, of feeling taken care of and protected, of being held within the hope conveyed by the other that everything will be all right. While this kind of parental caretaking or soothing forms an essential part of any counselling relationship, there is a further form of safety that also forms a necessary aspect of counselling: the sense of feeling safe enough to enter dangerous territory. This is similar to the trust that a person might have in a guide. To build the possibility for that kind of relationship, a counsellor needs to convey to the person an appreciation that they are aware that dangerous territory does exist, that they have the confidence and competence to survive a journey into such territory, and that they believe that the person can survive it too. A counsellor can signal that they feel able to move into painful areas of experience with the person by acknowledging what is at stake ('it's as if you want to let these feelings out but you fear that, if you did, the tears would go on for ever . . .'), and talking through what could be done to make the risk bearable, for example, taking the issue piece by piece, or agreeing to meet for a longer session.

For a counsellor, entering a relationship of trust can represent a challenge on two fronts. It is hard for a person to be trusted if they do not feel worthy of trust. From the counsellor's side, being willing to be available to another person in a counselling role implies believing in one's own capacity to deserve trust. Acceptance of this can be difficult for some counsellors. The quality of the relationships between a counsellor and his or her colleagues can play a key factor around the building of trust. If someone who is engaged in counselling work feels that their supervisor, or immediate colleagues, do not support them in this activity, their capacity to offer secure relationships to those seeking help can be seriously undermined.

At the same time, it is important for a counsellor to recognize that, most of the time, the people who come to them for help will not trust them unconditionally, and will continue to test them out, as a means of guarding against betrayal or disappointment. The issues that people bring to counselling are often topics or events that are hard for them to talk about, because of guilt, shame or embarrassment: it may require a high level of trust before the person feels safe enough to talk openly about what really matters.

Being genuine

From the perspective of the counselling skill model, people are driven to seek counselling because they have been silenced by the absence of other people in their life who will listen, or by the unwillingness or inability of people to engage in meaningful conversation around personal issues. The impact of either of these sets of circumstances is to leave the person with a sense of being invalidated: they are left feeling as if their experience, and their status as a person, does not count for anything and is worthless. To be more specific about the experience of invalidation, there are two broad types of relationship that can result in a person having a sense of not mattering. The first is where other people engage in pretence and dishonesty. The second is where others act in an impersonal and 'professional' manner.

Examples
Joe is 15 years old and has a learning disability that makes him depend on others to remind and assist him in fulfilling everyday tasks. He has lived with his mother, who has now become ill. Joe has moved in with his aunt and uncle. Although they are caring people, they seem unwilling to answer his questions about when his mother will come out of hospital, and when he can see her. They just tell him that she is 'doing well' and that he will be seeing her 'soon'. However, they are unable to hide their tension and anxiety. Joe becomes more afraid and angry.

Mathilde is 15. In her school she is a member of an ethnic minority group. She is bullied by one of the older children in the dominant group. Asked one day by her class teacher why she is withdrawn and upset, Mathilde begins to talk about the racial violence and harassment that she has experienced. When asked afterwards by a friend how the conversation with the teacher went, Mathilde replies, 'She asked all the right questions and said all the right things. She even wrote some notes and said she would follow it up. But I could see that she didn't care. She was just going through the motions. I think she was worried about being late for lunch. Don't worry – I won't speak to her again.'

In each of these examples, the person in the helping role has made an effort to respond constructively, but has hidden their own feelings behind a mask. In the case of Joe, his aunt and uncle were worried about their sister's illness and were trying to shield Joe from the reality of what was happening. In the case of Mathilde, the teacher felt furious, but impotent, but had been trained to respond to pupils in a neutral, unemotional manner. Both Joe and Mathilde were *mystified* by what was happening – they had no reliable data on which to judge how the other person felt about the issues that they were bringing up. Their responses – anger from Joe and avoidance from Mathilde – were inevitable in the circumstances.

One of the main things that a person is looking for when they seek counselling is for their experience to be *authenticated* by another person. Authentication can only take place when the listener responds in a humane and personal manner, which conveys fellow feeling. If a counsellor comes across as too detached, impersonal and 'professional', or as perpetually nice and agreeable, the person seeking counselling is always left wondering whether they are getting a 'real' response, or whether the counsellor's apparent empathy and concern are just an act. By contrast, the more that a counsellor is willing to state their true position on things, to disagree or challenge, to acknowledge uncertainty and confusion, express feelings, and set limits on what they are able to give or do, the more confidence the person will have that that the counsellor has a genuine interest in them.

One of the most important qualities of a helpful counselling relationship is emotional honesty. When someone is emotionally honest, they tend to be experienced as transparent, as not hiding anything. If, on the other hand, a counsellor is experienced as emotionally elusive or false, then the relationship tends to be undermined because the person is thrown into a state of doubt through beginning to wonder about what may be being left unsaid by the counsellor.

Caring

In deciding to enter a counselling relationship, a person is looking for someone who will *care* about them. The concept of care has been largely ignored or devalued within the counselling literature, probably because it might be taken to imply a lack of professional expertise and detachment. This is a pity because, as the philosopher Heidegger has pointed out, *caring* represents a fundamental aspect of involvement in the world: the experience of caring discloses what is important and has meaning for us.

In a counselling relationship, caring can be expressed by:

- paying attention to the person;
- anticipating the other person's needs;
- small acts of kindness;
- remembering information about the person's life;
- thinking about the person when they are not there;
- proceeding gently and slowly, and with patience – checking things out;
- putting one's own needs aside, in the interest of the other;
- genuine curiosity about the experience and views of the person;
- celebrating the person's achievements.

A further sense of the importance of care in counselling situations can be reinforced by considering that, in seeking counselling, a person is allowing themself to be someone who is fragile, vulnerable, in pain or lost.

Working collaboratively

One of the most important aspects of a counselling relationship is the extent to which the person and the counsellor are able to work together to tackle problems. A useful image of the counselling relationship is that of an *alliance*: the person and the counsellor are allies in the struggle to deal with difficult issues.

On the whole, during counselling, the person and counsellor proceed as if they were 'on the same wavelength' and working effectively together: the issue of the strength of the 'alliance' is rarely raised as a specific topic for discussion. Nevertheless, there are many points within a counselling conversation where the question of working collaboratively is highly relevant:

- At the start – does the person wish to begin a counselling conversation right *now*?
- During a session – are we in agreement around what we are trying to achieve in the long run (goals)?
- Are we in agreement over what we are trying to do right at this minute (tasks)?
- Is this the best way to work through this particular issue (methods)?
- Whose turn is it to talk?
- Is this the time to stop?
- Do we need to talk about this again? When?
- What could we each have done to make that discussion more helpful?

Each of these moments represents an opportunity to stand back from the immediate flow of conversation and interaction between the person and the counsellor, and reflect on what is happening. This activity can be understood as *metacommunication* – communicating and reflecting on the process of communication and the state of the relationship. A capacity to engage in metacommunication is a crucial aspect of collaborative working. An invaluable discussion of the nature of metacommunication in counselling can be found in Rennie (1998).

The nature of metacommunication can be illustrated by considering the usual shape and content of a conversation between a person and their counsellor. Most of the time in a counselling situation, both the person seeking help and the counsellor talk about the person's 'problem'. For example, a woman talking about her relationship with her teenage daughter might say: 'We just argue all the time. There doesn't seem to be anything we can do together that doesn't end up in a battle.' The person offering counselling might reply by saying: 'That sounds really frustrating; . . . it's as if there is a real barrier between you.' The person seeking help might then go on to say more about other aspects of this issue. In this example, the focus of the conversation is on the problem that has been identified by the person. This is probably the kind of conversation that happens most frequently in counselling encounters: the counsellor acts as a kind of sounding board, and reflects back to the person the main threads of what they have been exploring, in a way that helps them to expand on the issue and gain some perspective on it.

In addition to this kind of reflective response, it can be useful for a counsellor to build into their conversational repertoire the careful and consistent use of a slightly different way of responding to the person: *checking out*. The process of checking out introduces important possibilities for conveying value and affirmation to the person, and building the kind of relationship within which difficult issues can be explored safely. It can also have the effect of slowing down the interaction in a way that allows the person some opportunities to reflect on the feelings and thoughts that they are experiencing at that moment.

Checking out basically involves pausing within the flow of the conversation to test out assumptions about what is happening, or to inquire about the assumptions or the experience at that moment of the person who is seeking help. Rennie (1998) describes this activity as 'talking about the process of talking'. There are many different ways in which checking out or metacommunication can be helpful within a counselling session. Some of the most widely used forms of checking out are listed below, along with examples of how they might be used to enhance the interaction around 'my teenage daughter and I argue all the time' that was introduced earlier in this section:

> **Example**
> A woman talking about her relationship with her teenage daughter states, 'We just argue all the time. There doesn't seem to be anything we can do together that doesn't end up in a battle.' Her counsellor, a worker in a family support centre, responds: 'That sounds really frustrating . . . it's as if there is a real barrier between you.'

The counsellor's response is a fairly standard empathic reflection that picks up on the main feeling that she senses (the client's frustration) and seeks to find an image to capture the key relationship difficulty that is causing the problem (described by the counsellor as a barrier). However, there are a number of ways in which the counsellor might choose to use her response to the client as an opportunity to reinforce the collaborative nature of their relationship. There are at least four metacommunicative strategies that the counsellor could employ at this moment:

- *Check out the person's reaction to what the counsellor has just said.* The counsellor might wonder whether she had accurately understood the meaning for the person of the situation that was being described, and could check this out by saying: 'That sounds really frustrating; . . . it's as if there is a real barrier between you . . . . Although, as I hear myself saying that, I'm not sure whether I've got it quite right. I'm aware that there's a lot about your situation that I don't know . . . . Is "frustration" the right term, or would you use another word . . . . And maybe "barrier" is too strong?'
- *The counsellor being open about her strategies and intentions at that point.* The counsellor may be mindful of the fact that, although the person has mentioned a number of issues that are bothering her, she has a gut feeling that the situation with her daughter is probably the most important, or urgent, of these. This could be expressed by saying: 'I realize that in the last couple of minutes you've told me about lots of things that are hard for you at the moment. But it's what you said about your daughter that really struck home for me, because it seemed very painful for you, and I have sense that it might be the link between all these other things you mentioned. What's happening with your daughter sounds really frustrating; . . . it's as if there is a real barrier between you. My sense is that it might be useful to stay with this for a bit. What do you think? Does that feel right for you?'
- *Invite the client to focus on her own plans, strategies and assumptions.* The counsellor may not be sure about the agenda or goals of the person at this point in the conversation, so might say: 'The situation with your daughter sounds really frustrating; . . . it's as if there is a real barrier between you. But I'm not sure whether that's the thing

you want to look at more closely now. Is it? Or is there something else that's more pressing?'

- *Check out her assumptions about what the person might be thinking or intending.* Sometimes, a counsellor may come up with a theory, or a guess, about what might lie behind the thoughts or feelings that the person may be experiencing, but without having any real evidence to indicate whether these ideas are valid. Often, this kind of counsellor intuition can be sensitive and accurate, and provide a good guide for moving forward. On some occasions, however, the counsellor may have misunderstood the person. It is therefore important to check out any such theories. In this case, the counsellor may have a sense that the person blames herself in relation to her problem with her daughter. One way of acknowledging this might be to say: 'That sounds really frustrating; . . . it's as if there is a real barrier between you. As you were speaking about your daughter, I just had a strong feeling that you were blaming yourself for what was happening. Have I got that right, or is it something else?' The person might reply: 'I wouldn't call it blaming myself, it's more that I just don't feel adequate – I don't know what to do.' In this instance, the process of checking out has allowed the counsellor to see that her assumption was only partially correct: the person was being self-critical, but not to the extent of actually *blaming* herself.

Each of these metacommunicative strategies has the effect of standing aside from the immediate content of what is being said, to allow a few moments of sharing, discussion and reflection around aspects of the relationship between the counsellor and the person seeking help. In effect, these metacommunicative moves are offering openings to a question that could be summarized as: are we on the same wavelength – do we each understand and agree with what the other is trying to achieve right now? These moves are also consistently emphasizing the affirming and empowering stance of the counsellor in relation to the person. In effect, they are conveying ideas such as 'you are in charge', 'I believe that you are the person who knows what is helpful for you', 'I can only help you if you let me know if what I am doing is working for you'.

Regularly checking out with the person what they think, feel and want, and what you as a counsellor think, feel and want, has the possibility for achieving a wide range of positive outcomes in relation to talking through an issue. It implies to the person that they have choices, and that these choices are important to the counsellor and worthy of being taken seriously. It implies that the counsellor is doing their best to be sensitive and responsive to what the person needs at that moment, and might therefore be a person who can be trusted in the future. It suggests that the counsellor is someone who is genuinely curious and interested in the person, and in the totality of what the person might be thinking and feeling – the counsellor is not pursuing a fixed pathway or agenda. Checking out introduces slight pauses within the conversation, moments within which the person might shift slightly away from the problem and engage in reflection around what the problem means to them ('is this about blaming myself?'), or what they can do to change ('am I willing to look closely at this issue, right now?'). It also opens up an awareness that it may be acceptable to be wrong about some things, and that there are ways of surviving being wrong – a particularly helpful insight for people whose lives may be dominated by perfectionism.

The role of checking out or metacommunication can be important at points in counselling where the relationship, or topic being talked about, shifts in some way. For example, if a person talking about a practical issue, such as a patient talking to a nurse about treatment choices, or a student talking to a teacher about course options, conveys in some way that there is an emotional or personal dimension to the issue that they might wish to explore, then it is good practice to check out with the person whether they would at that moment like to explore their feelings in more depth; 'You seemed to me to have a lot of feelings as you were talking . . . there seemed to be tears in your eyes . . . . I was wondering if you wanted to take a few minutes with me to look at how these feelings might be a factor in the choices you need to make?' Depending on the circumstances, it may also be important to check out with the person how long they have to talk (or you have to listen to them) and any confidentiality limits that may apply. Similarly, it would often be appropriate to check out with the person that they have reached the end of a counselling episode. For example: 'From what you have told me, I think we can both understand why it is so essential for you to make the right decision at this point in your life . . . . Is there more you wanted to say about that side of things? Would it be OK to go back to thinking about the type of treatment/course that would be best for you?'

Metacommunication is an essential strategy in situations where the relationship between a person and a counsellor may have broken down or reached a point of impasse. It is not realistic to expect the counselling relationship to proceed smoothly at all times – there will inevitably be points at which a person feels that they are not getting what they need from the counsellor, or that the counsellor misunderstands them. At these moments, it is valuable for the counsellor to be able to 'hit the pause button' and invite reflection from both participants around what has been happening. It is particularly important for the counsellor to be willing and able to acknowledge their role in the difficulties that have arisen – a counsellor who insists on attributing the sole cause of any problems to inadequacies on the part of the person or client is not demonstrating a collaborative style of working and may come across as blaming and persecutory. A great deal of research into the topic of 'ruptures in the therapeutic alliance' has been carried out by the psychologist Jeremy Safran, whose writings includes a wealth of practical suggestions for how to resolve relationship breakdown between counsellors and those receiving help from them (see, for example, Safran, 1993; Safran and Muran, 2000).

At a deeper philosophical level, metacommunication is a good way of expressing some of the core values of counselling. Rather than viewing the counsellor and person seeking help as separate entities, the process of checking out suggests a sense of two people being in relationship with each other, and requiring to take account of each other's position in order to work effectively together. The idea of being a 'relational self', rather than an isolated, completely separate 'autonomous self' can be helpful to people who have difficulty in getting and giving support, and this simple conversational strategy can represent a useful and unthreatening way of introducing the possibility of relatedness into someone's awareness. The use of metacommunication emphasizes the worth of the person – their intentions, preferences and experience are being taken seriously.

Box 7.3   The relationship matters more than counselling techniques

In research carried out in Australia by Terry MacCormack and his colleagues (2001), counselling was offered to people who were receiving treatment for cancer. The counselling was fairly short term (maximum eight sessions) and was highly structured around specific therapeutic tasks that the patient was taken through by their counsellor. In the study, the effectiveness of two different types of therapy was compared. One form of therapy that was offered was cognitive behavioural therapy; the other approach consisted of relaxation and visualization exercises. Interviews were carried out with patients after they had received counselling. The results of the study were striking. Although the people who had received counselling praised the professionalism of their therapists and reported that the techniques that they had employed had been useful, all of them stated that what had been most important was to be able to spend time with someone who listened and cared. Some of the statements made by participants were:

I was able to talk and relate to her and trust her, and to talk about things . . . she helped me to keep going.

It was like I had another friend to talk to.

It was good to have someone objective to talk to, to get things off your chest.

He was safe and easy to talk to. So I could say anything and be honest about how I felt.

It was nice to have someone coming and talking to me . . . . The doctors are hopeless, and they're the ones you have the main contact with . . . . I asked for empathy [from my doctor] and he gave me none.

MacCormack *et al.* concluded that participants seemed to be saying that their counselling was 'primarily a "being with" or relational experience [that] . . . provided a unique conversational space to explore/discuss thoughts/feelings, and . . . occurred with an experienced and understanding professional who cared' (p. 58). The implications of this study are that 'being with' a person, being willing to listen, and being able to express genuine caring, are what matter most to people who are receiving counselling.

Theoretical frameworks for understanding counselling relationships

The central importance of the relationship has been widely accepted within the counselling literature. Within this body of theory and research there have been suggested a number of frameworks that can be applied in making sense of what happens between a person and a counsellor. The most relevant theoretical models for practitioners engaged in embedded counselling are the person-centred, psychodynamic, transactional analysis and multidimensional approaches. These sets of ideas can be regarded as comprising *tools for reflection*: concepts that can be used in training and supervision, and within the flow of everyday practice, as ways of making sense of what is happening in relationships with people seeking help.

The person-centred counselling relationship

The person-centred approach to counselling, originally developed by Carl Rogers in the USA in the 1940s, and more recently associated with the writings of Dave Mearns, Brian Thorne, Tony Merry and Germain Lietaer, among others, has been a major influence on the thinking and practice of many counsellors and people who use counselling skills in their work.

The key idea around which person-centred counselling is organized is that a person develops personal and emotional problems because of a lack of relationships within which they can be himself or herself. Instead, the person may have been exposed to relationships in which they have felt judged and not valued. The remedy for this, according to person-centred theorists, is to provide the person with a relationship within which they can grow and develop. Forming a relationship with the person is therefore an essential aspect of any counselling that is based in the person-centred tradition.

What makes a good relationship? Rogers and his colleagues suggested a set of necessary and sufficient conditions (also known as core conditions) that characterized a good relationship between a therapist and a person seeking counselling (the client):

- Two persons are in psychological contact.
- The therapist experiences unconditional positive regard for the client.
- The therapist is congruent or integrated in the relationship.
- The therapist experiences an empathic understanding of the client's internal frame of reference and endeavours to communicate this to the client.
- The communication to the client of the therapist's empathic understanding and unconditional positive regard is to a minimal extent achieved.

Each of these factors is important in the counselling relationship, and the absence of any one of them will undermine the bond between the counsellor and the person seeking help. For example, unconditional positive regard (which can also be understand as acceptance or a sense of being valued) is essential because a judgemental attitude on the part of the counsellor would merely replicate the key relationship factor that had brought about the person's difficulties in the first place. A positively 'prizing' or acceptant response from the counsellor, by contrast, clearly signals to the person that they are entering a different kind of relationship, one in which they are free to express their true feelings and preferences. Empathic understanding, which refers to a sense of being understood, with the counsellor being seen as able to view the situation from the perspective of the client, is important because it conveys to the person that the counsellor is interested in them, wants to understand, and is not seeking to impose their own ideas or advice on to the person. All of this encourages the person to keep talking, and to give voice to all aspects of their problem.

However, from a person-centred perspective, the single most important quality is *congruence* (also described as authenticity, genuineness or 'realness'). Congruence refers to the capacity of the counsellor to make use of their own experience within the relationship. This involves paying attention to the feelings (and thoughts, images and fantasies) that come up when the person is talking, and using these to inform a response to the person. Sometimes this will mean the counsellor sharing with the person what they are feeling. At other times, the counsellor will internally take note of what they are feeling, but not say anything about it at that moment. For example, if a person is in the process of talking about an issue, it may be unhelpful if the counsellor interrupts them to tell them how they are feeling at that moment.

Another key principle of the person-centred helping relationship is *non-directiveness*. This is an attitude or philosophy that the person-centred counsellor adopts. Rather than trying to guide or advise the person, the counsellor adopts a strategy of following them, paying very close attention and showing great interest, while letting the person take the lead. The idea here is that the person is the expert on their own life, and that the counsellor is like a companion on their journey.

If a counsellor is in touch with their own feelings and reactions, and relatively open in sharing these with the person, and is consistently following the person in an interested, warm, accepting and curious way, then they will come across to the person as having *presence* or being present for them. Presence can be seen as a mid-point between being *over-involved* (intrusively over-interested and identifying with the client) and being *under-involved* (cold, distant, detached and 'professional'). A counsellor who displays presence is, as Mearns (1997) puts it, in a good position to work at *relational depth* and form a relationship with the person that will enable them to explore difficult issues.

Carl Rogers summed all this up in the form of a list of characteristics of a helping relationship:

> Can I be in some way which will be perceived by the other person as trustworthy, as dependable or consistent in some deep sense?
> Can I be expressive enough as a person that what I am will be communicated unambiguously?
> Can I let myself experience positive attitudes towards this other person – attitudes of warmth, caring, liking, interest, respect?
> Can I be strong enough as a person to be separate from the other?
> Am I secure enough within myself to permit his or her separateness?
> Can I let myself enter fully into the world of his or her feelings and personal meanings and see these as he or she does?
> Can I accept each facet of this other person when he or she presents it to me?
> Can I act with sufficient sensitivity in the relationship that my behaviour will not be perceived as a threat?
> Can I free the other from the threat of external evaluation?
> Can I meet this other individual as a person who is in the process of becoming, or will I be bound by his past and by my past?
>
> (Rogers, 1961: ch. 3)

The image of the counselling relationship that has been developed within the person-centred approach has proved useful for practitioners working in a wide variety of settings. The key ideas within the model – acceptance, congruence/genuineness and empathy – embody a type of relationship which users experience as empowering and affirming.

Box 7.4   The counselling relationship from the perspective of the client

Ideas developed within psychotherapy approaches such as person-centred, psycho-dynamic and TA provide a valuable set of ways of making sense of the counselling relationship. However, these models are primarily formulated from the point of view of the counsellor and are limited in the extent to which they capture how the relationship is perceived by the person seeking help. In an intriguing study, Bedi *et al.* (2005) interviewed 40 clients, who had received counselling for a variety of problems, about their perceptions of their relationship with their counsellor. Specifically, participants were asked to describe 'the things that helped form and strengthen the counselling relationship'. What they said offers a view of the counselling relationship that differs in significant ways from the image provided by therapy theory. The single most important thing that counsellors did, according to these informants, was to use counselling strategies that were helpful. For example, one person said that the relationship was strengthened when his counsellor 'got me to make a list of my goals'. Although the research participants did mention a number of relationship-building aspects that would be predicted by existing theories of counselling skill – for instance, active listening and attentive body language – they also described a large number of processes that were unexpected. Near the top of the list was the counselling setting ('the counsellor decorated her office with little objects') and accentuating choice ('the counsellor allowed me to choose which chair I would sit in'). Also important for these people was a category of activity that Bedi *et al.* (2005) labelled 'service beyond normative expectation', or which might be otherwise characterized as deep caring, such as 'the counsellor saying to me, "call any time, or just come in any time, and there will be someone here, even if I'm not here".' On the whole, the people who took part in this study did not regard themselves as having much responsibility for building a good relationship, nor did they describe relationship building in terms of collaborative working together with their counsellor. The majority placed the responsibility for relationship-building squarely in the hands of their counsellors.

The psychodynamic perspective on the counselling relationship

Although psychodynamic theories of counselling have their origins in the writings of Sigmund Freud, contemporary psychodynamic thinking incorporates the ideas of many other figures, such as Erik Erikson, Donald Winnicott and others.

The key idea in any psychodynamically informed counselling is that a person's behaviour is driven or guided by *unconscious* factors: we are not aware of many of the reasons for our actions, or causes of our feelings. From a psychodynamic perspective, throughout their life a human being is exposed to situations of loss, attack, love and hate that evoke very strong, primitive or child-like reactions. These reactions are highly threatening, because: (i) a lot of the time they are not socially acceptable, and (ii) if we allow ourselves to consciously acknowledge these reactions we feel overwhelmed, ashamed or guilty. As a result, we use *defence mechanisms* (such as repression, denial and projection) to keep these troublesome wishes, emotions and images out of our minds, and to create an impression of being rational beings.

Within a psychodynamically informed approach to counselling, the counsellor makes use of the concept of defence in the following way. The relationship style of the counsellor is warm and accepting but fairly neutral. It can therefore be assumed that any feelings or fantasies (positive or negative) that the person has towards the counsellor are not triggered by the actual behaviour of the practitioner, but are evidence of *projection* on the part of the person or client. In a counselling situation, this kind of projection is defined as *transference*. The theory is that:

- being in a close relationship (with a counsellor) is threatening or anxiety-provoking in some way;
- because it stirs up feelings about other close relationships the person has had in the past;
- but it is hard to consciously acknowledge or own these feelings;
- so they are projected on to the counsellor in some way.

Example

Olaf is very sensitive to any hint of criticism from his counsellor. From the outset, he described his counsellor 'really down on me' and 'harsh'. Later in counselling, Olaf starts to talk about how his father always set high standards for him and never gave him praise.

In turn, the counsellor may have feelings about the person/client that are based in their own unconscious projections – these are described as *counter-transference*.

Example

Agnes is an occupational health nurse working with the fire brigade. She has a great admiration for firefighters, whom she regards as brave and manly. In health counselling situations where it may be appropriate for Agnes to challenge her firefighter clients (for instance, when they do not follow agreed rehabilitation programmes), she avoids challenging them, and finds excuses for their behaviour.

At the heart of psychodynamically informed counselling, therefore, is an expectation that the relationship between the person and the counsellor is unlikely to be 'nice'. The task of the counsellor is to provide a secure enough 'holding' environment or 'container' so that the person can feel safe enough to express the positive ('you are wonderful') and negative ('you are cruel and I hate you') feelings that might come up in relation to the counsellor. It is through working together with the counsellor to understand these reactions that the person can get to the point of making sense of the difficulties they have been experiencing in the relationships in their life (it is assumed that all emotional problems ultimately come down to relationships).

It is important to be aware that the theory of transference is controversial, basically because it undermines the idea that the person can be responsible for what they do, and that there can be genuine closeness or a real partnership between counsellor and person seeking help. The concept of transference can also difficult to apply in practice, because it requires a great deal of self-awareness on the part of the practitioner to be able to identify when transference or counter-transference reactions are taking place. Specialist counsellors or psychotherapists who use a psychodynamic approach typically undergo lengthy training and personal therapy in order to develop their capacity to work constructively with these processes. In terms of thinking about whether the concepts of transference and counter-transference are relevant in situations where counselling is embedded in other professional roles, it is helpful to take account of the intensity of the relationship that is likely to develop between the counsellor and the person seeking help. For example, in a one-off ten-minute conversation between a doctor and patient, it is more likely that the discussion will be task-oriented. By contrast, a residential social worker spending many hours each week with a group of adolescents in care, is much more likely to be drawn into areas of relationship difficulty and projection.

The transactional analysis approach to making sense of relationships

Transactional Analysis (TA) is an approach to psychotherapy that was developed by Eric Berne, Claude Steiner and others, in the 1960s. For practitioners whose counselling role is embedded within other professional duties, TA provides a uniquely rich and comprehensive theoretical language for describing and analysing the moment-by-moment interaction between the counsellor and the person seeking help, as well as a framework for understanding the troubled relationships that the person might be experiencing in their everyday life. The basic idea around which all TA theory is built is that the personality of any individual is organized around three distinct 'ego states': the Parent, Adult and Child (Stewart and Joines, 1987). The Parent aspect of the person consists of parental functions that have been internalized from their own mother, father and other caretakers. The two key dimensions of the Parent are critical standard setting, and nurturing. The Adult ego state is the part of the person that responds to the world in a logical, rational, information-processing manner. Finally, the Child in the person can be viewed as the remaining traces of how the individual experienced the world when they were very young. There are two dimensions to the Child – a fun-loving side and a hurt one. From a TA perspective, a psychologically healthy person will be able to have access to, and express, all of these ego states in appropriate situations. However, many people have developed in ways that make them more likely to rely on certain states than on others, so that, for example, they may be critical and distant (in Parent ego state) at a celebratory event that calls for a playful Child response.

The application of the ego state model to interactions between two people allows patterns of unsatisfactory or dysfunctional relating to be revealed and understood. For instance, if a person speaks from their Adult, and attempts to engage the Adult of the other person (perhaps through a request for information), but the other person replies in a whiny, hurt child kind of manner ('why are you always bothering me?'), the interaction is experienced by the first person as not quite 'right' in some way. Such a response is unlikely to lead to effective collaboration. In TA terms, such an interaction would be described as a *crossed transaction*. Other parts of TA theory develop these ideas in terms of understanding sequences of interactions (games) and patterns of relating that occur across a whole life (scripts). One of the advantages of TA theory, in contrast to some other models of therapy and human interaction, is that much of it is written using colloquial, vivid language, which is accessible and memorable for people who are seeking help – it is not just a theory for insiders. Although there are relatively few specialist TA counsellors and psychotherapists, many practitioners in areas such as health and education study TA at an introductory level and find it to be an invaluable tool for making sense of relationships and interactions that that are frustrating or stuck. Another useful facet of TA theory is that it is clear about its values and offers some fairly precise ideas about the goals of counselling.

Multidimensional relationship models

While the person-centred and psychodynamic theories of relationship appear to capture crucial aspects of what takes place within counselling or helping encounters, they do not seek to reflect the potential complexity of relationships between people. A moment's reflection on personal experience will make it clear that any relationship exists at a number of different levels. Moreover, it is not at all easy to make sense of these levels because our language does not provide a readily accessible set of constructs or categories for talking about relating. The psychoanalyst Erik Erikson was one of the first theorists to begin to formulate a comprehensive framework for understanding relationship patterns. Erikson adopted a developmental approach, which characterized human beings as passing through stages of psychosocial development that were defined by different relationship tasks. For example, in the first year of life, the key task for the infant is develop a sense of *trust* in other people. In early adult life, by contrast, the key task is to develop a capacity for engaging in an *intimate* partner relationship.

The approach taken by Erikson has been articulated more fully by the psychologist Ruthellen Josselson, who has constructed a model of relationship dimensions that is specifically oriented towards making sense of the types of relationship difficulties and issues that people might bring to counselling. Josselson (1996) suggests that there are eight main relationship dimensions:

- *Holding* – being there for another person, allowing another person to be there for oneself.
- *Attachment* – the emotional bonds, or enduring connection with another person.
- *Passionate involvement* – being aroused in a relationship, being excited, feeling pleasure, being physically touched.
- *Eye-to-eye validation* – affirmation, recognition of one's meaning and value in the eyes of another person.
- *Idealization and identification* – admiring another person, using them as a model or mentor, wanting to be like that person.
- *Mutuality and resonance* – being with another person, joining in together, doing things together, sharing the same feelings.
- *Embeddedness* – belonging, being a member of a group.
- *Tending and caring* – looking after, being dependent.

Josselson argues that an emotionally well-adjusted person will have the capacity to engage with others along any and all of these dimensions of relationship. Conversely, a person may develop relationships difficulties or have an absence of capability around any of the dimensions. It is easy to see that the models of relationship discussed earlier fail to address all of the dimensions identified by Josselson. For example, the person-centred approach provides a good framework for making sense of eye-to-eye validation and mutuality/resonance, while the psychodynamic model has a lot to say about attachment and idealization/identification. However, neither approach has a great deal to offer when it comes to understanding relationship issues arising from passion or tending/caring. It is perhaps significant, and not surprising, that counselling/psycho-therapy theories of relationship mainly consider relationship dimensions that may be directly played out within the counselling room. Practitioners offering counselling that is embedded within other roles are possibly more likely to catch sight of the expression of passion and caring in the lives of people with whom they are working, and may be better placed to engage with these issues.

Another multidimensional model can be used to analyse relationship issues in counselling is the framework used in structural analysis of social behaviour (SASB; Benjamin, 1987) and the interpersonal octagon (Birtchnell, 1999) approach. This per-spective specifically considers reciprocal patterns of behaviour that takes place between participants in a relationship. For example, a person who has a need for controlling and maintaining order is likely to seek out relationships with people who will reciprocate through having a need for care and protection. In terms of more negative or destructive forms of this pattern of relating, it could be argued that people who behave in ways that are intimidating and sadistic will gravitate towards people who may expect rejection and disapproval. Ultimately, these reciprocal patterns can be viewed as manifestations of the interaction between how close to others (or distant from others) a person prefers to be, and their preference for being powerful and dominant (as contrasted with submissive).

Although there is not space to examine these multidimensional approaches to relationships in more detail here, it should be possible to see that there exist well-established theoretical frameworks that can be applied to the job of making sense of relationships in counselling situations. These models can be used in two main ways. First, it is helpful for a counsellor to be aware of their own strengths and weaknesses in terms of relating to others. For example, a counsellor may be comfortable in relating to other people on the basis of mutuality and equality, but find it hard to respond when a person idealizes them, or demands to be taken care of. Second, when listening to the stories that a person seeking counselling tells about their life, it is useful to be able to pick out recurring patterns of relating, particularly if the person's problems in living seem to involve relationship difficulties.

Conclusions

This chapter has explored some of the activities and qualities through which a counsel-ing relationship may be built, and some of the ways in which it might be understood. Many of the issues discussed in this chapter – listening, trust, caring – may appear obvious, or come across as truisms. Surely it hardly needs to be said that a counsellor should be someone who is trustworthy? However, it cannot be emphasized often enough that a good relationship is ultimately what counselling is about. No matter how skilled a practitioner might be at exploring painful emotional issues and facilitating change, if the person does not trust the counsellor, and does not feel a bond and connection, then they will not open up enough to allow the knowledge, experience and competences of the counsellor to have much of an impact on them.

A counselling relationship can be understood as being based on a set of principles:

- *Being there for the person* – listening, being patient, curiosity, allowing the person to take the lead; as a counsellor, not using the counselling session to further your own agenda or gratify personal needs.
- *Being trustworthy* – being reliable and honest; maintaining confidentiality.
- *Caring* – having a genuine concern for the person; thinking about them between meetings; anticipating their needs.
- *Belief that change is possible* – being hopeful about the capacity of people to be in constructive and caring relationships, and in the ability of each person to make a positive contribution to society.
- *Reflexivity* – awareness of self in the relationship, i.e. the counsellor being able to monitor their own reactions to the person and to use this information to build a more effective helping relationship.
- *A collaborative stance* – whatever happens in a counselling session depends on the efforts and actions of both the counsellor and the person seeking help (and can be undermined by unhelpful attitudes and actions from either participant).

The expression of these principles within a counselling relationship serves three quite different functions. First, the establishment of a safe, caring, collaborative relationship enables the counsellor and the person seeking help to work productively on the resolution of problems in living. Conversely, the absence of such a relationship will seriously hinder anything that the counsellor and person are trying to achieve. This kind of relationship has been described as a working alliance. Second, for someone who is desperate or in distress, a counsellor can provide a form of basic human contact that is healing in itself. The medical anthropologist Norman Kleinman (1988) described the core of any counselling as 'empathic witnessing': the counsellor is another human being who is willing to be a witness to, and share, a person's suffering. Finally, sometimes the quality or depth of the relationship can be such that the person seeking help learns something new about the possibility of being close to another person, being accepted, loved or understood. These moments can trigger a fundamental shift in the person's capacity to form relationships. These three aspects of the counselling relationship can be prominent to a greater or lesser extent within work with different individuals. However, to be an effective counsellor requires a capacity to respond to all three types of relational demand. Maybe most people seeking help are satisfied with a solid working alliance, but there will occasionally be others who need a witness to their troubles, or who are looking to close gaps in their capacity to relate. It is therefore essential for anyone in the role of counsellor to be willing to look closely at their own relationship strengths and weaknesses.

The following chapters explore things that are *done* in counselling: talking through a problem, making a decision, planning behaviour change and so on. All of this material needs to be read in the light of what has been discussed in the present chapter; what can be done in counselling always depends on the potential of the relationship to allow it to be done. There is a reciprocal connection between the tasks of counselling – the action that is undertaken to make a difference to the problems in living of the person – and the quality of the relationship between counsellor and person. There needs to be at least the beginnings of a relationship that is strong enough to make the person feel sufficiently safe and supported to embark on exploring difficult issues in their life. Then, the process of exploring the issue has the potential to bring both participants together, and cement their relationship, around a shared task. Finally the successful completion of that task creates a relationship with a history of shared achievement. In practice, the task dimension of counselling and the relationship dimension are always inextricably linked – it is only in textbooks such as this, that they are separated out at a theoretical or conceptual level.

Questions for reflection and discussion

1. Take a few moments to think about the people with whom you have relationships that allow you to express yourself most fully. Describe the qualities of these people. To what extent do these qualities map on to the ideas introduced in this chapter?
2. In terms of the people to whom you offer a service, how often are you able to be congruent, authentic or fully 'present' with them? What is the effect on your relationship with your clients when you are able to be genuine with them? What are the organizational factors that facilitate or inhibit the expression of genuineness?
3. What are your strategies for repairing relationships that have become stuck or distanced? What else might you do in such situations?
4. How much do you care about the people that you meet in a professional role? How do you express your caring?
5. How helpful is the Freudian concept of transference for you, in making sense of interactions with people who come to you for help?

Further reading

Highly recommended are:

Josselson, R. (1996) *The Space Between Us: Exploring the Dimensions of Human Relationships.* Thousand Oaks, CA: Sage.
Mearns, D. and Cooper, M. (2005) *Working at Relational Depth in Counselling and Psychotherapy.* London: Sage.

Josselson's book offers a useful framework for making sense of relationship patterns in one's own life as well as within professional helping relationships. Full of vivid case examples, the book provides a rich vocabulary for discussing and reflecting on the meaning of different kinds of relationship. The book by Mearns and Cooper provides a clear explanation of the role of the relationship in any type of therapeutic work. The authors give vivid examples of their work with clients in a variety of settings –

long-term psychotherapy, as well as situations where counselling is embedded within another helping role.

Key reading on psychodynamic approaches to counselling relationships is:

Jacobs, M. (2005) *The Presenting Past*, 3rd edn. Buckingham: Open University Press.
Leiper, R. (2004) *The Psychodynamic Approach to Therapeutic Change*. London: Sage.

Key reading on the person-centred approach is:

Mearns, D. and Thorne, B. (1999) *Person-centred Counselling in Action*, 2nd edn. London: Sage.
Merry, T. (2002) *Learning and Being in Person-centred Counselling*, 2nd edn. Ross-on-Wye: PCCS Books.
Rogers, C. R. (1961) *On Becoming a Person*. London: Constable.
Tolan, J. (2003) *Skills in Person-centred Counselling and Therapy*. London: Sage.

Key reading on Transactional Analysis is:

Stewart, I. and Joines, V. (1987) *TA Today: A New Introduction to Transactional Analysis*. Nottingham: Lifespace Publishing.

The best source on the concept of metacommunication is:

Rennie, D. L. (1998) *Person-centred Counselling: An Experiential Approach*. London: Sage.

Further discussion of theories of counselling relationships can be found in:

Feltham, C. (ed.) (1999) *The Counselling Relationship*. London: Sage.
McLeod, J. (2003) *An Introduction to Counselling*, 3rd edn. Buckingham: Open University Press, ch. 12.

8

Having a useful conversation: 'just talking'

'It sounds like this keeps going round and round in your head. This picture of your grandfather being laid out. And you can't sort of share it with anyone. Is that right?'

'Aye, I've never told anyone about it. But I keep thinking about it all the time now.'

'I'm wondering if you'd like to talk a bit more about it now, with me? I'd like to hear more, if this would be a good time for you to talk about it. I know from what you've said to me before that you've been trying to be very positive about your treatment. But from where I'm sitting, this image of your grand-dad just seems . . . I don't know . . . frightening?'

'Naw, not frightening. Its more . . . I just keep wondering about him. He looked alone, even though he was in the middle of a room full of people.'

'He was alone?'

'Yes. It's funny. Just when he needed other people, he was alone.'

Introduction

The general task of counselling is that of enabling a therapeutic conversation to take place. Although a number of specific tasks, such as problem solving and behaviour change, may emerge from within the conversation, the baseline or 'default setting' for any counselling encounter is that of enabling the person to talk in a way that allows them to find meaning and possibility within the area of their life space that is troubling them. The aim of this chapter is to consider some of the strategies and methods that a counsellor can use to facilitate a meaningful or therapeutic conversation. It is essential to approach these suggestions from a starting point of awareness of personal experience. What are your own experiences of having been involved in meaningful conversation? What made these conversations memorable and full of meaning? Counselling ideas and methods are not a substitute for whatever it is a person has learned to do, but are better viewed as possibilities for adding to or refining existing strategies.

A counselling relationship provides space for a particular *type* of conversation, one that is a bit different from other conversations that a person may have experienced in their everyday life. A person is likely to want to seek out such a conversation because some kind of dilemma, conflict, issue or bad feeling has been present in their life for some time and they have not been able to resolve it. The experience of the person may include a sense of being burdened, of carrying alone a weight that is crushing. This experience is often accompanied by a sense that it would be helpful to talk about the issue, but the person may have no clear idea of how that conversation might proceed or what might come out of it. Quite possibly, the person has already attempted to talk about the issue with a friend or family member, or even with someone in a professional helping role, but without achieving very much.

Coming into the counselling encounter a person will probably have quite vague expectations about what they are looking for, other than to somehow feel better. It is important for anyone who is offering a counselling relationship to reflect on the implications of this starting point. People rarely enter counselling with a specific idea about what will happen. Nevertheless, reflection on the factors that lead people to want to enter a counselling relationship suggests that there are two main expectations that people hold. The first is that the conversation will be meaningful. The second is that the person they are talking to will offer something back – there will be a dialogue.

The wish to engage in a conversation that is full of meaning reflects a desire to make sense, to gain perspective on a problem or issue, to make connections between something specific that may be happening now, and the bigger picture of one's life. A meaningful conversation creates a more complete understanding of the issues that were discussed. Such a conversation is memorable, it lives on in the imagination of the person and can act as a point of reference. What makes a meaningful conversation possible is the simple fact that, once a person starts to talk – about anything – what they say contains a vast amount of *implicit* meaning, which can be brought into attention and awareness. The majority of ordinary, everyday conversation can be thought of as verbal table tennis – statements are rapidly batted back and forth between the protagonists without much pause for reflection. In a more meaningful conversation, such as a counselling session, the interplay between speakers is slowed down or even stopped, so that the meaningfulness of statements can be explored. For this to happen, the counsellor needs to be able to initiate a different way of talking. One of the core competences in counselling is to be able to subvert everyday ways of talking so that the person can engage in what is, for them, a new form of discourse that creates new meaning. A simple example of how counsellors subvert everyday ways of talking is that, in normal conversations, a disclosure by one speaker ('we spent Christmas at home') is usually followed by a matching disclosure by their conversational partner ('we went to my husband's family for Christmas'). In contrast, a counsellor would never automatically engage in matching disclosure, but would tend to say something in reply that would encourage the person to say more about the personal significance of the topic.

The wish to engage in a conversation in which the other person will offer something back reflects a desire to make contact, to share the burden, to enlist the fresh perspective of seeing an issue from a different vantage point. There is a special kind of emotional pain that is associated with being out of contact with other people; a fundamental difference between an issue which a group of people are tackling together, and the same issue being dealt with alone. We live in a predominantly individualist culture where the basic virtue of mutuality is losing ground. A counselling relationship seeks to introduce some mutuality into an issue by providing a space in which *we* (the person and the counsellor together) can talk something through. A dialogical counselling conversation can have additional significance because, on the whole, professional helpers such as nurses, doctors and teachers do not engage much in mutual dialogue, but instead listen, diagnose/assess and then tell the person what to do. There are many situations where this prescriptive approach is both necessary and effective, but in relation to personal troubles it tends not to be experienced as 'being offered something back'. All too often, the recipient of a prescriptive approach to helping has a sense of being categorized, slotted into a pre-existing system. A dialogical conversation, by contrast, is a two-sided, open-ended process.

The remaining sections of this chapter describe a range of strategies for conducting meaningful dialogical conversations in counselling contexts. This type of conversation can be regarded as the grounding for any form of effective counselling. Occasionally, more specific counselling tasks may emerge from this groundwork. Some of these are discussed in Chapters 9 and 10. However, it is important to appreciate that a meaningful conversation can, in itself, be experienced as very helpful. There are many counselling episodes where the counsellor may think that nothing much happened because their impression was that the person was 'just talking', but which the service user may have evaluated as extremely useful. Making meaning and making contact are simple principles but can make a big difference to people. The following sections explore some of the ways in which these ideas can be implemented within counselling conversations.

Empathic engagement

Empathy is a core building block of any meaningful counselling conversation. The concept of empathy has been central to the practice of counselling and psychotherapy ever since the pioneering research of the American psychologist Carl Rogers in the 1950s, which showed that that ability of a counsellor to empathize sensitively and accurately with the experience of their client was a major component in therapeutic effectiveness. Empathy refers to the capacity of one person to 'tune in' to the reality of another person, to 'walk in their shoes', to see the world from that other person's perspective. In counselling, this quality is most valuable in the context of an empathic *engagement* with the person. In other words, it is not enough to empathize silently: a good counsellor *communicates* their empathic understanding in a form that the person can receive. Empathy is, in fact, a subtle and elusive quality. It differs, for example, from sympathy or compassion. These are both valuable human qualities in their own right, but imply a rather narrower response, which expresses fellow feeling or solidarity for the suffering that a person is experiencing. Empathy, by contrast, embraces a wider attempt to take in all, or as much as possible, of the experiential world of the other person, not just the vulnerable or painful aspects. Empathy can also be confused with identification, in the sense that a counsellor might respond to a person by saying 'I feel, or have felt, that too' or 'that happened to me, therefore I know what you are talking about'. While empathy always encompasses some degree of willingness to identify with the person, perhaps by imagining what it would be like to be them, true empathic engagement seeks to go beyond those aspects of the other's experience that are familiar, and to find some means of connecting to aspects that are unfamiliar or different. An additional challenge in relation to empathic engagement is that it calls for a holistic response to the other, including cognitive, feeling and moral dimensions of the way the person experiences the world, and also an appreciation of the direction in which the person is moving.

In counselling, genuine empathic engagement *makes a difference* to the person who receives it. A useful way of understanding the importance of empathic engagement is through the idea of the person's 'track', as defined by Rennie (1998). When a person starts talking about an issue, it is as though they are on a 'track' – their account has direction and momentum. Non-empathic responses by a counsellor can throw the person off their track because they indicate to the person that the counsellor has not understood them. At such a moment, the person finds themself wondering whether they need to stop and explain things to the counsellor, or perhaps even thinking that there may be little point in talking to someone who does not latch on to what they are trying to say. Using an analogy from driving, consistent empathic engagement is about keeping the car on the road – a basic requirement for any kind of journey to take place.

Empathic engagement can have an impact on the person that goes beyond merely keeping the conversation on track. Vanaerschot (1993) has analysed the impact of accurate, sensitive empathic engagement in terms of a number of significant 'micro-processes' in the person:

- feeling valued and accepted as a person. Feeling confirmed in one's own identity as an autonomous, valuable person;
- learning to accept feelings by hearing another person put one's own feelings into words without shame or embarrassment;
- alienation is dissolved: 'I am not abnormal, different and strange – there is someone else who can understand me.';

- learning to trust one's own experience through the affirmation of that experience by the counsellor;
- focusing the person's attention on the core aspects of their issue or problem;
- facilitating recall of information. Previously 'forgotten' or 'repressed' aspects of the issue may surface;
- organizing information. The empathic statement may put things in order.

All of these processes have the effect of encouraging the person to deepen or thicken the story they are telling, by incorporating other aspects of their experience. The story that they tell and the conversation they have with the counsellor, therefore more fully represents their possibilities as a person, including their strengths as well as their problems. The opposite process occurs when the counsellor offers a response which is *not* empathic. When a counsellor responds in a way that is 'off the track', the person may 'defer' to the counsellor (Rennie, 1994) and behave as if what the counsellor said was sensible or useful. If this happens consistently, then the conversation can quite rapidly begin to lose any relevance for the person.

A counselling conversation can be significantly undermined by the expression of *false* empathy, in the form of statements such as 'I understand how you feel'. This kind of statement is an assertion of empathic engagement by the counsellor, rather than an actual demonstration. It does not provide the person with any evidence of the counsellor's understanding. When a counsellor makes an attempt to articulate what they understand, as in a statement such as 'you have been talking about the stress of your job, and I just have a sense that you are so tired', then the person has something to work with. It may be, in this example, that the counsellor has picked up the wrong feeling and that in reality the person feels angry, but at least the person has received evidence that the counsellor has understood something (I have bad feelings arising from job stress), and has an opportunity to put the counsellor right. A danger of false empathy is that it put the counsellor in the position of an all-knowing expert, which can then inhibit the development of a collaborative mutual exploration of issues. By contrast, real empathic engagement can quite often miss the mark. If a counsellor conveys a sense of tentativeness and genuine curiosity in their attempts to be engaged, and a willingness to be corrected, statements that miss the mark demonstrate the openness of the counsellor to a process of working together.

Empathic engagement is not something that can ever be finally and completely achieved – who can ever fully understand the experience of another person? It is more useful to view empathic engagement as a way of talking, a style of conversation. Empathic statements position the counsellor as interested and willing to learn, but not yet fully knowing. They position the person as interesting and worth knowing, and as having a rich and fascinating story to tell.

The following sections examine some of the practical methods through which empathic engagement can be facilitated in a counselling conversation.

Acknowledging what has been said: active and passive empathic engagement

The American psychoanalytic psychotherapist Leston Havens has written about the use of language in the process of empathic engagement. Havens (1978, 1979) makes an important distinction between *active* and *passive* empathic engagement.

Passive empathy occurs when the other person is openly expressing what they feel. The task of the counsellor here is to convey an acknowledgement of what is being said. Active empathy, on the other hand, takes place when the meanings being expressed by the person are more implicit. The task of the counsellor is then to bring forth these meanings and explore the ways in which they may be interconnected. Havens (1978) suggests that:

> in active empathy one searches out the other. There is 'a bold swinging into the life of the other' . . . one puts into language how one intuits the other is feeling. . . . [W]hen no feelings occur to us, we can actively search out the other's feelings until we are close.

> (pp. 340, 344)

> The waiting, feeling posture, in which one echoes some of the patient's statements and above all supports and echoes his feelings, is passive empathy . . . . One tries to be a 'pane of glass' . . . through which the other is seen . . . . We can place ourselves emotionally close to the other person, allowing the reverberations of feeling to occur, and then utter what occurs to us.

> (pp. 340, 344)

It is important to recognize that passive empathic engagement does not imply that the counsellor is doing nothing at all. The process that Havens describes 'allowing the reverberations to occur', or that Barrett-Lennard (see below) characterizes as the counsellor *resonating* to the person, requires that the counsellor listens, is open to what is heard, pays attention to their own feeling states, monitors the situation, finds appropriate moments at which to say something to the person, and carefully formulates what they say at these moments. Nevertheless, the counsellor is passive in relation to the ongoing flow of the person. Passive empathic engagement occurs when the person is very much 'on track', and talking with a purpose and direction.

At moments of passive empathic engagement, the counsellor may regularly offer *simple empathic statements*, such as:

- exclamations and non-verbal utterances ('mmm');
- ejaculations ('Good God!');
- adjectives of empathy ('awful', 'wonderful');
- translations ('it is/was a very difficult time . . .').

Statements such as this convey to the person that the counsellor is paying attention and is emotionally tuned in ('I am aware of at least some of what you are feeling'). These statement provide a kind of background message of encouragement along the lines of 'keep talking, I am with you'.

At other points in a counselling conversation it may be helpful to offer a slightly more *active* response, based on a process of 'searching out' the meaning of what the other person is saying. If the meaning of what the other person is saying is not clear, or the person seems stuck, it can be useful, in Havens' terms, to 'put into language how one intuits the other is feeling'. This will usually involve offering a *basic reflective statement* which encapsulates what the person has said, or at least the key points. Some of the most widely used sentence stems for this kind of response are: 'you're feeling that . . .', 'like right now . . .', 'you appear to be saying/feeling . . .', 'you convey a sense of . . .', 'it's as if . . .'.

For the counsellor, a basic reflective statement is an opportunity tentatively to check out what has been understood. If a person has been talking steadily for more than two or three minutes, a great deal of information may have accumulated, and several personal and emotional themes may have been flagged up. Reflecting back what has been understood allows the counsellor to attempt a preliminary organization of this material, and to communicate this to the person. In turn, it confirms to the person that the counsellor understands (or not) and allows the person to put the counsellor right, if necessary. The implicit message in a basic reflective statement is that 'I am listening to you, and tracking what you are saying, and this is what I think the key themes might be . . . . Are these correct?' While a passive empathic statement is like an instant echo of what the person has said ('I feel your pain . . .'), a basic reflection more actively enters the world of the speaker and seeks to find the right words to capture what might be happening there ('my sense is that what you are saying about your pain is . . .'). In some respects a passive empathic utterance can be seen as a kind of companionship, an acknowledgement of connection. By contrast, more active empathic statements evoke a sense of the counsellor as separate and slightly more detached: a reflective statement always implies that the one who is reflecting is separate, almost an observer of the speaker, and needs tentatively to check out whether they have understood.

Complex empathic statements: connecting threads of meaning

On the whole, simple empathic statements aim to let the person know that they have been heard, affirm their value as a person ('you are worthy of being taken seriously'), and begin to develop a way of talking together that acknowledges feelings and core themes. By contrast, *complex empathic statements* involve linking different themes in order to expand the conversation. There are many ways of doing this, including:

- 'Perhaps no one understands . . .' (empathizing with the difficulty of empathizing, and/or the difficulty that the client has in expressing their problem).
- 'You have been feeling . . . for such a long time, and you have decided to talk about it now . . .' (opening up the tension between a long-standing issue and the decision to do something about it now).
- 'No wonder . . .' (justifying and accepting the feelings in the light of the background situation).
- 'How awful to want both . . .' (bridging two or more memories or feelings, and acknowledging the way the person feels about it).
- 'You feel . . . because . . .' (making the link between a situation in the person's life and the feelings triggered by that situation).
- 'You feel . . . when . . . and then you cope with that by doing . . .' (making a link between a situation, a feeling triggered by that situation, and the person's response to that feeling).

- 'What has been happening is . . . and you feel . . . because you can see that in the future . . .' (making a link between a current situation and feelings associated with how the client thinks the situation will affect them in the future).
- 'It's almost as though there is a part of you that is saying . . . while another part, or maybe another voice in your head, is saying . . .' (beginning to identify different 'voices' or 'parts of the self').

These are just some of the many types of complex empathic statement that can be used. These statements open the possibility of talking about the tension and *multiplicity* in the person's life, by drawing attention to different parts or elements of an issue, as experienced by the person. They also draw attention to the potential for achieving *coherence* across different experiences, by tentatively inviting reflection on how these parts might fit together.

Complex empathic statements enable the person to begin to *make sense* of what had perhaps previously been a set of fragmented and chaotic experiences. In addition, these statements can invite an unblocking of ways of talking that may be repetitive and stuck. For example, a person may say (again and again) that 'I just can't make new friends . . . I just clam up when I meet someone new, and they must think I'm not interested in them.' Any of the ways of responding listed above might play a part in inviting a different conversation, such as:

Person: I just can't make new friends . . . I just clam up when I meet someone new, and they must think I'm not interested in them.
Counsellor: I get the sense that this difficulty with making friends has been around for a long time, and I'm wondering whether there is something that has made you want to talk about it now . . . . Is there anything different? My feeling is that there's part of you that feels stuck with this problem, and another part of you that wants to make things different, that hasn't given up trying to make friends. Does that seem to fit at all?
Person: Maybe it does. I'm just really fed up. I know what the problem is. I just don't seem to be able to do anything different. I haven't been able to figure out how to relax enough to be normal in these situations.
Counsellor: Is this something we could maybe look at together – how to do something different? How to relax and be normal? I'm wondering what that means for you. What is it like for you to feel normal? When does that happen for you? Is it that there are some situations where you feel OK?

In this example, the counsellor has had a sense that there are two sides to what the person has said, as if they were speaking with two voices: an 'up front' voice that is saying 'I am stuck and it is hopeless', and another voice in the background saying 'I have worked out some of this, I have some clues about what is happening, I still want to make things different for myself, I have some hope.' In identifying these two sides, or voices, the counsellor is creating an opening for the silenced voice (the voice of hope) to say more. Then, in expressing curiosity about the way the person understands being 'normal', the counsellor is building the possibility of making a connection between what the person does to be normal in some situations, and whether these skills and abilities might be applicable to situations of making friends.

Box 8.1   The importance of tentativeness

Often, the helpfulness of a counsellor statement may depend not so much on *what* was said as on *how* it was said. In a research study that investigated the verbal styles of counsellors, Kimberley Gordon and Shake Toukmanian (2002) analysed the degree of *tentativeness* in counsellor statements. Tentativeness was defined as a response that had 'an element of openness and uncertainty and is delivered in a manner that invites the client to elaborate and expand on what is being communicated' (p. 92). Typically, tentative statements would include a phrase such as 'I get a sense that . . .', 'I wonder if . . .' or 'I'm not sure, but . . .'. Gordon and Toukmanian found that counsellor statements that were rated high on tentativeness helped the client to explore an issue in more depth, compared with statements that were coded low on this quality. They argued that tentativeness on the part of the counsellor introduced 'beneficial uncertainty' into the awareness of the person seeking help, which encouraged curiosity and a search for additional information. A similar finding emerged from a study by Tarja Kettunen and her colleagues (2003) into the speech patterns of hospital nurses who were offering health counselling to patients. In this research, tentativeness was characterized by 'word repetition, incomplete sentences, stammering, pauses and even hesitation' (p. 333). These researchers reported that tentative speech patterns left room for the patient's ideas, invited exploration and softened the intrusiveness of some of the lines of questioning that the nurse was following.

The results of these research studies suggest that tentativeness can enhance the extent to which a counselling conversation functions to facilitate exploration of issues. It is essential to keep in mind, however, that there can also be occasions when tentativeness may not be the most effective strategy for a counsellor to adopt. For example, if a person has reached a new understanding and the counsellor wishes to help them to hang on to it and remember it, it may be best to make a clear, unhesitating, confident, non-tentative assertion of what has been understood or agreed. The reason for this is that while tentativeness may enable thoughtfulness, directness may enable memorability.

Empathic engagement as a process: the Barrett-Lennard model

Godfrey (Goff) Barrett-Lennard is an Australian psychologist who worked with Carl Rogers in the 1960s on some of the landmark research into the role of empathy in counselling (Barrett-Lennard, 1998). During that time, Barrett-Lennard had the opportunity to study what happened when a counsellor was able to engage empathically with a person seeking help. He came to the view that the best way to understand what was happening was to regard empathy as a cyclical process, comprising a series of moment-by-moment interactions between person and helper. His model (Barrett-Lennard, 1981, 1993) can be described in terms of a series of five steps, as set out in Table 8.1.

This simple model has a great deal of practical significance in relation to what a counsellor actually does during the process of empathic engagement. The model

TABLE 8.1 Barrett-Lennard's model of empathic engagement

	The person seeking help	*The counsellor*
Step 1	Is aware of an issue that they wish to explore	Open and attentive – signalling a readiness to hear what the person has to say
Step 2	Talks about the issue or concern	Actively listens, and allows the emotional meaning of what the person is talking about to physically 'resonate' in them
Step 3	Pauses to hear what the counsellor has to say	Expresses their understanding of what the person has said, usually in the form of a summary
Step 4	Receives what the counsellor has said and conveys their sense of the extent to which the counsellor's summary was accurate and helpful	Observes the person's response to their attempt to summarize and convey understanding
Step 5	Resumes talking . . . the cycle continues	Resumes attentive listening . . . the cycle continues

suggests that there are four key competences that the counsellor is required to deliver. These are:

- a readiness to hear the person – this requires being able to set aside any other distracting thoughts;
- an ability to 'resonate' – to allow the emotional meaning of what the person is saying to be felt at a gut level;
- a capacity to use language, to summarize accurately, sensitively, tentatively and succinctly their sense of what the person is trying to communicate;
- observational skill – watching and listening to how the client receives what has been offered. If the counsellor's response has been accurate, then there is often a visible sign of relief on the part of the client, as if they are saying 'yes, that's it'. If, on the other hand, the counsellor's response is not quite right, the client may look away, reply with a 'yes, but' statement or look confused.

This cycle of empathic engagement typically occurs several times within a counselling session. On each occasion, if the counsellor is successful in capturing enough of the essence of what the person is trying to say, then the person will gradually move into a deeper and more personal exploration of the topic. If, on the other hand, the counsellor continues to get it wrong, or not quite right, the client may lose the thread of what they are talking about, may stop trying to communicate, by moving on to more superficial topics, or may resort to more vivid and forceful language (for example, metaphors) to try to get their point across. In such a situation, a good counsellor will try to find some way to repair the situation and get the conversation back 'on track'.

The empathy cycle model not only provides a valuable set of guidelines for competences that counsellors can reflect on in supervision and practise in training, but also makes it clear why the concept of empathy is complex and hard to understand. The model suggests that there are three quite different vantage points in relation to estimating the level of empathic engagement in a counselling conversation. First, there is the counsellor's sense of how open and empathic they are being (steps 1 and 2). Second, there is the quality of empathy exhibited in what the counsellor says to the person (step 3) – this is what an external observer would mainly pick up on. Finally, there is the person's sense of whether they themself felt that what the counsellor has said did indeed 'hit the mark' (step 4).

Summing up empathic engagement

The previous sections have explored some of the ways in which meaningful conversation is based on a consistent willingness to engage empathically with the reality or 'world' of the person seeking help. In practice, empathic engagement is expressed through statements that a counsellor makes in summarizing what they have understood from what the client has been saying. It is not useful to try to learn a standard 'formula' for responding to clients, because this strategy is quickly perceived as lacking in genuineness. There are many different ways of being empathic. It is essential that each counsellor develops a style of 'being with' or 'tuning into' the person they are helping, that is consistent with their personality, role and cultural identity. However, when making an empathic reflection (or any other kind of statement), it is important to keep in mind two key questions:

- *What effect does what I am saying have on the therapeutic relationship?* Does the statement convey a sense of working collaboratively? Does it build the client's belief that I am someone who accepts and respects them, and will be open with them?
- *How does the statement impact on the client's attention?* What does the statement draw attention to (for example, am I influencing the person to focus on certain themes and drop others)? Do my words invite the person to reflect more deeply on their feelings and sense of self, or do they draw attention to external factors (for example, how other people have behaved to cause their problems)? Does the statement facilitate the person telling their own story, or does it distract them and put them 'off the track'?

Moment-by-moment empathic engagement, when done well, should have the effect of gradually building a net of shared understanding that allows the person to explore personal issues more deeply and extensively, and thereby generate connections between events, ideas and experiences in such a way that makes meaning and achieves understanding.

So far in this chapter, considerable attention has been given to the idea of empathic engagement. This is because it represents what is probably the single most important aspect of a counselling conversation. If a person has a problem in living that they wish to talk about, then what they want is someone who will really listen to them, and will do their best to understand the problem from the person's perspective. People want to be heard and understood. When this happens, a basic human connection takes place that is intrinsically supportive and healing. If this does not happen in a counselling conversation, then little else will happen because the person will have a sense of remaining isolated and silenced (whether they admit this or not) and the counsellor's response to the person will be based in an incomplete appreciation of their situation. We now turn to other strategies for facilitating meaningful conversation.

Telling the story

Probably the most basic counselling task is that of giving the person an opportunity to tell their story. When a person experiences a stressful or difficult situation in their life, there seems to be a natural tendency to want to tell the story of these events to at least one other person. Telling the story has a number of positive effects. Organizing a set of memories, images and feelings into a story enables the person to sort out a mass of information that might have previously been whirling around in their mind. The structure of a story allows the person to put these events into a cause and effect sequence ('he said this, and then I did that'), which links together action (what happened), intention (goals and plans) and emotion (what was felt). A story also usually includes an evaluative or 'moral' aspect, which weaves in how the person stands in relation to the events that are being recounted – whether they were pleasurable, disgusting or whatever. Quite often, a person will seek a counselling relationship within which to tell their story because they do not have anywhere else to tell it. The story that the person wishes to tell may be threatening or embarrassing to other people in their life, or it may be that the person is isolated and does not have access to other people who are willing to listen to what they have to say. The need to tell the story can also arise in situations where the person has been allowed to tell only a 'thin' or selective version of their story, and has not had the chance to give voice to a 'thick' version that expresses more fully what they thought, felt and did. One of the important outcomes of telling the story, therefore, is that it allows the person to begin to make sense of something that has happened, by organizing and ordering feelings and events into a sequence.

Another essential aspect of telling the story concerns the opportunity it affords for enlisting support and feedback. It is possible to imagine that there were significant evolutionary advantages for the human race in sharing stories of threatening (and other) events – the storyteller might be both asking for help and alerting other members of the group to potential danger. In a counselling situation, when a person tells a rich and vivid story of something that has happened in their life, it has the effect of allowing the counsellor to know them much better. A good story is like a snippet of film that takes the counsellor (or any other listener) inside the world of the storyteller. The sharing of a story therefore provides the counsellor with invaluable information about the person, which allows any subsequent response to be better grounded in the reality of the person's experience. If the story is truly heard and received, it also helps the person to know that someone else understands them and cares enough about them to be interested in what they have been through. The telling of the story therefore combats isolation and hopelessness.

Box 8.2   The health benefits of talking about a problem

Some intriguing and important research carried out by the American psychologist James Pennebaker (1997) has established that talking about a problem, or even merely writing about it, can produce significant health benefits. In a classic series of studies, Pennebaker and his team divided volunteers into two groups. One group were asked to write about an issue that was stressful for them, for ten minutes on four consecutive days. The other group was instructed to write about superficial topics. In neither case was anyone else (including the researcher) to read what had been written. A range of health measures were taken before the writing task, at the end and after a follow-up period. It was found that members of the group that who written about a stressful topic, even for this very limited amount of time, reported fewer health centre visits and better immune functioning at follow-up, compared with those who had written about unimportant topics.

In further research, the Pennebaker clinic investigated the impact of different ways of disclosing stressful events (for example, spoken rather than written). What they found across their extensive programme of research was that the impact of even quite minimal disclosure was quite significant: at the time of writing or talking about the problem, participants felt worse, but afterwards they were happier and healthier. How can this happen? Pennebaker argues that human beings have evolved to tell other people about their troubles as a way both of eliciting support and of disseminating information about potential threat across their social group. However, in the modern world there are many factors that inhibit people from telling others about their troubles and fears (for example, other people are too busy to listen). This inhibition results in autonomic nervous system activity, that becomes stressful if allowed to continue. In addition, active inhibition interferes with information processing – the person does not process the event properly, and is left with ruminations, dreams and other intrusive cognitive symptoms. In contrast, confronting the traumatic or stressful memory, by telling the story of what happened, reduces the physiological work put into inhibition, and enables the person to better understand and assimilate the event.

The skill of facilitating the telling of the story has a number of different elements. In a counselling relationship, the marker for the telling of the story may simply be that the person signals that an issue is concerning them, but then talks about that issue in a general way that does not give the listener much of a sense of what actually happened. This kind of process typically implies that a very thin version of a story is being offered, but there is a thicker and more meaningful version ready to come out. Usually, all that is required is an invitation, such as, 'I'm wondering if it might be helpful if you could tell me more about what happened, that led to the worries and concerns that you now have about this. Could you take me back to the beginning, when it all started?' A key factor at this point is to avoid any suggestion of asking the person to give an explanation, or to 'account for' what they did in any judgemental sense. The aim is, instead, to convey a genuine curiosity about what actually happened and what the person felt and did at each point. As the person begins to tell their story, it is usually helpful to indicate empathic interest by occasionally summarizing, reflecting back or giving a personal reaction response ('how awful', 'I can just feel how difficult that was'). It is important for the listener, as far as possible, to be able to follow and stay with the story. If there are gaps in the story, or the teller appears to head off at a tangent, it may be useful to intervene with a statement along the lines of 'I seem to have missed something there, you were talking about what he said to you and then you seemed to skip to what happened the next day – I'm not quite sure what the connection was . . .'. However, it is also important to keep in mind that people have different ways of telling their stories and that, by just continuing to listen, everything will become clear in the end. There are finely balanced judgements to be made, between interrupting and seeking clarification on the one hand, and giving the person space, on the other. On the whole, professional helpers, such as teachers and nurses, tend to control and constrain the opportunities that their clients have to tell their stories, because they are keen for the person to 'get to the point'. Being patient and allowing the person to tell their story in their own way, can therefore have the effect of reinforcing the idea that this is a relationship in which they are being offered more freedom to talk things through.

The end point of the storytelling task will often take the form of a coda, which brings the conversation back to the present moment, such as '. . . and that's why I told you that I kept feeling so frustrated last week'. There may often be a pause in the conversation at the end of the story – as though the teller can stop for breath or look around having finished something that needed to be done. This moment is highly significant in terms of what the counsellor does next. During the telling of the story, the teller has 'held the stage' and in all likelihood the counsellor has said little. At the completion of the story, it is the counsellor's turn to say something. There are basically two types of response that a counsellor can make. First, the counsellor needs to acknowledge the story and also to respond to the implications of the content of the story. In most circumstances it is crucial to acknowledge the story before attempting any kind of discussion of what it might mean. As mentioned in the previous chapter, the medical researcher Arthur Kleinman (1988) has written very sensitively about a process that he describes as *empathic witnessing* – one human being responding to the troubles, pain and suffering of another human being. This kind of fundamental affirmation of the experience of the teller, and of their courage in telling the story, can be tremendously meaningful for a person. The counsellor can convey this sense of basic acceptance by staying for a few moments with their feeling of the story as a whole, and how it has affected them, and by putting some of this into words. It can be useful to try to find some kind of name or phrase that sums up the story as a whole (for example: 'the battle you have had to be your own person in the face of everyone else's expectations') because this creates a shared reference point that both person and counsellor can employ if they want to return to the events and feelings of that story at a future date.

The second task for the counsellor is to work with the person to explore the meaning and implications of the story. Following the telling of a story, there is often much for the person and counsellor to reflect on: a story will often encompass many significant threads of insight into a person's life and how they cope with events. A story can be viewed as an opening, or invitation into the person's subjective world. It can therefore lead on to other counselling tasks, such as making sense or making a decision.

Example

An example of telling the story as a task within a counselling relationship is the time when James, a 14-year-old school student, talked about his problems to his form teacher, Stan. At that stage in his life, James had a reputation in the school for being 'difficult' – he would sometimes defy teachers, either by ignoring what they asked him to do or by replying in a sarcastic or joking manner. This behaviour had resulted in most of his teachers becoming more strict with him, and regularly checking his work, which in turn triggered further 'difficult' responses. One afternoon, Stan was supervising James during a period of after-school detention. The two were alone in a classroom, so Stan took the initiative in asking James if he would be willing to tell him his side of the story. After a bit of coaxing, James began to open up and told his story. He talked about himself as a person who believed in fairness and in doing his best. He recalled the first time he had experienced trouble with a teacher. It had been a year ago. James had worked hard on a project and had felt that his teacher had singled him out for attention by asking him questions about it in front of the whole class. He remembered being so afraid that he was quite unable to say anything in reply to the questions that the teacher had asked him. He then worried about the situation the whole weekend, hardly sleeping or eating. The following week, when another teacher had asked him a question in class, 'I just snapped, and said something stupid.' He talked about how he now felt trapped in a situation that was getting worse with every day. It took about twenty minutes for this story to come out. Stan responded by acknowledging how painful and worrying it must be for someone with the high standards of James to be 'stuck in a trap' of this kind. He added that he appreciated the fact that James had felt able to let him have such a clear picture of what had been happening. Once he had said these things, they were both ready to look at possible strategies for changing the way that James viewed teachers and they viewed him.

Talking together: building a dialogical conversation

A good counselling conversation is carried out in a spirit of *collaboration*. The person and the counsellor come together as allies, forming an alliance to work together to overcome the person's problems in living. This alliance is constructed through language. The way that the person and counsellor talk together has the effect of positioning them as co-workers, which in turn allows the knowledge, skills and imagination of each of them to be brought to bear on the task. One of the most important methods for facilitating dialogue is the use of *metacommunication*, which was discussed in Chapter 7. By talking in ways that reflect on the process of talking (communicating about communicating – for example, 'I wondered what you felt when I made that suggestion'), a counsellor is in effect assembling micro-moments of dialogue within whatever other conversation is going on. This section examines some of the other conversational strategies that can be employed to promote and sustain collaborative talk.

Evoking places outside the self

Many counselling conversations can be characterized as 'face-to-face' or 'I–you' encounters. The person talks about themself ('I feel . . .', 'I think . . .') and the counsellor responds with statements such as, 'my impression is that . . . you feel that . . . you think that . . .'. This kind of interaction can evoke an image of a tennis game or chess match, where two protagonists face each other and are in competition. In a counselling situation, which depends for its success on a collaborative approach, this type of conversational structure can be unhelpful. An alternative way of talking can involve introducing the idea that there is a place outside of the self of the person, which the counsellor and person can explore together. The place can be in some sense either 'out there' or, if 'inside' the person, is a part of the self that can be observed by another (presumably more rational or in-control) part. Examples of such statements include:

> 'So your world is a place where . . .'
>
> 'When you stay in touch with that felt sense inside, it feels as though it is saying . . .'
>
> 'The situation is that . . .'
>
> 'That anger has become a part of your life . . .'
>
> 'That was one time when you were able to defeat perfectionism . . .'

Each of these statements introduces the idea of a place or territory that can be explored together: 'your world', 'the situation', 'that felt sense inside', 'that anger', 'perfectionism'. There are big differences between using this linguistic strategy to explore a 'situation' (where the conversation is directed into talk about other people, and the whole environment in which the person operates), a 'felt sense' (where the conversation may move in the direction of inner feelings) or 'perfectionism' (which draws attention to an imagined entity that exists in the world and in the person), in terms of the subsequent focus of the conversation. However, all of these sentence forms position the person and the counsellor as co-inquirers, as if sitting side by side to look at the same thing together.

Externalizing the problem

The conversational strategy of evoking an external entity or place which the person and counsellor can, as it were, address together or side by side, forms a central element of the *narrative therapy* approach developed by Michael White in Australia and David Epson in New Zealand, and their colleagues. An accessible introduction to their methods can be found in Morgan (2001). Within this approach, a basic linguistic move is to position the person as separate from the problem. Once this has been accomplished within the conversation, it then becomes possible to pursue two therapeutically rich lines of inquiry: (i) the influence of the problem on the person, and (ii) the influence of the person on the problem. Narrative therapists describe their method of exploring these issues as *relative influence questioning*.

Example

Katerina was a woman whose life appeared often to be on the point of imploding. She was a single parent of three school-age children, with a full-time low-paid job. She admitted that it was difficult to 'keep it all going' at the best of times. These were certainly not the best of times – Katerina had broken her leg in a fall and her mobility was severely limited. The community nurse who visited her weekly noticed that Katerina appeared to be emotionally tense, and asked her if she wanted to talk. Katerina began to speak about how angry she felt most of the time, and her remorse about shouting at her youngest son on a regular basis: 'I don't know what it's doing to him, but I just can't stop myself'. On being invited to talk more about 'the anger', Katerina described it as 'rage and fury' that was exhibited in 'shouting and saying nasty stuff'. The nurse asked whether the rage and fury were always around, or whether there were times that Katerina was free from them. She described a couple of occasions when her son had been naughty but she had been able to deal with him calmly. The nurse then explored with Katerina her perception of the effect that 'rage and fury' had on her life, and also how she had been able to resist the temptation to allow 'rage and fury' to overcome her on these occasions with her son. In asking these questions, and talking in this way, the nurse was positioning 'rage and fury' as external to Katerina, and developing a conversation that emphasized her capacity to control this set of emotions.

The method of externalizing the problem is a powerful conversational strategy because it makes it more possible for the person to talk about their strengths and capabilities (how they have been able to minimize or defeat the problem in the past) in a form that allows for humour ('not that boring old rage and fury again') and creativity ('my children have composed the "rage and fury song", which they have started to sing if they think its coming close').

Using the words 'I' and 'we': self-involving statements

It can be valuable to reflect on the use of pronouns in counselling conversations, for example the use of the word 'I'. There are many subtle ways in which the type of relationship that is on offer is shaped through the use of pronouns. For instance, when people discuss their problems with professional helpers, such as nurses, doctors and teachers, helpers will seldom use the term 'I' to refer to themselves. Individuals in their professional roles typically avoid any self-reference and construct what they have to say around 'you' statements ('you have said you have a headache, so the best thing would be for you to take a painkiller') or objective statements ('the X-ray shows that you have broken your ankle'). This kind of discourse positions the helper as a neutral, impersonal figure, who is a representative of the organization or system and a purveyor of objective, reliable, advice. By contrast, in intimate personal conversations, such as between friends or family members, the word 'I' is used a great deal:

'I have a headache.'
'So do I.'
'I think it's because the room is so stuffy.'
'I'll open the window.'

This kind of ongoing self-reference is a means of constructing a conversation in which both speakers are positioned as entitled to be fully present, in terms of being allowed to have and express opinions, needs and personal experiences – it creates an ethos of intimacy, in contrast to the ethos of detachment found in conventional professional relationships.

In a counselling relationship it is important for the counsellor to be emotionally in contact with the person, and this requires a way of talking that makes appropriate use of 'I' statements, for example:

> 'As I get it, you felt that . . .'
>
> 'I gather . . .'
>
> 'I feel that. . .'.

These statements can be defined as *self-involving*, in that they begin to acknowledge or imply that 'I am here, as another person, trying to understand you'. More fully self-involving statements can introduce reference to the counsellor's inner processes and reactions:

> 'As I was listening to you, I was aware of so many reactions – sadness, anger, weariness – and I began to get a feel for how much has been happening for you . . .'
>
> 'I have been trying to follow, but I'm aware you are saying a lot of things that fit together in complex ways . . . . Let me check that I've got it right . . .'
>
> 'There were many things you said, but the one that really hit me was . . .'

These kinds of statement support collaboration and relationship-building, in that they convey a sense of being willing to be honest with the person, and of letting them know something of what the counsellor is thinking and feeling in relation to the person. These statements can also function as a model of emotional problem-solving and interpersonal communication skills, by demonstrating non-defensiveness and openness in a relationship and a demonstration of how to operate collaboratively.

There has been a great deal of research carried out into counsellor self-disclosure – the sharing by a counsellor of personal information during a counselling session with a client. The findings do not provide a straightforward answer to the question of whether counsellor self-disclosure is helpful or hindering. It seems that there can be occasions when *biographical* self-disclosure, which involves the counsellor revealing facts about their life ('I have been divorced . . . am gay . . . am a member of the Baptist Church . . .') can be enormously helpful for some clients in making the counsellor more 'human' and in contributing to a lessening of a sense of being alone. However, it also seems clear that there are some clients who do not appreciate biographical self-disclosure because it can make them doubt the motives and competence of their counsellor. There seems to be a general consensus that substantial biographical self-disclosure on the part of a counsellor is rarely helpful, whereas well-timed, limited biographical sharing can be of value.

The question of counsellor disclosure of biographical similarity with the person seeking counselling is a major issue in relation to the delivery of counselling services. There are many counselling organizations and agencies, in fields such as alcohol and drug abuse, bereavement and loss, health problems such as cancer and AIDS, and marital counselling, that are staffed by people whose lives have been touched by the particular problem around which the agency offers a service. These services are widely used because people are reassured by the idea that they will see a counsellor who has some first-hand experience, who has 'been there'. On the other hand, different people who have been affected by something like HIV and AIDS may still have quite different stories to tell. It is for this reason that it is risky for counselling to become over-reliant on biographical similarity – a counsellor who places too much emphasis on the fact that they have personally experienced an issue may contribute to silencing those aspects of the person's experience that might differ from those of the counsellor. Too much biographical self-disclosure can also begin to reverse the balance between who is helping and who is being helped. This is a real possibility in counselling situations where the person seeking counselling has a history of taking care of other people and hiding their own vulnerability. Such a person can easily shift into a frame of mind where they start to question whether the counsellor is strong enough to be exposed to their pain. In contrast, counsellor disclosure of immediate responses to the person, in the form of self-involving 'I' statements, is generally well-received by clients.

Another way of using the 'I' pronoun that contributes to the development of a personal conversation is for the counsellor to give voice to the 'I' of the person. An example of this would be:

Person: It's just hard to deal with the demands of the children, what they need all the time, as well as looking after my mother. You just feel like there's no time for anything. You're tired all the time.

Counsellor: When I hear you speaking, what I'm hearing is 'I'm so tired. I'm run ragged. I can't cope any more with my children and my sick mum needing me all the time'.

This kind of statement is an empathic reflection, but one which changes the 'you' statements of the person, which slightly distance her from her feelings and experiences, to an 'I' statement that is more direct and may evoke further expression of what this situation is like for this person. The fact that the counsellor is voicing the 'I' of the person is a demonstration of the willingness of the counsellor to be in the world of the person and to speak from within that world. If the counsellor in this example had dispensed with the introductory lead-in phrase 'when I hear you speaking . . .' and instead responded immediately with 'I'm so tired . . .', the effect would have been even more marked. This kind of use of 'I' is almost like a momentary fusion of person and counsellor.

Finally, the use of the word 'we' in a counselling conversation introduces the possibility that the 'I' of the counsellor and the 'I' of the person might jointly engage in a task together. There are many occasions when this can be helpful, such as:

Person: I don't know what to do about these debts. I owe money on several credit cards, and now I've got a gas bill that I don't know how I'm going to pay.

Counsellor: Is this something we could look at together? We could make a list of all your income and debts, and see whether we could come up with a plan. Would that be helpful?

The invitation that is being implicitly extended, in using a 'we' statement, is that both participants will be involved in the task. In the above example, the counsellor might take on the role of writing down information that was supplied by the person and then initiate discussion around priorities.

Questioning

In the context of counselling, the use of questioning raises a number of difficult and complex issues. Questions are an integral part of everyday conversation and can be used for a range of purposes: to obtain information ('what time does our train arrive in London?'), to get people to explain or justify their actions ('why on earth did you buy that sofa?') and to reflect on abstract philosophical issues ('what is the meaning of love?').

One of the leading figures in counsellor education and training, Allen Ivey, emphasizes that effective counselling depends on the *intentional* use of language (Ivey and Ivey, 1999). What Ivey is getting at is that skilful counselling requires the counsellor to be sensitively aware of the impact that their communication might have on a person, and as far as possible choose ways of speaking that are facilitative, rather than otherwise. Nowhere is this more true than in relation to the use of questioning.

There are times when the use of questions can be perceived by a person seeking help as valuable. For example, questions can convey the genuine curiosity of the counsellor. Sometimes people want to talk but find it hard to get started; they will appreciate questions that help them to open up. However, too much or the wrong type of questioning can have the effect of closing the conversation down. The reason why questioning can be problematic in counselling is that any question constructs a rela-tionship of control: the questioner is in control because they are directing the attention and awareness of the other person towards coming up with an answer. Being asked a question momentarily overrides the agency and 'track' of the person answering, and forces them to think about what the questioner has asked. Even rejecting the question ('sorry, I don't want to think about that right now') diverts the person from the flow of their thinking and feeling for the time it takes to ponder the question and formulate the response. Questioning therefore does not fit well within a way of talking that seeks to demonstrate empathic engagement. The essence of being empathic lies in actively checking out with the person that you understand what they are trying to express, in a way that encourages a deepening of the conversation.

A question such as 'when did the problem start?' may be heard by the client as a gentle invitation to keep talking. On the other hand, it may be heard in a more con-frontational or even authoritarian manner, as 'I am interviewing you ... give me the facts.' One of the difficulties with questioning is that there is a (usually hidden) statement behind every question. So, a question such as 'when did the problem start?' will almost always arise from the counsellor's assumption or hypothesis that the start of the problem was significant. Rather than put this as a question (which hides the hypothesis) it is often better to use a form of words that allows the counsellor's meaning and intention to be more transparent, such as 'from what you are saying,

I keep thinking that I don't really have a clear idea of when the problem started in the first place. It would help me to get a feel for how this whole difficulty hangs together if you could say a bit more about that.' Turning a question into a statement does two things: (i) it emphasizes that the person seeking help is the expert on their own life, and is in control, and (ii) it builds a collaborative relationship, by sharing aims and assumptions whenever possible.

It is important to recognize that there are different types of question that can be used in counselling, including:

- *Closed questions*, intended to elicit specific information. Examples are: 'have you reported this incident to the police?', 'how often has this happened in the past?'
- *Open questions*, intended to encourage the person to expand on a theme or topic. Examples are: 'what other feelings did you have when all that was happening?', 'how have you learned to deal with this when it has happened in the past?', 'what led up to this . . . how did the situation develop?', 'what happened next?'
- *Hypothetical questions*, intended to encourage the person to consider new possibilities (Newman, 2000). Examples are: 'if you were able to deal with this situation, what would you do?', 'if we were having this conversation in five years' time, what would your life be like?'

Questions have an important role to play in counselling. The point to keep in mind is that questions are powerful interventions, which can have a strong impact on the helper–helped relationship, and also on the inner process and focus of attention of the person seeking help.

Topic shifts

A conversation is always *about* something. The idea of the *topic* of a conversation is often used to refer to the subject that is under discussion when people talk. A conversation can address a single topic or a number of topics. In counselling, the topic that the person talks about can be another person, for example 'my mother' or 'my relationship with my mother', or it could comprise an issue or problem, such as 'loss' or 'feeling afraid'. A significant topic of a counselling conversation can sometimes be self – 'how I feel about myself'. Sensitivity to *topic shifts* can be a valuable tool in building meaningful conversation.

There are two aspects of topic shifting that are particularly important in counselling. The first is when the person engages in a topic shift that they do not account for. Usually, if someone is talking about, for instance, their relationship with their mother, and then shift to talking about loss, they will briefly explain the transition to their listener: 'all that stuff about how caring my Mum was has made me think about how much I have missed her since she died'. If, on the other hand, the person changes topic without offering any kind of explanation, it is possible that there is something *unsaid* that would deepen the conversation and the counsellor's understanding of the person if it could be brought into the open. For example, if a person shifted abruptly from talking about 'mother' to talking about 'loss', without saying why, the counsellor might try to check out what had happened:

Counsellor: Can I just hit the pause button for a moment? I was aware that you were telling me about how caring your mother was, and then you seemed to be quiet for a few seconds, then moved on to something quite different, around feelings of loss. I was wondering what was happening at that moment.

Person: I was getting tearful and I didn't want to cry here. I was starting to realize something – I don't let people take care of me, and my Mum was the only person who ever did that for me. That's too painful to admit. I guess I diverted myself into something a bit less painful, to put you off the scent.

In this instance, what had been unsaid at the point of shifting topic was enormously important in terms of the relationship between the person and the counsellor ('is this a relationship where I can cry and be cared for?') and the relationship between the person and other people in general ('what is the cost of not allowing other people to care for me?').

A second aspect of topic shifting that is important in counselling concerns occasions when a topic change is initiated by the counsellor. Unintended and unexplained counsellor-led topic shifts are seldom helpful because they can easily throw the person off the track of what they were saying, and cause them to circle around the topic trying to find the thread of their thought or meaning. Such topic shifts can often arise from counsellor questions. If a counsellor is listening to a person and is beginning to think that perhaps the person is avoiding talking about an important topic, it is much better to signal this tension and create a situation where the person can choose the direction in which they wish the conversation to go at that moment, by saying something like:

> I am aware that I'm sitting here listening to you telling me about your boyfriend, and I keep thinking that you haven't said anything about that crucial job interview you went to last week. I just wanted to flag up, given that we don't have long to talk today, that I'd like to hear about what happened, if you feel that would be OK for you.

When initiating a topic shift, it can be useful for a counsellor to internally monitor their reasons for making this move. For example, the counsellor seeking to shift from the boyfriend topic to the job interview topic might briefly reflect on what this said about their assumptions about the goals of counselling or their feelings about the person's relationship with the boyfriend ('I feel bored when she talks about him . . . why could that be?').

Sensitivity to topic shifting can also encompass curiosity about what is happening when a topic disappears from the conversation. In counselling, a person will tend to move on from a topic when they have said all they need to say, when the issue associated with the topic is resolved to their satisfaction. However, the person may also drop a topic because they believe that the counsellor does not want to hear about it ('I stopped talking about my gay lifestyle because I could see it was making you uncomfortable . . .').

The rhythm of a therapeutic conversation

Counselling is a situation where two people talk with each other. However, closer examination of the process of interaction that occurs reveals that there are aspects of the back-and-forward flow or rhythm of the conversation that can contribute to learning and development. There are two aspects of the flow of conversation within counselling that seem particularly significant. The first is the moment-by-moment talking and listening that takes place. The second is concerned with longer segments of conversation that can span several minutes.

The American psychologist and psychotherapy researcher Robert Russell has made a major contribution to understanding the role of language and talk in counselling (Czogalik and Russell, 1994; Russell, 2004). In his research study, the transcripts of therapy sessions are analysed to identify the characteristics of how the person and the counsellor are using language – how they are talking and what they are talking about. The most widely prevalent pattern of talk that was uncovered could be described as *objective information exchange*. In this, the person described what was happening in their life and listened to how the counsellor responded to what they had said. What makes this way of talking helpful? Russell (2004) has suggested that this pattern represents the rhythm of dialogue in its most basic form. He points out that the earliest socialization processes to which infants are exposed consist of just this type of rhythmic exchange of speaker and listener roles, in the context of mother–infant interaction – it is a fundamental building block on which all development depends. In a counselling situation, Russell argues that this rhythm allows the person to 'recalibrate' or fine tune the balance between their voice and their ear.

Another rhythm unfolds over a longer period of time. A number of research studies have found that, in a typical counselling session, the person will begin by describing a general problem ('I worry too much about just about everything to do with being a student'), and then, after a while, will provide the listener (the counsellor) with a specific example of an occasion when the problem manifested itself ('for instance, I couldn't make up my mind whether to tell you about this problem, because you are my tutor and you would think I was stupid. I had decided to talk to you about it at the tutorial last week, but . . .'). After the story of a specific incidence of the issue is complete, the person will move on to evaluate and reflect on the meaning of the event ('so, you see, I'm just neurotic . . .'). The research and theory that has generated an understanding of this pattern of talk is summarized in McLeod (1997b). Why is this pattern of talk useful? This kind of storytelling provides a counsellor with several opportunities to learn more about the person and to engage in collaborative exploration of their problem. The opening phase, where the problem is described in general terms, allows the person and the counsellor to develop a shared understanding of the issue, the person's goals and the context of the problem in the person's life. The next phase, where the person offers a concrete narrative example, provides a great deal of detail about what the person feels and does, and the roles taken by other people. The closing phase opens up possibilities for discussing how the person makes sense of the problem.

Awareness of these rhythms has great practical significance for counsellors.

It is important for a counsellor to be able to tune into the style and pace of the person, rather than trying to force the person's pattern of talk into the way the counsellor prefers to talk. Because they are in a position of relative power and control, it is very easy for a counsellor to cut across and undermine the rhythm of a conversation, for example, by not allowing the person to finish, asking factual questions, rather than patiently waiting for specific narrative examples to emerge or not speaking during the pauses when the person is expecting a response. Another area of practical significance arises when the counsellor observes that the person's rhythm is uneven or has gaps in it. For example, sometimes a person in a counselling session will not tell a specific, vivid story that exemplifies their problem. It is helpful for the counsellor to think about why this has happened. It may be that the person does not feel safe enough to take the risk of being known and exposed by disclosing a detailed example. Alternatively, a person may talk in a way that includes little or no evaluation or reflection. Again, it is useful for a counsellor to give some thought to what this might mean.

Although this discussion of linguistic rhythms has focused mainly on the patterns of language use, it is also essential to pay attention to the physical expression and embodiment of these phenomena. These rhythms can be seen in the movement that a person makes, the pace, tone and quality of their voice, and the synchrony between the movement and gesture of the person, and those of the counsellor. The conventional arrangement of person and counsellor sitting in static chairs, facing each other at a slight angle, may serve to inhibit awareness of the embodied nature of this rhythmic interplay because it tends to close down the amount of physical movement and range of vocalization that are possible. Counselling methods that make use of drama, dance, ritual, music or the outdoor environment have the potential to bring an appreciation of these rhythms much more into the foreground.

Discursive positioning

Within psychology, philosophy and the social sciences, somewhere in the 1960s and 1970s there took place what has come to be known as the 'narrative turn'. Previous to this shift, there had been a tendency to attempt to understand individuals, and social life, in objective terms, for example, by trying to measure characteristics of people (such as 'intelligence' or 'mental health') or determine the factors that caused people to act in the way they did (for example, genetic inheritance, external reinforcement). What happened at the point of the narrative turn was the realization that, as human beings, we largely create the realities we live in, through language and talk. We construct identities by telling stories about ourselves, and the groups to which we belong. These identities and realities are constantly being maintained and re-created through conversation and other ways of using language (for instance, writing). This sea-change in thinking about people resulted in the emergence of some valuable new ideas which can be applied in counselling situations. One of the most fertile of these ideas is the notion of *discursive positioning*.

To understand the concept of discursive positioning it is necessary to start with the idea of *discourse*. Although there are some arguments about what this term means, and how it should be used, the broad view is that within any culture there exist well-established ways of talking about certain issues. These ways of talking, or discourses, comprise ideas and beliefs, and also linguistic forms (such as key words and phrases, and forms of speech). To claim an identity as an individual, and to explain or account for one's actions, it is necessary to *position* oneself in relation to prevailing discourses. For example, within western society there is a strong thread of Christian discourse, which contains within it a fundamentalist wing that asserts that abortion is morally wrong. However, also within western culture there are discourses of liberalism and feminism, which assert (in slightly different ways) that it is a woman's right to choose. We are all familiar with this debate, and with the forms of language (arguments, imagery, justifications) that are brought to bear by each side. Each of us will, from time to time, find ourself being called upon to position ourself in relation to these discourses. An individual can position themself either by simply adopting a mainstream discourse (such as that promoted by the Catholic Church) or by making an effort to assemble different discourses into a personally coherent account (this would be necessary, for example, for anyone who views themself as both Catholic and liberal).

The concept of discursive positioning was first introduced by the Oxford philosopher Rom Harré and his colleagues (a collection of their key papers can be found in Harré and Van Langenhove, 1999), and is increasingly used by social psychologists as a means of exploring the relationship between the individual and society. Examples of how positioning theory may be applied to counselling can be found in McLeod (2004b), Monk and Sinclair (2004), and Winslade (2005).

An awareness of positioning can be valuable in enabling a counsellor to help a person find new ways to talk about an issue. This benefit results from the two moves that it allows the counsellor to make. First, the counsellor can invite the person to more fully articulate and explore the position that they have adopted. This can be helpful because the person may never have explicitly considered the way they have positioned themself in relation to a topic. The person may discover, as a result, that their position is not consistent with positions they have espoused in other areas of their life. Second, within a conversation, a counsellor can offer other positions, which allow the person the opportunity to try out new vantage points on areas of their life. Some examples of these moves are included in the discussion below.

Inviting reflection on positioning

Inviting reflection on positioning has been described by Winslade (2005) as *discursive empathy*. Rather than empathically reflecting back to the person the meaning, or emotional content, of what they have said, in this kind of empathic response the counsellor reflects back the discursive position that the person has adopted.

Example
Duncan is a manager in a successful IT business. He has had a heart attack and is undergoing rehabilitation that involves a combination of exercise, physiotherapy and lifestyle change. The nurse who is co-ordinating Duncan's rehabilitation programme meets with him weekly to check his progress. They have the following conversation:

Nurse:	Would it be OK if we looked at your activity diary now, so we can see what you have been able to do over the last few days?
Duncan:	Here it is. You will see that I had a couple of meetings with the section heads in my office. Just to see how they were getting along. I was worried about how they were coping.
Nurse:	That wasn't part of the rehab plan, was it? I thought you had decided to wait a bit longer before making contact with people at work?
Duncan:	You're right. But I just felt that I should do it. I guess I felt responsible – like I was just leaving them in the lurch.
Nurse:	I'm thinking that this sense of responsibility is a big thing for you. I've heard you mention it before. You often say that you 'should' be doing this or that. What's that about for you?
Duncan:	I suppose I do say that a lot, now that you mention it. I've always felt that I should be responsible.
Nurse:	Could you tell me what that means for you? Feeling responsible?
Duncan:	It's like I should look after people. I should do the right thing by other people.
Nurse:	Do you have any idea where that comes from in your life?
Duncan:	Well, yes, now that I think about it. That sense of responsibility comes from the church. Growing up in a family that had that sense of service to the community. One of my uncles and a grandfather were ministers. You had to sacrifice yourself to others. It was never acceptable to put yourself first. I remember my grandmother saying, over and over again, 'who do you think you are?' whenever anyone put themself first. All of us in the family are locked into this, I think.
Nurse:	So this way of thinking about things, this 'service to the community' . . . I'm wondering how relevant it is to the situation you are in now. I'm thinking, well, this is a situation where you might be needing to put yourself first. At least for a while.

In this dialogue, the nurse counsellor invited her patient to reflect on the way he positioned himself morally in relation to his work colleagues. Quite quickly, their discussion opened up a space in which Duncan was able to identify the discourse within his own life that he was drawing upon in order to account for his actions. Once he had identified the discourse and noted some of the ways that it structured his actions, the nurse counsellor, in turn, was able to ask him to begin to consider whether there might be alternative ways of positioning himself that would be more consistent with his goal of recovery. In long-term counselling or psychotherapy there could be some significant learning for Duncan as he begins to reflect on the implications of positioning himself in this manner in relation to a discourse of self-sacrifice. In the more limited counselling space provided by the rehab nurse, the interaction reported here was sufficient to give both Duncan and his nurse counsellor a handle on how to deepen their conversation on occasions when self-sacrifice re-entered the picture.

Offering a different position

Another way of working with positioning is to rephrase what a person has said so that it embodies a different position. This strategy does not invite the person to reflect on the discursive context of their way of talking, but much more directly manoeuvres the person into trying out an alternative conversational stance. The most straightforward example of this kind of counselling method can be found in relation to discourses of agency/passivity. Almost all counsellors have developed their own ways of making the kind of move that is illustrated in the following example.

Example

Student: The course is too much for me. There is too much work to do. The other day the lecturer said that we needed to hand in our lab report by the end of term, and it's just impossible. I'm just hopeless at it. There's no way I'm going to get through.

Tutor: Right, so what you are saying is that you are feeling a lot of pressure of work right now, and you are wondering whether you can handle it. Is that the main thing?

Student: Yes, it's just too much. There isn't enough time. The books are never in the library when you need them. It's just impossible.

Tutor: OK, these are extra pressures – not enough time and books not being in the library. So you're saying to yourself something like, 'I just won't be able to get it done'. Is that right?

Student: Yes.

Tutor: I was wondering if we could maybe just break this down step by step. That would help me to understand the challenge that you are facing. Would that be alright? If we looked at it step by step?

Student: OK.

Tutor: Right, well, if we look at it from the point of view of getting the lab report in. What does the lab report involve, for this module?

Student: I've been working with a small group, to complete a microbiology experiment on cell growth. Each of us needs to write our own separate analysis of the data.

Tutor: Could you break that down for me a bit? What has your bit of it involved? What have you being doing?

Student: My job is to use the microscope to make readings, and then I write them in a lab book . . .

Tutor: . . . and that has been OK?

Student: Yes, there hasn't been any problem with that. In fact, the lab assistant said I had done that well.

In this passage, a student who is seeking help from his personal tutor begins by positioning himself as a passive victim of external forces (the course, the lecturer, the library, his own inadequacy). It would be possible for the tutor to engage empathically with this discursive position, for example, by inviting the student to explore the meaning of pressure, or blame, in his life. However, the tutor here has decided that the priority is to help the student to complete the relevant assignments, and anticipates that the best way for the student to achieve this is through adopting a position of agency. The tutor therefore offers the student a different way of talking about the issue, a discourse of agency. This is carried out by describing the student's report of problems as something he is saying now, by using the linguistic construction 'so what you are saying is that you are feeling . . .'. Here, the counsellor is translating a statement originally framed by the student within a discourse of passivity ('it's just impossible') into a discourse of agency, in which the capacity of the student to be responsible for his actions is foregrounded: 'what *you are saying* is that you are feeling a lot of pressure of work right now, and *you are wondering* whether you can handle it'. The counsellor's restatement of the issue introduces the idea of personal agency in the use of the words 'saying' and 'wondering'. Later, the counsellor invokes another discursive move, which is to shift the conversation away from a total, or totalizing description of a whole situation, described in general terms, and into the direction of descriptions of specific actions taken by the student at different stages ('looking at it step by step'). Acquiescing in this move requires, or at the very least encourages, the student to talk about his problem in terms of what he did in response to specific sub-tasks. From the tutor counsellor's perspective, this new way of talking about the issues opens a space where he can observe and affirm both positive action that the student has taken, and examples of skills and resources that the student can bring to bear on the sub-tasks that are proving harder to complete. Once the way of talking about the problem has shifted in this way, possibilities for change, and solutions, tend to emerge naturally within the conversation.

A final aspect of discursive positioning comprises the way that the counsellor and person seeking help position themselves *in relation to each other*. For example, in the case of the nurse working with Duncan on rehab planning, it would have been easy for her to position herself as a health advisor only, and merely reinforce the importance of keeping to the agreed rehab schedule. Similarly, the tutor meeting with the distressed student might well have spoken from the position of the 'voice of the university', by telling him how it was important to work hard, make sure that he is at the library when it opens and so on. In both of these cases, the helpers positioned themselves, instead, within a discourse of collaboration and curiosity, and invited the people they were helping to talk on these terms.

Box 8.3   Holding a meaningful conversation in a situation of extreme difficulty: the challenge of Alzheimer's disease

People who have Alzheimer's disease typically experience a number of severe problems in relation to communicating their ideas and feelings. The cognitive effects of this neurological illness include an increasing difficulty in finding words and a gradual deficiency in memory. These problems are exacerbated by the attitudes of other people towards anyone who has been diagnosed as suffering from dementia – the person can quite rapidly be categorized as not capable of making sense or of making decisions on their own behalf. The person's frustration at this treatment, which may be expressed in the form of emotion, will typically be regarded as just yet another manifestation of the disease. In turn, this reaction will lead to the person becoming more frustrated. As their frustration increases, their memory and linguistic capacity are affected. They are trapped in a cruel cycle. In recent years, research carried out by Steven R. Sabat and others has cast a fresh light on the communication process in people diagnosed with dementia. Sabat (2001) spent a great deal of time with people with severe dementia symptoms and developed new understandings of the interplay between the speaker and listener in this situation. He argues that the key to holding an effective conversation with a person with dementia relies on taking an *intentional stance* towards the other. What this means is that the speaker is positioned as someone who is trying to convey an intelligible message. In addition, to enable effective communication to take place, the listener should engage in a process of *indirect repair*, which he defines as referring to 'inquiring about the intention of the speaker, through the use of questions marked not be interrogatives but by intonation patterns, to the use of rephrasing what you think the speaker said and checking to see if you understood his or her meaning correctly' (pp. 38–9). Sabat (2001) argues that 'the responsibility for effective communication between people lies with the listener as well as with the speaker' (p. 39). The work of Sabat contains many examples of people with dementia who had been perceived as hardly able to communicate with those around them, but who started to be able to make good sense once these principles were applied consistently. This research has important implications for counselling. Although very few people who seek counselling help are afflicted by Alzheimer's disease or other neurological problems, the majority of them do have trouble in expressing the complexities of what they feel and think, and the events in their life that have contributed to their problems. Counsellors have a lot to learn from Sabat's unique study of people with dementia: the ideas of 'intentional stance' and 'indirect repair' can usefully be applied in a wide range of counselling situations.

Opening the door: using vivid language, imagery and metaphor

Being willing to listen closely to another person is an essential aspect of any counselling role. However, as well as being open to hearing the *whole* of what a person is expressing about the issues or problems in their life, it is useful to be ready to tune into the *way* that a person talks about their problem. There are many aspects of a person's way of expressing themselves that can be informative about their emotional state – for example, their tone of voice, posture, and the pace and volume of their talk. One of the most useful dimensions of communication, from a counselling perspective, is the occurrence of vivid imagery and metaphor within the person's description of their troubles. It is always worthwhile to take mental note of the types of images a person uses. Sometimes an image can be so striking that it is worth inviting the person to elaborate on it. In these situations, if a word or phrase seems to stand out from the what the person is saying, then it is almost certain that it conveys a lot a of meaning for the person.

The image or metaphor in these occasions almost operates as shorthand for a longer story that the person could tell. Inviting them to describe the reality of the image or metaphor can be an effective way to allow the story to be told.

Example

A teacher who is experiencing a high degree of work stress, and has a variety of physical ailments, including chronic back pain, has visited his GP three times in the past month for prescriptions for painkillers, none of which have made much difference. On this occasion, the GP suggests that it might be helpful to look at whether similar problems had happened before in the patient's life and how he had coped in the past, and moves temporarily into a counselling mode:

Person: I had a really bad time a few years ago, and my back was playing up then too. It was really difficult to get through that, and its always in the back of my mind. Sometimes now I just feel as though I'm skating on thin ice – it would not take much and I would fall back into all that awful stuff I was feeling then. I wouldn't call it depression, but . . .

Counsellor: Would it be OK if we just looked a bit more at what you just said there? My attention was really drawn to that phrase you used – 'skating on thin ice'. It just seems such a vivid image, it really hit me, because it seems to really catch what that situation means to you. I remember you have used an image like that before, when you came to see me last week, to describe your situation. Would it be OK with you to stay with that image for a few moments? I'd be interested to learn more about what that means to you – 'skating on thin ice' . . .

The counsellor is here expressing curiosity and interest, and using meta-communication/checking out in negotiating agreement over staying with the metaphor.

Person: That's OK. When you mention it, I realize that it's something I say a lot.

Counsellor: Right, well maybe you could begin by telling me where you are skating – on a rink, a river . . .?

The counsellor encourages the person to 'dwell in' the metaphor, to explore its sensory qualities, to begin to let the story unfold: what went before; what is happening now – who, where, how, why; how will it end?

Person: That's funny, its definitely a frozen lake, with mountains on either side.

Counsellor: Are you going fast, slow . . .?

Person: I'm skating very deliberately. Not fast or slow. I mustn't stop.

Counsellor: You mustn't stop? What would happen if you stopped?

Person: If I stopped I would be more likely to fall through the ice. I must keep going.

Counsellor:	So, if you stopped there would be the risk of . . . what?
Person:	It would just give way.
Counsellor:	And then?
Person:	I would freeze. I would be pulled down. I just wouldn't last for ten minutes. It would be the end.
Counsellor:	So you must keep going. Are you OK if you keep going? How do you keep going?
Person:	If I can get to the other side I'll be fine. I'm not sure how I keep going. I grit my teeth and tense my muscles. If I relaxed for even a moment I'd be gone.
Counsellor:	So you keep going, trying to get to the other side. And is that far away – the other side . . .? What's it like over there?
Person:	Quite far, but I can see the people there.
Counsellor:	The people . . .?
Person:	Yes, there are people there who are trying to help me to get to the other side. Giving me advice. I know I'll be all right if I can make it over to where they are, so they can take care of me.
Counsellor:	So these people are really rooting for you?
Person:	Yes, definitely.
Counsellor:	Thanks for that. I know it may seem silly to be talking about skating and so on, but it did seem to me that what you were saying there was somehow important. What came over to me was that you have to keep moving, very carefully and deliberately, or you will disappear into a depression like you had before, but there are people who can help, if you can get to them. Is that right?
Person:	Yeah, that's it in a nutshell.
Counsellor:	It's making me think that maybe the pills I've been prescribing you are only part of the answer. Could we look at what would be involved in actually getting this support that's on offer from these people?

In the remaining time in the consultation, the conversation between the stressed teacher and his doctor centres around the possibility of taking some time off work, and how this time might be used to make contact with people who would be sources of support. The GP suggests that an appointment could be made with the cognitive behavioural therapist who visits the practice, who could be another source of support and who might have further ideas about dealing with work pressure. Until the very end of their conversation, they do not make use of the word 'depression', both of them choosing to use the person's own terminology of 'the ice' to refer to the problem.

This example illustrates some basic features of the use of metaphor and imagery within counselling conversations. The metaphor that was generated by this person – skating on thin ice – could easily have been ignored by the helper. It is a fairly commonplace image, which can be taken for granted. However, it can be seen that, for this person, in the context of what he had said before (mainly describing lists of symptoms), this image was vivid and conveyed new meaning. The metaphor functioned like a door into the individual world of the person seeking help. The counsellor can choose to open this door, or not.

The majority of powerful, evocative metaphors refer to physical, bodily qualities (Lakoff and Johnson, 1999), and as a result an invitation to the person to put these concrete aspects of the metaphor into words ('describe where are you skating . . . how far away is the other side?') is likely to allow the person to become more aware of their own bodily sensations (emotions and feelings) that are bound up in the imagery.

Metaphors also provide opportunities to develop the relationship between the person and the counsellor, through working together to explore the meaning of the metaphor. The image can then become a shared language between them – on any future occasion they would both understand what was at stake if they used the term. Research by Angus and Rennie (1988, 1989) into the use of metaphors in counselling showed that what people found helpful was when their counsellor collaborated with them around a joint discussion of the meaning of the image or metaphor.

Because they are vivid and out of the ordinary, metaphors are highly memorable. After a counselling session a person is more likely to remember a vivid metaphor than they are to remember other topics and ideas that have been discussed. Metaphor can therefore help to link together counselling and everyday life.

George Lakoff and Mark Johnson have made a significant contribution to the understanding of metaphor (Lakoff and Johnson, 1980, 1999). They have suggested that each metaphor both highlights and hides meaning. In other words, a metaphor draws attention to particular aspects of an experience, while pushing other aspects into the background. So, for example, the image of 'skating on thin ice' that was used earlier highlights the ideas that the person is busy and active, and is visible to other people. It is a metaphor that perhaps makes it harder to see and appreciate a side of this person's stress and depression that is reflected in being alone, hidden and safe. From a counselling perspective, it can be useful therefore to listen out for counter-metaphors, or examples of images that describe a very different set of experiences. It can also be helpful to invite such images, by using such prompts as 'if you weren't on that frozen lake, where would you like to be?'. However, rushing prematurely into the elicitation of alternative or counter-metaphors, before an initial metaphor has been fully explored, runs the risk of not being respectful of the person, by not being willing to join them where they are now and, instead, rushing them in the direction of where the counsellor thinks they *should* be headed.

The use of metaphor in counselling allows the possibility for making use of important human resources, such as imagination, creativity and the capacity for play. 'Metaphor talk' in counselling can often be energizing and connecting, and can lead to new discoveries.

Conclusions: how and why 'just talking' can make a difference

This chapter has explored the idea of using a counselling space for 'just talking' – helping the person to put their problem in living into words. Different sections of the chapter have examined various ways that a counsellor can try to engage in conversation that is as meaningful and productive as it can be. But, in the end, this is all about 'just talking'. While the following chapters introduce and discuss some of the *specific* tasks that may emerge from a process of talking, it is essential for anyone engaged in offering counselling relationships to realize that, most of the time for most people, 'just talking' is a hugely valuable activity. Having a meaningful conversation about a topic of personal significance can be regarded as the basic *general* task of counselling. Why is this? How can it be that 'just talking' can make a difference? As a means of drawing this chapter to a conclusion, it is relevant to review the reasons why talk, in itself, may be therapeutic or healing, or may lead to learning and change. Some of the key factors are summarized below.

- *The counsellor as someone to talk to*. Probably the most valued testimony that a client can pay to a counsellor is to regard them as a person who is always worth talking to, whom they will seek out when they need to talk something through. Knowing that there is a person within one's social network who can function in this way is a source of great strength.
- *An opportunity for reflection*. A person who chooses to talk about a problem is already actively engaged in trying to make sense of their situation and to find solutions. The act of talking creates many opportunities for further, deeper and different reflection. As the person talks, they are mapping out their story, and describing their experience. As they do this, they are listening to their own words, and reflecting on the meaning and implications of what they have said. A speaker listens to what they are saying in a way that is fundamentally different from merely thinking about things (having a dialogue 'in your own head'). The person also has an opportunity to reflect on how the listener responds to what they say in terms both of their moment-by-moment interest and reactions and of their verbal replies.
- *Discovery of implicit meaning*. What a person says almost always carries more meaning than they are aware of at the time. This phenomenon can be demonstrated by recording and transcribing any interview or counselling conversation, and analysing all the possible meanings that are expressed in each utterance. A counsellor who is closely listening to what a person is saying will usually be able to pick up and feed back, meanings that go slightly beyond what the person assumed that they were saying. For example: 'you talk about feeling sad, and at the same time I'm wondering if you are also perhaps angry or resentful'. Alternatively, a person may become aware of implicit meanings by reflecting on what they have said: 'it was only when I really started to talk about it that I realized that I am actually really annoyed about what happened'. The consequence of this kind of process is that, as a person talks, the problem may become more 'meaning-full', and they develop a 'thicker' story that allows them to connect current troubles to other themes, events and resources in their life.

The next two chapters introduce a range of counselling tasks arising from specific issues around maintaining or repairing a personal niche within a culture and society However, 'just talking' can be regarded as a general task, which is always being carried out during a counselling session, whatever else might be happening. A useful, or *therapeutic* conversation occurs when a person is able to talk about a problem or issue in a way that allows new possibilities to come into view. This kind of conversation can be regarded as healing or therapeutic because it contributes to a sense of resolution or closure of a wound, a source of pain. A therapeutic conversation goes beyond a mere reporting or cataloguing of troubles, and involves using the presence of, and connectedness with, another person in a supportive and life-enhancing dialogue.

This chapter has described a number of ways of deepening conversation: empathy, sensitivity to stories, attention to positioning, metaphor and rhythm. However, the single most important aspect of a therapeutic conversation is the experience of being having someone *listen*: good counsellors are good listeners. The reason that listening is so powerful is that it creates an experience, for the person seeking help, of being with another person in relation to their problem in living. For the person seeking help, there are always significant parts of their experience, or their story, that they have had to carry alone. The more that the helper listens, the more the problem emerges as something that they both know. It is almost as if the problem, and the pain, fear, shame and confusion that accompanies it, begins to be brought into being in the room between them. Once this happens, they can begin to 'walk around' the problem together, examining it from different angles and deciding what to do with it. To some extent, listening is about information gathering, about learning about the facts of what happened in the person's life, who was involved, how the problem grew. However, more than that, it is about being willing to enter the life of the other, by being a companion and a witness. Listening, in the fullest sense, is always personal, it always involves an emotional and a moral commitment by one person to another. The person seeking counselling is making a commitment to being known, and the counsellor is investing themself in a willingness to know.

The importance of 'just talking' cannot be overemphasized. Time and again, people who have used counselling report that what was helpful was the chance to talk, to have someone listen, to be heard, to share embarrassing secrets. However, within the flow of conversation there are sometimes specific tasks that may come into focus. The reason why these tasks emerge is that a counselling conversation always takes place in relation to some life goal, and always has the purpose of advancing that goal. It is as if, when engaged in 'just talking' about a problem, the person is looking out for ideas on what to do about the problem. Often, the solution to a problem emerges from talking, or even arrives fully formed. Sometimes, though, there may be a sense that an answer or solution is possible, but that it needs to be worked out in a more structured or planned manner. It is to an examination of these occasions, when counselling is oriented towards a clear-cut issue, that we turn in the following chapters.

Questions for reflection and discussion

1. What are your own experiences of having been involved in meaningful conversation? What made these conversations memorable and full of meaning? What can you learn from these experiences that you can apply in counselling situations?
2. Reflect on the feeling of being truly understood. Identify one recent occasion when you felt that another person really understood what you were experiencing. How did they

express their empathic engagement with you – how did you know that they understood? What was the effect of their empathic sensitivity on your relationship?

3. What kinds of questioning strategies do you employ in your work with people who come to you for help? Over the course of a day, make a note of the types of questions you ask. Can you identify statements behind these questions? To what extent are these questioning strategies effective and 'intentional' – are there alternative ways that you could use to achieve your conversational goals?

4. What metaphors do you use most often in your conversations at work? What metaphors do your colleagues and clients use? What meanings are highlighted and hidden by these metaphors? Are there occasions when you deliberately extend the use of a metaphor over a number of conversational turns? How helpful has this been?

Suggestions for further reading

Key reading on the concept of empathy is:

Mearns, D. and Thorne, B. (1999) *Person-centred Counselling in Action*, 2nd edn. London: Sage.

A valuable source of ideas on the role of metaphor in counselling is:

Rennie, D. L. (1998) *Person-centred Counselling: An Experiential Approach*. London: Sage. Ch. 5.

The most accessible introduction to the work of James Pennebaker can be found in:

Pennebaker, J. W. (1997) *Opening Up: The Healing Power of Expressing Emotions*, rev. edn. New York: Guilford Press.

Copies of research studies carried out by Pennebaker's group have been lodged on his website:

http://homepage.psy.utexas.edu/homepage/faculty/pennebaker/Home2000/JWPhome.htm

There have been a number of studies that have used micro-analysis of conversational sequences to develop new insights into what happens in counselling interactions between health professionals and patients. These papers are technically quite demanding but go more deeply into the issue of what makes an effective helping conversation than the present chapter has been able to do. Examples include:

Karhila, P., Kettunen, T., Poskiparta, M. and Liinatainen, L. (2003) Negotiation in Type 2 diabetes counseling: from problem recognition to mutual acceptance during lifestyle counselling. *Qualitative Health Research*, 13: 1205–24.

Kettunen, T., Poskiparta, M. and Karhila, P. (2003) Speech practices that facilitate patient participation in health counselling – a way to empowerment? *Health Education Journal*, 62: 326–40.

Pilnick, A. (2003) 'Patient counselling' by pharmacists: four approaches to the delivery of counselling sequences and their interactional reception. *Social Science and Medicine*, 56: 835–49.

9

Resolving difficult feelings and emotions

Introduction: understanding emotion • Types of emotion tasks in counselling • Methods for working with emotions in counselling • Making use of supervision • Conclusions • Questions for reflection and discussion • Suggestions for further reading

Yes, you're right
Like my granddad
I'm alone at the same time as being surrounded
By people
Who love me.
Sometimes it's unbearable.
Sorry.
It's like
A different kind of pain
That I carry around.
Some really bad feelings.
Right here.
It's different from the cancer pain.
Sometimes I almost
Want
To go away and cry
Sorry.

Introduction: understanding emotion

On the whole, we live in a world in which rationality is valued and emphasized over emotion. There are a number of reasons for this. Emotion is an immediate, bodily response to a situation, which has direct and clear implications for action. For example, fear triggers flight. Most of us live in complex, crowded urban environments in which we are constantly faced with multiple competing stimuli and rules, where a thoughtful, considered response is usually most effective. In this environment, a spontaneous emotional response is likely to lead to trouble. We therefore learn, early on, to suppress our emotions in the interest of getting along with people. In the past, individuals tended to learn about people and relationships through face-to-face contact, such as listening to another person telling a story or viewing a drama being enacted on stage. In these situations, the bodily emotion of one person can be directly communicated to others. In contrast, in contemporary societies, we largely learn about people and relationships through watching television or reading novels. Both of these are emotionally 'cool' and disembodied media. When watching a television programme, we are placed in the position of a distant observer, rarely able to connect with the subjective physical emotion and feeling of any individual actor or character. We are also in a position of being able to switch off at any moment and make the character disappear.

Despite the uneasiness and ambivalence about emotion that permeates much of our culture, it is essential to recognize that feelings and emotions are an essential part of life. One of the most important functions of a counselling relationship is that it provides a space in which there is permission to feel, and to express emotions. It may be useful to regard emotion and feeling as sources of meaning or as signal systems. An inherent aspect of being human is the capacity to perceive, think and reason, to use concepts and ideas to guide action. Parallel to this system of cognitive information processing and decision making, there is an emotion-based system that operates directly on various bodily functions such as heart rate and respiration. While cognitive processing sorts information in terms of possibly thousands of concepts and categories available in language, the emotion system sorts information in terms of a smaller set of categories that have been biologically wired in through evolution: anger, fear, joy, loss, pleasure, disgust. From a counselling perspective, therefore, feeling and emotion always have some *meaning* in relation to what is happening in a person's life space or personal niche. Feeling and emotion are bodily signals that provide information about the basic attitude or action tendency of the person towards an event, other person or situation. For example, certain emotional responses are part of a basic biological 'fight–flight' response, indicating that there is something in the environment that is threatening and which evokes either anger (destroying the threat or making it go away) or fear (escaping from the threat). The emotional reactions that people tend to want to explore in counselling are those where the meaning of the emotion is not clear to the individual, either because the emotion state is fleeting and vague, consisting of a general sense of emotional pain, or is confused/confusing (why do I keep feeling angry and losing my temper?). When a person knows and accepts what they feel about something, then they usually do not seek counselling.

Box 9.1   The pervasiveness of hurt, pain and suffering

A central theme within the counselling and psychotherapy literature has been a recognition that emotional pain, understood as an undifferentiated state of hurt and suffering, lies at the heart of the life difficulties experienced by many people. Theorists who emphasize the importance of emotional pain also tend to place great importance on the simple virtue of allowing people to express their pain and to be heard. One of the hidden traditions within the counselling field has been the practice of 'co-counselling', which was first developed in Seattle in the 1950s by Harvey Jackins (Kauffman and New, 2004). Co-counselling is a form of peer self-help in which people take turns to talk about themselves and to listen. There are well-established guidelines that enable this to be carried out in a safe and respectful manner.

The primary aim of co-counselling is to allow the expression, or discharge of hurt, in an environment of acceptance. The research of Bolger (1999) into the experiences of people who have had troubled childhoods reinforces this view. Bolger concluded that 'the individual feels psychological pain at the moment when he/she becomes separated from a significant other' (p. 357), and that over time this pain may become covered up, and contribute to a sense of self as 'broken'. Miller (2004) has forcefully argued that contemporary psychology and medicine have largely denied the pervasiveness of pain and suffering, and have sought instead to define a reality in which symptoms can be eradicated by 'interventions'. The implications for counselling of the work of these writers and theorists are highly significant: there is no counselling method that will eradicate the reality of pain and suffering, and make it go away. Although a sense of hope and optimism about the possibility of change is an essential element of effective counselling, any counsellor working with a person around emotional issues needs to start from a position of acceptance of suffering as part of life.

The reason why feelings and emotions are often vague and confused is that people may have grown up in a family or wider cultural environment in which particular emotions were unacceptable. For instance, many men have learned that it is not 'manly' to feel sadness and loss, or even fear. Many women have been socialized into believing that is not appropriate for them to feel angry. As a result, men may feel afraid or disgusted about any possibility of feeling or expressing sadness. Women may feel fear and self-disgust about any possibility of feeling or expressing anger. Instead of sadness, men may get angry. Instead of anger, women may get anxious or fearful. While these are very broad generalizations, which should never be simplistically applied to individual lives, they do illustrate a basic truth about emotion, which is that *the emotions or feelings that a person exhibits may hide or protect other emotions or feelings that are harder to acknowledge.*

It can be useful to take account of the concept of *authenticity* with respect to feeling and emotion. When a person is expressing genuine feelings, what they say has a sense of being authentic and will have a direct emotional impact on anyone in contact with them. For example, even listening to a radio interview with a grieving disaster victim, whom one has never met, is many thousands of miles away and speaking in another language, can be a profoundly moving experience. By contrast, attending a family funeral accompanied by weeping relatives can evoke a sense of detachment. When a person expresses a genuine or authentic feeling or emotion, there is typically a physical sense of relief or release, and a sense of resolution in relation to the issue or problem that is associated with that emotion. These are valuable indicators of whether a feeling or emotion is primary, or may be a secondary emotion that masks a more basic one. It is rarely helpful to challenge a person seeking help on the grounds that they are expressing false or pretend emotions. The emotions they are expressing are real enough to them, at that moment, and worthy of consideration and respect. The point here, for a counsellor, is to be willing to listen to their own gut sense that there *may be more to come*.

The Canadian psychologist Les Greenberg has made a major contribution to developing an understanding of the role of feelings and emotions in counselling (Greenberg *et al.*, 1993; Greenberg, 2001). He uses the term 'emotional processing' to convey the idea that what a counsellor should be trying to do is to collaborate with the person seeking help to allow the meaning of an emotion to unfold bit by bit. This is achieved, essentially, by staying with the emotion and looking at all its different aspects. Any counselling method that is used in work around emotions is trying to do just this – to help the person to reflect on what the emotion is, where and when it happens, what it leads to and what it means.

It is valuable to make a distinction in counselling between *feeling* and *emotion*. Both are part of the same embodied, internally sensed way of responding to the world. Both are sources of meaning and information. However, feeling can be regarded as an ever-present inner sensing that can be referred to at any moment. Feelings are typically multifaceted: there are many sides to what one feels in a situation, or many threads of feeling of which a person may be aware. Emotion, by contrast, is more specific. It takes over the body, and can usually be identified as one thing, for example, anger. In counselling, feelings are always part of the equation. For a counsellor, understanding what a person is talking about is hugely influenced by the feelings the person conveys and by what is felt by the counsellor themself while listening. In counselling, strong emotion occurs less often. When it does occur, though, it demands attention. Effective counselling skill requires the courage to be willing to be with another person when they are expressing strong emotion, as well as the sensitivity to be able to enter the person's everyday feeling-world.

Types of emotion tasks in counselling

There are three broad categories of counselling task that involve working with feeling and emotion. These are:

- *Exploring feelings that are elusive, vague or hidden*. The marker for this task arises when the person may have a vague sense of how they feel about an issue, but be unable to put this into words or to stay with the feeling long enough to know what it is about. Sometimes, a person may claim that they do not feel anything at all. The counselling task here is to bring what is felt sufficiently into awareness for it to become a source of meaning and information that can be useful to the person. For example, Gina, a supervisor in a medical laboratory, consulted her human resources (HR) manager about how best to handle one of the technicians who was persistently late in arriving for work. Following Gina's account of the issue, the HR manager asked her, 'I can see that the facts here are fairly straightforward. But there seems to be something else around too. Maybe this isn't relevant, but as you were talking I found myself wondering how you felt about this person.' This question threw Gina off balance. She replied that she was not aware of having any particular feelings about this colleague. The HR manager asked her whether she would be willing to pause for a second or two and reflect on any feelings that she might be aware of at that moment. After a brief silence, Gina laughed and said that, yes, she realized that she was very fond of this technician: 'She reminds me of my own daughter, she is very warm and affectionate, and makes a big difference to the team – she is the one all the others will turn to if they need to talk about something.' In discussing the situation further, Gina became able to recognize the ways that her unwillingness to admit her liking for her colleague had resulted in her taking too formal and rigid an approach to the lateness problem, which in turn prevented her from holding the type of 'friendly' conversation with her that might have resolved the problem in a creative fashion. For Gina, becoming more aware of how she felt was the vital clue to the solution of her difficulty.

- *Giving expression to emotions that are being held back*. If a strong emotion is stimulated by an event, it seems that there is a basic human need to express that emotion in some way. If the emotion is not expressed or released, the person may have a sense of incompleteness or 'unfinished business' which can interfere with normal functioning. The idea that emotions demand expression, and that it can be psycho-logically and physically damaging to hold back emotion, can be traced to the ancient Greek theory of *catharsis*. The marker for this kind of task may simply be that the person recognizes that there are emotions near the surface: 'I just need a good cry' or 'I feel so angry inside but I just can't do anything with it'. The counselling task involves creating the conditions for, and facilitating, the safe release of the emotion. For example, Ali was a refugee who had fled with his family from an oppressive regime. Safe in Britain, and waiting for his work permit to be finalized, Ali began to visit his GP every two weeks with a series of ailments – back pain, stomach spasms, headaches. On one of these visits, the GP asked Ali if he thought that it might be helpful to book a longer consultation, to give them more time to talk about Ali's situation and about whether these different illnesses might be linked in some way. Ali readily agreed, and on his way out of the room joked, 'You'd better watch out doctor. Have some tissues ready for our next meeting. Once I start to talk, I have five years of tears waiting to come out.' At the beginning of their next consultation, the GP invited Ali to tell him the whole story of what had happened to him in leaving his country and travelling to Britain. Within a few moments, Ali was in tears, as he described scenes of fear, torture and loss. The doctor moved his chair alongside Ali and placed his hand over Ali's hand. He encouraged Ali to keep talking, to continue with his story and occasionally reassured him that 'you are alright now, you are safe here'. At a follow-up consultation one week later, Ali reported that 'it was the first time I have felt well in years. I have been busy with voluntary work and looking after the children, and haven't been thinking about headaches and back-aches at all.'

- *Limiting or managing the expression of emotions that are experienced as being out of control.* The emotion-focused tasks that have been described above share an aim of learning how to bring buried or suppressed feelings into awareness, and accepting what they may contribute to a person's participation in life. By contrast, another type of emotion-centred task in counselling can comprise the effort to control the experiencing, expression and enactment of emotions that are regarded by the person as being unwelcome, or out of proportion to the situations in which they find them-self. For example, Alistair was a policeman who had worked on a motorway patrol for several years, witnessing on a routine basis fatal road traffic accidents. His colleagues and his wife had noticed that he seemed to be 'on a hair trigger', and likely to become verbally, and occasionally even physically, angry at the slightest provoca-tion. Persuaded to consult the force occupational health physician, Alistair could not be convinced to accept a referral to a psychologist: 'I'm not mental, I just need to sort this out.' The occupational health doctor decided to invite Alistair to return for a longer consultation, to explore the issue further. At this meeting, he asked Alistair of he would be willing to look at whether there was a pattern to his anger episodes. Alistair agreed, and, after describing three recent incidents in which he had 'lost his head', began to see that he needed further help in order to regain his self-control in work situations. He said: 'There are times when I need to take command of people and speak in a clear loud voice to give them directions for their own safety, but I can see now that I am going much too far.' The remainder of the session was spent discussing what he could expect from a clinical psychologist and the process of the referral.

These three forms of 'emotion work' can be the main focus of counselling in some instances, or may be subsidiary to other tasks. For example, helping a person to deal with a relationship problem may often involve feelings of anger or loss with reference to a troublesome 'significant other'. The third emotional processing task described above – limiting the expression of emotions that are experienced as being out of control – can usefully be considered as a type of behaviour change task (see Chapter 10). The remainder of the present chapter discusses some of the methods that can be used in counselling when a person is seeking help to make sense of feelings and emotions that are vague and elusive, or are being held back.

Methods for working with emotions in counselling

A variety of methods can be used to facilitate the awareness and expression of feelings and emotions, and exploration of their meaning. The followings sections briefly described some of the strategies that may be helpful in this kind of work.

Developing a sensitivity to feeling and emotion

Some counsellors seem to operate as if the emotional life of the people they are trying to help was irrelevant. These are counsellors whose responses predominantly lead the person in the direction of talking about what they *do* and what they *think*, rather than what they *feel*. They do not pay attention to emotion cues or invite the person to explore feelings. This is a very limited approach to counselling, which is missing out on important information about the significance of events in the person's life. Some other counsellors seem to operate as if emotional expression and catharsis were their primary goal. This is not effective either, as a general rule. Both research and practical experience suggest that feelings are always linked to situations, relationships and events, and that what is helpful is not just to express the raw emotion, but also to learn more about what the emotion *means*, what it says about the situation, relationship or event in question. There may be some occasions when a person needs just to express and 'let go' of a strong buried emotion, but this is a rare event in counselling. Usually, what is more helpful is to enable the person to make use of their emotions as a guide to action. In a sense, a lot of counselling is about the development of what Daniel Goleman (2005) has called 'emotional intelligence', which involves making it possible for the person to be more aware of their emotions and what they mean. To be able to offer this to a person seeking help, anyone in a counselling role needs to be aware and sensitive around the flow of feeling and emotion within their relationship with the person.

Counsellor competence around the awareness of feeling and emotion is based on a willingness to *listen for feelings* at all times during a counselling encounter. Listening for feelings primarily means being sensitive to the feeling words that a person uses and weaving these into the conversation. However, it can also involve being on the alert for the *absence* of feeling words. Some people have difficulties in dealing with problems in living because they are unable to refer to their feelings or consciously acknowledge how they feel. The classic example is the person who may be very attached to the people in their life, but never tells them how much they love them or care about them, or enjoy their company. A state of lacking feeling words has been labelled 'alexithymia', and people with psychosomatic complaints are often alexithymic. A sensitive counsellor may find that a person's body language, tone of voice, or even the events they are describing, hint at a feeling that they seem to be unable to put into words. In these circumstances, it can be helpful for the counsellor tentatively to offer feeling words for the person to 'try out for size'.

In a counselling situation where it is possible to maintain a relationship with a person over an extended period of time, the counsellor may find that the person keeps coming back to the same feeling state again and again. They may consistently get angry, feel tired, get depressed, or whatever, no matter what trigger situation they are in. Recurrent feelings that appear to be not quite appropriate to the situation can often be a sign that there are buried feelings. What seems to happen is that a person can 'specialize' in emotional states that they are familiar with, rather than enter other emotional states that may seem to them to be scary and out of control. The counsellor should, at these times, be as sensitive as possible to the presence of possible hidden feeling states, for example, by catching the flash of anger that accompanies an expression of repetitive sadness.

Box 9.2   Making sense of recurring patterns of feeling: the concept of 'rackets'

Transactional Analysis (TA) is a good source of ways of describing the kinds of psychological and interpersonal processes that trouble people in their lives. In TA theory, it is assumed that people who live productive and healthy lives will have access to, and appropriately express, a wide range of emotions – anger, fear, sadness, happiness – in response to different situations that they encounter. Many of us, however, tend to return to the same feeling state, no matter what the situation. In TA language, such recurrent patterns of feelings are described as *racket feelings*, which are defined as 'a familiar emotion, learned and encouraged in childhood, experienced in many different stress situations, and maladaptive as an adult means of problem-solving' (Stewart and Joines, 1987: 209). This phenomenon is explained in terms of a process of *rubberbanding*. The assumption is that, when under stress, a person is swiftly and unconsciously catapulted back into what they learned to do as a child, as a way of coping with scary situations. The emotional state that then emerges is the one that was functional, as a child, in gaining parental support and care.

There is another aspect of racket theory that is also significant as a means of understanding apparently inappropriate or self-defeating emotional responses, which is the idea of *stamps*. The concept of 'psychological trading stamps' is now somewhat dated. It refers to the practice of supermarkets in the 1960s of encouraging trade by giving customers stamps that were pasted in books and cashed at a later date. (Now this is done through loyalty cards.) The point about stamps is that they are saved up and traded in at a later date. The application to emotional life is that some people may feel racket feelings, but not express them at the time, while storing them up for an emotional outpouring in the future. The person or people who are the recipients of the eventual emotional cashing-in are typically surprised by the intensity of feelings which may be unleashed – they do not realize how much patient collecting lies behind the emotion event that they are witnessing.

These ideas from TA theory are certainly not the final word in relation to the question of recurring patterns of feeling and emotion, but they are stimulating and thought-provoking, and show how ordinary language can be employed vividly to express quite sophisticated ideas about emotional dynamics in a way that can communicate with many people who are seeking help around such issues.

Finally, one of the best ways for any counsellor to heighten their awareness of feelings and emotions in a counselling session is to *listen to their own feelings*. There are at least three ways in which the counsellor's own feelings comprise a vital source of information about what is happening in the counselling relationship. First, a counsellor who listens to their own feelings may become aware that what they are feeling consists of a feeling that they brought into the counselling session and that has nothing to do with what the person seeking help is talking about. For example, a person in an embedded counselling role may be feeling frustrated and angry because of some work hassles. There is a danger that these feelings may get in the way of tuning into the emotional world of the person seeking help. Part of sound preparation for a counselling session involves setting aside personal emotional processing in order to be able to concentrate on what the other person is feeling. Second, what a counsellor feels when with a person seeking help can often take the form of emotional *resonance*: it is as if the counsellor is resonating like a tuning fork to the feelings being emitted by the other person. Therefore, a lot of the time in counselling, how the counsellor is feeling may be a good clue to how the person is feeling at that moment (although this always needs to be checked out). Third, what the counsellor feels in response to a person may be *how other people also feel in relation to that person*. For example, if the counsellor feels angry or annoyed with the person, it may be that other people (their friends, family, work colleagues) sometimes feel the same way too. This awareness can be used, carefully, to explore questions such as: What is this person doing to make me feel angry? Do I respond in the same way as others do? (Which others, and in what circumstances?) And what does this response do in terms of the kinds of relationships this person has with these people?

Emotional sensitivity in counselling is a matter of mastering dual attention: listening to oneself at the same time as listening to the person seeking help. This is why training in counselling places such an emphasis on what is sometimes called personal development work. A huge part of this personal development consists of learning about one's own emotional life, as a means of being better able to tune into the emotional worlds of others.

Creating an environment that is conducive to the expression of emotion

If a person is using counselling to work on an emotion or feeling, it is probable that they are embarrassed, ashamed or inhibited about acknowledging or expressing that area of emotional life. If the person was *not* embarrassed or ashamed, the chances are that they would be able openly to display that emotion in everyday life. It is therefore helpful to make sure that the person feels safe enough to express emotion. For instance, the person may be reassured to be told that the counsellor is comfortable with the expression of feelings, or that they can go at their own pace, or have plenty of time for this task. The person may be worried about whether anyone outside the room will hear them, or see them when they leave, or whether there are facilities (tissues, a washbasin, mirror) for putting on a face for the outside world. It is probably easier to express feelings in a soft environment, for example, a cushioned armchair that can be hit or stroked, rather than in an office furnished with hard upright chairs. The counsellor, too, may have concerns in these areas – 'what if my colleagues hear shouting coming from my office?', 'if this person breaks down, I'm sure I will start to cry too, and how will I be able to be ready for my next patient?'

Using the person's 'feeling language'

Sensitivity to the language with which the person talks about their experience can provide a number of possibilities for facilitating feeling and emotion. One of the ways that people avoid getting in touch with their feelings is too talk quickly or shift topics frequently. People sometimes do these things because they may be aware at some level that talking slowly, or staying with a topic, would mean that the felling or emotion associated with that topic, or that was being felt at that moment, might become overwhelming. Many 'standard' counselling responses, such as reflecting back what the person has said, allowing silences, and talking in a gentle, measured voice, can have the effect of slowing the person down and helping them to keep in touch with what they are feeling at that moment. There may be specific words, phrases or images that are evocative for the person. Often, these phrases and images will be embedded in the person's speech, produced by the person as they talk about an issue. From the counsellor's perspective, these words can almost jump out of the conversation and very obviously possess a great deal of meaning. The counsellor can reflect these words or images back to the person, or may even invite the person to repeat them, and report on what happens when they try this.

Paying attention to what the person's body is saying and doing

Because feeling and emotion are bodily phenomena, there are several ways that careful attention to what is happening at a physical level can be used in emotion work. When a person uses an emotion word, it can be helpful to invite them to indicate where that feeling is located in their body, and then to focus their awareness on that part of the body and what they feel there. Bodily movement is an important means of expressing emotion – when we are happy we dance and when we are angry we hit things. When a person refers to a feeling or emotion, or seems to be feeling something, it can be valuable to draw their attention to any gestures or movements that seem to accompany the feeling, and either to give words to that movement ('what is your clenched fist saying?', 'if the fingers that are stroking your other arm had a voice, what would they say?', or perhaps repeat and exaggerate the movement ('clench the fist more, and hold it there for a few moments – what happens when you do that?'). Breathing is closely linked to the expression of feeling and emotion. A highly effective way of controlling or choking off an emotion is to hold one's breath or breathe as shallowly as possible. By contrast, the release of emotion is typically accompanied by long, deep breaths, sighs and yawning. There may be times when a counsellor can become aware that a person is holding their breath, or is breathing as little as possible. At these moments, it can be useful to point this out to the person, and invite them to breathe deeply and regularly, perhaps also breathing along with them for a few seconds. Another bodily indicator of emotion is stomach rumbling. Some counsellors believe that stomach rumbling, in the absence of overt hunger, is a signal that there is a deeply held, buried feeling struggling to be expressed. If asked, and if they are not too embarrassed, a person will often be able to report on the feeling or desire that lies behind the rumbling.

Using enactment

When a person wishes to express strong feelings, but finds it hard to let go, it may be helpful to use *enactment*. Usually, a strong emotion is felt *in relation to* another person. For instance, someone may feel angry with a colleague or feel the loss of a parent. In these circumstances, it can be difficult to enter the emotion fully when merely talking to a counsellor – there can be a tendency for the person to talk *about* their feelings, rather than enter directly into them. A face-to-face counselling conversation is also a situation in which a person will probably be exerting a certain amount of self-control and will be monitoring what they say, rather than allowing themselves to be lost in or taken over by feelings. Inviting the person to perform their feelings, through enacting their interaction with the object of their emotions, can be an effective strategy for facilitating emotional expression. The person can be asked to imagine that they are talking directly to the other person: 'what do you want to say to him or her? Just talk to them as if they were here'. There are several variants of this method, such as imagining the other were sitting on a chair, allowing the other to answer back, and encouraging repetition of key statements: 'say it again – she's not listening to you'. (This counselling strategy is often described as two-chair work – see Greenberg *et al.*, 1993.) During this kind of enactment, it can be helpful if the counsellor sits alongside the person, rather than opposite them. This has two effects. First, it reinforces the enactment, and makes it possible for both the person and the counsellor to speak to the other. Second, it creates a situation where the person is not expressing strong feelings directly at or towards the counsellor – it may be embarrassing to express anger directly to a counsellor when the person knows that the true target of their anger is someone else. A further variant on the method of enactment can involve expressing feelings through a letter written to the other person. This letter may be brought to a later meeting with the counsellor, may be kept or may be ritually destroyed, to represent the act of moving beyond the feelings that it carries. People may find it useful to write letters on consecutive days, as a way of allowing all of their feelings to emerge, bit by bit.

Experiential focusing

The psychologist, philosopher and psychotherapist Eugene Gendlin has developed a method of *experiential focusing*, which is widely applicable is situations where a person is struggling to make sense of, or give expression to, a feeling or emotion (see Cornell, 1996; Gendlin, 2003; Purton 2005). Gendlin argues that the meaning of any situation, relationship or event in which a person is involved is captured in a bodily 'felt sense' to which the person can refer. The felt sense includes a wealth of *implicit* meaning, not all of which is explicitly known or understood by the person at any particular point. If a person can be enabled to stay with (or *focus* on) their felt sense of a situation, then the layers of meaning that are bodily present can begin to be symbolized and consciously known. Usually, symbolization occurs in the form of language – the person finds words and phrases that emerge from the felt sense and seem to capture threads of its meaning. However, symbolization can also take the form of an image, sound or bodily movement. For Gendlin, the activity of helping a client to focus on an unclear felt sense comprises a basic therapeutic process that occurs in virtually all forms of effective counselling. This is because a central problem that many people have in their lives is that of not allowing themselves to stay close to what they are feeling for long enough to allow the broader personal meaning of what is happening in their life to emerge. Gendlin would argue that people avoid focusing on their felt sense of a problem by blocking their internal awareness by incessantly talking, being 'busy' or not paying attention to bodily feelings and sensations. The group of practitioners associated with this approach have developed a set of simple procedures for helping people to access their felt sense and make use of what they find there. They have encouraged the use of these focusing instructions in peer self-help communities worldwide (see Boukydis, 1984), and with clients experiencing a variety of health problems. Experiential focusing is a method that is readily incorporated into counselling that takes place embedded within other professional roles. Gendlin's (2003) book *Focusing* provides clear guidelines on how to use this method. These guidelines are also available on the Focusing Institute website: http://www.focusing.org/.

Personal and family rituals

A ritual is an activity or routine that is invested with special significance by a person or group of people. Human beings have always used rituals as ways of dealing with conflict and for marking life transitions. For people seeking to resolve emotional difficulties, ritual may represent a valuable means of expressing troublesome feelings in a controlled setting. For example, a person who is troubled by feelings of depression and hopelessness may counter these emotions by starting each day with a set of yoga exercises which symbolize hope and renewal. In Talmon (1990: ch. 3) the story of a client, Mary, is described. Mary was angry with her father for a variety of reasons, and wished to exclude him from her life. Together, she and her husband, along with the counsellor, devised a ritual in which Mary read out, with powerful emotion, a 'decree of divorce' from her father, while the counsellor set on fire a photograph of her father, accompanied by music played by her husband. This ritual, carried out during a counselling session, had an enormous impact on Mary in signalling a transition from a self that had been dominated by her father, to a new self that was free and ready to enter a different phase of her life. Within the counselling and psychotherapy literature there are many examples of rituals that have been devised for different therapeutic purposes (Imber-Black and Roberts, 1992; McMillan 2006) and which can be adapted for use in microcounselling situations. Ultimately, in a counselling setting, the rituals that will make most sense for a person are those that are co-constructed, that take shape from the ideas of the counsellor and person seeking help working together, rather than anything that is 'off the shelf'.

Using CBT techniques to control emotions

If a person seeks help around the goal of controlling emotions, it may be valuable to consider the use of cognitive behavioural therapy (CBT) techniques. Cognitive behavioural therapy encompasses a range of methods that have been designed for, or can be adapted to, the task of emotional self-control. Some of the CBT techniques that can be applied in this situation include the following:

- Keeping a diary of when and how 'emotion events' occur – with the aim of identifying what triggers them off and what seems to prevent them.
- Exploring an emotional event in detail and working backwards step by step through the sequence of events that preceded it. This can then lead to working together to find ways of interrupting the emotion-inducing sequence (for example, by saying to oneself to 'keep calm', or by thinking about a pleasant image).
- Finding alternatives to the emotion. For example: 'if you did not get angry/burst into tears/freeze with fear, what else could you do?').
- Learning relaxation skills. In many situations, being able to move into a previously learned relaxation or breathing routine can give the person a few moments to

pause and reflect on their choices (for example, whether to express the troublesome emotion or do something else).

- Identifying the thoughts and processes of 'self-talk' that trigger emotions. For example, someone may make themself angry because they tell themself that other people are looking down on them – this is an irrational or dysfunctional thought that can be challenged by the counsellor.

The particular usefulness of CBT techniques lies in its applicability in working both with people who do not want particularly to understand their emotion, but are interested just in controlling it, and with people who prefer a more structured, rather than exploratory, approach to counselling. People who are scared or embarrassed about expressing their feelings in the presence of the counsellor may also prefer a CBT approach, which on the whole does not require any kind 'here-and-now' emotional expression. There are many self-help books and websites that provide CBT-based information on how to control emotions. The movie *Anger Management*, starring Jack Nicholson and Adam Sandler, depicts, in a somewhat extreme way, how some of these techniques can work in practice.

Expressive arts as tools for working with feelings and emotions

Emotion issues often centre around the fact that feelings and emotions are processes that take place in a reality that is largely outside of the verbal. Once emotion-oriented counselling gets to the stage where the person can talk about their feelings, either most of the work has been done (or the person has switched into intellectualizing about their feelings, and the opportunity has been lost). The expressive arts comprise a mode of engaging with emotional experience that can powerfully tap into non-verbal ways of knowing and communicating. For example, the availability of a lump of plasticine or similar material can give a person an opportunity to allow their hands to express their feelings in the moulding of a shape. The availability of paper and crayons can allow image and colour to be utilized. These arts tools are readily accessible and are non-threatening to most people who are seeking counselling. In some situations, more complex forms of expressive activity, such as drama or dance, may also be possibilities.

Cultural resources

The task of working on feelings and emotions may take place solely within a counselling session or may include activities that the person decides to pursue elsewhere within their life space. The direct work of the counsellor, in relation to feeling and emotion, can therefore in some cases be restricted to planning and rehearsing where and how the person might feel safe to express strong emotion. There exists a broad range of cultural resources and settings that can be facilitative for someone struggling to resolve an emotional issue. As mentioned earlier, letter-writing can represent a powerful means of channelling feelings. Other forms of writing, such as poetry, can also be used. Other people may opt to express rage and anger by shouting at a football match, or in the privacy of their car, or allow tears to come by visiting a graveside or spending some time looking at photographs of loved ones. A hugely valuable source of emotional healing for many people is music – listening to, or playing, a piece that evokes a certain emotional state may allow a person to stay with that state long enough for its personal meaning and significance to emerge and be worked through. Films, which can be purchased or borrowed on video or DVD, can allow a person seeking to come to terms with an emotional issue to enter imaginatively into the world of a character who is also experiencing such an issue, and vicariously to participate in the process of resolution as experienced by that character. Novels can supply a similar sort of learning – the key here is not to suggest to the person seeking help that they should copy the way that a character in a film or novel has dealt with their emotional difficulties, but that the story can represent one *possible* way of coping. For people who are stuck in an emotional impasse, the idea that there are different possibilities can be liberating. Another important cultural resource is self-help and self-improvement books, for instance around such themes as coping with grief, being more assertive and willing to express anger, or dealing with fear.

Box 9.3   Cultural differences in emotional expressiveness

In a study by Kamer Shoaib and Jennifer Peel (2003), 45 Kashmiri women living in Oldham, England, were interviewed about their views of counselling. Some of these women were users of counselling or mental health services, whereas other were not. Interviews were conducted in the language preferred by the participant. One of the main themes to emerge from this study was the difficulty that many of these women had in translating statements about their emotional life into English. Some Kashmiri emotional terms did not have any meaningful English-language equivalent. The authors noted that 'many poignant phrases for emotions made use of the head and the heart, for example ... "emptying the heart", "in my head the weight will lighten" and "my heart's pain will reduce" ' (p. 92). These findings confirm the results of other studies of emotional expressiveness in members of Asian and other non-western cultural groups. In these cultures and languages, emotions are not denoted by psycho- logical terms such as 'anger' or 'anxiety', but tend largely to be indicated by reference to parts of the body such as the head, heart and stomach. Moreover, some forms of feeling appear to be culture specific and may be extremely difficult to understand or appreciate from a different cultural standpoint. The result of these differences in emotional expressiveness has meant that, within healthcare systems dominated by practitioners from majority western cultural groups, minority clients have often been offered interventions that are not appropriate. When working with a person from another cultural group, it is therefore important for a counsellor to be curious and open in relation to how feelings and emotions are described. These are also opportunities to learn new ways of thinking about feelings. After all, 'emptying the heart' is a phrase that, as Shoaib and Peel (2003) suggest, is indeed poignant, and which for many people who are not Kashmiri may capture a vital truth about the experience of sadness and loss.

Using silence

The end point of a 'working with emotion' task will normally be when the person decides to stop. This may occur when there are no more feelings to come out or when the person has done as much as they can on that occasion. Following an 'emotion event', it is probable that a person will view the world in a different light and have some new insight into their problem. However, they may not want to talk much at that moment. If counselling is taking place in a situation where a series of meetings is possible, it is usually better that any kind of extended reflection around the meaning of any emotions and feelings should be saved by the counsellor for another day: forcing reflection and analysis could interfere with the emotional learning that has taken place.

Making use of supervision

It is important to be aware that a counsellor working in this territory is likely to be affected by the expression of strong emotions and painful feelings. Human beings have a capacity to 'resonate' to the feeling states of others. A counsellor who is accompanying a person in a counselling task that involves an opening up of emotion is inevitably affected by this process and needs to be ready to deal with it through such means as doing their own 'talking it through' by consulting colleagues or a supervisor. It can be particularly useful for the supervisor to be sensitive to the feelings that a counsellor expresses when describing their work with a client. Often, the feelings that the counsellor brings into a supervision consultation can be understood as the client's emotions that they are 'carrying' or have 'picked up'. It may need another person, such as a colleague or supervisor, to point this out, to enable the counsellor to become aware of what has happened.

For those whose counselling is embedded in another professional role, working with a person around emotion-focused goals and tasks may be the hardest aspect of their counselling role. This is because most professional roles, such as that of teacher, nurse or social worker, require the performance of rationality and control, whatever the circumstances. Much professional training involves socialization into subtle (or not so subtle) methods of 'cooling out' clients or colleagues who might be becoming too 'heated' that are characteristic of life in large bureaucratic organizations (Hochschild, 1983; Fineman, 1993). The emphasis in counselling, of being willing to move into the 'danger zone' of emotion and trouble, can represent one of the most challenging areas of interface between the values and practices of counselling and those that exist within day-to-day organizational life. Supervision and consultation are invaluable as ways of resolving the issues that arise around this interface.

Conclusions

Difficulties with emotions lie behind many, or even all, of the main categories of psychological problems for which a person might seek help from a counsellor or psychotherapist. Depression can be understood as a sadness/anger problem. Anxiety is about fear. Relationship problems stem from anger. Low self-esteem can be understood as feeling ashamed to share what you really feel. Being willing and able to move beyond vague diagnostic categories such as depression or anxiety, and get closer to what is really bothering a person, is a major counselling competence. Working with emotions can be likened to stepping out of 'talking about' problems in living, and stepping into the danger zone where these problems are actually *felt*. This step also takes the person and the counsellor closer to the lived reality of the person's life space or personal niche. This is because emotions are always, ultimately, linked to people, events and objects within that niche. Being sensitive to the person's feelings and emotions allows the counsellor to get beyond general statements such as 'I feel anxious a lot of the time', to more specific statements such as 'I am afraid of my boss, he is a bully'. It is through talking about these specifics that the person and the counsellor can find some leverage in relation to ways of changing what is happening.

It is possible to see that there are many strategies that can be employed in counselling situations in order to help a person who is experiencing difficulty around acknowledging or expressing feelings and emotions. When the task faced by the person seeking help is that of expressing and exploring emotions, the skill of counselling lies in being willing to talk, to create a space in which feelings and emotions can be allowed a voice in the conversation: the range of methods described in this chapter are merely ways of facilitating such a conversation. As always, the potential impact of any method depends on the strength of the relationship between the counsellor and the person seeking help.

Questions for reflection and discussion

1. How comfortable are you with the expression of emotions? Are there emotions around which you feel relatively comfortable, and other emotions that are hard for you to express or hear? What are the implications of your personal emotional profile for your work as a counsellor?
2. What is the emotional profile of your workplace? Which emotions are allowed, and in what circumstances? Which emotions are suppressed? What happens to people who express taboo emotions in your office or clinic? What are the implications of your organizational emotion profile for you as a practitioner, and for the people who use your service?
3. Over the course of a convenient period of time (an hour, a day), keep a note of the emotion and feeling terms that people use in their conversations with you (and you use in your conversations with them). Are there any patterns that you can identify? For example, do people from different ethnic groups seem to talk in different ways about

feelings? What has been the effect on you and your interactions with others, of specifically listening for emotions?

4. One of the important psychological theories of emotion, touched on at various points throughout this chapter, is that individual people tend to have emotions in which they 'specialize' and feel or express a great deal, but that these 'preferred' or familiar emotions conceal deeper emotions that may be experienced as shameful or threatening. To what extent would you say that this theory holds true for you personally, or for other people that you know well? If this theory is valid, what are its implications for your work with people who seek counsel from you?

Suggestions for further reading

One of the key issues in emotion work, for counsellors as well as for people seeking help, is to develop an understanding and appreciation of the role of feeling and emotion in everyday life. We live in world that values rationality and control, and many people need to be persuaded that taking their emotions seriously, as a source of information about values, preferences and life choices, is a worthwhile thing to do. The series of books on emotional intelligence by Daniel Goleman and his colleagues has helped many people to recognize the importance of emotions. A useful text to start with is:

Goleman, D. (2005) *Emotional Intelligence*. New York: Bantam Books.

An approach to making sense of emotion that is more explicitly grounded in research can be found in the work of the psychologist Keith Oatley:

Oatley, K. and Jenkins, J. M. (1996) *Understanding Emotions*. Oxford: Blackwell.

Many counsellors have found that the focusing approach of Eugene Gendlin supplies them with a practical, flexible starting point for responding to different kinds of emotional dilemmas. The basic book on this approach is:

Gendlin, E. T. (2003) *Focusing: How to Open up your Deeper Feelings and Intuition*. New York: Rider.

The work of Les Greenberg represents an invaluable source of insight into the role of emotions in counselling. A key book is:

Greenberg, L. S. (2001) *Emotion-focused Therapy: Coaching Clients to Work through their Feelings*. Washington, DC: American Psychological Association.

10

Learning to do something different: working together to change behaviour

Introduction • Why behaviour change is hard to achieve • Doing something different: step-by-step tasks • Counselling methods for facilitating behaviour change • Personal contexts of change • A narrative perspective on behaviour change • Conclusions • Questions for reflection and discussion • Suggestions for further reading

'I've been thinking about what you said – about being alone and at the same time surrounded by people.'

'I know, that's a big thing for me.'

'I was wondering – do these people know how you feel about what's happening for you? Who have you told? Who have you *really* told?'

'Not any of them, not really. I see what you're getting at – how can they help if they don't know what I need. It's what you keep saying to me: "asking for what I want . . . taking care of myself . . . not being the strong man all the time". All that stuff.'

'Exactly. Would it be useful to take a few minutes to look at how you could start to tell them? For example, what's stopping you, and what you could do different?'

Introduction

It has been emphasized throughout this book that a counselling relationship is based on listening, following, being receptive, and giving the person a space in which they can begin to develop their own solutions to problems. It is essential to remember that 'just talking' can make a real difference to a person. Often, the primary counselling task that a person is seeking help to fulfil is simply that of *talking*, of putting feelings, concerns and hopes into words. However, there are other occasions within a counselling relationship when the person may have a very specific idea of what they want to work on, or work out, in terms of a habit or pattern of behaviour. This chapter focuses on the counselling goal of *behaviour change*. The topic of behaviour change includes a wide range of issues that people may present in counselling, encompassing quite specific, self-contained habits such as 'keeping my paperwork up to date', through more far-reaching behavioural patterns, such as weight loss or smoking cessation, changes in interpersonal relating ('how do I stop getting into arguments with my co-workers?'), and changes that embrace many aspects of a person's life ('how do I live now that my spouse has died?'). We live in a society in which the pace of change appears to be ever-increasing. Indeed, the rise of psychology as a discipline within the twentieth century can be viewed as a cultural response to the need of ordinary people to get a handle on the challenge of how to change and adapt in the face of new work patterns and social norms. As a result, the counselling and psychotherapy literature contains a proliferation of ideas about how to facilitate change. Some of these ideas are presented in this chapter. Emphasis is placed on the importance of breaking the change process into a series of achievable tasks designed to progress towards the ultimate goal. However, first, we consider the key question: why is it so difficult to change behaviour?

Why behaviour change is hard to achieve

One of the major differences between counselling, understood as a skilled and intentional activity, and the type of everyday help giving that takes place between people who are friends or family members, lies in the way that behaviour change is understood. From a common-sense perspective, if someone has a problem, then the obvious response is to suggest or advise that the person should do something different. This advice is often backed up by personal experience of the type 'when that happened to me, what I did was . . .'. From a counselling perspective, hoping to achieve anything useful with this kind of advice is usually futile, the reason being that, for most people, changing a pattern of behaviour that has perhaps been established over several years is a difficult thing to achieve. While simple advice on behaviour change may indicate that the listener cares enough to try to find a solution to the complainant's problem, and is doing their best to help, it will rarely lead to any significant or sustained shift in what the person actually does. But why is behaviour change so hard?

There are at least three reasons why changing behaviour is difficult. First, a person's behaviour tends to develop in balance with their social environment. In other words, the significant people in an individual's life have come to expect that the person will behave in certain ways, and the subtle 'reward system' that takes place in interactions between people (in the form of approval, affirmation and avoidance of criticism) consistently maintains or reinforces established patterns of behaviour. Our behaviour is shaped to a large extent by the situation that we are in, and self-initiated change (such as one person saying to another, 'I wish I could take more exercise') will normally run against the grain of situational forces, such as the cost, time and effort of joining a fitness club.

The second reason why it is hard to respond effectively to a request for help with behaviour change is that *if it was easy for them to change, they would have done it already*. For example, on the whole, people do not feel that it is necessary to talk through with anyone their desire to change the kind of soap they use. That is because it is easy to choose another brand of soap, try it out and decide whether you like it. A student asking for help to change their study skills behaviour, by contrast, is a markedly different scenario. Here, the person seeking help would be motivated by a fear of failure (or actual failure) and would usually have tried out various approaches to setting up a study regime, but without success. Asking for counselling help from a professional, around a behaviour change issue, is therefore normally preceded by a history of unsuccessful attempts to change – the person has already tried all the obvious solutions.

A third reason why behaviour change is difficult is that the person may well have a personal investment in staying the way they are. No matter how much a person may protest that they really want to change, there will be some part of their sense of who they are that identifies with their present pattern of behaviour. Doing something radically different can be frightening – it is a step into the unknown. So, no matter how much a student may want to become better organized and achieve good grades, if they have a sense of themselves as 'someone who just passes and is one of the crowd', then attaining A grades and being noticed by tutors may be quite threatening.

Box 10.1   The limited value of making helpful suggestions as a means of enabling behaviour change

Transactional Analysis (TA) theory includes an elegant analysis of the limitations of advice giving as a strategy for facilitating behaviour change. Berne (1964) suggested that it made sense to regard sequences of apparently self-defeating interactions between people as psychological 'games'. Within his model, a game is a series of interactions between two or more people that leads to a well-defined, predictable outcome in the form of an experience of frustration or some other negative emotion. Berne regarded games as a substitute for genuine relating between individuals. He believed that, although people often are afraid to engage in honest and intimate interaction with others, we all nevertheless have a basic need for social contact, and a game provides a structure for such contact without running the risk of too much closeness. In his book

Games People Play, Berne identifies a large number of psychological games, ranging from all-encompassing long-term life games ('Alcoholic', 'Now I've Got You, You Son of a Bitch'), to more benign or briefer interaction sequences such as 'Ain't It Awful'. One of the games that can occur frequently in counselling situations is 'Why Don't You – Yes But' (YDYB). In this came, a person asks for help or advice, and the other players make suggestions. For example:

Person: My life is so stressful, I feel tired all the time and my social life is suffering. What can I do?

Counsellor: Why don't you keep a diary and look at how you could cut down on your work commitments?

Person: I've tried that – there's nothing I can change.

Counsellor: So what about looking for another job?

Person: I can't afford to take a drop in salary, so that's not realistic.

Counsellor: What about trying some relaxation tapes or meditation?

Person: I've tried them too – finding the time to do them just makes me more stressed . . .

This kind of interaction is clearly futile as a piece of counselling. But what makes this kind of suggestion giving so hopeless? Using the ego states described in TA theory, Berne argues that the apparently rational, Adult-to Adult request made by the person seeking help in fact conceals a different kind of transaction – between a needy Child and someone (the counsellor) who is unwittingly pushed into the position of all-knowing Parent. The pay-off for the person initiating the game is that the helper will always prove to be inadequate (none of their suggestions will be worth following up), which then leaves the instigator reinforced in a basic sense of being someone who cannot be helped. In other words, the game allows the person to maintain a superficial contact with another person without being called upon to explore what is really true for them – in this case a deep feeling of hopelessness and despair about their life.

It can be seen that, in this case, almost any kind of counselling response – empathic reflection, open and curious questioning, encouragement to say more – would be more useful than giving suggestions. It does not matter how sensible and valid the suggestions might be, because they have not arisen out of a shared process of problem solving based on mutual understanding, they will almost certainly be met with a polite and appreciative response of 'yes, but . . .'.

It should be emphasized that, although behaviour change is an important goal for many people who seek counselling, it is a mistake to assume that change is necessarily what someone wants from this kind of help. As well as change, the goals of counselling include acceptance, understanding and meaning making. Indeed, in many cases it is impossible to bring about change in the absence of these less tangible outcomes.

This chapter provides an overview of the tasks and methods that are associated with the crucial counselling goal of helping someone to change a troubling or self-defeating pattern of behaviour. The aim of the chapter is to provide tools and strategies that make it possible to move beyond just contemplating change, and arrive at the point where actually doing something different can become a reality. The ideas in this chapter are grounded in a recognition that change is always difficult, and that people require an approach that is sensitive to their own individual ideas and experiences of what has worked for them in the past, and what will be helpful now. There are different pathways of change that work best for different people. A good counsellor is always responsive to the preferences of the person seeking help and willing to be flexible. The chapter, like the rest of the book, takes the position that it is the quality of the relationship between the helper and person seeking help that is most important. Changing anything significant about the way that one responds to the world can be viewed as embarking on a painful and arduous journey, which is eased by the presence of another person who is willing to be a companion and guide.

The next section of the chapter discusses some of the key step-by-step-tasks associated with behaviour change: making sense of the problematic behaviour, working out how the problematic behaviour fits into the person's life as it is, imagining how things could be different, and issues of readiness, support, implementation of change and avoiding relapse. In embedded counselling, it is unlikely that the counsellor will have opportunity to work through all of these tasks with the person seeking help, because to do so would take a long time. However, it is well within the scope of embedded counselling to assist a person with specific tasks, appropriate to where they have reached in their quest to 'do something different'. This is followed in the subsequent section by an exploration of three of the most widely used change strategies employed by counsellors: dissolving the problem (by understanding it), setting targets and implementing a behaviour change programme, and finally identifying and utilizing personal strengths and resources. The chapter then turns to examine *personal contexts of change* (frequently encountered life situations that produce pressure for change). The contexts discussed are: dealing with difficult relationships, decision making, undoing self-criticism and enhancing self-care, and negotiating life transitions such as bereavement. The chapter closes with a brief reflection on narrative perspectives on behaviour change.

Doing something different: step-by-step tasks

Looking at the process of behaviour change as a journey serves as a reminder that this activity necessarily consists of several steps. An essential weakness of advice giving is that it offers the person seeking a help a one-step solution. In effect, advice is saying to a person 'just do this one thing and you will be all right'. A counselling approach, by contrast, is based in an appreciation of the complexity of change. Competence as a counsellor involves recognizing that the goal of behaviour change can only be achieved through the completion of a number of sub-tasks. One implication of this perspective is that it makes it possible to see more clearly the contribution that can be made by microcounselling conversations, where counselling is embedded in another practitioner role and time may be short. Sometimes, a practitioner counsellor may not be able to see a behaviour change goal through to completion, but may nevertheless be able to assist the person to fulfil one or more tasks that are necessary elements of the whole sequence. Because behaviour change is often difficult, a person may choose to tackle it by attempting one step or task at a time.

Example

The necessity of tackling behaviour change in a step-by-step manner is illustrated in the experience of Donald, who had suffered heart failure. He had been told that his future survival depended on his ability radically to alter his lifestyle by cutting out smoking, alcohol and fatty foods, and introducing a diet regime. In hospital, Donald received health advice from the nurses, physiotherapist and nutritionist attached to his ward, and seemed highly motivated to put his new programme into action. However, on his first check-up with his GP, it became apparent that he was not keeping to the recommended diet and exercise schedule. He agreed to have brief fortnightly meetings with the practice nurse, to support him in bringing about these vital changes to his behaviour. The nurse asked him to keep a food and exercise diary, which they discussed at each visit. However, she also checked out the barriers to change in Donald's life. It emerged that he saw himself as an 'action man' who 'worked hard and played hard'. Asked what this meant in practice, he admitted that it meant working long hours at the office, and drinking on Friday and Saturday with his friends at the pub. The nurse invited Donald to talk about how he felt about this. He spoke of being 'trapped' between two sides of himself – the side that wanted to stay healthy, and the side that thought he 'could survive anything'. The nurse also asked him how his friends would react if he stopped drinking and smoking. He replied: 'Well, they would give me a hard time, but in the end they would accept it – one of the others went through something similar – he gets called "the driver" now.' They then discussed how he could overcome these barriers, and the nurse made a point of asking him about these issues at every subsequent appointment. Only then were they able to move to the difficult and demanding tasks of changing Donald's diet – giving up foods he liked and, through trial and error, replacing them with foods that were good for him – and gradually building up his exercise regime. It took him six months. At a later consultation, his GP congratulated him on his progress and asked him what had made the difference. He replied: 'It was the nurse, I couldn't let her down.'

Just as in the case of Donald, meaningful behaviour change is hard work – there is no magic wand that can be waved that will instantly make everything different. The counselling tasks that are described in the following sections represent a number of ways of breaking down an overall goal of behaviour change into a set of sub-tasks. In effect, all of these sub-tasks can be seen as ways of slowing down the process of behaviour change, so that the person ends up with an approach to their problem that takes into account as many factors as possible, rather than consisting of the kind head-long rush to 'do something different' that often leads to disappointment and a sense of defeat. Although the tasks described below are in a logical order, starting with those that address barriers to change, then moving to implementing and finally maintaining change, it is not helpful to assume that a person will work through them in a logical sequence. Some people will only want help with one or two of the tasks – they will be well able to do the rest themselves. Other people will shuttle back and forth between tasks as they slowly find their own way forward.

Making sense of problematic behaviour: identifying underlying personal conflict

One of the key tasks associated with behaviour change is to make sense of what it is in the person's life that is motivating them to want to change. The desire to change behaviour will usually begin with a person's felt dissatisfaction with they way that they are esponding to a current situation. Some examples of counselling conversations that may suggest the need to make sense of problematic behaviour are:

> 'Why do I let him treat me like a doormat? How can I become more assertive?' (Woman speaking to a worker at a domestic abuse project)

> 'I don't seem to be able to organize myself. Every time my caseload increases, my filing system collapses. If only I could manage my time better.' (Social worker during a meeting of a peer support group)

> 'No matter how much I tell myself it's stupid, and no matter how much I want to stop, every time I see a sharp object, I immediately start to think about how I could use it to cut myself. I just wish I could stop doing that – one day it will go too far.' (Prison inmate talking to a member of a suicide and self-harm helpline)

> 'I fly off the handle with my son whenever we talk about the business and where it is going. What on earth makes me do that? I can't control my anger.' (Owner of a family manufacturing company during a meeting with a business consultant)

Making sense of a puzzling personal reaction to a situation is a counselling task that is generally marked by a self-questioning statement along the lines of 'why am I doing this, and how can I do something different?' It is often enough for the practitioner counsellor to reply to such a statement by saying something along the lines of, 'is this something we could look at together?' or 'do you think it might be helpful to take a few minutes to talk about that a bit more?'

In a counselling situation of this type, where the ultimate goal is to be able to act in a different way in a particular situation, the person will usually express two different, yet linked, tasks. On the one hand, the person is puzzled about why it is they are engaging in behaviour that they do not like. On the other hand, the person wishes to change their response and acquire a different behavioural pattern. Normally, a wish to make sense is a precursor to taking action and indicates that the person is not quite ready to change their behaviour: they want first to understand why it is they are acting as they are.

A further consideration that is worth bearing in mind when counselling around the task of *making sense of a problematic reaction* is that the issue that the person is describing is essentially one that is based on a *self-split*. In effect, the person is saying that part of them does something, while another part of them is critical of that activity. This duality or tension in the person's experience of self is central to understanding the problem. It is as if the person is arguing with themselves. If the task of *making sense* is to be successfully completed, it will at some stage be necessary to invite the person to consider the issue in these terms. It is therefore helpful if, from the outset, the counsellor is on the alert for clues concerning the nature of this underlying conflict. If the person is intending to move on to engage in the further task of changing their behaviour, it will undermine their ability to achieve change if, in effect, they are still arguing with themself.

There are various methods that a counsellor can employ when working with a person on the task of making sense of a problematic experience, such as 'just talking', drawing a map or diagram of what happened, or acting out the key event. However, Greenberg *et al.* (1993) suggest that what seems to work best is to invite the person to talk about their puzzling or problematic reaction in a way that highlights what actually happened on one specific occasion, including the feelings and emotions that are associated with that event. This approach consists of two stages. First, by telling the story of a specific event in detail, from an 'I' position ('I did this, and felt that . . .'), the person is drawn into re-experiencing what happened, on a moment-by-moment basis. This way of talking yields a rich description of how the person thought and felt at each point, and highlights the intentions of the person, making it possible to identify the competing intentions that were in play ('I wanted to run away, but at the same time I was telling myself that I needed to face up to the challenge'). The second stage of the task involves making sense of the event in terms of the conflict between these competing intentions, or parts of the self, and finding a way of making a bridge between them, so that these different and contrasting impulses or beliefs can work together and be in dialogue, rather than in conflict.

Example

The unfolding of this way of tackling a *making sense of problematic experience* task can be seen in the relationship between Melissa, a business consultant, and Kamaljit, a businessman who was seeking advice around the process of transferring control of his manufacturing company to his son Kenny. During a point in the consultation where Melissa and Kamaljit were reviewing the timetable they have agreed for the handover, Kamaljit mentioned that he was worried about some of his recent tendency to 'fly off the handle' with his son over 'really trivial incidents'. He stated that: 'I just cannot understand what is happening. We have been working together perfectly well. He knows more about the business than I do. Why have I suddenly started to lose my temper like this? Do you think that I should go on one of these anger management courses?' Melissa wondered whether this statement might be a marker for an underlying issue that could be crucial to the successful management of the business plan and decided that it might be useful to spend some time exploring the topic in more depth. She asked Kamaljit whether he thought that it might be worth spending a few minutes looking at these occasions where 'your temper enters the equation', with the aim of 'maybe getting to the bottom of what is happening here'. He agreed. Melissa then invited him to select one incident where he had flown off the handle, and to describe to her in detail what had happened, as if it was happening in the moment. With some difficulty, and frequent prompting to remain 'in the moment', he began to re-enter his experience of an angry moment a few days previously:

Kamaljit: I am sitting at my desk. Kenny comes in with a copy of a contract he has been working on with a new supplier, for me to sign. I read through it. Just a few pages. It's fine. I look up. He is checking his email on his mobile phone screen. I get really angry with him and tell him that he should pay more attention, and that this is no way to behave in a business meeting.

Melissa: How did he react to that?

Mamaljit: He apologized and put the phone away.

Melissa: I'm wondering what was happening for you at that moment you got angry? What were you thinking and feeling?

Kamaljit: Oh, the usual. I don't matter any more. They don't need me.

Melissa then invited Kamaljit to explore the meaning, for him, of the sense that 'they don't need me' at this stage of his life. Quite quickly, he was able to identify ways in which he continued to be needed, and might be needed more in his post-retirement future, as well as aspects of his work role that were being lost. By expressing both sides of this tension within his sense of his own core self or identity ('I am someone of value, who looks after everyone in the family' versus 'I am over the hill and they don't need me'), he arrived at a more balanced under-standing that helped him to make sense not only of these specific incidents with his son, but also more broadly of his feelings about the changes that were taking place in his life as a whole.

In this example, Melissa possessed sufficient counselling skill to be aware that Kamaljit's mention of flying off the handle with his son might be a marker for an aspect of his life that would repay further exploration. The manner in which Kamaljit referred to the events that had taken place with his son conveyed that these occurrences were puzzling for him, in being out of character (that is, not the result of a general behaviour pattern or trait) and inappropriate (not a rational response to the immediate situation). The events were therefore difficult to reconcile or integrate with his usual story of who he was, and how his life was lived. The implication was that his response to his son meant something significant, and that this meaning would be worth knowing about. In her response to Kamaljit, Melissa needed to check out that he acknowledged that his reaction to his son was problematic, and that he was willing to look at it further with her, at that moment. After all, he may not have felt safe enough with Melissa to allow their conversation to go down that path. When he confirmed that he wished to look at the matter further, she made a tentative suggestion concerning a *method* by which he might do this (by telling the story, in detail, of an incidence of the problematic response).

The end point of effective completion of this particular counselling task occurs when the person arrives at a new or enriched appreciation of what it was about them that made the situation such a problem. In the case of Kamaljit, by understanding the factors behind his problematic anger reaction, he was able to change without difficulty the way he responded to his son – simply by reminding himself, and inviting his son to remind him, of the meaning that these situations held for him. If he had attempted to develop ways of managing and controlling his anger (that is, moved straight into planning behavioural changes), in the absence of this stage of making sense of his problematic actions, he would probably have continued to suppress his painful feelings of 'not being useful and more'. The chances are, in such a scenario, that the part of him that did feel hurt and unheard would have undermined his efforts to change, with the result that any anger management programme would have been ineffective.

How does the problematic behaviour fit into your life as it is?

Another approach to helping a person to make sense of a pattern of behaviour that they wish to change is to invite them to suspend their opposition to the problem and to reflect instead on what the presence of the problem does for them. The underlying assumption here is that anything a person does must have a function in their life. In order to pursue such a conversation, it can be helpful to employ the language of *externalization* of problems, introduced in Chapter 8. For instance, to return to the case of Kamaljit, it might be useful to ask him about when the anger visits him, and how it influences his life and his relationships with others. He might reply that the effect of the anger is to 'keep Kenny in his place' and to 'delay the time when Kenny takes over the company'. Another way of talking about this kind of process is to invite the person to think about what the problem does for them or what the pay-offs are for them, of having had this problem over a period of time. It would be unusual for anyone consciously to develop a problematic pattern of behaviour as a means of achieving a payoff or reward, and a person seeking help would most likely reject any such suggestion. It is therefore important to engage in this kind of conversation with sensitivity. The idea is not to interrogate the person, in an accusatory fashion, but to gently open up a topic for reflection and consideration.

There are several reasons why this counselling task can represent an important step in successful behaviour change. First, it allows the person to begin to map out what they may *lose* by changing how they act in some situations. This can be a catalyst for starting to think about how these needs might be taken care of in alternative ways. Second, if the person can look closely and honestly at what their problem does for them, they may well come across some surprises – pay-offs that they had not previously thought about. Such discoveries can be helpful in promoting hope, since the person may be enthused by the idea that they are now doing something different rather than merely repeating what happened during previous attempts to change. Finally, the question 'how does the problem influence you?' prepares the ground for the reverse question, 'how do you influence the problem?' This line of conversation, which is discussed more fully later in this chapter, brings into focus the active capacity of the person to do different things in certain situations, rather than being always dominated by 'the problem', and can represent a fertile means of enabling the person to accept that they may, indeed, have the power within them to do something different.

Imagining how things could be different

When a person is seeking help to change their behaviour, an important counselling task centres on the exploration of what it is that the person actually wants to achieve. At the moment of seeking help, the person may be so burdened by the existence of a troublesome pattern of behaviour that all they can think about is getting rid of it. Their approach to change is dominated by a sense of what they do *not* want to do – *not* eat as much, *not* be a doormat, *not* get angry. Any behaviour change plan based on 'not doing' is doomed to failure because the only way that real change will happen is if the person is able to replace the unwanted behaviour with a new pattern of behaviour. The trick, in the end, is always to acquire, practise and master the new behaviour, rather than just suppress the old pattern. It may be useful to think in terms of training for a sport. If a person is trying to become better at playing tennis, they may go through a phase of being dominated by what *not* to do – don't hit the ball into the net, don't hit it beyond the baseline and so on. This kind of learning strategy tends to have limited success. Someone can only become a competent tennis player by having a positive image of what it is they want to achieve. This positive image can come from watching a top tennis player or, even better, through coaching that gives the person a feel for what it is like to hit a good shot. The key is that the person gains a vision of what it is they are striving for and can assess their performance against that ultimate end point thereby making adjustments to what they do in order to get closer to the ideal. All effective sports coaching involves this kind of *cognitive rehearsal* of good performance.

In a counselling context, therefore, if a person has identified a goal of changing their behaviour in some way, it is useful to listen for an opportunity to invite the person to talk about what it is that they actually want. This task can be entered by questions such as 'how would you like it to be?' or 'what would your life be like (or what would you be doing differently) if you changed this pattern of behaviour?' The Skilled Helper counselling skills model developed by Gerard Egan (2004) includes a valuable analysis of the process of working with the person to identify their 'desired scenario'. The solution-focused approach to therapy (see O'Connell, 1998) employs the 'miracle question' for this purpose. The client is asked to imagine that a miracle has taken place overnight, and their problem has been completely eradicated. They are then invited to describe what their life is like. (Before using the miracle question, it is important to study or, even better, receive training in how it is used by solution-focused therapists – it is a powerful method, but needs to be applied at the right time and in the right way, otherwise the client may become confused about what is being suggested.) Other ways of enabling the person to identify their preferred behaviour are to ask if there are any individuals whom they would take as models or whether there have been times in their life when they exhibited the behaviour that they are now seeking to acquire (or re-acquire).

There are several ways in which holding a conversation about the detailed specification of a new or amended pattern of behaviour can be helpful. It allows the person to be clear about what they are trying to achieve, and at the same time to share this vision with their counsellor. Usually, it leads to a detailed description of the preferred behaviour, in place of a general or global description, which outlines specific small changes that can be accomplished one at a time. It can instil hope in, and be motivating for, a person to disclose to someone what it is that they really want, and to have this desire taken seriously. Finally, this kind of conversation opens up the possibility of using imagination in a creative and positive way. Rather than imagining terrible things that may happen ('I will be stuck like this for ever'), the person can playfully imagine good outcomes and a better life.

Are you ready?

A great deal of research and clinical experience in counselling and psychotherapy has shown that the issue of *readiness to change* represents a key factor in any work around behavioural change. The exploration of the person's views around their readiness to do things differently is therefore an important counselling task. Many practitioners have found it useful to employ the *stages of change* model developed by James Prochaska and

Carlo DiClemente (2005). From their experience in working in a health arena in which many patients were resistant to changing illness-promoting behaviours, such as smoking and drinking alcohol, these psychologists developed the idea that there are major differences between people in relation to their readiness to change. They formulated a five-stage model of the change process to account for these differences. Their model is known as the 'transtheoretical' approach because it intentionally integrates ideas from various schools of therapy into an overarching framework. The stages of change observed by Prochaska and DiClemente are:

1. *Precontemplation.* The person has no immediate intention to make changes in relation to the behaviour that is problematic. For example, someone who is a heavy smoker may be aware that their behaviour is a health risk, but is not yet willing to face up to the possibility of quitting.
2. *Contemplation.* At this stage, the person has decided to change their behaviour, but at some point in the future, for example at some point within the next six months.
3. *Preparation.* The person has taken some initial steps in the direction of behaviour change. For example, a person seeking to stop smoking may have collected information about the availability of cessation clinics, nicotine patches and so forth.
4. *Action.* The person has changed their problematic behaviour for less than six months, and is still in a position of consolidating their new patterns of behaviour and avoiding temptation.
5. *Maintenance.* The person is avoiding relapse, or coping with episodes of relapse, over a longer period of time.

As further time elapses, and the problematic behaviour or habit is defeated, the person can be viewed as entering a *termination* stage – the problem is no longer relevant to them, and they do not need to give it any attention.

The value of the stages of change model, in relation to working together to do something different, is that it suggests that quite different counselling tasks may be required at different stages of the change process. For example, the tasks for the person at the precontemplation phase may include raising awareness by collecting information, and validating and accepting the person's point of view and state of readiness (rather than establishing a critical or coercive relationship). The tasks at the contemplation stage may include decision making, and exploring the meaning of the person's ambivalence.

Example

David is a retired engineer who is a volunteer member of a Circle of Support and Accountability, set up to enable the reintegration into society of high-risk sex offenders. For more than two years, David has been a member of a small group of volunteers, drawn from all walks of life, who have met on a weekly basis with Simon, a 30-year-old man who had received two jail sentences for sexual offences with young boys. David learned about the stages of change model during the training course he attended, and has found that it helped him to make sense of what he calls the 'learning curve' that has taken place between Simon and his team of supporters. 'At the start, it was very much a matter of talking about the consequences of what he was doing, and making sure that he knew that we would be using our contacts in the neighbourhood to check that he was meeting the conditions of his probation contract. As time went on, though, what we talked about started to shift quite dramatically. There were some really emotional times, when he was looking at himself really deeply. More recently, it has been mainly a matter of providing support for what he calls his "new life".'

Further information about the stages of change model, and its application in counselling, can be found in Prochaska and DiClemente (2005). These authors have also published a self-help guide based on the principles of the model (Prochaska *et al.*, 1994). For practitioners whose counselling is embedded in other work roles, the most useful aspect of the stages of change model probably lies in the ways in which it can be applied in understanding the difference between the point at which a person is actively committed to changing their behaviour, and the prior stages where they may be vaguely aware of a need to change but are not yet ready to commit themselves. There are many microcounselling situations in health and social care settings in which practitioners routinely work with people who are precontemplative – for example, in relation to smoking cessation, weight loss, domestic violence, and alcohol or drug abuse. Practitioners operating in these settings may find it helpful to consult the literature on *motivational interviewing* (Miller and Rollnick, 2002), which offers a set of strategies intended to facilitate/motivate the individual to move beyond precontemplation and contemplation, and to engage with the tasks associated with preparation for change and then action.

Do you have the right kind of support?

It is difficult to make significant behavioural changes on one's own, through planning and willpower. Lack of support from other people constitutes an important barrier to change and ensuring that adequate social support is available represents an important counselling task for many people seeking help around a behaviour change goal. The role of the counsellor can involve checking out with the person the amount of support that is available and how accessible it is. It may be valuable to rehearse or run through strategies for enlisting support. Part of this task may involve discussion about the ways in which the counsellor can offer support. In some counselling situations it may be possible to meet with key supporters, to explore their perceptions of how they can help. Support may come from individuals already within the person's social network, such as family, friends and work colleagues, or may encompass new people, such as members of self-help groups. Support may be dispersed over a number of people or be concentrated on one main 'ally'. Support may be provided face to face, by telephone or by email. If the person seeking help has difficulty in identifying potential supporters, it may be useful to invite them to think about 'who would be least surprised to hear about your success in changing this behaviour?' There is no special counselling method that is associated with the task of ensuring support – this is a task that relies on the person and the counsellor being willing to spend some time on it, and pooling their ideas.

Implementing changes

At the point when the person begins to make changes in their life, it is important that everything possible has been put in place to ensure success. It is usually a good idea for a counsellor to run through some typical situations that may occur, as a means of refining the person's strategy for change and also as a way of checking that the person's expectations are realistic (for example, that it is not a 'complete disaster' if it goes wrong the first time), including their plans for accessing support (to celebrate success, or to talk through what happened if they were not successful). It can be useful for the person and the counsellor to enact likely scenarios, or at least talk through them, as a form of rehearsal. It can also be valuable for the person to write down their plan or a checklist. This talk can be initiated by the counsellor with a question such as, 'would it be useful to go through what will happen tomorrow when you . . .?' It is important for the counsellor to keep the focus on concrete behaviour (what the person will actually do), rather than allowing the conversation to slide into statements of motivation, will and intention ('I'm really up for it this time', 'I know I'm ready').

Anticipating and preventing relapse

The *stages of change* model developed by Prochaska and DiClemente (2005), introduced earlier in this chapter, suggests that relapse is an almost inevitable consequence of most attempts to change behaviour – it is very difficult indeed to continue to do something different without ever slipping back into old ways. An essential counselling task, therefore, when a person is on the point of implementing change, is to consider the issue of relapse. It is usually helpful to explain the concept, and to be candid about the likelihood that some relapse will occur at some point. The questions that may need to be discussed include: How will you know if relapse has happened? What are the factors that might make you vulnerable to relapse? What will you do if you have a relapse? How will you use support at these times? What can you learn from a relapse episode about your change strategy? One of the biggest dangers associated with relapse is that the person will 'catastrophize' the situation, and jump to an extreme conclusion such as 'I'm no good' or 'it's a waste of time, this isn't going to work', and abandon all the good work that they have done up to that stage. The more that the counsellor has been able to introduce the idea that relapse is normal, routine, predictable and surmountable, the less likely it is that the person will jump to a catastrophic interpretation of what has happened. It is always important to keep in mind that a person engaging in behaviour change that they consider to be significant enough to merit the help of a counsellor, will in all probability be in a state of high emotional vulnerability when they begin to try out new ways of doing things and will as a result perceive a relapse as a major setback.

Planned follow-up sessions, where possible relapse incidents can be explored, can be a valuable source of support for the person if the counsellor is in a position to offer ongoing contact.

The aim of the preceding sections has been to introduce some of the tasks most frequently involved in counselling where behaviour change is a goal. The underlying theme is that of the counsellor building a relationship with the person that is characterized by a willingness to be close to them in every step of the behaviour change journey, and being curious and questioning about every aspect of the process. The next section looks at some well-established behaviour change methods.

Counselling methods for facilitating behaviour change

At the point when a person seeking help is clear that their goal is to change an aspect of their behaviour, and has identified at least some of the component tasks that are necessary to move towards that goal, it is helpful to invite the person to think about *how* they believe would be the best way, for them, to accomplish their objectives. There are four main strategies that have been used by counsellors to facilitate behaviour change: dissolving the barriers to change, planning and setting targets, activating resources, and setting up a project. These strategies are discussed in the following sections.

Exploring and dissolving barriers to change

One method of bringing about change that has been advocated by many counsellors and psychotherapists, is based on the idea that, if a person has enough insight and understanding in relation to whatever it is that is motivating or causing them to act in a dysfunctional manner, they will be free to behave in ways that are more life enhancing and productive. This approach is associated with long-established forms of counselling and psychotherapy, such as psychodynamic psychotherapy and person-centred counselling. The key idea is to focus not on the problem behaviour, but on the person who is engaging in that behaviour. For example, someone who abuses alcohol may have a history of emotional neglect and abuse, and may have low self-esteem. From this perspective, binge drinking may be viewed as almost emotionally and interpersonally necessary for the person as a means of assuaging emotional pain and living up to other people's views that they are 'no good'. In this approach, counselling that concentrates on programmes to encourage 'alternatives to drinking' is missing the point: it is the sense that the person has of who they are that needs to change. There is no doubt that this approach can be effective. However, it can take a long time and requires the establishment of a strong, ongoing relationship with a counsellor. It therefore may not be a realistic option in many embedded counselling settings where there may be a great deal of pressure on time and other professional tasks to fulfil. Nevertheless, in these settings, dissolving barriers to change may still be an important method in relation to sub-tasks (described earlier in this chapter) such as *making sense of problematic behaviour* and *imagining how things could be different*.

Cognitive behavioural methods: setting targets and implementing a programme

The behaviour change methodology that is believed by many specialist counsellors and psychotherapists to be maximally effective in facilitating behaviour change, and is backed up by a substantial amount of research, is *cognitive behavioural therapy* (CBT). Attractive features of this approach, for many practitioners and clients, are that it is business-like and down to earth. The key idea in CBT is to analyse the behavioural patterns of the person (the problem behaviour and the new preferred behaviour) in terms of an A-B-C formula: *antecedents, behaviour* and *consequences*. Anything that a person does on a regular basis is regarded as being elicited or triggered by a stimulus or situation (antecedent) and reinforced or rewarded by its consequences. This formula is the basis for a simple yet effective behaviour change method. The first step is to collect information, over a period of time, concerning the exact, detailed problem behaviour that is exhibited by the person, the situations in which this behaviour occurs, and the consequences that follow from it. The next step is to devise a programme in which the problem behaviour is gradually eliminated or extinguished, while at the same time the desired behaviour is gradually introduced. The third step is to ensure that the new behaviour is maintained in different situations over a period of time, rather than abandoned when the going gets tough.

The A-B-C formula encourages the person seeking help and their counsellor to devote their attention, initially, to two areas: antecedents and consequences. These are the crucial points of leverage in relation to the problem behaviour.

Example

Trudy was a school support worker who was called in to work with Andy and his family, on account of Andy's problem with school attendance. Trudy spent a long time listening to the family, asking them to describe exactly what it was that happened on school days, and showing a lively non-judgemental curiosity in everything that they had to say. At the end of this phase, she brought out a sheet of flipchart paper and some pens, and started to map out what she thought was going on, while inviting the family members to add details or make corrections. She made a list down the centre of the page of all the activities that Andy engaged in on a typical day when he did not go to school – his reason for not wanting to go, the argument with his parents, the parents going to work, Andy having the house to himself, watching TV and so on. In a different colour, she made a list on the left-hand side of the page, of the possible triggers for these events. For example, non-school days were more likely to happen when Andy had not done his homework, or there was a test, and unresolved arguments were more likely if both parents needed to be at work earlier than usual. On the right-hand side of the page, in a third colour, Trudy listed some of the consequences of Andy's behaviour – falling behind in his work and feeling panicky, enjoying daytime TV, being on the receiving end of sarcastic comments from teachers, assembling an impressive collection of music downloads, missing out on lunch and games with his friends, and so on. As she was doing this, all of the members of the family started to make connections, and imagine alternatives. For instance, a parent staying at home for two days would have the time to make sure that Andy did his homework in the evening, and to help him with it, as well as making staying at home seem less attractive for Andy, since he would not be able to watch TV and download music from the PC. It also became apparent how stressful, demanding and challenging some aspects of Andy's school life were, and how important it would be to make sure that he received regular rewards in recognition of his efforts. At the end of one meeting, all of the members of the family came away with new behaviours that they agreed to initiate, which were listed in a page pinned to the kitchen noticeboard. Trudy agreed to meet with them two weeks later, to check on their progress.

The CBT literature contains a wealth of ideas for behaviour change techniques, and workbooks that can be used by counsellors and clients in relation to specific behaviour change problems. However, at its heart, CBT is a common-sense approach that relies on the application of some simple, yet powerful, ideas, in a systematic manner. Like any other method, it works better when there is a good relationship between the person seeking help and the counsellor – notice how respectful and accepting Trudy was in a counselling situation where it would have been all too easy to be drawn into taking sides and to condemn Andy's 'laziness' or inadequacy.

Activating personal resources

A quite different method of working with a behaviour change task is to pay attention to occasions when the problem behaviour does *not* occur, rather than the occasions when it *does*, or episodes when the person has dealt with the problem behaviour successfully, rather than when they have failed to deal with it. The underlying assumption behind this strategy is to activate the person's existing resources and strengths, rather than focusing on their weaknesses. This general approach is associated with solution-focused therapy (O'Connell, 1998) and narrative therapy (Morgan, 2001). The key idea is that there will almost always be times when the person has been able to behave differently (narrative therapists describe such events as 'unique outcomes' or 'glittering moments'), and that the widespread human tendency to become preoccupied with problems will have obscured these achievements. The job of the counsellor, therefore, is to assist the person to identify the moments of success in relation to the problem behaviour, and then to build on the personal resources that are behind these 'glittering achievements'. This method can be difficult to implement if the person seeking help is so gripped by a sense of the total control exerted by the problem that they cannot (or will not) allow even the slightest possibility that good moments do occur. On the other hand, it has the potential to be highly energizing and liberating because (i) the solutions that are generated are wholly the product of the person, rather than being suggested or 'set up' by the counsellor, and (ii) it wholly ignores the failures and deficits of the person and celebrates their achievements.

Behaviour change as a project

A lot of the time, people struggle to change their behaviour because the things they are trying to alter have become ingrained habits that have, over a long period of time, become second nature – the person is hardly aware that they are doing the action that they wish to modify or eradicate. One of the ways of organizing the series of tasks that may need to be carried out for behaviour change is to regard the whole enterprise as a project. Viewing the change process as a project can help the person to distance themselves from an undermining sense of failure when their change efforts do not immediately work out for the best. Talking about the task as a project can also help the person and the counsellor to work together – each of them is making suggestions in relation to a shared endeavour. The image of a project also brings to mind the metaphor of building something new, which may involve dismantling previous structures, making plans, reviewing progress, celebrating achievements and so on. Using 'project' language can have the effect of externalizing the problem, and provide a channel for the person's creativity and imagination.

Box 10.2   The role of homework assignments in behaviour change

Having a really good discussion, within a counselling session, of how and what to do differently, and how to change problematic behaviour, is of little value if the person then does not implement any changes in their everyday life. One of the useful strategies for bridging the gap between the counselling room and real life is the practice of agreeing on *homework* tasks. Homework tasks in counselling can be suggested by the person or by the counsellor, and can range from quite structured and formal tasks, such as writing a journal or completing worksheets, to more informal or flexible tasks such as 'listening to other people more', 'practising slow and deep breathing as a way of coping with my anxiety' or 'visiting my grandmother's grave'.

There has been a substantial amount of research carried out into the process of agreeing homework tasks in counselling (see, for example, Mahrer *et al.*, 1994; Scheel *et al.*, 1999, 2004). Although homework is often considered as a method that is primarily employed by cognitive behavioural therapists, there is plentiful evidence that counsellors using a wide variety of approaches are all likely to use homework with at least half of their cases (Ronen and Kazantzis, 2006). Based on a review of the research evidence, Scheel *et al.* (2004) have developed some useful guidelines for using homework in counselling. These include: the homework assignment to be based on collaboration between counsellor and client; describing the task in detail; providing a rationale for why the task will benefit the person; matching the task to the person's ability; writing down the task; asking how confident the person is about fulfilling the task, and if necessary modifying the task accordingly; trying out the task during the session; asking, at the next meeting, how the person got on with the task; celebrating or praising the person's achievement of the task. In some counselling situations, it is also possible to use reminders to maximize the chances that the task is carried out. For example, a number of smoking cessation projects phone patients between sessions to check on their progress. Also, counsellors who use email contact, with clients, as an adjunct to face-to-face contact, can quite easily send a brief email reminder message between meetings.

Personal contexts of change

The discussion in this chapter so far has looked at some general tasks and methods that are associated with the goal of working together with a person to bring about changes and help them learn to do something different. However, the behaviour change issues that trouble people tend to be linked to a particular set of situations or contexts that arise again and again in counselling work. This sections explores how behaviour change can be facilitated in relation to these contexts. The contexts that are examined are: relationships, decision making, self-care and coping with transition. Competence as a counsellor requires developing an understanding of how these situations arise and how they can be handled in the specific client group with whom you work.

Dealing with difficult or painful relationships

One of the tasks that can sometimes emerge in counselling is that the person wishes to explore practical difficulties in relating to others, for example around communication, assertiveness or making friends. These are general difficulties, occurring in all relationships, rather than a problem within a specific relationship. This kind of task overlaps with other tasks that are discussed in this section, for example changing behaviour or enhancing self-care, but is distinctive because of it focuses on a central theme of interpersonal skill.

> ### Example
> As a social worker in a busy local authority department, Lisa's job involved liaison with several other organizations to secure services that would meet the care needs of her clients. Her role required her to keep her senior social worker informed about any new initiatives involving other agencies, so that he could make sure that the social work department was adopting a consistent and coherent set of procedures and standards. This time, something had gone badly wrong. Attending a meeting with representatives of another agency, the senior social worker learned about a set of projects that Lisa had developed with them, but had not told him about. Furious, and claiming that 'this isn't the first time this has happened', he insisted that the human resources department get involved, to the extent of issuing a formal warning to Lisa around her work performance. The human resources staff member who met with Lisa arranged to have a long session with her. In their conversation, Lisa explained that, while she felt that she was a good social worker in terms of her work with clients, she felt 'at a loss' in terms of relating to her colleagues in the department. She had no friends on the team, and so lacked informal support and information networks. She felt highly anxious every time she needed to communicate on any topic to the senior social worker or anyone else in authority. Invited to give some examples of what happened when she tried to communicate with colleagues, Lisa described a series of scenarios characterized by persistent inability to be heard by others. She said that she had long ago given up trying to do anything about this 'paralysing fear'.

There are several methods that can be used by a counsellor when working with a person on the task of developing interpersonal skills. Some of these methods are described below.

Analysing critical incidents

A critical incident is an example or instance of any type of event that a person finds problematic. While talking in general terms about interpersonal situations that are troubling may be useful in enabling the person to begin a process of exploring this topic, and in allowing the counsellor to gain a sense of the overall scope of the problem and the person's depth of feeling in relation to it, in the long run little will change unless the person becomes more specific. Descriptions of critical incidents can be elicited by questions such as 'can you give me an example of one time when that happened?' or 'can we look together at what happened at one of these meetings?' It is helpful if the counsellor can work with the person to tease out their behavioural 'script' for that situation, building up a picture of the whole sequence of what happened by collecting information on:

- Who was involved – what was the situation (context)?
- What the person thought and how they felt, and what their plans and goals were before the event?
- What actually happened – what did the person think, feel and do at each moment, and what did other participants appear to be thinking, feeling and doing?
- What happened next – how did the situation or interaction end or resolve itself, what did the person feel about what had happened, what did they learn?
- How typical this incident was – how did it differ from other similar incidents?
- What the person thinks they did well – given that this was a difficult situation for them, what did they think, do or say that they felt pleased about?
- Whether the person has a preferred outcome – what would they have liked to happen?

It is best if this information emerges naturally as the person tells their story of the incident, rather than the counsellor conducting an interview in which the person is responds to a series of questions. The aim is to instil a spirit of mutual exploration and problem solving that will carry over into a phase of identifying alternative strategies, and then trying them out. Moving into this phase can be initiated by the counsellor first summarizing what he or she has learned (empathically engaging and checking out) and then asking the person whether describing the incident has led them to be aware of anything they might do differently in order to achieve a better outcome. After the person has identified some new strategies, the counsellor may wish to make some additional suggestions. It is important that, if at all possible, the counsellor does not lead off and offer suggestions for change before the person does. If any of the person's difficulties are around the issue of assertiveness, then it will be hard for them to disagree openly with the counsellor and there is a danger that they may go along with suggestions that are well meant, but off the mark. Once an agreement has been reached about some different behaviours and strategies that might be tried out, the conversation can move on to a discussion of where and how they might be applied in practice.

Identifying unique outcomes

An alternative method for working with interpersonal and social skills difficulties is not to focus on an instance of the problem (critical incident analysis), but to take the opposite approach and find some examples of occasions where the person coped well. Narrative therapists, such as Michael White and David Epston, use the terms 'unique outcomes' and 'glittering moments' to refer to episodes that stand out for the person as being times when they were not defeated by a problem, but managed to resist it. Identifying unique outcomes is made easier if the person and counsellor have together been able to come up with a phrase they can use to refer to the 'problem'. For example, in the case introduced above, the social worker, Lisa, talked about being overcome by 'paralysing fear'. Her counsellor might invite her, then, to find examples of times when she had managed to resist the fear in some way, or when it had perhaps not been present at all. For people who are locked into a self-defeating pattern such as 'paralysing fear', it may take some time to think of examples of counter-instances. However, because of the inherent resourcefulness and creativity of individuals, such instances always exist. Once the person has identified a glittering moment, the counsellor can invite them to describe what happened, perhaps using some of the questions from the critical incident method outlined earlier. This can lead to a discussion around such themes as 'what do you do to invite paralysing fear into your life?', 'what do you do that keeps paralysing fear at bay?' and 'who would not be surprised to hear about your success in overcoming paralysing fear?'. These questions introduce various possibilities for the person taking charge of the situation, by recognizing how they allow the problem into their life, what is involved in living a life in which the problem does not play a role, and what sources of support exist to help them to maintain a problem-free life. Further details on this method of working with interpersonal (and other) difficulties can be found in Morgan (2001).

Rehearsal and role play

From a counselling perspective, the issue of interpersonal and social skills is unusual in that it represents an area in which the problem can be readily enacted within the counselling room itself. If a person is having difficulties with making friends, and is describing how they would ask someone they have met at the gym to meet them for a cup of coffee, it is relatively easy for the counsellor to say something along the lines of, 'Why don't we try something? To let me get a better idea of what you would do in this situation imagine that I am Shona, whom you have met the aerobics class. You are wanting to get to know her better, so you decide to invite her to have a cup of coffee after the class. What would you say? . . . Say it to me, as if I was Shona . . .'. This method has the potential to produce detailed information about the strategies that the person uses in this kind of situation. This material can then be discussed in terms of what might be done differently and so on. One of the advantages of role play and rehearsal is that this sort of activity can be both energizing and expressive, and deepen the person's engagement in the counselling process.

Self-help manuals

We live in a society characterized by a high degree of social mobility and change. As a result, many people feel uncertain about how to deal with everyday interpersonal and social situations, ranging from telling someone that you are annoyed with them (anger management) to organizing a dinner party. This pervasive uncertainty around social rules and etiquette generated a massive library of self-help books, some of which may have a role to play in counselling. It may be helpful for a counsellor to refer to such books or to recommend a book to a person. Some people are happy to work through a self-help text on their own, whereas others may prefer to use a book as a supplement to face-to-face counselling sessions. Practitioners working in particular areas may find that self-help books on communications and relationship topics are available for their specific client group, and reviewed in their specialist professional journals. Most public libraries carry good stocks of self-help books. Some of this material is also available on the internet.

Using community mentors, supporters and role models

A person who is struggling to deal with an interpersonal or relationship issue may find other people within their social world who can help them in a variety of ways. Often, they may have overlooked the potential value of these people, and may need the assistance of a counsellor to activate these resources. The narrative therapy tradition (Morgan, 2001) and the community support approach developed by Milne (1999) represent useful sources of ideas about how to facilitate engagement with mentors, supporters and role models. For example, a narrative therapist will encourage a person to make contact with resourceful individuals within their social network by asking a question such as 'who would be least surprised to hear about the success you have had in overcoming this problem?', and then urging the person, if practicable, to bring their 'supporter' up to date with what they have achieved.

In relation to any of these methods, the key challenge, when working on an inter-personal skill task, lies in not becoming too prescriptive and directive. The counsellor may be able comfortably to perform the skill that is troubling the person, or may possess a clear idea of how the skill should be performed, and can fall into the trap of telling the person what to do rather than working through the issues collaboratively, step by step. The counsellor can be a valuable resource ('here's what I might say in that situation . . .'), but always needs to be aware that they might not be the best, or only, model for the person. If a counsellor becomes too much like a teacher when carrying out this sort of task, they limit the extent to which the person has agency and owner-ship, or is in control, and may fix the relationship between the counsellor and person.

A useful image for a counsellor in relation to this type of task is that of functioning as a coach. A coach prepares their player for times when they are on their own, faced with the real business of the game. A coach is encouraging and supportive, and helps the player to build images of effective plays. However, a coach also knows that there are many occasions when the player will lose and uses the experience of losing as a source of potential learning. The fields of counselling/training around interpersonal skills issues and of sports coaching have converged in recent years to form an area of practice known as *life coaching*. For any counsellor whose work involves regular requests from people to explore interpersonal and social skills issues, the literature and training courses in the area of life coaching provide an invaluable source of ideas and methods.

In Lisa's case, the human resources (HR) manager asked her if she would be interested in meeting for a couple of brief sessions to talk though the difficulties she was having around communicating with colleagues, or whether she would prefer to look at other possibilities, such as referral to the employee assistance programme (EAP) counselling service provided by the local authority. Lisa decided that it 'wouldn't do any harm' to meet with the HR manager to see if that would help and then, if necessary, try some-thing else later. The HR manager asked Lisa to tell her about specific examples of when she had, and had not, been paralysed by fear when interacting with colleagues, and to talk her through what her approach would be if the HR manager was her senior and she had to convey some crucial information to her. It became apparent to both of them that Lisa had a strange unwillingness to look at other people when she was talking to them. She admitted that she preferred to deal with people over the telephone, so she would not need to look at them. The HR manager, in her counselling role, pointed out that 'not looking' could have the result of cutting Lisa off from important information around how people were reacting to what she was saying. She agreed that this might be true. They acted out a brief scenario of reporting to a manager, one with no looking, and one with continuous eye contact. Lisa agreed that she 'felt less paranoid' in the second scenario. She agreed to try this out over the next week and then come back to discuss it further. In the second meeting, she reported that 'looking' had made an enormous difference. This second meeting focused on identifying people in Lisa's life whom she could tell about this accomplishment and then the rest of the session was spent talking about the general stressfulness of a social worker's job.

Decision making: finding, analysing and acting on information

Behaviour change may involve making choices, and in many circumstances a decision-making process will require collecting and appraising different sources of information. In some professional roles that involve a counselling element, decision making may comprise a counselling task that arises on a regular basis. For example, health professionals working in the fields of HIV testing, genetic screening and termination of pregnancy, social workers arranging residential care for elderly clients, and teachers exploring career and further education options with their school students, are all faced with the requirement to assist people through a decision-making process.

The single most useful method that can be employed in relation to decision making is probably 'just talking'. Making it possible for a person to look at a choice from all angles, and explore how they feel about all the options, in a situation where the listener has no preconceived ideas about which course of action is right or wrong, is enormously helpful. Sometimes, it can be valuable to offer some structure to the activity of decision making. A common-sense cultural resource that many people find useful is to construct a form of balance sheet – a piece of paper where the factors for and against each choice are listed and may then be weighted in terms of which is the most important. A slightly more elaborate version of a balance sheet is a force-field analysis, where the forces pressing in different directions can be mapped on a piece of paper. This technique can be helpful in identifying the sources of different forces ('it's my mother who wants me to follow option A, whereas its my boyfriend who is pressing me to take option B'). In some situations, for example, when a person is thinking about a career choice, a SWOT (strengths, weaknesses, opportunities and threats) analysis may be valuable. The value of any of these 'mapping' techniques is that they slow down the decision-making process, thus allowing more time for reflection. They also allow the person to generate a comprehensive analysis of the factors involved. Finally, written maps 'externalize' the task, enabling the person and counsellor to work side by side to come up with ideas and move them around on the page.

Another useful strategy in relation to decision making is to introduce the concept of *implications*. Using a brainstorming approach ('let's just imagine – without censoring any ideas that come up – what might happen if you decided to . . .'), or a mapping technique, the person can be encouraged to look beyond the immediate consequences of a decision and to consider the long-term consequences. Alternatively, it may be that some imagined catastrophic long-term consequences ('if I quit this job I'll never find another one') can be seen as being not too awful once they are openly discussed with a counsellor.

In some counselling situations, a conversation about making a decision may circle around the issue for a long time without any decision ever being made. If this happens, it can be worth looking at whether the current decision reflects a more fundamental conflict or tension within the person's life as a whole.

Example

Steve is a community support worker who has spent a lot of time supporting Gareth, a retired single man who persistently has trouble with neighbours who are noisy and inconsiderate. Typically, Steve ignores the insensitive behaviour of his neighbours, or at best writes them a polite note (which they ignore). In their conversations, Steve encourages Gareth to express his anger and annoyance, to let his neighbours know how he really feels. Gareth thinks about this, and replies, 'I know that letting myself get angry with them would be a much better way to get the message across. Every time we meet, I know that I end up deciding to do this. But I just can't do it. I was always taught that emotions are a waste of time, or even destructive.' What has been happening with Gareth can be understood in terms of a lifetime tension within his sense of who he is, between the wish to feel and express emotion, and wish to be 'good' and calm. The Transactional Analysis theorists Mary and Robert Goulding (1997) explain this position as arising from a decision that Gareth would have made in his childhood (the decision to 'not feel'). From their perspective, the reason why his difficulties with his neighbours are so hard for Gareth is that their actions have created a situation in which he is on the point of making a *redecision* ('it's acceptable and useful to express emotions'). This perspective can be useful in counselling because it acts as a reminder that arriving at a decision is not merely a matter of working through the practical implications of what is the best thing to do right now – sometimes making a decision can require revisiting core existential decisions (safety vs freedom; autonomy vs relatedness; trust vs suspicion) around which a person's identity or sense of self is constructed. In a relationship where counselling sits alongside other professional tasks and roles, there may not be enough time or space to work through the issues raised by the existential dilemmas that accompany difficult decisions. However, it does not do any harm to point them out and to work together around finding other people and places where they may be resolved.

During the process of working through a decision-making task, one of the responses that the person may well appreciate from the counsellor is a degree of supportive *challenging*. We live in a society in which the big decisions are arrived at through democratic or judicial processes that involve one side challenging the evidence and arguments put forward by the other. Most people, when faced with a decision, will recognize the value of a 'critical friend' or 'devil's advocate' role. Of course, the primary task of the counsellor is to maintain a supportive and collaborative relationship, so it is important to make sure that challenging does not become over-adversarial in ways that might undermine or threaten that relationship. The most effective challenging is based on a capacity to gently point out possible inconsistencies or contradictions in what the person has said ('from what you are saying now, the key factor seems to be X . . . but it seemed to me from what you were saying a few minutes ago, the key factor was Y – I'm not sure how these factors fit together for you'). Another type of facilitative challenging can involve pointing out when the person might be avoiding some aspect of the decision ('you have written down all these for and against statements on the balance sheet – I'm aware that we have discussed all of them apart from these statements in the corner that you wrote in a red pen').

Box 10.3   Weighing up information and making a decision: Sally's story

The story of Sally is described in a short case study written by a GP, Trisha Greenhalgh (2001). Sally was a successful businesswoman in her thirties who consulted her GP over 'the loss of "white stuff" from both nipples'. Sally's boyfriend had discovered, through the Internet, that this symptom might indicate a brain tumour. Her GP confirmed that the 'white stuff' was in fact milk, and began a process of collecting research-based information about the possible causes, consequences and treatment for this condition (galactorrhoea). Over two further consultations they discussed the information that was available and agreed on further tests that were carried out. Their exploration of the significance of the 'white stuff' allowed Sally an opportunity to disclose more about her life as a whole, and in particular her ambivalence around her boyfriend's wish that they should buy a larger house and start a family. At the end of this consultation episode, Sally and her GP agreed that the tests had not uncovered any underlying disease, that the symptoms could present in healthy women and that no treatment was necessary. In a final meeting, with Sally's boyfriend present, the GP suggested that they might wish to meet with the counsellor attached to the practice, to explore their respective concerns around starting a family.

This case illustrates very effectively the interplay between information, the meaning of the information for both the person seeking help and the professional helper, and the important life issues that can emerge through the process of weighing up options in terms of personal values and goals. It also illustrates the limits in terms of the kind of counselling that can be provided by a busy health professional such as a GP. Although Greenhalgh was well aware of the issues that Sally faced around long-term commitment and possible motherhood, she also realized that she did not have the space in her schedule to explore these issues in any depth, so made a referral to a specialist counsellor.

Enhancing self-care and undoing self-criticism

One of the underling themes of almost all counselling is the issue of *self-care*. The concept of stress is widely used by people to refer to an experience of accumulated pressures. These can be understood as challenges or demands that cannot be immediately dealt with, but which add up over time into a catalogue of worries, a burden. From a perspective of making sense of the individual as living within a personal niche, a sense of pressure or stress can be interpreted as reflecting the energy and effort that it takes to hold the niche together. This effort is exerted to avoid two outcomes that are generally regarded as undesirable. The first is to become dependent, to seek shelter within the niche of another person or group, rather than bear the responsibility for keeping one's own niche functioning. The other undesirable outcome is to 'break down', for the niche to fragment and collapse, and to be left vulnerable and unprotected. While there are times when it may be in a person's best interests to depend on others or to break down, on the whole, people work hard to prevent these eventualities: they take care of themselves. Each of us has our own personal repertoire of self-care strategies that we employ in order to deal with the stresses of life. At times of trouble, these strategies may be stretched and even found to be inadequate. A key question for any counsellor to consider, when listening to a person talking about a current crisis, is to wonder about the self-care strategies that the person is using, why they might not be effective, and what other strategies they might use (for example, methods of self-care they have employed in the past, but have neglected or forgotten).

The notion of self-care reinforces the distinction between counselling, on the one hand, and advice giving on the other. In advice giving, a problem is 'fixed' – a solution is found and that is the end of the matter. Counselling, by contrast, is always *person*-centred, as well as *problem*-centred. In counselling, the aim is not merely to resolve a specific issue now, but also to enable the person to learn enough to be able to cope with similar problems in the future. Effective counselling, therefore, involves paying attention to the person's repertoire of self-care strategies, and finding ways to support and extend them. It can be useful to think of self-care as having two sides. One aspect of self-care consists of positive actions that the person undertakes in order to live a fulfilling and healthy life. The other aspect consists of self-undermining and self-critical actions that are destructive of a fulfilling and healthy life. Many (or most) behaviour change goals that people present in counselling will involve sub-tasks around self-care and undoing self-criticism. For example, a person seeking to change a pattern of alcohol abuse may need to work on positive self-care tasks, such as finding alternative ways to meet people and have fun, and also on undoing a critical inner voice that says 'you are a loser anyway – it doesn't matter if you have another drink'.

Negotiating a life transition

Many of the examples of working together to do something different that have been discussed in this chapter have referred to situations where the person made a decision to change a fairly specific and well-defined set of behaviours – such as losing weight, getting more exercise, becoming more sociable. However, there are other behaviour change issues that are on a different scale. People tend to have periods in their life when little change takes place, and then other periods that are characterized by fairly dramatic shifts from one status or way of living to another, when their personal niche is disrupted in a major way. The idea of *transition* is a valuable concept in counselling because it provides a way of thinking about large-scale personal change events. Transitions can be unexpected and unplanned, or relatively predictable. Examples of sudden transitions are:

- losing a job;
- winning the lottery;
- becoming ill;
- divorce;

- the loss of someone close to us;
- termination of pregnancy;
- moving to another area or country.

In addition, there are predictable or 'normative' changes built into the life course, that inevitably affect all (or most) of us, such as:

- leaving home;
- becoming a parent;
- retirement from work.

An understanding of the process of transition is valuable for anyone in a counselling role, because it is at such moments of transition that people feel the need to talk to someone outside of their immediate situation, who can help them to gain a perspective on what is happening. Negotiating a difficult life transition represents an important counselling task. While there are a number of specialist counselling agencies that offer help to people undergoing specific transitions, such as marital separation and divorce, relatively few people make use of them. There are also many transitions that do not fall readily into the terms of reference of these agencies. For these reasons, many people experiencing transition look for counselling help from whatever professional source is available to them, such as a nurse, doctor or social worker.

There are several useful models of transition and crisis that have been developed (see Hopson and Adams, 1976; Hopson, 1989; McAdams, 2000; Sugarman, 2003, 2004). These provide a useful framework for making sense of the experience of the person seeking help. All of these models suggest that a person in transition goes through a series of stages of readjustment such as:

1. Shock – exhibited either as excitement ('this is great') or numbness ('its not really happening').
2. Provisional adjustment – the 'honeymoon period'.
3. Gradual loss of confidence. Increase in depression ('I can't cope').
4. Crisis point – despair and hopelessness.
5. Reconstruction/rebuilding a new life: either accepting the new situation and reconstructing self/identity (leading to a higher level of confidence/competence than at the start), or quitting and giving up.

When using a transition model, it is essential to be flexible – in any individual case the progression from one stage to another may occur quickly or take a long time, and the individual may skip stages or repeat them.

The implications of this kind of transition model for the work of the counsellor are that it:

- draws attention to the fact that transition involves ups and downs – it is not a smooth process;
- suggests that it may not be of any use to attempt counselling during the shock phase – the person is dealing with an overload of new information and will not be able to process it – at this stage, basic safety and care are crucial, as is forming a

relationship that the person may be able to use for counselling purposes at a later date;
- implies that helping a person through a transition involves paying attention to (i) letting go of previous attitudes, relationships and behaviours, (ii) changing behaviour (for example, learning new skills, making new friends) and (iii) cognitive restructuring (learning to see oneself in a different light).

For any counsellor working with a particular group of people seeking help, it is important to become attuned to the specific ways that the transition cycle plays out in the lives of that set of people. For instance, in bereavement it may take many months or even years before a person is ready to reflect on the implications of their loss, whereas in students beginning studies in another country the pressure to adjust and to deal with the experience of transition is immediate. There are also major differences in the level of social support and acceptance associated with different types of transition. A person who becomes ill is typically able to access many different forms of support. By contrast, some women undergoing termination of pregnancy may not feel able to tell any of their friends and family about their decision, and as a result may be left on their own with painful emotions.

Examples of episodes of embedded counselling around transition issues

The following examples illustrate some of the counselling goals, tasks and methods that can be associated with working together around life transitions.

Hector has had a successful career as a supervisor and manager in an engineering company for many years. Now, five years short of his expected retirement age, he has developed a number of health problems that are making it impossible for him to function effectively at work. In his meetings with an occupational health doctor, to assess his condition, he persistently minimizes the severity of his problems and continues to talk as though he will soon be able to return to work as before. The doctor points this out to him, adds that he has been wondering what Hector feels about the prospect of taking early retirement, and asks him if he would find it helpful to talk about this during their next meeting. Hector agrees that this would be useful. When they meet, the doctor invites Hector to tell him about what he will lose when he gives up his job, and what he will gain, what will be missing in his post-retirement life and what the new possibilities will be. At the end of their conversation, Hector comments that, 'I've got more of a handle on the situation now – I can see that I was assuming that my social life would come to an end when I left the company.'

Margaret and her three children had lived on a Caribbean island that was largely destroyed by a volcanic eruption. Evacuated by the Navy, they ended up in Britain being taken care of by a church group who provided housing and other support for refugees. Although Margaret and her children spoke English, they had great difficulty in understanding the accents of the people in the neighbourhood within which they had been located, or of being understood by them. The country seemed dark, damp and unwelcoming. Over the space of two years, a small team of support workers helped Margaret and her children to reconstruct their lives, using a combination of assistance in practical issues around work, health and education alongside a willingness to take time to listen and talk.

Judith is several weeks into the first year of senior school. She enjoyed the junior school, where she knew everyone and had a good relationship with her class teacher. However, the transition to senior school has been very difficult. She feels as if she has been separated from her friends, is unable to make new friends, and has not come to terms with the demands of the timetable and homework. The teacher responsible for support and guidance notices Judith's isolation and distress, and asks if she would be willing to meet during the lunch hour. When invited to talk, Judith bursts into tears and describes a long list of problems. With Judith's permission, the teacher makes a list of these problems and suggests that they might look at how they can deal with them one at a time. Over the next three weeks, they come up with a set of coping strategies that Judith can employ, and keep monitoring how they can be applied within the different difficult situations that Judith encounters during her school, day. By the Christmas break, Judith has settled in, and at their final lunchtime meeting her teacher brings in a special cake to celebrate her achievements.

These brief examples show how some basic behaviour change methods can be applied in working with a person around a transition issue. Judith's teacher uses her own adaptation of CBT methods, culminating in the use of a ritual (eating together) to mark the completion of the change in personal status that had taken place. With Hector, one good, meaningful conversation was enough to make a difference, whereas with Margaret and her family a team of support workers developed relationships that were supportive and resourceful.

Bereavement as a prototypical transition

Bereavement is a particularly important type of transition, and it is essential that any-one who undertakes a counselling role should take some time to reflect on the nature of bereavement and the issues involved in trying to support a person who is experiencing personal loss. Although there are a number of specialist bereavement counselling services, the evidence from research suggests that formal bereavement counselling is not effective in many cases (Schut and Stroebe, 2005; Stroebe *et al.*, 2005), and that it is mainly those people with complicated and severe grief reactions that are helped by formal, regular scheduled therapy. Why is this? One of the factors is undoubtedly that, as an almost universal human experience, there are many cultural resources available to people to help them cope with their grief (Walter, 1999; Hockey *et al.*, 2001). For example, religious rituals and teachings are immensely valuable for many people during their experience of loss. There are also many novels and films that sensitively present healing images of the meanings of death. Another factor that appears to be associated with the lack of effectiveness of bereavement counselling is that some services are offered on an 'outreach' basis, where all people in a community who have been bereaved are routinely invited to receive counselling. This kind of service, where the person has not made a deliberate decision to seek help, appears to be particularly unhelpful on the whole (Schut and Stroebe, 2005), although clearly they will some-times make contact with individuals who do benefit from counselling, but who may be unwilling or unable to go out and look for it themselves. The implications of this research are that, first, it seems likely that professional nurses, doctors, teachers and others who may be the first line of support for people who have been bereaved, and are sensitive enough to respond to moments when the person wishes to talk, have a par-ticularly important role to play. Second, it is essential for those offering embedded counselling to be aware of situations where the person is undergoing complicated grief, where the loss has perhaps triggered underlying issues, and to be in a position to make a referral to a specialist service.

Box 10.4   Trauma as an extreme form of transition

In recent years, post-traumatic stress disorder (PTSD) has been identified as a distinct psychiatric condition, and various treatment approaches have been developed to address it (Meichenbaum, 1994; Scott and Stradling, 2006). Post-traumatic stress disorder occurs when the person has been exposed to a highly traumatic and threaten-ing event. The typical signs of PTSD are intrusive memories of the events, such as flashbacks, alongside attempts to avoid thinking about what had happened. Avoidance can sometimes only be achieved by self-medication through alcohol and drugs. The person suffering PTSD tends to lose trust in the world, and experiences even minor setbacks and stresses as highly threatening. This set of symptoms can lead to sleep loss and fatigue, secondary relationship problems, difficulties at work, and depression. Although the literature on PTSD tends to be dominated by high-profile trauma-inducing events, such as involvement in warfare, or being the victim of terrorism or natural disaster, there is, in fact, a surprising amount of 'everyday' traumatic stress around. Events such as car accidents, domestic violence, bullying, sexual violence, robbery and childbirth can lead to PTSD reactions, so it is not unusual to come across people who are suffering from undiagnosed or mild traumatic stress. Part of the preparation for a counselling role requires being informed about the specialist services that are available locally for people experiencing PTSD. Usually, clinical psychology provides a good source of expertise in this condition. However, it is also worth reflecting on the meaning of traumatic stress disorders, and what the disorders can tell us about other, less dramatic forms of transition. At the heart of the PTSD response is the need to cognitively process information that is not readily assimilated into the person's way of making sense of the world. When we encounter a routine life difficulty or irritation (the car won't start), we can usually make sense of it quite readily (the battery is flat). By contrast, when something traumatic and completely unexpected happens (I was waiting in the queue at the bank and a masked man with a gun rushed in), then it is hard to make sense of what all this might have meant ('Could I have died?', 'What would have happened to my children?', 'Why me?', 'Could I have done anything different?'). What is required is to find a way to construct a coherent story or narrative around what happened. This can be achieved by slowly remembering and piecing together an account of the event, but reliving the event may be very hard because each strand of memory is associated with fear and terror.

Because so much has been written about bereavement work, there exists a wide and varied literature on the use of counselling in this context. Two widely used bereavement counselling texts are Worden (2001) and Lendrum and Syme (2004). Early models of bereavement tended to be organized around the idea that the person experiencing loss passed through a series of stages of learning to cope. More recent thinking has tended to question the notion of fixed stages and replaced it with the idea that dealing with bereavement confronts the person with a set of tasks. These tasks may differ in salience for each individual and may be carried out in no particular order. An influential model has been formulated by Worden (2001), who has identified four key bereavement tasks:

- to accept the reality of the loss;
- to work through the pain of grief;
- to adjust to an environment in which the deceased is missing;
- to emotionally relocate the deceased and move on with life.

An alternative model has been proposed by Stroebe and Schut (1999), who discuss two broad categories of task: loss-oriented and restoration-oriented. Loss-oriented tasks include dealing with the intrusion of feelings of loss and despair, and letting go of ties with the deceased person. Restoration tasks include doing new things and developing new relationships. Clearly, in any individual case, the mix of tasks will be unique.

Bereavement is a prototypical transition issue because it encapsulates a set of issues that are present in virtually all transition situations. Working with a person experiencing a significant life transition necessarily involves some looking backward, at what has been lost, as well as looking forward at new opportunities and a new sense of self. There is almost always strong emotion involved in transition work because of the strength of attachment that the person has towards whatever it is that has been lost. Transition work may often involve engaging with cultural support systems and rituals, some of which may be helpful and some of which may not. And counselling around transition issues raises questions for people in counselling roles around how active they should be: does the person's distress really require professional assistance, or might such assistance interfere with the operation of naturally occurring informal systems of help?

A narrative perspective on behaviour change

As a counsellor, it is a mistake to become so preoccupied with the task of behaviour change that one forgets or neglects the more fundamental task of giving the person a chance to tell their story and be heard. There are many ways in which behaviour change can be understood as a particular form of storytelling. The founders of narrative therapy, Michael White and David Epston (1990) have always talked about behaviour change in terms of a process of *re-authoring*. For them, a person's identity or sense of self is constituted by the stories that the person tells about themselves or are told about them by other people. From this point of view, the person seeking to change their behaviour is developing a new story to tell about who they are (for example, the old story may have been 'I am someone who struggles to pass exams' and the new story might be organized around a narrative of 'I am someone who has learned how to manage the stress of exams'). Once the new story has been created by the person, perhaps through working together with a counsellor, the next step is to try it out on audiences. After all, other people need to know that 'I do well in exams' – if they are still telling the old story of the person as an exam-flunker, this will undermine the person's efforts to do something different.

The implications for a counsellor of adopting a re-authoring perspective are that it becomes important to listen carefully to the stories that a person tells about themself. Are they success stories or are they failure stories? If they are failure stories, what new material can be introduced into the storyline that will allow the person to tell it as a success story? The principal method that narratively oriented counsellors use to assist people to construct success or solution stories is to encourage them to identify their own strengths and resources. For example, the counsellor may ask the person with an exam-taking issue if there were ever occasions when they had done well in an exam or even had coped with an anxiety-provoking situation. The person's answers to these questions are clues to resources and strengths, which can then become the building blocks for a new story. However, even cognitive behavioural therapy (CBT) methods can be understood in narrative terms. The careful analysis of the problem behaviour, agreement around behavioural targets, and plans for how to meet these targets, are all designed to produce an experience of success for the person. This experience is then woven into their story who they are and what they can do – it is re-authoring by another route.

There is another significant dimension to the concept of re-authoring: its political side. In a lot of cases, the problems that people have, and the behaviour that they want to change, are the result of stories that *other people* have told about them. Frequently, these other people are authority figures such as parents, teachers, social workers and psychiatrists. The stories may be reinforced by being framed in bureaucratic or medical language, and enshrined in massive case files. For example, someone with a problem around exams may turn out to have based their self-story as a learner around the fact that 'my Dad told me I was stupid – he told the teachers too, and they believed him'. For such a person, arriving at the point of being able to tell their story in terms of statements such as 'I am intelligent, I am a competent learner' is a matter of personally authoring their own story, rather than having it authored by someone else. The person becomes the *authority* on their own life.

Narrative ideas are also relevant to an understanding of transition issues arising from experiences such as bereavement or the onset of illness. One of the common themes in these types of transition difficulties can be understood as the experience of *narrative disruption* (Kleinman, 1988; McLeod, 1997a). A key characteristic of a stable life is that the person is able to able to tell a coherent story about who they are and what their life is about. When the structures of that life are radically disrupted, however, the person is left without words. Their story does not fit any longer. Hector, the factory manager introduced earlier in this chapter, lived his life within a narrative that might be summarized as 'I work for the company, I play golf every week with the other managers in my division, I bring home a good salary, I go on holiday to Spain twice each year . . .'. Faced with an illness that stops him from going to work, and which will soon reduce his income by half, this narrative no longer applies as a description of Hector's life. In asking him to talk about what his life might be like following retirement, his occupational health doctor, in a counselling role, is seeking to help Hector to construct a new life narrative for himself. In a case of severe and total life disruption, as occurred with Margaret and her children, the profound loss of so many elements of a pre-existing life history may make it hard for the person even to talk about themself. At these moments, the strong emotions that a person may be feeling may be almost impossible to channel into words. Moreover, there is a loss of any sense of future, since a life narrative provides a structure for talking about 'who I was, who I am now, and who I want to be in the future'.

The concepts of narrative disruption and reconstruction have been widely used in studies of the psychology and sociology of health and illness, as a means of understanding the personal experience of disease and the ways that illness cuts people off from those around them and forces a reappraisal of identity and relationships. These processes have been powerfully documented in a classic study by Gareth Williams (1984), and in a series of investigations by the sociologist Arthur Frank (1995, 1998, 2000), some of them based on his personal experience of cancer. These studies provide an invaluable resource for counsellors working with people who are living with health problems, in demonstrating the importance for those who are undergoing this kind of transition of just talking about their situation, and having another person who can work with them to construct a new narrative. It is only through the painful and lengthy process of finding the words to articulate the experience, and making connection with discourses that allow new ways of talking, that a person can gradually build a new story for their life.

Conclusions

It is impossible in a chapter of this length to do justice to the huge topic of facilitating behaviour change. The aim has been to provide an outline of some ideas and methods that may be used in embedded counselling relationships. The themes that have been emphasized within the chapter are:

- Behaviour change is difficult to achieve, and there are many barriers to achieving this type of goal.
- Effective and lasting change requires a step-by-step approach, with the ultimate goal of behaviour change broken down into a number of constituent tasks.
- There is no one right method to facilitate change – people differ a great deal in terms of the change processes that are meaningful to them. A good starting point is usually to inquire about what the person has done to initiate and implement changes in their life in the past.
- It is seldom effective to try merely to eradicate or extinguish unwanted habits – what works better is to replace these behaviours with alternative activities.
- Each of the various change methods that are written about by professional psychologists and psychotherapists can ultimately be reduced to a set of common-sense

strategies, which can readily be applied by practitioners whose counselling role is embedded in other wok functions.

• The single most important thing that a person in a counselling role can do for anyone who is seeking to change their behaviour is to function as a supporter and ally in their journey. The quality of the relationship is crucial in helping the person to persevere with their change objectives.

The example of bereavement can be used as a framework for understanding other types of behaviour change. In bereavement, as in all forms of behaviour change, there are basically three things that need to be done. First, it is necessary to let go of the past. This may involve making sense of what has happened, and grieving for the person who has gone and the self that was brought into being through the relationship with that person. The second task is to deal with what is happening now, the chaos of a life that may be missing one of its foundation stones. Third, it is necessary to plan for the future, to build a new repertoire of behaviours and relationships. The example of bereavement is particularly important and evocative for a number of reasons. It evokes the image of people grieving differently – there are huge individual and cultural differences in the way that people respond to death. It evokes an appreciation of the cultural, social, family and interpersonal networks of meaning, relationship, belief and ritual that help people to make the necessary changes to their lives following a bereavement. Coping with loss is always done together as well as done alone. The meaning of bereavement, and the potential avenues for dealing with it, depend on the personal niche within which an individual lives their life. All of these aspects are true of any kind of behaviour change.

Questions for reflection and discussion

1. Identify one occasion when you attempted to change your own behaviour in some way. What strategies did you use? What worked and what didn't work for you? How well do the ideas presented in this chapter help you to make sense of your own behaviour change experience?
2. What are the self-critical, sabotaging or undermining statements that you make to yourself? In what ways do these statements prevent you from taking care of yourself sufficiently? How might you lessen the effects of these statements?
3. What are the types of behaviour change issues that arise for the people with whom you work as a practitioner? What are the methods that you have found to be most and least effective in facilitating change with these individuals? On the basis of what you have read in this chapter, what other methods might be valuable?
4. Reflect on your own experience of bereavement. What helped you to cope? What was unhelpful? What have your learned from this experience that you can use in your role as a counsellor?

Suggestions for further reading

There are many excellent books on cognitive behavioural therapy. Particularly recommended are:

Grant, A., Mills, J., Mulhern, R. and Short, N. (2004) *Cognitive Behavioural Therapy in Mental Health Care*. London: Sage.

Kanfer, F. H. and Goldtsen, A. P. (1991) *Helping People Change*, 4th edn. Needham Heights, MA: Allyn & Bacon.

The best introduction to narrative approaches to behaviour change is:

Morgan, A. (2001) *What is Narrative Therapy? An Easy-to-read Introduction*. Adelaide: Dulwich Centre.

A book which combines cognitive behavioural and person-centred ideas about behaviour change, and which is widely used in practitioner training, is:

Egan, G. (2004) *The Skilled Helper: A Problem Management and Opportunity Development Approach to Helping*. Belmont, CA: Wadsworth.

11

Dealing with difficult situations in counselling

Introduction • Dealing with difficult situations: some general guidelines • The concept of boundary • Ethical dilemmas • Ethical decision making • Risk and self-harm • Losing it • Referring on • When confrontation may be necessary • Conclusions • Questions for reflection and discussion • Suggestions for further reading

Do you remember
The first time we met
You told me about confidentiality
And you asked me if I had ever
Felt
At risk, you said
Of harming myself.
You know
Once and for all
Well
I can tell you
Now
That of course I do
I think about it a lot

Doesn't everyone
In my situation?

Introduction

A central theme within this book has been the idea of the counselling space. It has been argued that counselling represents a unique and invaluable form of support with respect to life in complex societies, through making available a relationship which offers a blame-free, safe space for reflection on problems in living, and the development of solutions. Earlier chapters have examined what is involved in creating such a space and then using it for different kinds of purposes. The aim of the present chapter is to consider some of the issues involved in *maintaining* a counselling space, particularly in relation to threats to its integrity and functionality. This chapter looks at *difficult situations* – moments in counselling where it may become impossible to continue with a counselling or therapeutic conversation.

It is important for a skilled counsellor to be able routinely to monitor what is happening in the counselling relationship, to be aware of any possibility that a threat to the space may be building up. In order to be able to respond to the person in a caring and responsible manner, anyone in a counselling role should have a clear idea of their strategies for dealing with difficult situations. For this reason, *preparation* for offering a counselling relationship should always involve a process of working through worst case scenarios, so that the counsellor is as ready as they can be to cope with any difficult situations that may arise. In these situations, the person seeking help may be at their most vulnerable, so it is especially important for their counsellor to have a clear idea of how they will handle whatever comes up.

In this chapter, a range of difficult situations are described, with suggestions offered for ways of responding to them. Within the limits of this chapter, it is not possible to provide an exhaustive coverage of all of the strategies that might be employed in dealing with these scenarios. In many cases, organizations will have their own protocols for handling difficult issues, which will draw on resources that may be available locally, for example, the immediate involvement of a more experienced colleague. Further information and ideas for dealing with difficult situations can be obtained from the list of suggested reading at the end of the chapter.

Dealing with difficult situations: some general guidelines

An ability to deal appropriately with difficult situations that can arise in counselling requires *preparation*, in three main areas. These are: developing a capacity to *anticipate* problems; being able to work out the moral, ethical and practical *implications* of different courses of action; and possessing a set of *practical strategies*.

Anticipating problems is the kind of competence that probably develops only through immersion in an area of work, over a period of time. In relation to counselling, it refers to the kind of practical knowledge and 'case lore' that comes from talking with other practitioners, taking part in case discussions, and reading both case histories and books or articles on ethical dilemmas and risk assessment. Curiosity about these aspects of the counselling role can help in the development of sensitivity to *possibilities* – if the person is saying this now, then where might it lead in future? Being able to work out the *implications* of implementing alternative courses of action in a difficult situation is an invaluable skill – for example, the section below on ethical decision making includes suggestions for how implications may be explored in a systematic way. Finally, there are some difficult situations that can be dealt with by having a plan or set of *practical strategies* in place, a predetermined protocol for what to do if a particular kind of 'counselling disaster' happens. For example, if a person in the middle of a counselling session begins to exhibit the signs of a panic attack (which may appear to be similar to a heart attack), there are some straightforward practical measures that can be put into action (these procedures are described later in this chapter). If a counsellor is able to apply these measures, there is every chance that the counselling session may be able to proceed. If, on the other hand, the counsellor does not know what to do, then the session may need to come to an end while external assistance is sought.

The concept of boundary

Counselling can be understood as giving a person a safe space, outside of the demands and pressures of everyday life, within which they can choose to talk about a problem in living – a 'bubble' within which the person feels free to say whatever they want, without fear of consequences. In helping to create such a space, a counsellor is in effect building a barrier or setting a *boundary* between the counselling conversation and the rest of the person's life: what is said during the counselling session stays there. Also, different rules apply within the counselling space. For instance, it is acceptable to say the unthinkable, or express feelings or wishes that be unacceptable to others. Most of the time, counselling conversations and relationships can be contained within this space or boundary without too much difficulty. On the whole, a counsellor and a person seeking counselling possess a shared understanding of what they are doing together and of the limits of their relationship. Sometimes, however, threats to the integrity of the space, or to the clarity of the boundary between counselling and everyday life, can emerge. Examples of such situations include:

- Either the person, or the counsellor, wishes to extend the relationship into friendship and may suggest meeting on a social basis.
- There may be pre-existing links between the person and the counsellor (they may have a 'dual relationship') and these different roles become muddled. For instance, a university tutor offers to meet with a student to provide supportive counselling on a regular basis. The student goes along with this, because he does not want to offend the tutor and risk getting a poor essay mark; the tutor realizes the student's essay is a fail, but does not want to add to his troubles by giving a poor mark. This situation soon begins to intrude on the counselling relationship, as a hidden agenda that cannot be talked about.
- The helping capacity of the counsellor may be impaired or limited in some way – the counsellor may feel threatened or out of their depth.

- Other people may be clamouring to be informed about what is being said in counselling sessions.
- The person may express needs that cannot be effectively resolved through counselling and that require urgent action. For example, the person may disclose an intention to harm themself or others, or may exhibit high levels of emotion that lead to their being unable to look after themself at the end of a counselling session.

Dealing effectively with events such as these is never easy. They represent a set of genuine dilemmas in which a counsellor is faced with making choices between different courses of action that each have advantages and disadvantages. For instance, there have been many occasions where a genuine friendship has developed between people who first met as counsellor and client. Surely, also, people who are adult should be free to choose who becomes their friend. Yet, at the same time, a journey into friendship is inevitably a journey away from a counselling relationship. It is not always easy to determine what is the right thing to do.

Because of the significance of the kinds of scenario that have been outline above, it is essential for anyone involved in offering counselling relationships to have a clear understanding of the boundaries that are appropriate to the work that they are doing. It can be useful, as a counsellor, to take some time to visualize, or map out on a piece of paper, the boundaries within which one is working. In any counselling situation there are usually boundaries in operation around:

- Time. When does counselling happen? How long does it go on for? How are the start and finish points signalled?
- Space. Where does counselling take place? how private is this space (is there anyone else there)? How are the edges of the space marked off?
- Information. Who gets to hear about what has been said in the counselling session (confidentiality)? How is information recorded? what information is held?
- Intimacy. How close is the relationship? How willing is the counsellor to be known? Is touch permissible?
- Access. What kind of contact is possible between counselling sessions? What happens if the person feels a need to talk with their counsellor between sessions?
- Safety. The safety of the person and/or the counsellor both within and outside of formal meetings. For example, what happens if the person becomes violent or threatens suicide?

For each of these boundaries it can be helpful to map out: (i) what the boundary is; (ii) who decides on the boundary, and how it is decided or negotiated; (iii) how the person seeking help learns about the existence of the boundary or is invited to negotiate it; and (iv) what happens if the boundary is violated.

Careful attention to boundaries is particularly important when the counselling is embedded in another helping role, such as that of nurse, teacher or social worker. In stand-alone specialist counselling, many of the boundaries listed above are defined in terms of the basic procedures of the counselling agency, for example, weekly one-hour sessions, leaflets to clients explaining confidentiality, the counsellor never having any other relationship or contact with the client outside of sessions. In embedded counselling, by contrast, there is always some level of dual relationship between counsellor and person seeking help, and some degree of improvisation is required in relation to time, space and access. It is therefore essential for anyone engaged in embedded counselling to do as much *preparation* as possible in advance of offering a counselling relationship, in terms of thinking through boundary issues and defining personal and organizational limits. It is also crucial for anyone engaged in embedded counselling to use supervision and support on a regular basis, as a means of keeping boundary issues under review. Getting it wrong, in relation to boundary issues, can be hurtful and damaging both for people seeking help and for counsellors. For a person seeking help, being led to expect confidentiality and then finding that information has been passed on, or being led to expect an ongoing relationship and then being left high and dry, can be felt as a betrayal. For the counsellor, any sense of having betrayed a person seeking help can be highly stressful and undermining of professional self-belief.

The concept of boundary is vital in relation to making sense of what is happening, and what may need to be done, when things seem to be going wrong within a counselling relationship. When the imaginary boundary round a counselling relationship dissolves or is breached, the space collapses and counselling ceases to be possible. Each of the difficult situations discussed in the following sections of this chapter can be understood as representing different types of boundary issue.

Ethical dilemmas

The moral basis for the practice of counselling can be expressed in different ways. Counselling is informed by a set of core *values*, such as respect for the person, and belief in a person's capacity to develop and learn. It is also informed by a set of *ethical principles*, which are largely similar to the ethical codes found in all health and caring professions. Ultimately, these values and ethical principles reflect the fact that both good and bad things can happen in counselling. While it is the goal of counselling to help people to fulfil themselves, and live constructively with others, it is also quite feasible that there can be occasions when counselling can be experienced as harmful, exploitative or manipulative.

The key ideas that underpin professional ethics are:

- autonomy – the person is regarded as an individual who has the right to make their own decisions;
- doing good and avoiding harm;
- justice and fairness – making sure that people are treated equally.

There is an excellent discussion of these principles, and their application within counselling, available on the ethical guideline pages of the British Association for Counselling and Psychotherapy website (www.bacp.co.uk). In practice, these ethical factors have a number of implications for the way that counselling is carried out. The main ways that ethical considerations influence counselling practice are considered below.

Informed consent

When someone is seeking help, before the actual counselling commences it is the responsibility of the counsellor to ensure that the person is sufficiently informed about what is on offer and what might happen.

Examples of conversations around informed consent

Alicia, 15, attends a youth club likes and trusts the community education worker who runs the club. One evening, when the club is quiet, she starts to talk about her problems at school. The youth worker says that she is very happy to talk about these issues, but that Alicia needs to know that she is only around one evening each week, and so she cannot guarantee that they could talk every week. She checks out how Alicia feels about this, and whether she might prefer it if the youth worker helped her to make an appointment at a local young person's counselling service.

A GP suspects that Mike, an unemployed man who has visited regularly with a variety of physical ailments, is bottling up a lot of feelings about how his life has worked out, but is afraid that other people might see how vulnerable he is. At one consultation, he suggests to Mike that it might be helpful if they took a bit more time to look at what was going on in his life that might be making him feel bad. He adds: '. . . of course, there could be things that are upsetting to talk about. Maybe you would want to think about whether you want to go into these things right now. Sometimes it can be better to make an appointment at the end of my afternoon clinic, when the place is quiet and we can have more time. What do you think? It's up to you.'

Elsa starts to tell her social worker about why she has taken her children out of the family home and moved in with her mother. Before Elsa gets into her stride, the social worker intervenes to say: 'I know you know this, but I'm just reminding you that if you tell me anything that's around harm to any of the children, I would have to do something. I don't have any choice about that. I'm really happy to talk all this through with you – we've got at least an hour if we need it – but any abuse or harm has to be reported. Is that OK?'

In these examples, the person in the role of counsellor is providing the person seeking help with the information that they need in order to make an autonomous decision about whether they want to proceed. In these particular examples, the counsellor was acting on the basis of an assumption that the person already possessed a reasonably good understanding of counselling and knew what they were looking for. There are some occasions where this would not be the case and a counsellor might need to take quite a long time to tell a person what was involved in counselling, to the point where that person was capable of making a truly informed choice.

Being aware of one's limits as a counsellor

The ethical injunctions to do good and avoid harm are closely linked to the question of counsellor competence. For example, there are many people who work in education, health and social services who get to know clients who have had experiences of sexual or emotional abuse in childhood. Sometimes, the practitioner may feel a strong urge to help the person, by listening to their story and perhaps trying to help them to come to terms with what has happened. This is a very caring response, but there are times when it may not represent the best course of action. If a person has been assaulted in childhood, the resulting sense of lack of trust, and perhaps self-hatred, may permeate many aspects of the person's life. Talking through all of that may take a long time, may involve strong emotions, and requires a great deal of persistence and consistency on the part of the counsellor. Any nurse or other practitioner faced with such a situation needs to consider whether they are capable, in terms of the time they can give, and their confidence and competence as a counsellor, to accompany their client on such a journey. Starting on such a journey, and then pulling back, clearly has the potential for hurt. At the same time, ignoring what the client has said about their abuse, for fear of 'getting in over my head' also has the potential for hurt or harm. What is appropriate will depend on the circumstances. For instance, in one situation it may be best to work with the person to find a psychotherapist. In another situation, a nurse or social worker might be able to get sufficient supervisory back-up to offer supportive counselling for a period of time. Another set of issues around counsellor competence arises from what might be described as *temporary impairment*. For example, a counsellor who has recently experienced the loss of a close family member is unlikely to be much help to someone with a bereavement issue. A counsellor who is burnt out, stressed or tired is unlikely to be in a good position to offer ongoing help to someone. Being aware of one's limits as a counsellor is much easier when the practitioner has been using regular supervision or consultancy support and there is someone who is close enough to the counsellor to challenge their attempt to be 'heroic', rather than helpful.

Taking care around dual relationships

Much of the theory, literature and training that informs contemporary counselling practice is based on an assumption that the counsellor and the person seeking help are, or should be, strangers. The assumption behind this view is that the quality of the relationship, in terms of trust and confidentiality, is of paramount importance, and that any contamination of that relationship with other kinds of ties should be avoided at all costs. This approach has the advantage of creating a pure kind of counsellor–client relationship, in which all that the counsellor knows about the person is what they say during their weekly session, and the person can feel secure that whatever they say in counselling is safely and securely insulated from the rest of their life. Although this kind of formulation is neat, and elegant, it flies in the face of several different types of 'dual relationship' situations where counselling appears to thrive:

- rural communities, where everyone knows everyone else;
- self-contained subcultures within urban areas (for example lesbian, gay, bisexual and

transgender communities) where people choose to see counsellors who share their own values and lifestyle;
- various types of therapeutic communities, where counsellors and clients may live and work together;
- counselling embedded within other practitioner roles (for example, nurse, teacher, priest).

Although there are plentiful examples of counselling being delivered effectively within a dual role relationship, anyone with experience of providing counselling within such a setting knows that taking care around role boundaries is essential. After all, there would be no one who would claim that counselling could reasonably take place between close family members, such as a husband and wife, or parent and child. The crucial moral and ethical factor that represents the biggest challenge for any counselling dual relationship lies in the principle that counselling must be *in the interests of the person seeking help*. When the counsellor has some other kind of involvement with the person, it is necessary to be alert to any possibility that the counsellor might be responding on the basis of what would be right *for them*, rather than what would be right for the person.

Sensitivity to cultural differences in moral standpoint

The types of ethical issue that arise in counselling situations can often be associated with distinctive ideas about right and wrong that are based in cultural beliefs and attitudes. It is important, therefore, for practitioners to be sensitive to the ways that cultural difference can lead to ethical dilemmas. One of the most important dimensions of cultural difference, that can often have an impact on ethical practice, concerns the individualism–collectivism dimension. Western cultures and, in particular, the middle-class segments of such cultures, tend to view life from the perspective of the individual. The rightness of a decision or course of action, therefore, is based on whether the consequences are beneficial for the individual. In most other cultures, people view the world from a more collectivist point of view, and a decision is evaluated in terms of what 'we' should do, or whether it benefits 'all of us'.

Ethical decision making

Deciding what to do when an ethical dilemma comes up in a counselling situation, is not at all easy. There are many sources of information available about ethical principles (see, for example, McLeod, 2003: ch. 15). The websites of counselling organizations such as the British Association for Counselling and Psychotherapy also carry detailed codes of ethical practice. However, ethical codes have limited practical value: the ethical dilemmas that confront practitioners are either so obvious that they do not require consultation of published sources, or so complex and sensitive that the written guidelines do not provide a straightforward guide to action.

When trying to arrive at a solution to an ethical dilemma, it can be useful to apply a step-by-step decision-making framework:

1. *Collect all relevant information.* This will include information about the situation, the preferences and resources of the person seeking help and yourself as the counsellor, and the possible views of other people who might be affected by the outcome.
2. *Consider who benefits from different courses action.* Identify the benefits of what could be done, from the points of view of the person, the counsellor and others.
3. *Consider the consequences.* Identify the consequences of any action, from the points of view of the person, the counsellor and others.
4. *Identify duties.* To whom does a duty exist in the case being examined? For example, does the counsellor have a primary duty or responsibility to the person, or to a wider group, such as the person's family or society as a whole? To whom does the organization within which the counsellor is employed have a duty or responsibility? What is the counsellor's duty to themself?
5. *Consult.* Use consultation with others, for example, a counselling supervisor or mentor, or published sources, to develop a more complete understanding of duties, benefits and consequences, and to check out your own assumptions in these areas.
6. *Decide.* Bring together these various factors into a preliminary plan of action.
7. *Test the plan.* Consult again, to check how the plan appears to other people (including the person being helped). Evaluate your plan from the perspective of Stadler's (1986) tests of universality, publicity and justice, by reflecting on the following questions:
   (a) Would I recommend this course of action to anyone else in similar circumstances? Would I condone my behaviour in anyone else? (Universality)
   (b) Would I tell other counsellors what I intend to do? Would I be willing to have the actions and the rationale for them published on the front page of the local newspaper or reported on the evening news? (Publicity)
   (c) Would I treat another client in the same situation differently? If this person was a well-known political leader, would I treat them differently? (Justice)

In practice, there are occasions when a counsellor may feel that a decision needs to be made immediately and there is not enough time to work through the steps outlined above. However, even when this happens, it can be valuable afterwards to sit down and work out the intricacies of duty, benefit and consequence that were at stake, and to use consultation – ethical dilemmas are an important topic in consultation and supervision, as the following examples demonstrate.

Examples of conversations around ethical dilemmas

Grania is a nurse who has been providing counselling for some time to James, a patient who has a long-term problem and who has needed to talk about how the illness had affected his image of himself as someone who took care of others in his family. He brings in an expensive gift. He knows that this is something that Grania would like, and he knows that she knows that he would know this. In responding to her patient, Grania is open about her pleasure in being offered this gift, and also her difficulty, as a practitioner bound by health service rules, in being able to accept the gift without consulting her line manager and supervisor. She encourages

James to share his feeling around the gift-giving and her response. They agree that Grania will consult on the question of the gift, and that they will discuss it further at their next meeting. In the meantime, Grania is aware that the gift may be an expression of a strong wish on the part of James to be the caretaker and provider, and reflects on how and when (and whether) it would be useful to explore that idea with him.

Ian is a community support worker who has been counselling someone for six months who has a serious medical condition. He has a similar medical problem himself. At the start of his contact with this person, Ian decided not to mention his own health problem to the client. However, he is now finding it extremely difficult to carry on with the counselling because what the client is talking about reminds him of his own pain and despair, and he keeps wanting to cry during sessions. Ian imagines that it would be overwhelming for his client if he now began to share his own condition, and manufactures a rationale for handing the care of this person over to a colleague. The client is mystified about what has happened and feels rejected.

Miranda is a youth worker attached to a secondary school. The school has a specialist counsellor and has a rule that any child under 16 needs to have parental permission to receive counselling. Miranda has just finished a group workshop for a class of 15-year-old children, on relationship skills. At the end, one of the students, Kaya, comes up to her and launches into the story of her problems. When asked about whether she has considered using the specialist school counsellor, Kaya says that her parents had not given her permission to see the actual school counsellor, 'so I chose to speak to you instead'. Miranda acknowledges the difficult situation that Kaya finds herself in, and talks for a few moments about the reason why parental approval is necessary. She asks Kaya if she would be willing to tell her what happened when she asked for her parents' approval, and whether it would be helpful if Miranda perhaps met with her parents and Kaya together to review the situation.

These dilemmas illustrate the potential complexity of situations that may be ethically problematic in counselling. The dilemma that is presented to the counsellor is *their* problem. In each case, the person seeking help is trying to get what they need, but in a way that places the counsellor in a difficult position. The task for the counsellor is to acknowledge the dilemma, while remaining focused on maintaining an ongoing counselling relationship with the person. The scenario that described the ill counsellor (Ian) exemplified the importance of anticipating potentially difficult situations – Ian chose to ignore an aspect of the counselling relationship (his own health status) that had the potential to undermine his capacity to provide a safe space for counselling. The longer that time went on, the harder it became for him to do anything about the situation.

The following sections of this chapter explore difficult situations that are more clearly a problem for the person seeking help. These are situations in which risk of some kind is involved, where the person becomes impaired during the session, or where the person's needs are too great to be addressed in a meaningful way through counselling.

Risk and self-harm

One of the most challenging situations for a counsellor is when a person seeking help talks or acts in a way that suggests they may be at risk of harming themself or another person. There are several different forms that that risk may take in counselling. The person may:

- plan to take their own life;
- be engaged in self-harming behaviour such as cutting, purging, starving, alcohol or drug abuse, unsafe sex;
- be engaged in, or planning to, inflict harm on another person (which may include the counsellor), through physical, verbal or sexual violence, harassment or stalking, criminal activity or unprotected sex (for instance, in cases of HIV/AIDS infection).

While it is necessary to acknowledge that a person may have the right to kill themself or possibly even to threaten other people whom they perceive to have wronged them, it is also necessary to take into account that when a person refers to risky behaviour *to a counsellor* or other practitioner, they are almost certainly asking for help to avoid doing anything harmful. It is therefore essential for anyone acting in a counselling role to be prepared to respond constructively, actively and immediately.

In any of the types of harm listed above, a counsellor needs to arrive at a position on whether it is helpful to proceed with counselling or whether the situation requires some other kind of intervention. In order to make this kind of decision, a counsellor should be able to (i) listen out for indications from the person that some kind of harm may take place; (ii) engage the person is conversation around their intentions, and the meaning that the harm event holds for them; (iii) estimate the level of risk; (iv) implement strategies for avoiding harm.

On many occasions where harm is an issue, the person seeking help may be quite open and explicit about what is in their mind. At other times, however, the person may convey their intentions in a disguised, vague or metaphorical way of talking. There is some evidence that counsellors are not particularly sensitive at picking up subtle clues about harmful behaviour. In a study carried out by Reeves *et al.* (2004), a group of highly trained specialist counsellors were recorded in sessions with 'standardized clients', who had been instructed by the researcher to talk vaguely about suicidal intentions. Very few of the counsellors followed up the implicit cues the clients were expressing around suicidal intentions within the sessions. One explanation for this finding could be that these counsellors were more tuned into the positive aspects of what their clients were saying and less focused on negatives. Another explanation was that they lacked skill and confidence in initiating conversations around risk.

The key point here is that potentially risky behaviour may be exhibited in a variety of ways. For example, a person who has intentionally cut her arms may not say anything to a counsellor about this, but may have bandaged arms or wear a long-sleeved pullover on a warm day. A person may talk about someone to whom he bears a grudge with clenched fists and angry gestures. A person may share fantasies or images of death or destruction. In any of these cases, it is important for a counsellor to be willing to pause the counselling conversation, share their concern with the person and ask the person what they specifically have in mind.

Serious suicidal behaviour is rare, and it is unlikely that a practitioner involved in offering counselling would come across more than two or three cases over the course of their career, unless they were working in a specific area such as psychiatry or a suicide helpline. It is important for counsellors to prepare for the possibility of working with suicidal people through training, reading and study, rather than relying on first-hand experience. Excellent accounts of theory, research and personal experience around suicide can be found in Williams (1997) and Jamison (1999). The writings of Firestone (1997a, b) are particularly useful in relation to understanding the ways that different levels of suicidal intent are expressed in the language and imagery that a person might use. Firestone suggests that there exists a suicidal or self-destructive 'voice' to which practitioners can learn to be sensitive.

Assessing the severity of suicidal risk is far from being a precise science. Guidelines for sifting evidence of suicidal thoughts and intentions can be found in Hall and Platt (1999), Joseph (2000), Neimeyer *et al.* (2001) and Palmer (2002). The key indicators of high risk are:

- evidence of previous attempts;
- current suicidal thoughts and plans;
- access to means and opportunity;
- attitude towards help;
- current or past mental health problems;
- current circumstances and quality of support available from professional and informal supporters;
- current alcohol and drug use;
- recent life events or anniversaries;
- hopelessness and negative attitude towards the future;
- male aged between 16 and 30.

In general, counselling may be relevant for a person when their expression of suicidal intent is vague, when the person and their circumstances are known to the counsellor, and when the person is actively engaged in help-seeking. Otherwise, it is essential to give serious consideration, in collaboration with the person if at all possible, to organizing ongoing support in which the person's safety can be ensured while they find a way through their current difficulties.

Other forms of risk, such as deliberate self-harm and violence to others, need to be approached in a similar fashion. Violent behaviour carries with it the additional challenge that the person may become violent towards the counsellor. It is necessary for counsellors to be prepared to deal with the rare occasions when people seeking help become violent or abusive. Strategies for dealing with this kind of eventuality include having colleagues available who can offer assistance, an alarm system, and an ability to use techniques of de-escalation, in which the person is responded to in a calm, accepting manner.

Losing it

Suicidal and violent behaviour are possibilities that may occur in any kind of helping agency. In situations where suicidal or violent intentions emerge, practitioners whose counselling is embedded within other professional roles should be able to draw upon procedures and protocols that have already been put into place within their place of work. There is another type of crisis, however, that is more specifically associated with counselling, which can be characterized as 'losing it'. This kind of episode occurs when a person is exploring a life problem that has a strong emotional content, and reaches a stage at which they become overwhelmed by fear to the point that they become unable to continue to engage in rational dialogue. It is as if the person's psychological processes close down, to keep them safe, and they become out of touch and detached from what other people consider to be reality. There are three main forms of 'losing it' that can take place in counselling sessions:

- panic attacks;
- dissociation;
- hallucinatory and delusional behaviour.

Each of these phenomena makes it hard, or impossible, to continue pursuing any of the counselling tasks described in Chapters 8, 9 and 10 because effective involvement in such tasks requires a capacity to respond to another person and engage in some kind of collaborative conversation or dialogue. When a person has 'lost it', they have withdrawn from dialogue with external others and are largely focusing on some aspect their own inner experiencing.

Panic attacks are associated with a set of reactions that take place when a person experiences high levels of anxiety in a specific situation. Typically, a person will have a panic attack when they feel trapped and enclosed, with no possibility of escape. This may happen in a lift, aeroplane or any other enclosed space. A counselling session, where a person might have a sense of being 'on the spot' or under pressure, can quite easily be experienced in this kind of way. What seems to happen in a panic sequence is that the person begins to have thoughts of being trapped and powerless, which then in turn trigger physical 'flight' response, characterized by fast, shallow breathing. This physiological activity quickly produces a set of other physical symptoms, such as pins and needles in hands and arms, pressure across the chest and faintness. The person then pays attention more and more to these symptoms, which are experienced as highly alarming and generate an even higher level of thoughts about being out of control or even of dying. In turn, these thoughts lead to even faster, shallower breathing, and more physical symptoms. A panic attack is a spiral that can lead to loss of consciousness or actual flight (the person runs away, or tries to). The person will subsequently be motivated to avoid the situation that triggered the attack, and will be even more fearful if required to enter that situation. There are several accessible sources of information on managing panic, which are of value for both counsellors and those seeking help (for example, Silove and Manicavasagar, 1997; Ingham, 2000; Baker, 2003).

Dissociation can be regarded as a cognitive process for dealing with overwhelming threatening thoughts (for example, memories of highly distressing and traumatic events) and emotions by not allowing these thoughts and emotions into awareness. The person achieves this by focusing their attention on something that is neutral or safe, as an alternative to what is threatening and painful. There are usually two processes that enable a person to do this. First, the person may attempt to stop breathing. This cuts off their awareness of what they are feeling and almost makes time 'stand still'. Second, the person may find an image in their mind to attend to, or may focus on an apparently meaningless object in the room, such as a radiator or a light bulb. From the perspective of the counsellor, the person will be experienced as having 'gone away' – they will act as if they do not hear what the counsellor is saying, and are almost unaware of the counsellor's presence. A less extreme variant of this pattern can occur when a person deals with threatening thoughts and emotions by changing the topic of conversation – from the perspective of the counsellor this activity is experienced as a lack of continuity or coherence in the conversation.

Hallucinations and delusions can be viewed as ways that a person has developed for dealing with persistent impossibly difficult and stressful thoughts and emotions. What seems to happen is that these thoughts and emotions become organized into voices that the person hears, imaginary people or objects that they see, or belief systems around which they organize their life.

There is a set of basic methods for responding to these difficult situations. In essence, a counsellor confronted with any of these types of 'losing it' response needs to be able to engage constructively at the *cognitive, bodily* and *social/interpersonal* levels. At a cognitive level, the person is likely to be generating a steady stream of 'self-talk' (things that they are saying to themselves in their head, or that are being said by voices or internalized critical others) that are quite destructive and negative – for example, 'I can't cope', 'I am going to die', 'I am worthless'. It can be helpful for a counsellor to keep talking, in a calm and reassuring manner, and to introduce more positive self-statements into the person's awareness, such 'you will be all right', 'my sense is that you are afraid now, but we can see this through together'. It may be that the counsellor can introduce hopeful images or statements that the person has shared on a previous occasion. It may also be helpful for the counsellor to offer an explanation of what is happening and what can be done, such as 'I think that what you were beginning to talk about was something that is very frightening for you, and now you need to cut yourself off from it by . . .', 'I think what might be helpful now could be if you listen to me and . . .'.

Another important area for a counsellor to attend to is the physical or bodily response of the person, particularly their breathing. People who are in a process of 'losing it' are often breathing fast and shallow, or slowly (holding breath). It can be useful for a counsellor to draw the person's attention to their breathing ('I'm aware that you seem to be . . .') and instruct them in breathing regularly and deeply. For example, it may be effective to invite the person to 'breathe with me – in as far as you can – one, two, three, four, five, six, seven – and out again – one, two . . .'). In panic situations, it can be useful for a person to breathe into and out of a bag, or their cupped hands, as a means of reducing their oxygen intake. In some situations, the person's posture may be frozen, or hunched over (which inhibits breathing) and it can be useful to encourage them to begin to move, perhaps to walk.

Finally, a common feature of these ways of coping is a withdrawal of contact from the other, and a retreat into a private world. It can be helpful to encourage the person to look at the counsellor, to engage in eye contact, and (if appropriate in the context of the relationship) to touch. Accompanied by calm, confident talking on the part of the counsellor, the re-establishment of interpersonal contact can both enable the person to pay less attention to their own inner processes, and to gain a sense of safety and security ('there is someone here I can trust and rely on') that can make whatever it was that was scary seem a bit more bearable.

These three basic methods are not, in themselves, going to eliminate panic, dissociation or voice-hearing from a person's life for ever; they are simply strategies for helping someone who is seeking counselling to manage their thoughts and feelings in the moment, so that they may, if they choose, continue to engage in a counselling conversation.

Within western society, experiences of panic, dissociation and hallucination are often addressed through psychiatric interventions, such administration of drug treatment, or by specialist psychotherapeutic interventions such as cognitive behavioural therapy (CBT). Although the methods being described here are consistent with a psychiatric or CBT approach, they are better viewed as a crisis-management strategy, designed to enable the person to make use of a counselling relationship and space to talk. In most cases, it will be helpful to explore with the person the potential value of receiving specialist help for their panic, voice-hearing or dissociation. It is therefore important for anyone offering a counselling relationship to be informed about the possibilities for such specialist help that are available within their community, and the procedures for making referrals.

Box 11.1   Working with people who are hard to reach

Sometimes, a person may be looking for help with a problem in living, but experience great difficulty in expressing what they need. Such individuals may have a life that is characterized by general communication problems, for example, people who have learning difficulties or Alzheimer's disease. Other people may be incapacitated by temporary states of fear, anxiety or voice hearing, which may make it hard for them to stay focused on a conversation. The American person-centred therapist Garry Prouty has developed some useful methods for making basic emotional and interpersonal contact with people who are hard to reach. He recommends that a counsellor faced by a person who is withdrawn or unable to communicate effectively should concentrate solely on making concrete and literal empathic reflections. Prouty (2000) describes five types of basic contact-making reflections:

- *Situational reflections* – statements of the counsellor's awareness of the person's situation or environment. For example: 'you are sitting on the sofa'.
- *Facial reflections* – statements that seek to capture the pre-expressive feelings of the person, as embodied in their face. For example: 'you are smiling'.
- *Word-for-word reflections* – restatements of single words, sentences and other sounds made by the person.

- *Body reflections* – the counsellor moves their own body to match the postures or movements made by the person.
- *Reiterative reflections* – if any of the previous types of statements appear to be effective in establishing contact, they are repeated.

The assumption behind these literal empathic reflective methods is that the person has for the moment lost contact with the external world, and that if recontact is to occur, it needs to begin with simple moves that are unthreatening, under the control of the person, and uncomplex. Of course, it is essential to offer these statements in a gentle and respectful manner. Prouty (2000) offers an example of his work with an older woman, Dorothy, who was an institutionalized resident of a psychiatric facility. She mumbled for about ten minutes, while Prouty reflected back whatever words he could make out. Then, she made a clear statement, 'come with me', which Prouty again reflected back. She then led him to the corner of the room, and they stood there silently for some time. She put her hand against the wall and said 'cold'. He put his hand on the wall too, and repeated 'cold'. He noted that 'she had been holding my hand all along; but when I reflected her, she would tighten her grip' (p. 69). Dorothy's words then gradually began to make more sense: 'I don't like it here. I'm so tired . . . so tired' (with tears).

Further information about this method can be found in Peters (1999) and Prouty *et al.* (2002). What it offers is a disciplined and caring means of patiently staying as close as possible to the experience of someone who is withdrawn, until the point where they feel able to enter into a reciprocal relationship.

Referring on

Being willing and able to refer individuals to other sources of help is an essential competence for any practitioner who is offering counselling that is embedded in another professional role. The kinds of factors that can bring the issue of referral into the frame are when the person seeking help:

- needs more time than the counsellor is able to give or more frequent meetings;
- is primarily looking for practical information and advice, rather than an opportunity to talk things through;
- describes problems in living that the counsellor believes are beyond his or her capacity to work with;
- might gain a lot from making use of a specialist agency where there are practitioners available who have a wealth of knowledge and experience in relation to the type of problem the person has described (in other words, there is somewhere better for them to go);
- is involved in a prior relationship with the counsellor that would be incompatible with the creation of a secure and confidential counselling space.

It is important to realize that counselling, as envisaged in this book, is a generic form of helping, through which, in principle, many types of problems in living can be addressed by many different types of practitioner. The strength of counselling is that, compared with other forms of help, it is flexible and accessible – a matter of talking to someone who is equipped to listen and engage in a therapeutic conversation. However, it is also necessary to recognize that there exists a huge array of professional and voluntary groups and agencies that have developed knowledge and skill in helping people to deal with specific types of problems. There is little point in any counsellor struggling to help someone with a problem when there are other practitioners available who may have better resources in relation to that problem.

The key steps in the referral process, for a counsellor, are: (i) knowing what alternative resources are available; (ii) engaging the person in a discussion around the possibility of seeing someone else; and (iii) making the referral and managing the 'passing over' stage. These are all quite sensitive tasks.

Part of the work of preparing to offer counselling relationships involves building up a network of agencies to whom people may be referred, and keeping this database updated. It is necessary, for any service or agency, to know about the type of client they are willing to work with, the kind of service they offer, how a person can access the service, who pays and the waiting time. It can be extremely useful to make contact, formally or informally, with someone who works in the service, so that any detailed issues can be explored on a personal basis if and when a referral needs to be made. It is also helpful to collect information about the service that could be read by the person seeking help, for example leaflets and website details. This level of detail is required because the person seeking help may be in a state of urgency and neediness that could make it hard for them to tolerate ambiguity or uncertainty ('I think the CBT service should be able to help you but I'm not sure whether you need to be referred by your GP'), and because there is a tendency for specialist services to be inaccessible owing to long waiting times, complex referral routes, cost (private practice clinics) or location (only based in big cities and, therefore, out of reach of people in rural areas or unable to pay travel costs).

Making a suggestion to a person that it might be valuable to consider an alternative source of help, represents a sensitive moment in a counselling relationship. Almost certainly, if a counsellor has reached a point where referral might seem useful, they will have learned quite a lot about the person and begun to form a relationship with them. From the perspective of the person seeking help, having opened up to a counsellor it can be very hard to hear a referral suggestion as anything other than a form of rejection ('I don't really want to see you again') or as a sign of personal deficiency ('I must be too crazy for her . . .'). To minimize these reactions, it is useful for a counsellor to be as open as possible about their reasons for bringing up the topic of referral and to allow sufficient time for the issue to be explored collaboratively.

At the point of making a referral, it is important to do everything possible to prepare the person for the new form of help they will receive ('what you will find is that the therapist in the CBT clinic will work in a different way from me. For example, they will probably expect you to do homework assignments, such as keeping a diary . . .'). It is also essential to make clear to the person the information that has been transmitted to the new therapist – they may assume that a new helper will know everything about them or be upset that they know anything at all. It can also be valuable, in some circumstances, to continue to see a person for a while after they have started to work with a different practitioner, or to arrange to see them at some time in the future to 'catch up' on developments in their life. These practices can also help to soften any sense of rejection.

It is perhaps easiest to think of referral as involving access to specialist professional services. However, there are many other sorts of community resource that may be just the right environment for a person. These can include self-help groups and networks, church groups, educational programmes and political action groups. Community resources can also include individual people who have their own personal story to tell around overcoming a problem.

When confrontation may be necessary

The fundamental standpoint for any counsellor is that of collaboration – standing alongside the person and being their ally as they seek to resolve problems in living. Sometimes, however, it may be necessary to take a more oppositional stance, and to challenge or confront a person. There are a number of situations in which the difficulty that the counsellor is experiencing in remaining an ally of the person seeking help are so distracting to them that confrontation is inevitable. These situations can include:

- when the person is lying to the counsellor;
- when the person continues to engage in self-destructive actions, despite extensive exploration around the underlying issues;
- when the person is using the counselling to gain external advantage – for instance, a student who appears to attend counselling only to secure a note that will justify an extension on an essay deadline;
- when the person is exploiting or threatening the counsellor, for example using the counsellor as an object of sexual arousal.

In each of these situations, and in other situations that might be imagined, the integrity of the counselling space is at stake because if the counsellor does not do something then they will be unable to continue with any degree of authentic self-respect.

When challenging or confronting a person, it is important for a counsellor to make 'I' statements and take responsibility for their own judgements and feelings. It is also important to confront only in a context where the person has been otherwise valued or affirmed, to prevent the possibility of coming across as persecutory. It is helpful to be specific about which actual behaviour triggered a particular reaction, for instance using the formula: 'when you said/did . . . I felt/thought . . .', and to avoid 'totalizing' statements that generalize about the whole of the person. In other words, it is best to separate the issue or behaviour from the person as a whole.

When confronting someone, check out that the recipient has heard what you are saying and understands your key points. It is also essential to take care of safety issues – it is clearly not a good idea to confront someone with a history of violence while alone in a building. The experienced psychotherapist Irvin Yalom (2002) has written that his rule of thumb is, wherever possible, to 'strike while the iron is cold'. In other words, confronting from a state of anger or frustration, or when the person is angry or upset himself or herself, may result in a situation where neither side can be heard, with the result that the viability of the relationship may be threatened.

Confronting is generally a frightening experience for counsellors, who tend to be people who want to be liked and to be seen as helpful. It can therefore be particularly important for anyone involved in a counselling role to make use of consultation and supervision in respect of this kind of episode. However, explicit confrontation is rare in counselling. Challenge and disagreement can be regarded as intrinsic parts of the process of dialogue that is the bedrock of good counselling. Confrontation, on the other hand, is something stronger. It is not part of routine counselling practice, but is an action that arises from a threatened breakdown of the counselling space.

Conclusions

A central theme that has run through this chapter is the idea of *crisis* – difficult situations in counselling tend to be those in which there is a crisis to be resolved, either a crisis in the life of the person seeking help, or a crisis in the relationship between the person and the counsellor. In responding to crisis, it is important not to assume that the acute difficulty being experienced is necessarily characteristic of the person (or the relationship) as a whole. As James and Gilliland (2001: 21) put it: 'crisis is a perception of an event or situation as an intolerable difficulty that exceeds the person's *immediately available* resources and coping mechanisms'. In other words, the person may be able to draw on resources and coping mechanisms that are not immediately available but that can be brought to bear on the situation.

Crisis episodes in counselling, when the safe space of the relationship is under threat, are likely to elicit a complex mix of emotions, thoughts and action tendencies. At a point of not knowing how to cope, a person may express anger and hostility, anxiety and fear, or sadness/loss, depending on the meaning of the situation to them. Their thinking may be dominated by a sense of being violated, they may be thinking ahead to the possible consequences of what is happening, or their thinking may be oriented towards the past, and fixated on terrible events that cannot now be recovered or put right. In relation to their behaviour, the person may be actively trying to resolve the crisis event, they may seek to evade or escape the event, or they may be immobilized by it, perhaps even engaged in behaviour that is unproductive, self-defeating and disorganized. Any of these patterns and reactions can be experienced during difficult situations in counselling, by the person and possibly also by the counsellor. In such circumstances, it is particularly important for a counsellor to be able to draw on principles and strategies that they have been worked out in advance (preparation and training) and to be able to make use of the support of colleagues.

Another theme that threads through the issues discussed in this chapter is the degree to which difficult situations represent a challenge to the values and collaborative stance of a counsellor. At times when the person seeking help is happy to engage in a two-way conversation about the problems in their life, it is a relatively straightforward task for the counsellor to treat the person as an equal partner, respect their agency, believe in their capacity for growth and development, participate in joint decision making, and so on. At the crunch points, for example, when the person is suicidal, is fearful and withdrawn to the point of not being able to leave their chair, or furious at what they perceive as a betrayal of a counsellor who has told them they will need to see someone else, the balance changes. At these points, it may be necessary to be quite directive, for example, by questioning the person about their plans for suicide, or being clear about the limits of their caring and commitment ('I'm sorry, but I am just not able to give you the time that you need'). At the same time, in taking control and exerting authority to maintain the safety of the person (or their own safety in their role as counsellor), a counsellor should to be mindful of the fact that at some point in the future a more collaborative way of working will need to be re-created.

Difficult situations are not smooth or easy. They are hard work and even scary. However, they provide opportunities for taking the relationship between a person and a counsellor, and the bond of trust between them, much further. None of the difficult situations described in this chapter are trivial. On the contrary, they reflect real challenges to people, sometimes even challenges of life and death. Being able to work through these challenges successfully, even if untidily and with difficulty, can bring people together and can be the source of much learning.

Questions for reflection and discussion

1. What kinds of ethical dilemma have arisen for you in relation to your counselling role? How have you resolved these issues? In your view, what effect have these ethical issues had on the people who consult you for help? How relevant or valuable for you are the guidelines for ethical decision making provided in this chapter?
2. Reflect on the types of people with whom you interact in your work setting. What are the risk issues presented by these people? What strategies do you employ for assessing risk, and ensuring the safety and well-being of service users?
3. What are your procedures for referring people on to specialist services? How do you know whether these procedures are satisfactory for the people who are referred?
4. What is your own experience of being confronted by someone in a position of authority, in a work setting? Did this episode lead to a productive conclusion? What did the person do, in confronting you, that was constructive, and what did they do that was destructive?

Suggestions for further reading

The literature on crisis intervention contains a great deal of wisdom and practical knowledge around how to approach difficult situations in helping relationships. Particularly recommended are:

James, R. and Gilliland, B. (2001) *Crisis Intervention Strategies*, 4th edn. Belmont, CA: Wadsworth.
Kanel, K. (1999) *A Guide to Crisis Intervention*. Belmont, CA: Wadsworth.

The 'tidal model' of mental health includes useful suggestions about how to respond constructively to situations when a person is at risk of suicide or self-harm:

Barker, P. and Buchanan-Barker, P. (2005) *The Tidal Model: A Guide for Mental Health Professionals*. London: Brunner-Routledge.

Creative and effective approaches to working with people who hear voices are described in a useful book by the founder of the Hearing Voices Network, an important self-help organization:

Romme, M. and Escher, S. (2000) *Making Sense of Voices: A Guide for Mental Health Professionals Working with Voice Hearers*. London: Mind Publications.

Other innovative strategies for understanding and being helpful in relation to the kinds of personal crises that are generally described as 'mental health issues' are reviewed in the *This is Madness* series:

Newnes, C., Holmes, G. and Dunn, C. (eds) (1999) *This is Madness: A Critical Look at Psychiatry and the Future of Mental Health Services*. Ross-on-Wye: PCCS Books.
Newnes, C., Holmes, G. and Dunn, C. (eds) (2000) *This is Madness Too: A Further Look at Psychiatry and the Future of Mental Health Services*. Ross-on-Wye: PCCS Books.

A book that contains a comprehensive analysis of ethical issues in counselling situations is:

Bond, T. (2000) *Standards and Ethics for Counselling in Action*, 2nd edn. London: Sage.

12

Putting it all together – doing good work

Introduction • Counselling embedded within other professional roles: integrating knowledges • Using supervision, consultation and support • Affirming difference and diversity • Assembling a toolkit of methods • The role of training and continuing professional development • Avoiding burnout • Personal therapy for counsellors • Making use of research and inquiry • Conclusions • Questions for reflection and discussion • Suggestions for further reading

Can I have a few minutes to talk about Bob? Older man. Been seeing him every couple of weeks for six months. Usual stuff – medication, dealing with questions, tests. He had never talked about what it all meant to him. Tremendous family support. Last week it all poured out. What? Yes, of course – *what* poured out? I guess the main thing was about dying, which he knows at some level, but not at another. But the immediate thing was letting his children know how he felt about them. All the things he wanted to say before it was too late. He's feeling himself getting more tired and not facing up to anything. Never been one to get emotional. Anyway, he came up with the idea of making a speech at his birthday party. We talked a bit about what he might say. He thinks they'll video it. Sorry – it's bringing it all back. At one point he said something like 'it's getting so bad I might take things into my own hands'. Yes, I asked him about harming himself. He said he would never actually do that. I believed him. What do you think? Is it worth going back to that next time I see him? What? What's it bringing back for me? Where do you want me to start?

Introduction

In earlier chapters, a number of dimensions of counselling skill have been discussed. In order to explore these dimensions, it has been necessary to separate them out and examine them in turn. In practice, however, when actually working with someone engaged in the process of talking though an issue, all of these different aspects of counselling skill need to fit seamlessly together. On the whole, the best way to integrate different facets of counselling skill – as with any other skill – is simply to do it. Each time that a counsellor enters into a helping relationship with a person is an opportunity for learning and contributes to building up a reserve of practical knowledge. However, there are some specific issues that can emerge at the stage of moving from primarily learning about counselling to that of primarily practising it. These issues include: developing a counselling approach that is consistent with other professional roles within which it might be embedded; purposefully making use of consultation and supervision; developing a personal style in the form of an individual toolkit or repertoire of methods; engaging in continuing professional development; dealing with the stress of the work; making use of research and inquiry.

Counselling embedded within other professional roles: integrating knowledges

A useful concept to have emerged in social science in recent years, and which has been exploited by narrative therapists, is the idea of *knowledges*. Rather than thinking of knowledge as a single, unitary body of concepts and information, which implies a fixed truth, it has been argued that it is more appropriate to recognize that different groups of people possess their own distinctive 'knowledges' around any topic. The idea of knowledges implies that there can be different truths on a subject, reflecting diverse standpoints and perspectives. Narrative therapists have further developed this concept in their use of the term 'insider knowledges', to draw a contrast between 'expert' or 'objective' knowing, and the personal knowledge that is held by people who have first-hand experience of a subject. For example, although textbooks can provide a wealth of expert knowledge on depression, this may not correspond to the 'insider knowledge' that is possessed by someone who has known depression in their life. Narrative therapists argue that the problems are often compounded by the tendency of professional helpers to impose 'expert knowledge' on them and not take their personal 'insider knowledge' seriously. It is easy to do this, since expert knowledge derives authority from being based on research and contained in books on library shelves, whereas insider knowledge can only claim the authority of the voice of the individual person, or perhaps a group of service users speaking up collectively.

The concept of knowledges has a great deal of relevance for anyone involved in offering counselling within the context of another professional role, such as a nurse breaking off from wound care to allow a patient to talk through his feelings about the way that his disfigurement has impacted on his life, or a teacher finding time to explore a pupil's options in responding to bullying. In any such situation, the person offering counselling is required to take into account three different forms of insider knowledge:

- counsellor knowledge;
- nurse or teacher knowledge;
- personal knowledge.

These three sources of insider knowledge refer only to what is happening inside the awareness of the counsellor. In addition, the counsellor will have an appreciation of the insider knowledge of the person seeking help.

Knowledges are inevitably complex, and consist of networks of ideas, concepts, memories, practices and so on. In order to highlight the potential for tension between knowledges, it can be useful to consider a 'knowledge' as comprising a specification for *how to understand* something and *what to do* about it. For instance, the nurse in the example earlier, caring for a patient with a disfiguring facial wound who has indicated that he wishes to talk about his feelings, might momentarily be aware of a range of potentially conflicting reactions:

- Counsellor response: 'How can I create a space for safe exploration of this issue?', 'He trusts me enough to open up how he is feeling', 'How much time do we have?', 'Is this a private enough place to talk?'
- Nurse response: 'Could this be a side effect of the medication he is receiving?', 'Is he depressed?', 'Should I consider a psychiatric referral?', 'I don't have time for this right now.'
- Personal response: 'I would feel awful if that had happened to me', 'If I was in his situation I would just want to cry', 'I can't handle this – it's too heavy.'

Each of these responses is based on a different type of insider knowledge. One of the biggest challenges for anyone involved in providing counselling that is embedded within another work role is to develop strategies for acknowledging and making use of *all* of the knowledges that are available to them. As a nurse in a uniform, busy changing the dressing on a patient's wound, it would be impossible to move straight into a counsellor role and ignore the realities of the nurse–patient relationship. At the same time, a counselling conversation that was not informed by the personal experience of the counsellor would run the risk of being detached and distanced.

There is little research into the way that 'embedded' counsellors deal constructively with the challenge of conflicting knowledges. One of the most obvious strategies is *sequencing* – applying different knowledges in turn. For example, the wound care nurse could enter into a counselling conversation, close that conversation, then ask about side effects and other possible symptoms of depression. In contrast, it seems likely that many people who work in human service occupations such as education and teaching, who may possess sensitivity and skill in counselling, find it virtually impossible to shift out of the dominant knowledge stance of their profession and tend to suppress any awareness they might have of the emotional needs of their clients, service users or patients.

Some practitioners choose to build opportunities for counselling into their work with clients by deliberately integrating counselling 'invitations' into their everyday practice. In this way, the practitioner can set the scene for counselling, rather than being in a position of being asked to respond to counselling needs at times when it is difficult to do so. For example, a teacher can let her students know that she is available for one-to-one consultation at a specific time each week, or a community nurse visiting patients in their homes can try to schedule time on a regular basis for a cup of tea and conversation with each patient, once nursing tasks have been completed.

Within the mainstream professional counselling community, there has been some concern about counselling that is offered in the context of other roles, for example by health, education and social care staff. From the point of view of a practitioner of 'stand-alone' counselling, there are a number of potential dangers associated with 'embedded' counselling:

- the person receiving counselling may be unclear about what is happening and what to expect, if their helper is playing different roles at different times;
- the person offering counselling may get out of their depth;
- the boundaries of the counselling relationship, for example, around the confidentiality of what is said, may become blurred.

It is easy to imagine situations where embedded counselling can run into difficulties.

Example

Susan is a university student who has a good relationship with one of her tutors. During one tutorial, Susan talks about why it is so difficult for her to speak in seminars, and begins to make a connection between what she feels like in the seminar room, and feeling 'exposed and weak' during a time in her childhood when she had been sexually abused. Her tutor does her best to help Susan to talk this through, but is personally upset and shocked by what she is hearing. Some of this reaction transmits itself to Susan, who is reinforced in her core self-belief that she is 'different' and 'strange'. In future tutorials, the tutor subtly conveys the message that she does not wish to hear any more about Susan's abuse story. Even worse, she mentions what has happened to a colleague who does not appreciate the sensitivity of the situation, and then tells other colleagues. Susan comes to believe that she is being treated 'with kid gloves' by the staff in the college.

It is important to be aware of the challenges faced by offering a counselling space within the context of other relationships. The case of Susan illustrates the damage that can be done when a teacher or other worker drifts into a counselling role without sufficient thought about what might be involved. The model of counselling skill provided in this book specifies the steps that need to be taken to ensure that embedded counselling is safe:

- careful preparation;
- negotiation and construction of a bounded 'space';
- focus on key counselling tasks;
- awareness of the limits of what can be achieved;

- a resource/referral network;
- consultative support or supervision for the counsellor.

If these elements are in place, then both practitioners and the people they work with can be confident that useful and constructive outcomes can be achieved.

The main theme of this section has been the potential sources of tension between a counselling role and other roles such as those of doctor, teacher or social worker, and the importance of thinking through the implications of the different knowledges that are associated with these roles. However, it is also essential to acknowledge that there can be significant advantages associated with embedded counselling, compared with a stand-alone counselling role. A nurse or teacher is likely to possess a fair amount of information about a person and the key facts of their life history, some of it gained through first-hand observation. As a result, at the point where that person seeks to talk through a problem in living, the person will know that their nurse counsellor or teacher counsellor possesses this information, and will therefore be able to get straight to the point in terms of what is bothering them. By contrast, a specialist counsellor has no prior knowledge of the life of a client who makes an appointment to see them, and will need to spend some time acquiring this information. This may be awkward for the client, because what they really want is help for their problem, rather than spending time explaining their life history. Also, an embedded counsellor may well have a richer appreciation of a person's life, from having seen that person in different everyday situations, in contrast to the more limited appreciation possessed by a specialist counsellor who must rely on the verbal reports of what is happening 'out there' provided during the weekly therapy hour.

Another significant advantage of embedded counselling is that the person seeking counselling is in a position to make an active and deliberate choice of whom they decide to talk to. For example, someone who has a health problem may interact with several different health staff – doctors, nurses, physiotherapists, cleaners and porters. They can decide who seems trustworthy and who is on their wavelength in advance of taking the risk of opening up about how they feel. By contrast, a person entering specialist counselling is normally allocated to a counsellor or psychotherapist whom they have never met before, and with whom they need to build a relationship of trust very quickly. Although there is no research evidence on this question, it would seem likely that people who decide to seek counselling help from someone with whom they already have some dealings, such as their GP, spiritual advisor or educational tutor, do so on the basis that they feel that they possess good evidence of the helpfulness, genuineness and reliability of that person.

A final potential advantage of embedded counselling is that the professional knowledge of the helper may be relevant and useful in relation to their counselling role. For example, when a school pupil asks for some time to talk to one of his teachers around a bullying problem, then it is likely that the teacher will possess a sophisticated map or framework for understanding the dynamics of bullying and the types of strategies that are available. This framework is not an abstract set of ideas, but is peopled by the teacher's images and memories of numerous bullying cases and scenarios that they have encountered in the past. This professional knowledge can represent a tremendous resource in counselling. The skill of counselling, in this situation, involves making use of this knowledge in a way that is responsive to the individual person seeking help, rather than 'prescribing' a fixed solution. However, this framework represents a 'knowledge' that a counsellor working in a therapy agency or centre would be unlikely to possess, or to possess in such depth.

The issue of knowledges opens up a crucial arena for reflection and planning for anyone involved in providing counselling in the context of another helping role. To be an effective counsellor in this sort of setting requires finding ways of resolving tensions between competing knowledges and harnessing points of synergy. Achieving these goals will always involve the use of consultation and supervision, because there are inevitably aspects of the roles and knowledge frameworks that any of us occupy that are so taken for granted that we can lose sight of their existence. The cost of *not* arriving at an appropriate integration of roles and knowledges can be high, for the counsellor as well as for the person seeking help. Returning to the case of the college student, Susan, who drew her tutor into a conversation about childhood abuse, for which the tutor was not well prepared to handle. How stressful was that for the tutor? How did she cope afterwards, with her feeling that she had let Susan down?

Using supervision, consultation and support

One of the distinctive accomplishments of the counselling profession in Britain has been its insistence on the key principle that anyone who is involved in a counselling role must receive regular supervision from an experienced colleague who is not their line manager. This principle reflects an appreciation that the task of engaging on a one-to-one basis with the life difficulties of another person presents a set of challenges that cannot be effectively resolved alone. There is a lot happening in a counselling session, and it is invaluable to know that there is someone else available to act as a sounding board for questions such as 'have I missed anything?', 'is there anything else I can be doing to help?' and 'how can I make sense of the complex and confusing story I am hearing?' Supervision is also a place where the personal impact of the work can be explored, and the counsellor can receive support and develop strategies for self-care. Inevitably, the stories of some people seeking counselling will trigger memories and emotions in the counsellor, linked to similar types of experience in their own life. In addition, the emotional and relationship needs and patterns of some people who come for counselling can invite unconscious reciprocal responses on the part of the counsellor, which may not be helpful. For example, someone who copes with their difficulties by getting into arguments with other people, that reinforce a position that 'I need to deal with everything on my own because no one understands me', may talk about their concerns in a way that subtly irritates the counsellor and leaves a strong residue of emotion at the end of the counselling session. Supervision provides a place for exploring this: 'what is happening that makes me feel angry every time that Ernie tells me about his problems?'

The separation of supervision and line management is important because the focus of line management supervision is usually on the performance of the individual in relation to organizational goals, whereas the focus of counselling supervision is more exploratory, supportive and personal. Effective counselling supervision requires that the counsellor should feel free to admit possible mistakes and disclose personal vulnerabilities – it is harder to do this with someone who may be responsible for continuing your contract or recommending you for promotion. There is obviously an overlap between management supervision and counselling supervision – for example, a counselling supervisor needs to be able to communicate their concerns, and have them acted on, if they believe that a supervisee is not working effectively – but, on the whole, it has proved most useful to keep these roles separate.

There are a number of different ways that supervision can be organized. Many people who work in counselling roles arrange to meet their supervisor for one ninety-minute session each month, with the option of telephone or email consultations in emergencies. Some counsellors meet as a group with a supervisor, typically for a longer period or on more occasions, each month to ensure that each member receives sufficient individual time. Other counsellors meet in peer supervision groups, whereas some belong to networks where they can call on other members for consultative support. Accredited counsellors operate within professional codes of conduct that specify the amount of supervision that is required, and the level of qualifications and experience of supervisors. At present, such guidelines do not exist for practitioners who provide counselling within the context of other work roles. This situation can lead to difficulties for such counsellors in terms of getting their managers to agree to the allocation of dedicated supervision time, or to reimburse supervisors.

When arranging supervision, it is important to recognize that different counsellors have different supervision needs. Just as people have different learning styles and coping strategies, they have different ways of engaging with supervision (see Weaks, 2002). The supervision style or needs of a counsellor may shift through their career, for example as they become more experienced, or are faced with different client groups.

Box 12.1   What happens in supervision?

Just as a counsellor creates a space within which the person seeking help can explore and resolve a wide range of different types of problems in living, a supervisor provides a similar kind of space for a counsellor. There are many aspects of the work of a counsellor that may usefully be addressed in supervision. Hawkins and Shohet (2000) have devised a model of supervision that is widely used within the profession. They suggest that supervision can have three broad functions: education, support and management. The *educative* dimension of supervision relates to such aims as understanding the client better and exploring methods of working with the client's problems. The *supportive* dimension refers to the task of becoming aware of how the emotions and needs of the person seeking help have had an impact on the helper, and avoiding burnout. The *management* dimension is concerned with ensuring that the highest standards of care and service are maintained. Hawkins and Shohet have observed that these functions can be explored by reflecting on seven distinct areas:

1. The content of what the person seeking help was talking about.
2. The strategies, interventions and methods used by the counsellor.

3. The relationship between the counsellor and the person seeking help.
4. The counsellor's personal reactions to the person seeking help.
5. The relationship between the counsellor and the supervisor.
6. The supervisor's personal reactions to the counsellor.
7. The organizational and social context of the counselling.

The relevance, in supervision, of areas 5 and 6 (what is happening during the super-vision session) lies in the significance of a phenomenon known as 'parallel process': the re-enactment in the supervision relationship of issues being played out in the counselling relationship. An example of parallel process might be if a person seeking help found it hard to talk about their problem, and then in turn their counsellor was vague or hesitant in describing the case within the supervision session.

Most supervision is carried out through talk – discussing the work that the counsellor is doing. However, as in counselling, supervision can be facilitated using a number of different methods. For instance, Lahad (2000) describes the use of expressive arts techniques within individual and group supervision contexts.

Underpinning effective supervision is the establishment of a good relationship between supervisor and supervisee. The evidence from research on supervision suggests that counsellors' experiences of supervision is polarized to a significant extent. There are some counsellors who find supervisors with whom they are able to form a strong, productive and supportive partnership, and from whom they never wish to part. There are other supervisor–supervisee relationships that seem almost to enter a downward spiral, in which the counsellor becomes reluctant to share any evidence of difficulty or vulnerability with their supervisor, and the supervisor becomes more and more critical of the counsellor. This kind of experience can be highly damaging for counsellors, because it can take some time to decide to withdraw from such a relationship, given the authority of the more experienced supervisor, and the tendency to accept that their criticism might be soundly based. The book by Lawton and Feltham (2000) includes a useful analysis of the factors involved in abusive or unhelpful supervision. Although the majority of experienced counselling practitioners are able to offer satisfactory supervision or consultation to colleagues, in recent years a number of supervision training courses have been set up, which are invaluable in enabling would-be supervisors to become aware of the complexities of the supervisor role and the issues involved in constructing appropriate supervision contracts (Page and Wosket, 2001).

When constructing a supervision or consultation system it is helpful to build in diversity and choice. Ideally, over a period of time, any person in a counselling role should be able to work with different supervisors, and gain experience of different modes of supervision and support (individual, group-based, face-to-face, online). Supervision and consultative support also need to be viewed in a broader context of continuing professional development and learning, in which practitioners view themselves as *reflective practitioners*. Reflecting on practice is an activity that should be integral to practice, in the from of thinking through different courses of action, keeping a personal learning journal, writing notes and attending training events. Formal supervision probably works best when it leads to self-supervision: the best supervisor is the one with whom one can carry out a conversation in one's head and arrive at a productive answer to an immediate dilemma. It is also important to recognize that there can be significant organizational barriers to the development of an effective supervision network. Particularly within a busy organization, such as a health centre, in which counselling does not play a central role within the service that is provided for clients, but is embedded within other practitioner activities, it can be all to easy to argue that there is no time for supervision, or that supervision is a 'luxury we can't afford here'. In other organizational settings, there may be a blame culture, or an over-bureaucratic approach, that makes it hard to achieve authentic supervision relationships. Hawkins and Shohet (2000) provide an excellent discussion of organizational barriers to supervision and make a number of suggestions for ways in which supervision can contribute to the creation of a learning organization.

Affirming difference and diversity

A central theme of this book, and within counselling theory and research more broadly, has been the importance of the relationship between the counsellor and the person seeking help. This relationship is mainly understood and discussed, in the counselling literature, in terms of patterns of interaction (for example, the person speaks and the counsellor reflects back what they hear) and values (for example, the aim of the counsellor is to respect, accept and empathize with the person). These aspects of the counselling relationship are intentional: the counsellor purposefully sets out to establish relationship qualities, such as empathy and acceptance. However, there is another crucial dimension of the relationship that is beyond the intentional reach of either participant. Both the person seeking counselling and their counsellor are positioned within society – each of them has a social identity that is displayed in the way they talk, dress, look and act. The social identity of any individual is necessarily complex, consisting of such factors as age, sex, social class, ethnicity, race, sexual orientation, religion, health status and disability status. Every one of these factors has a social meaning, with implications for the way that a person views themself and the way that they are viewed by others. Some of these factors are visible and overt (skin colour, sex), whereas others are either harder to discern or may even be actively concealed (sexual orientation, social class).

Each of these social identity factors contributes to the construction of the relationship between a person and a counsellor.

Examples
Gary is a gay man who has had some difficulties at work and is under a lot of stress. He visits his doctor to ask for some antidepressant medication and a sick note. While he is there, he feels that it would be useful to fill in his GP on some of the detail of what has been happening in his life. He stares at the GP: 'Can I tell him I am gay? He looks straight. That must be a picture of his kids on the desk. I couldn't

stand it if he came over all politically correct on the surface and homophobic underneath.'

Anjali is a nurse whose Indian grandparents died during the famine of 1943 that came about as a result of British exploitation and misrule. She is visiting the home of Alec, an upper-class Englishman to whom she is providing palliative care. Alec is upset about his isolation and loneliness, so Anjali invites him to tell her about better times in his life. Alec starts to talk about the old days in India, when he was an administrator in Bengal . . .

Gemma is 15 years old, at school, and upset about her clumsiness in the gymnastics class. Her physical education teacher finds an opportunity to talk with Gemma on her own, and asks her what it is that is bothering her. Gemma replies: 'How could you understand? You can't remember what it's like.'

In each of these examples, a potentially strong and supportive relationship between a person and a practitioner is brought to a halt around the issue of difference. One of the biggest challenges in relation to continuing to do good work over a period of time is to retain curiosity about difference. It is all too easy, in any kind of professional role, to develop fixed images of 'types' of clients and service users. To combat this tendency, it is necessary to be active in seeking out ways of sustaining a sense of curiosity and positive affirmation, for example, by attending training events on this theme, working with colleagues from different cultural groups, and engagement with relevant areas of politics, history and art.

Assembling a toolkit of methods

The importance of counselling *methods* (what to do to achieve goals) has been highlighted throughout this book. Probably, when beginning to offer counselling, any practitioner will rely on a limited set of methods – some acquired during training, and others based on personal experience of life. Over the course of a career, one of the enjoyable aspects of continuing professional development can be that of acquiring awareness and competence in new methods. Perhaps one of the key messages of this book is that there are many, many things that a counsellor can do to be helpful. There are methods that have been devised by psychologists and psychotherapists, methods that are drawn from the arts, business, education, sport and many other fields. It may be valuable to accumulate a collection of 'counselling objects' – buttons, stones, driftwood, toys – that can assist the depiction of emotions and life situations. It can be useful to collect metaphors, images and stories that seem relevant to the client group with whom one is working.

The role of training and continuing professional development

There are many pathways that can be followed to gain training in counselling. Because the field of counselling practice is broad and diverse, different types of training and learning experience have evolved within different settings. Nevertheless, probably the most common training route is that a person may begin by engaging in a brief introductory course, of perhaps 20–30 contact hours, in the context of initial professional training in a field such as nursing, medicine or education, or at an evening class. The next step is often to enrol on a more extended course, of 100–150 contact hours, that may extend over a year. This kind of programme typically leads to the award of a certificate, and is oriented towards the learning needs of people whose counselling is embedded in another occupational role. The material in this book is primarily intended to support people at the certificate stage of training. There are large numbers of people within the workforce who have received counselling training at introductory and certificate levels. Beyond that level, it is possible to enter a professional training programme, leading to accreditation as a specialist 'stand-alone' counsellor. These programmes usually consist of 400 contact hours, over two or more years, and lead to the award of a first degree, diploma or master's degree. Finally, practitioners who have gained a certificate or diploma usually engage in ongoing continuing professional development amounting to a minimum of at least three days each year.

All of these training experiences should offer some combination of four key elements of learning:

- A framework (in other words, theory, models and research) for making sense of practice.
- Practical work, either with real clients and service users, or involving other members of the course in the role of counsellor and client.
- Reflection on the personal meaning and implications of the topics that are being addressed.
- Professional issues such as avoiding harm, negotiating consent, maintaining confidentiality, and working in different organizational contexts.

Although the balance between these elements will depend on the aims and duration of any specific course, before enrolling on a course it is essential to determine whether all of these principles have been incorporated into the design of the programme. For example, within counselling, distance learning courses are of limited value because meaningful practical work requires face-to-face contact, as does personal reflection that builds on feedback from others. While distance learning approaches such as e-learning online packages can be useful to facilitate learning around theory and research, they are only effective on counselling courses when they form part of a broader programme that includes face-to-face participation.

For most people who take part in counselling courses, the most significant contribution to their learning comes from the experience of working closely with a small group of fellow learners over a period of time. The types of issues that are covered on any counselling course (What is a helping relationship? How do learning and change take place? What are the personal, ethical and professional boundaries that are relevant to my role?) are the same issues that are played out in the relationships between members of the group. It is important to recognize that these are fundamental existential issues that are not at all easy to pin down. The challenge of facing these issues is made easier by being a member of a group that is working together on the same set of tasks. When selecting a course, therefore, it is important to consider the extent to which the structure of the programme makes it possible for groups to form and work effectively together. For example, there are many training workshops advertised that provide opportunities to receive training from well-known figures in counselling and psychotherapy. Often, however, these workshops are highly didactic, and consist of lectures and demonstrations conducted in front of a large audience, with little or no time allowed for participants to get to know each other. These workshops may well be interesting and stimulating, but do not provide the conditions for assimilating what has been learned into one's personal practice.

Finally, it is unlikely that a counselling course will be of any lasting value if what is taught is delivered from a position of *certainty*. Holding a dogmatic belief in a set of ideas can result in a style of practice in which the person fits the theory, rather than one in which the theory is applied responsively to fit the person. In their research into counsellors who were widely recognized by their colleagues as being the best in their locality, Thomas Skovholt and his colleagues found that two core themes that emerged across the practitioners they interviewed were an openness to new learning and a continuing interest in people (Jennings and Skovholt, 1999; Ronnestad and Skovholt, 2001; Skovholt and Jennings, 2004). Even though some of the 'master therapists' who were interviewed identified themselves as operating within specific models, all acknowledged that they questioned the assumptions of their theoretical approaches, and had always been willing to learn from, and about, other approaches to therapy. This pattern was also apparent in a study of experienced therapy practitioners carried out by Donald Polkinghorne (1992). The findings of these studies would appear to have two broad implications for counselling training. They imply that a good training programme is one which promotes a critical, questioning approach in which different perspectives on issues are explored. In addition, the value of a course can be measured in terms of the extent to which it opens up possibilities for lifelong learning, in the form of self-initiated inquiry that unfolds even after the end of the training.

Box 12.2   Putting it all together – doing good work at an organizational level

It is difficult to sustain the delivery of good quality counselling to clients within the context of a busy healthcare organization, in which practitioners are required to juggle multiple roles and pressures. A paper by Stein *et al.* (2005) describes the development of a programme within Kaiser Permanente, one of the biggest health providers in the USA, which was devised to ensure that doctors engaged empathically, effectively and in a culture-sensitive manner with the emotional and clinical needs of patients. The programme evolved over a seventeen-year period, and included training workshops designed to be accessible to doctors and relevant to their needs, the use of patient satisfaction surveys to collect of data on the use of communication skills by practitioners, and the creation of a group of 'communication consultants' – physicians or psychologists selected on the basis of their outstanding interpersonal skills who provided a supervisory and coaching role with colleagues. A particularly innovative feature of the programme was the adoption of a memorable phrase that captured the key elements of the Kaiser Permanente approach: 'the four habits model'. Practitioners were trained in interpersonal competences related to good practice with regard to four main areas of interaction with patients: *invest in the beginning, elicit the patient's perspective, demonstrate empathy*, and *invest in the end*. Taken together, these four habits encapsulated the dimensions of counselling skill that were considered to be most relevant to the role of a primary care physician within that specific organizational setting. The habits model provided a readily understood language that all the doctors across the organization were able to use to discuss and reflect on their practice, and explained what was needed in practical terms that helped to address the criticism of many physicians that such issues were merely 'touchy-feely' irrelevancies.

The article by Stein *et al.* gives a detailed account of the strategies that were used by the champions of this approach within Kaiser Permanente to maximize its chances of being taken seriously, such as building on success, enlisting the support of senior managers, using research evidence to convince tough-minded clinicians that inter-personal skills made a difference to health outcomes, and linking salary increases to ratings of patient satisfaction.

Avoiding burnout

The practice of counselling is stressful. There are several factors that appear to be par-ticularly associated with counsellor stress:

- Typically, counsellors work in settings where the potential need (that is, number of people seeking help) is greater than the resource that is available to meet that need, and so there is a pressure to work long hours or to find space to see another person.
- Quite a lot of the time, either counselling appears to make little positive difference to the person seeking help, or the benefit that does result is hidden from the counsellor. For example, following a helpful counselling session, a person may decide that they do not need to return to see the counsellor again, with the consequence that the counsellor never learns about their good news.
- Some people who engage in counselling have very harrowing and tragic stories to tell, or live in states of terrible emotional pain. Being exposed to these realities inevitably has a powerful impact on a counsellor.
- Most counselling is carried out on a one-to-one basis, under conditions of con-fidentiality; this can lead to counsellor isolation and lack of social support, and a sense of being exposed ('I am responsible for what happens to this person') in comparison with other occupations where teamwork is possible.

The intensity and relative importance of each of these sources of stress will depend on the setting in which counselling is being carried out. For example, workers in agencies dealing with women who have been abused are regularly exposed to high levels of emotional pain, but can usually depend on strong collective support from colleagues. By contrast, a nurse in a busy hospital ward may be less likely to encounter stories of abuse, but will probably experience a high workload, time pressure, and lack of emotional support from colleagues.

There are two main patterns of stress that appear to be prevalent in people who do counselling work. The first of these can be described as burnout (Maslach and Leiter, 1997; Leiter and Maslach, 2005). The theory of burnout was developed by the psychologist Christina Maslach to account for the effect on people of working in 'human service' or helping professions. Maslach suggests that people enter these professions with a passion to help others. Over time, the emotional consequence of always giving to others results in the passion to help becoming burned out. It is as if the energy and motivation of the person have been used up. The main symptoms of burnout are: a sense of emotional exhaustion; a tendency to treat clients in a detached way, as objects or 'cases', rather than as people; and a deep disillusionment or lack of personal accomplishment ('it's all a waste of time . . . I have being doing this job for ten years and nothing has changed . . .'). A counsellor who is burned out is therefore merely going through the motions and not really engaging with the people with whom they are working. This state also has serious negative implications for the private life of the person and their capacity to sustain close relationships. Burnout is a type of stress that gradually accumulates day by day and week by week, when people care for others without taking care of themselves.

A second form of stress that can occur in those involved in offering counselling relationships has been described as *secondary traumatization*. This type of reaction takes place when counsellors work with people who have been traumatized (Morrissette, 2004). When a person has been through an awful event, such as torture, natural disaster, war and the like, a range of psychological consequence can occur. Often, the sensory images of the event are so frightening that they cannot readily be assimilated into the person's memory. Images of the event continue to be intrusively re-experienced, and then locked away or avoided, as the person's cognitive processing struggles to integrate what has happened into their pre-existing understanding of the world. What this means, for a counsellor, is that when the person does begin to talk about these awful events in a counselling session, the images and re-experiencing, and levels of fear, are so strong that is as if the counsellor is a witness to the original event. A counsellor may find that they cannot get the person's phrases, or their story, out of their mind. Another process that can take place arises from what Janoff-Bulman (1992) has called 'shattered assumptions'. When a person has experienced events that should 'never happen', then their basic assumption of trust in the world as a safe place and people as good, is shattered. A counsellor working with such a person is faced with having to overcome that person's basic lack of trust, and may also find that the person's story has, in turn, shattered or threatened their own belief in a safe and good world. One of the hazards of counselling, therefore, is the danger of developing secondary traumatization, which can be expressed in a lack of trust in people, recurring images of cruelty and destruction, and general hyperalertness to any source of potential threat.

Although there has been a considerable amount of research into sources of stress in counselling and the ways that counsellors cope, the findings of these studies are contradictory and hard to interpret, and it is not easy to arrive at any generalizations. It seems likely that the process of stress in counsellors is often subtle and hidden. People who develop an interest in counselling, and readily offer counselling relationships to others, generally view themselves as possessing a good level of self-awareness and capacity to deal with stress. Probably this is true, much of the time, and results in effective self-care in the majority of counsellors. However, it may also lead to an unwillingness to acknowledge difficulty and vulnerability, in the interest of maintaining a facade of competence. There are many strategies open to counsellors for keeping burnout hidden, for example by adopting a detached, distanced approach to service users, becoming preoccupied with professionalism, or moving away from front-line work and concentrating on supervision, training and administration. A significant proportion of counsellors find they reach a point at which they cannot continue working, and undergo personal crisis, illness, time out and re-evaluation of personal goals. Sometimes, these practitioners learn a great deal from their crisis, and return stronger and more resilient.

The studies that are available of stress in counselling have focused on the experiences of full-time specialist counsellors and psychotherapists. There has been no research into stress and burnout in people whose counselling role is embedded in other work roles. In general, nursing, teaching, social work and other professions in which embedded counselling takes place are high-stress occupations. In these roles, it may be that the demands of responding to the counselling needs of clients and patients cranks up the overall stress level another notch. On the other hand, it may be that at least some practitioners in these areas view the counselling dimension of their role as providing a degree of meaning and balance to their work, and therefore as something that acts as a buffer to other pressures.

The discussion of stress and burnout in this section has concentrated mainly on the impact of this kind of work on the counsellor. It is also essential to be aware of the effect of counsellor stress on the person seeking help. Spending time with a burned out counsellor is unlikely to be satisfying. A tired nurse in a casualty department can probably record blood pressure and administer injections at an acceptable level of reliability. A tired counsellor, by contrast, is only minimally open to relationship.

Personal therapy for counsellors

Over the course of their career, almost all specialist professional counsellors and psychotherapists undergo one or more episodes of therapy. For therapy practitioners, the experience of being a client is usually referred to as 'personal therapy'. While people in general go to see a therapist (counsellor or psychotherapist) because they wish to deal with a problem in living, counsellors go to see therapists not only to deal with troubles but with the additional goal of learning about counselling. Being a client is one of the best ways to understand how the counselling process works (and doesn't work). In the client's chair, it is possible to watch what one's counsellor is doing. It is also possible to monitor one's own reactions to what the counsellor has said and done, both in the session itself and in the days or weeks following a session. A thorough analysis of the role of personal therapy in the development of practitioners can be found in the book by Geller *et al.* (2005). The book also includes some very interesting and readable chapters by well-known therapists describing the therapists' own experiences of receiving therapy. One of the contributors is Clara Hill, who is a leading figure in the area of counselling skills and in counselling research.

Making use of research and inquiry

In modern industrial societies, characterized by high levels of social and technological change, there is an expectation that new knowledge and information will constantly be generated by research, and that competent practitioners will continue to update their approach by being 'research informed'. The domain of practice-based research can be viewed as a continuum. On one end are large, theory-driven or policy-driven studies carried out by full-time researchers based in universities. There are also many smaller-scale studies carried out by practitioners. At this end of the continuum, which is con-cerned with knowledge generation, research is an activity in which a person is actively involved, a form of complex problem solving. At the other end of the continuum, research is a product that is consumed. Detailed research reports can be read in research journals. Less detailed reports can be found in professional journals. Digested research knowledge finds its way into textbooks.

Within the counselling world, the tendency has been that the majority of practi-tioners admit to being not very interested in research. The products of research are viewed as boring, inaccessible, irrelevant, and too abstract or theoretical (Morrow-Bradley and Elliott, 1986). Counselling practitioners report that their work is better informed and updated through consultation with colleagues and supervisors, partici-pation in skill-based workshops, and learning from clients, than it is by reading or doing research. The depth of the research–practice gap in counselling is surprising for practitioners from highly research-based professions such as nursing and medicine, where being research-informed is a routine part of working life. It is important to bear in mind, however, that there is much less research into counselling, in contrast to the vast amount of health research that has been carried out. Also, the fact that many medical interventions can be compartmentalized into separate elements (for example a drug, a specific surgical procedure) means that it is easier to carry out studies that produce results that can be slotted in to everyday practice. It is rare that a research study in counselling yields knowledge that can immediately be applied in practice.

There exists a range of different research approaches that can be employed in looking at the process and outcome of the use of counselling skill in embedded situations. Hill (2001) provides examples of research into various aspects of counselling skill using a variety of research techniques. There are a number of questionnaires that measure practitioners' own perceptions of their counselling skill competence (Hill and Kellems, 2002; Lent *et al.*, 2003), and service users' perceptions of the quality of the counselling relationship offered by practitioners (Mercer *et al.*, 2004, 2005). Several research studies have recorded interactions between practitioners and people seeking help for personal issues, and have analysed the competences that have been demonstrated in these episodes, for example in relation to language use (see, for example, Gallacher *et al.*, 2001; Karhila *et al.*, 2003; Kettunen *et al.*, 2003). Many studies, cited throughout this book, have interviewed service users, and also practitioners, around their experience of receiving or providing counselling. In one innovative study, Glowa *et al.* (2002) directly assessed the effectiveness of doctors' counselling skills by sending simulated patients into a hospital clinic. There is therefore no shortage of ways of investigating the use of counselling embedded within other roles. There are also many studies that have evaluated the effectiveness of training in counselling skill. What is lacking are comprehensive reviews of research into embedded counselling, specialist journals that encourage the publication of studies on this topic (other than the important *Patient Education and Counseling* journal in the healthcare field), and theoretical models that enable the findings of different studies to be synthesized into clear guidelines for practice. As a result, the literature around research in embedded counselling is fragmented and difficult to translate into practice. Nevertheless, despite this barrier, it is essential for practitioners in professions such as health, education, the clergy and criminal justice to work together to establish a more substantial research base to support this area of work.

Making use of research and inquiry is a valuable way to stand back from practice and to engage in constructive and critical reflection. It is also a good means of learning about the ideas and methods developed by colleagues in other places – it makes it possible to keep abreast of best practice.

Conclusions

This final chapter has discussed a number of themes that may appear obvious to many readers – there is nothing new about the idea that training and supervision are important in professional work, or that it is a good idea to develop strategies for coping with stress and avoiding burnout. What this chapter has attempted to do is to place these fundamental truths of good practice within a counselling context: in some respects people who open themselves to the distress of others do have distinctive training and support needs. There are perhaps two overarching ideas that provide a useful overview to the issues that have been discussed not only in this chapter, but in the book as a whole. The first is the notion of *craftsmanship*. A good counsellor, no matter whether the context they operate in is high-end private practice or the corner of a busy inner-city health clinic, functions as a craft worker. The satisfaction of the job comes from making the best of the materials that are available, and in producing something that is valued by customers and fellow workers. The essence of craftsmanship is attention to the task in hand, the gradual deepening of skill over time, and pride in a job well done. The other important concept is *resourcefulness*. Throughout this book, the idea has been highlighted that people encounter problems in living because they lack the resources to resolve difficulties that arise in their lives. People seek help because their resources are not sufficient to cope with the situation in which they find themselves. The same analysis can be applied to the role of the counsellor. Virtually anyone can be an effective counsellor to a limited set of people – those people whose problems and assumptions about change most closely match the helping resources of that practitioner. However, in the longer term, anyone who wishes to offer counselling to a wide range of people needs to expand their repertoire of helping resources. It is hoped that this book represents an invitation to resourcefulness and a gateway to thinking about, and trying out, some of the multitude of resources for counselling that exist within our culture.

Questions for reflection and discussion

1. Think about the professional context in which you work. What are the different knowledges that influence your counselling role? How do you integrate different knowledges in practice – what strategies do you use? What are the areas of tension between different knowledges?
2. Reflect on occasions when you have personally been a recipient of care. Identify episodes in which practitioners who were looking after you responded appropriately and sensitively to your feelings and personal concerns (or failed to do so). What impact did this have on you, as a person receiving care? What might have been the organizational factors that either supported or undermined good work from these carers?
3. Thinking back through the book as a whole, what are the questions that have emerged for you about how counselling can best be applied in the situation in which you work, with the people who come to you for help? In what ways might research inform the effectiveness of your work? If possible, access a database and search for research that might be relevant to your counselling role. If no relevant research has been carried out, what research might you like to do yourself (in an ideal world, given suitable time and support) – what would your research questions be, and what methods might you use to pursue these questions?

Suggestions for further reading

Skovholt and Jennings have written a fascinating book that explores many aspects of 'doing good work'. Although the book is based on interviews with specialist psychotherapists, rather than practitioners whose counselling is embedded in other roles, it contains much that is applicable in embedded counselling settings:

Skovholt, T. M. and Jennings, L. (2004) *Master Therapists: Exploring Expertise in Therapy and Counseling*. New York: Allyn & Bacon.

Anyone interested in reflecting on what is involved in training/learning in relation to developing counselling skills, might consider reading:

Mearns, D. (1997) *Person-centred Counselling Training*. London: Sage.

Mearns, D. and Cooper, M. (2005) *Working at Relational Depth in Counselling and Psychotherapy.* London: Sage, ch. 8.

Two of the most widely used and respected books on supervision are:

Hawkins, P. and Shohet, R. (2000) *Supervision in the Helping Professions*, 2nd edn. Buckingham: Open University Press.
Page, S. and Wosket, V. (2001) *Supervising the Counsellor: A Cyclical Model*, 2nd edn. Hove, Sussex: Brunner-Routledge.

References

Aldridge, S. and Rigby, S. (eds) (2001) *Counselling Skills in Context*. London: Hodder & Stoughton.

Angus, L. and McLeod, J. (eds) (2004) *The Handbook of Narrative and Psychotherapy: Practice, Theory and Research*. Thousand Oaks, CA: Sage.

Angus, L. E. and Rennie, D. L. (1988) Therapist participation in metaphor generation: collaborative and noncollaborative styles. *Psychotherapy*, 25: 552–60.

Angus, L. E. and Rennie, D. L. (1989) Envisioning the representational world: the client's experience of metaphoric expressiveness in psychotherapy. *Psychotherapy*, 26: 373–9.

Argyle, M. and Kendon, A. (1967) The experimental analysis of social performance. In L. Berkowitz (ed.) *Advances in Experimental Social Psychology*, Vol. 3. New York: Academic Press.

Baker, R. (2003) *Understanding Panic Attacks and Overcoming Fear*. London: Lion Hudson.

Baker, S. B., Daniels, T. G. and Greeley, A. T. (1990) Systematic training of graduate level counselors: narrative and meta-analytic reviews of three programmes. *Counseling Psychologist*, 18: 355–421.

Barker, P. and Buchanan-Barker, P. (2005) *The Tidal Model: A Guide for Mental Health Professionals*. London: Brunner-Routledge.

Barkham, M. (1989) Brief prescriptive therapy in two-plus-one sessions: initial cases from the clinic. *Behavioural Psychotherapy*, 17: 161–75.

Barkham, M. and Shapiro, D. A. (1989) Towards resolving the problem of waiting lists: psychotherapy in two-plus-one sessions. *Clinical Psychology Forum*, 23: 15–18.

Barkham, M. and Shapiro, D. A. (1990) Exploratory therapy in two-plus-one sessions: a research model for studying the process of change. In G. Lietaer, J. Rombauts and R. van Balen (eds) *Client-centered and Experiential Psychotherapy in the Nineties*. Leuven: Leuven University Press.

Barrett-Lennard, G. (1981) The empathy cycle – refinement of a nuclear concept. *Journal of Counseling Psychology*, 28: 91–100.

Barrett-Lennard, G. (1993) The phases and focus of empathy. *British Journal of Medical Psychology*, 66: 3–14.

Barrett-Lennard, G. (1998) *Carl Rogers' Helping System: Journey and Substance*. London: Sage.

Bauman, Z. (2004) *Wasted Lives: Modernity and its Outcasts*. London: Polity Press.

Bedi, R. P., Davis, M. D. and Williams, M. (2005) Critical incidents in the formation of the therapeutic alliance from the client's perspective. *Psychotherapy: Theory, Research, Practice, Training*, 41: 311–23.

Benjamin, L. S. (1987) The use of Structural Analysis of Social Behavior (SASB) to guide intervention in psychotherapy. In J. C. Anchin and D. J. Kiesler (eds) *Handbook of Interpersonal Psychotherapy*. New York: Pergamon.

Berman, L. (1993) *Beyond the Smile: The Therapeutic Use of the Photograph*. London: Routledge.

Berne, E. (1964) *Games People Play: The Psychology of Human Relationships*. Harmondsworth: Penguin.

Birtchnell, J. (1999) *Relating in Psychotherapy: The Application of a New Theory*. London: Brunner-Routledge.

Bohart, A. C. (2000) The client is the most important common factor: clients self-healing capacities and psychotherapy. *Journal of Psychotherapy Integration*, 10: 127–48.

Bohart, A. C. (2006) The active client. In J. C. Norcross, L. E. Beutler and R. F. Levant (eds) *Evidence-based Practices in Mental Health: Debate and Dialogue on the Fundamental Questions*. Washington, DC: American Psychological Association.

Bohart, A. C. and Tallman, K. (1996) The active client: therapy as self-help. *Journal of Humanistic Psychology*, 3: 7–30.

Bohart, A. C. and Tallman, K. (1999) *How Clients Make Therapy Work: The Process of Active Self-healing*. Washington, DC: American Psychological Association.

Bolger, E. (1999) Grounded theory analysis of emotional pain. *Psychotherapy Research*, 9: 342–62.

Bond, T. (1989) Towards defining the role of counselling skills. *Counselling*, 69: 24–6.

Bond, T. (2000) *Standards and Ethics for Counselling in Action*, 2nd edn. London: Sage

Bordin, E. S. (1979) The generalizability of the psychoanalytic concept of the working alliance. *Psychotherapy: Theory, Research and Practice*, 16: 252–60.

Boukydis, K. M. (1984) Changes: peer counselling supportive communities as a model for community mental health. In D. Larson (ed.) *Teaching Psychological Skills: Models for Giving Psychology Away*. Monterey, CA: Brooks/Cole.

Branch, W. T. and Malik, T. K. (1993) Using 'windows of opportunities' in brief interviews to understand patients' concerns. *Journal of the American Medical Association*, 269: 1667–8.

Brown, L. S. (2005) Feminist therapy with therapists: egalitarian and more. In Geller, J. D., Norcross, J. C. and Orlinsky, D. E. (eds) *The Psychotherapist's Own Psychotherapy: Patient and Clinician Perspectives*. New York: Oxford University Press.

Bylund, C. L. and Makoul, G. (2002) Empathic communication and gender in the physician–patient encounter. *Patient Education and Counseling*, 48: 207–16.

Cameron, D. (2004) Communication culture: issues for health and social care. In M. Robb, S. Barrett, C. Komaromy and A. Rogers (eds) *Communication, Relationships and Care: A Reader*. London: Routledge.

Cardemil, E. V. and Battle, C. L. (2003) Guess who's coming to therapy? Getting comfortable with conversations about race and ethnicity in psychotherapy. *Professional Psychology: Research and Practice*, 34: 278–86.

Carkhuff, R. R. (1969a) *Helping and Human Relations. Vol. 1: Selection and Training*. New York: Holt, Rinehart & Winston.

Carkhuff, R. R. (1969b) *Helping and Human Relations. Vol. 2: Practice and Research*. New York: Holt, Rinehart & Winston.

Carrell, S. E. (2001) *The Therapist's Toolbox*. Thousand Oaks, CA: Sage.

Cash, R. W. (1984) The Human Resources Development model. In D. Larson (ed.) *Teaching Psychological Skills: Models for Giving Psychology Away*. Monterey, CA: Brooks/Cole.

Christopher, J. C. (1996) Counseling's inescapable moral visions. *Journal of Counseling and Development*, 75: 17–25.

Cooper, M. (2003) *Existential Therapies*. London: Sage.

Cooper, M. (2005) Young people's perceptions of helpful aspects of therapy: a pluralistic model of therapeutic change. Paper presented to the Conference of the European Society for Psychotherapy Research, Lausanne, Switzerland, March.

Cornell, A. W. (1996) *The Power of Focusing: Finding your Inner Voice*. New York: New Harbinger Publications.

Cowen, E. L. (1982) Help is where you find it: four informal helping groups. *American Psychologist*, 37: 385–95.

Cowen, E. L., Gesten, E. L., Boike, M., Norton, P., Wilson, A. B. and DeStefano, M. A. (1979) Hairdressers as caregivers: a descriptive profile of interpersonal help-giving involvements. *American Journal of Community Psychology*, 7: 633–48.

Czogalik, D. and Russell, R. L. (1994) Key processes of client participation in psychotherapy: chronography and narration. *Psychotherapy: Theory, Research, Practice and Training*, 31: 170–82.

Dickson, W. J. and Roethlisberger, F. J. (1966) *Counseling in an Organization: A Sequel to the Hawthorne Researches*. Boston, MA: Graduate School of Business Administration, Harvard University.

Dienemann, J., Campbell, J., Landenburger, K. and Curry, M. A. (2002) The domestic violence survivor assessment: a tool for counseling women in intimate partner violence relationships. *Patient Education and Counseling*, 46: 221–8.

Egan, G. (2004) *The Skilled Helper: A Problem Management and Opportunity Development Approach to Helping*. Belmont, CA: Wadsworth.

Eide, H., Frankel, R., Haaversen, C., Vaupel, K., Graugard, P. and Finset, A. (2004) Listening for feelings: identifying and coding empathic and potential empathic opportunities in medical dialogues. *Patient Education and Counseling*, 54: 291–7.

Engebretson, J. (2000) Caring presence: a case study. *International Journal for Human Caring*, 4: 211–23.

Etherington, K. (ed.) (2001) *Counsellors in Health Settings*. London: Jessica Kingsley.

Feltham, C. (1995) *What is Counselling?* London: Sage.

Fineman, S. (1993) Organizations as emotional arenas. In S. Fineman (ed.) *Emotion in Organizations*. London: Sage.

Firestone, R. W. (1997a) *Combating Destructive Thought Processes: Voice Therapy and Separation Theory*. Thousand Oaks, CA: Sage

Firestone, R. W. (1997b) *Suicide and the Inner Voice: Risk Assessment, Treatment, and Case Management*. Thousand Oaks, CA: Sage

Frank, A. (1995) *The Wounded Storyteller: Body, Illness, and ethics*. Chicago: University of Chicago Press.

Frank, A. (1998) Just listening: narrative and deep illness. *Families, Systems and Health*, 16: 197–212.

Frank, A. (2000) Illness and autobiographical work: dialogue as narrative destabilization. *Qualitative Sociology*, 23: 135–56.

Gabriel, L. (2005) *Speaking the Unspeakable: The Ethics of Dual Relationships in Counselling and Psychotherapy*. London: Routledge.

Gallacher, T. J., Hartung, P. J. and Gregory, S. W., Jr (2001) Assessment of a measure of relational communication for doctor-patient interaction. *Patient Education and Counseling*, 45: 211–18.

Geller, J. D., Norcross, J. C. and Orlinsky, D. E. (2005) *The Psychotherapist's Own Psychotherapy: Patient and Clinician Perspectives*. New York: Oxford University Press.

Gendlin, E. T. (1984) The politics of giving therapy away: listening and focusing. In D. Larson (ed.) *Teaching Psychological Skills: Models for Giving Psychology Away*. Monterey, CA: Brooks/Cole.

Gendlin, E. T. (2003) *Focusing: How to Open up your Deeper Feelings and Intuition*. New York: Rider.

Gergen, K. J. (1990) Therapeutic professions and the diffusion of deficit. *Journal of Mind and Behavior*, 11: 353–68.

Giddens, A. (1991) *Modernity and Self-identity: Self and Society in the Late Modern Age*. Cambridge: Polity Press.

Glowa, P. T., Frasier, P. Y. and Newton, W. P. (2002) Increasing physician comfort level in screening and counseling patients for intimate partner violence: hands-on practice. *Patient Education and Counseling*, 46: 213–20.

Goleman, D. (2005) *Emotional Intelligence*. New York: Bantam Books.

Goodman, G. (1984) SAHSAtapes: expanding options for help-intended communication. In D. Larson (ed.) *Teaching Psychological Skills: Models for Giving Psychology Away*. Monterey, CA: Brooks/Cole.

Gordon, K. M. and Toukmanian, S. G. (2002) Is *how* it is said important? The association between quality of therapist response and client processing. *Counselling and Psychotherapy Research*, 2: 88–98.

Gordon, T. (1984) Three decades of democratising relationships through training. In D. Larson (ed.) *Teaching Psychological Skills: Models for Giving Psychology Away*. Monterey, CA: Brooks/Cole.

Goss, S. and Antony, K. (eds) (2003) *Technology in Counselling and Psychotherapy: A Practitioner's Guide*. London: Palgrave Macmillan.

Goulding, M. N. and Goulding, R. L. (1997) *Changing Lives through Redecision Therapy*, rev. edn. New York: Grove Press.

Grant, A., Mills, J., Mulhern, R. and Short, N. (2004) *Cognitive Behavioural Therapy in Mental Health Care*. London: Sage.

Grayson, A., Miller, H. and Clarke, D. (1998) Identifying barriers to help-seeking: a qualitative analysis of students' preparedness to seek help from tutors. *British Journal of Guidance and Counselling*, 26: 237–54.

Greenberg, L. S. (1992) Task analysis: identifying components of intrapersonal conflict resolution. In S.G. Toukmanian and D.L. Rennie (eds) *Psychotherapy Process Research: Paradigmatic and Narrative Approaches*. Thousand Oaks, CA: Sage.

Greenberg, L. S. (2001) *Emotion-focused Therapy: Coaching Clients to Work through their Feelings*. Washington, DC: American Psychological Association.

Greenberg, L. S. and Geller, S. (2001) Congruence and therapeutic presence. In G. Wyatt (ed.) *Rogers' Therapeutic Conditions: Evolution, Theory and Practice. Vol. 1: Congruence*. Ross-on-Wye: PCCS Books.

Greenberg, L. S., Rice, L. N. and Elliott, R. (1993) *Facilitating Emotional Change: The Moment-by-moment Process*. New York: Guilford Press.

Greenberger, D. and Padesky, C. A. (1995) *Mind over Mood: Change how you Feel by Changing the Way you Think*. New York: Guilford Press.

Greenhalgh, T. (2001) Narrative and patient choice. In A. Edwards and G. Elwyn (eds) *Evidence-based Patient Choice: Inevitable or Impossible?* Oxford: Oxford University Press.

Greenhalgh, T. and Hurwitz, B. (eds) (1998) *Narrative-based Medicine: Dialogue and Discourse in Clinical Practice*. London: BMJ Publications.

Grohol, J. M. (2004) *The Insider's Guide to Mental Health Resources Online*, 2nd edn. New York: Guilford Press.

Guerney, B. G., Jr (1984) Relationship enhancement therapy and training. In D. Larson (ed.) *Teaching Psychological Skills: Models for Giving Psychology Away*. Monterey, CA: Brooks/Cole.

Hall R. C. and Platt D. E. (1999) Suicide risk assessment: a review of risk factors for suicide in 100 patients who made severe suicide attempts. *Psychosomatics*, 40: 18–27.

Harré, R and Van Langenhove, L. (eds) (1999) *Positioning Theory*. Oxford: Blackwell.

Hart, N. (1996) The role of tutor in a college of higher education – a comparison of skills used by personal tutors and by student counsellors when working with students in distress. *British Journal of Guidance and Counselling*, 24: 83–96.

Havens, L. (1978) Explorations in the use of language in psychotherapy: simple empathic statements. *Psychiatry*, 41: 336–45.

Havens, L. (1979) Explorations in the use of language in psychotherapy: complex empathic statements. *Psychiatry*, 42: 40–8.

Hawkins, P. and Shohet, R. (2000) *Supervision in the Helping Professions*, 2nd edn. Buckingham: Open University Press.

Hill, C. E. (ed.) (2001) *Helping Skills: The Empirical Foundation*. Washington, DC: American Psychological Association.

Hill, C. E. (2004) *Helping Skills: Facilitating Exploration, Insight and Action*, 2nd edn. Washington, DC: American Psychological Association.

Hill, C. E. and Kellems, I. S. (2002) Development and use of the Helping Skills measure to assess client perceptions of the effects of training and of helping skills in session evaluation. *Journal of Counseling Psychology*, 49: 264–72.

Hochschild, A. (1983) *The Managed Heart: The Commercialization of Human Feeling*. Berkeley: University of California Press.

Hockey, J., Katz, J. and Small, N. (eds) (2001) *Grief, Mourning and Death Ritual*. Buckingham: Open University Press.

Hofstede, G. (2003) *Culture's Consequences: Comparing Values, Behaviors, Institutions, and Organizations across nations*, 2nd edn. Thousand Oaks, CA: Sage

Hofstede, G. J., Pedersen, P. B. and Hofstede, G. (2002) *Exploring Culture: Exercises, Stories and Synthetic Cultures*. Yarmouth, ME: Intercultural Press.

Honos-Webb, L. and Stiles, W. B. (1998) Reformulation of assimilation analysis in terms of voices. *Psychotherapy*, 35: 23–33.

Hopson, B. (1989) Life transitions and crises. In N. Niven (ed.) *Health Psychology*. Edinburgh: Churchill Livingstone.

Hopson, B. and Adams, J. (1976) Towards an understanding: defining some boundaries of transition dynamics. In J. Adams, J. Hayes and B. Hopson (eds) *Transition: Understanding and Managing Personal Change*. London: Martin Robertson.

Hubble, M. A., Duncan, B. C. and Miller, S. D. (eds) (1999) *The Heart and Soul of Change: What Works in Therapy*. Washington, DC: American Psychological Association.

Illich, I. (2001) *Medical Nemesis: The Expropriation of Health*, rev. edn. London: Marion Boyars.

Imber-Black, E. and Roberts, J. (1992) *Rituals for our Times: Celebrating Healing and Changing our Lives and Relationships*. New York: HarperCollins.

Ingham, C. (2000) *Panic Attacks: What they are, Why they Happen and What you can Do About Them*. Glasgow: HarperCollins.

Ivey, A. E. and Galvin, M. (1984) Microcounseling: a metamodel for counselling, therapy, business and medical interviews. In D. Larson (ed.) *Teaching Psychological Skills: Models for Giving Psychology Away*. Monterey, CA: Brooks/Cole.

Ivey, A. E. and Ivey, M. B. (1999) *Intentional Interviewing and Counseling: Facilitating Client Development in a Multicultural Society*, 4th edn. Pacific Grove, CA: Brooks/Cole.

Jacobs, M. (2005) *The Presenting Past*, 3rd edn. Buckingham: Open Universty Press.

James, R. and Gilliland, B. (2001) *Crisis Intervention Strategies*, 4th edn. Belmont, CA: Wadsworth.

Jamison, K. R. (1999) *Night Falls Fast: Understanding Suicide*. New York: Vintage.

Janoff-Bulman, R. (1992) *Shattered Assumptions: Towards a New Psychology of Trauma*. New York: Free Press.

Jennings, L. and Skovholt, T. M. (1999) The cognitive, emotional and relational characteristics of master therapists. *Journal of Counseling Psychology*, 48: 3–11.

Jevne, R. F., (1987) Creating stillpoints: beyond a rational approach to counselling cancer patients. *Journal of Psychosocial Oncology*, 5: 1–15.

Jevne, R. F., Nekolaichuk, C. L. and Williamson, F. H. A. (1998) A model for counselling cancer patients. *Canadian Journal of Counselling*, 32: 213–29.

Joseph D. I. (2000) The practical art of suicide assessment: a guide for mental health professionals and substance abuse counselors. *Journal of Clinical Psychiatry*, 61: 683–4.

Josselson, R. (1996) *The Space between Us: Exploring the Dimensions of Human Relationships*. Thousand Oaks, CA: Sage.

Kagan, N. (1984) Interpersonal process recall: basic methods and recent research. In D. Larson (ed.) *Teaching Psychological Skills: Models for Giving Psychology Away*. Monterey, CA: Brooks/Cole.

Kanel, K. (1999) *A Guide to Crisis Intervention*. Belmont, CA: Wadsworth.

Kanfer, F. H. and Goldtsen, A. P. (1991) *Helping People Change*, 4th edn. Needham Heights, MA: Allyn & Bacon.

Karhila, P., Kettunen, T., Poskiparta, M. and Liinatainen, L. (2003) Negotiation in Type 2 diabetes counseling: from problem recognition to mutual acceptance during lifestyle counselling. *Qualitative Health Research*, 13: 1205–24.

Kauffman, K. and New, C. (2004) *Co-counselling: The Theory and Practice of Re-evaluation Counselling*. London: Brunner-Routledge.

Kenny, D. T. (2004) Constructions of chronic pain in doctor–patient relationships: bridging the communication chasm. *Patient Education and Counseling*, 52: 297–305.

Kettunen, T., Poskiparta, M. and Karhila, P. (2003) Speech practices that facilitate patient participation in health counselling – a way to empowerment? *Health Education Journal*, 62: 326–40.

King, A. (2001) *Demystifying the Counselling Process: A Self-help Handbook for Counselors*. Needham Heights, MA: Allyn & Bacon.

Kinman, C. J. and Finck, P. (2004) Response-able practice: a language of gifts in the institutions of health care. In T. Strong and D. Pare (eds) *Furthering Talk: Advances in the Discursive Therapies*. New York: Kluwer.

Kirkwood, C. (2003) The persons-in-relation perspective: toward a philosophy for counselling in society. *Counselling and Psychotherapy Research*, 3: 186–95.

Kleinman, A. (1988) *The Illness Narratives: Suffering, Healing and the Human Condition*. New York: Basic Books.

L'Abate, L. (2004) *A Guide to Self-help Workbooks for Mental Health Clinicians and Researchers*. New York: Haworth.

Lago, C. and Thompson, J. (1996) *Race, Culture and Counselling*. Buckingham: Open University Press.

Lahad, M. (2000) *Creative Supervision: The Use of Expressive Arts Methods in Supervision and Self-supervision*. London: Jessica Kingsley.

Lakoff, G. and Johnson, M. (1980) *Metaphors we Live By*. Chicago: University of Chicago Press.

Lakoff, G. and Johnson, M. (1999) *Philosophy in the Flesh: The Embodied Mind and its Challenge to Western Thought*. New York: Basic Books.

Larson, D. (1984a) *Teaching Psychological Skills: Models for Giving Psychology Away*. Monterey, CA; Brooks/Cole.

Larson. D. (1984b) Giving psychology away: the skills paradigm. In D. Larson (ed.) *Teaching Psychological Skills: Models for Giving Psychology Away*. Monterey, CA: Brooks/Cole.

Lawton, B. and Feltham, C. (eds) (2000) *Taking Supervision Forward: Enquiries and Trends in Counselling and Psychotherapy*. London: Sage.

Lazarus, A. A. and Zur, O. (eds) (2002) *Dual Relationships in Psychotherapy*. New York: Springer.

Le Surf, A. and Lynch, G. (1999) Exploring young people's perceptions relevant to counselling: a qualitative study. *British Journal of Guidance and Counselling*, 27: 231–44.

Leiper, R. (2004) *The Psychodynamic Approach to Therapeutic Change*. London: Sage.

Leiter, M. P. and Maslach, C. (2005). *Banishing Burnout: Six Strategies for Improving your Relationship with Work*. San Francisco, CA: Jossey-Bass.

Lendrum, S. and Syme, G. (2004) *Gift of Tears: A Practical Approach to Loss and Bereavement in Counselling and Psychotherapy*, 2nd edn. London: Brunner-Routledge.

Lent, R. W., Hill, C. E. and Hoffman, M. A. (2003) Development and validation of the counselor activity self-efficacy scale. *Journal of Counseling Psychology*, 50: 97–108.

Linden, S. and Grut, J. (2002) *The Healing Fields: Working with Psychotherapy and Nature to Rebuild Shattered Lives*. London: Frances Lincoln.

MacCormack, T., Simonian, J., Lim, J., Remond, L, Roets, D., Dunn, S. and Butow, P. (2001) 'Someone who cares': a qualitative investigation of cancer patients' experiences of psychotherapy. *Psycho-Oncology*, 10: 52–65.

Mahrer, A. R., Gagnon, R., Fairweather, D. R., Boulet, D. B. and Herring, C. B. (1994) Client commitment and resolve to carry out postsession behaviors. *Journal of Counseling Psychology*, 41: 407–44.

Malchiodi, C. A. (ed.) (2004) *Expressive Therapies*. New York: Guilford Press.

Maslach, C. and Leiter, M. P. (1997). *The Truth about Burnout: How Organizations Cause Personal Stress and What to Do about It*. San Francisco, CA: Jossey-Bass.

McAdams, D. (2000) *The Person*, 3rd edn. New York: Harcourt.

McGoldrick, M. (1998) Belonging and liberation: finding a place called 'home'. In M. McGoldrick (ed.) *Re-visioning Family Therapy: Race, Culture and Gender in Clinical Practice*. New York: Guilford Press.

McLellan, J. (1991) Formal and informal counselling help: students' experiences. *British Journal of Guidance and Counselling*, 19: 149–58.

McLeod, J. (1990) The client's experience of counselling and psychotherapy: a review of the research literature. In D. Mearns and W. Dryden (eds) *Experiences of Counselling in Action*. London: Sage.

McLeod, J. (1997a) Listening to stories about health and illness: applying the lessons of narrative psychology. In I. Horton *et al.* (eds) *Counselling and Psychology for Health Professionals*. London: Sage.

McLeod, J. (1997b) *Narrative and Psychotherapy*. London: Sage.

McLeod, J. (1999) Counselling as a social process. *Counselling*, 10: 217–22.

McLeod, J. (2003) *An Introduction to Counselling*, 3rd edn. Buckingham: Open University Press.

McLeod, J. (2004a) The significance of narrative and storytelling in postpsychological counseling and psychotherapy. In A. Lieblich, D. McAdams and R. Josselson (eds) *Healing Plots: The Narrative Basis of Psychotherapy*. Washington, DC: American Psychological Association.

McLeod, J. (2004b) Social construction, narrative and psychotherapy. In L. Angus and J. McLeod (eds) *The Handbook of Narrative and Psychotherapy: Practice, Theory and Research*. Thousand Oaks, CA: Sage.

McLeod, J. (2005) Counseling and psychotherapy as cultural work. In L. T. Hoshmand (ed.) *Culture, Psychotherapy and Counseling: Critical and Integrative Perspectives*. Thousand Oaks, CA: Sage.

McMillan, D. W. (2006) *Emotion Rituals: A Resource for Therapists and Clients*. London: Routledge.

Mearns, D. (1997). *Person-centred Counselling Training*. London: Sage.

Mearns, D. and Cooper, M. (2005) *Working at Relational Depth in Counselling and Psychotherapy*. London: Sage.

Mearns, D. and Thorne, B. (1999) *Person-centred Counselling in Action*, 2nd edn. London: Sage.

Meichenbaum, D. (1994) *Treating Post-traumatic Stress Disorder: A Handbook and Practical Manual for Therapy*. Chichester: Wiley.

Mercer, S. W., Maxwell, M., Heaney, D. and Watt, G. C. M. (2004) The consultation and relational empathy (CARE) measure: development and preliminary validation and reliability of an empathy-based consultation process measure. *Family Practice*, 21: 699–705.

Mercer, S. W., McConnachie, A., Maxwell, M., Heaney, D. and Watt, G. C. M. (2005) Relevance and practical use of the consultation and relational empathy (CARE) measure in general practice. *Family Practice*, 22: 328–34.

Merry, T. (2002) *Learning and Being in Person-centred Counselling*, 2nd edn. Ross-on-Wye: PCCS Books.

Miller, G. (1969) Psychology as a means of promoting human welfare. *American Psychologist*, 24: 1063–75.

Miller, R. B. (2004) *Facing Human Suffering: Psychology and Psychotherapy as moral Engagement*. Washington, DC: American Psychological Association.

Miller, W. R. and Rollnick, S. (2002) *Motivational Interviewing: Preparing People for Change*, 2nd edn. New York: Guilford Press.

Milne, D. L. (1999) *Social Therapy: A Guide to Social Support Interventions for Mental Health Practitioners*. Chichester: Wiley.

Milne, D. L. and Mullin, M. (1987) Is a problem shared a problem shaved? An evaluation of hairdressers and social support. *British Journal of Clinical Psychology*, 26: 69–70.

Monk, G. and Sinclair, S. L. (2004) What's love got to do with it? Managing discursive positions and mediating conflict within a heterosexual love relationship. In T. Strong and D. Pare (eds) *Furthering Talk: Advances in the Discursive Therapies*. New York: Kluwer.

Morgan, A. (2001) *What is Narrative Therapy? An Easy-to-read Introduction*. Adelaide: Dulwich Centre.

Morrissette, P. J. (2004) *The Pain of Helping: Psychological Injury of Helping Professionals*. London: Routledge.

Morrow-Bradley, C. and Elliott, R. (1986) Utilization of psychotherapy research by practicing psychotherapists. *American Psychologist*, 41: 188–97.

Neenan, M. and Dryden, W. (2005) *Cognitive Therapy in a Nutshell*. London: Sage.

Neimeyer, R. A., Fortner, B. and Melby, D. (2001) Personal and professional factors and suicide intervention skills. *Suicide and Life-threatening Behavior*, 31: 71–82.

Newman, C. F. (2000) Hypotheticals in cognitive psychotherapy: creative questions, novel answers, and therapeutic change. *Journal of Cognitive Psychotherapy*, 14: 135–47.

Newnes, C., Holmes, G. and Dunn, C. (eds) (1999) *This is Madness: A Critical Look at Psychiatry and the Future of Mental Health Services*. Ross-on-Wye: PCCS Books.

Newnes, C., Holmes, G. and Dunn, C. (eds) (2000) *This is Madness Too: A Further Look at Psychiatry and the Future of Mental Health Services*. Ross-on-Wye: PCCS Books.

Norcross, J. C., Santrock, J. W., Campbell, L. F., Smith, T. P., Sommer, R. and Zuckerman, E. L. (2003) *Authoritative Guide to Self-help Resources in Mental Health*, rev. edn. New York: Guilford Press.

Oatley, K. and Jenkins, J. M. (1996) *Understanding Emotions*. Oxford: Blackwell.

O'Connell, B. (1998) *Solution-focused Therapy*. London: Sage.

Orford, J. (1992) *Community Psychology: Theory and Practice*. Chichester: Wiley.

Page, S. and Wosket, V. (2001) *Supervising the Counsellor: A Cyclical Model*, 2nd edn. Hove, Sussex: Brunner-Routledge.

Palmer, S. (ed.) (2001) *Multicultural Counselling: A Reader*. London: Sage.

Palmer S. (2002) Suicide reduction and prevention. *British Journal of Guidance and Counselling*, 30: 341–52.

Pedersen, P. (2000) *A Handbook for Developing Multicultural Awareness*, 3rd edn. Alexandria, VA: American Counseling Association.

Pennebaker, J. W. (1997) *Opening Up: The Healing Power of Expressing Emotions*, rev edn. New York: Guilford Press.

Peters, H. (1999) Pre-therapy: a client-centered/experiential approach to mentally handicapped people. *Journal of Humanistic Psychology*, 39: 8–29.

Pilnick, A. (2003) 'Patient counselling' by pharmacists: four approaches to the delivery of counselling sequences and their interactional reception. *Social Science and Medicine*, 56: 835–49.

Polkinghorne, D. E. (1992) Postmodern epistemology of practice. In S. Kvale (ed.) *Psychology and Postmodernism*. London: Sage.

Pope, K. S. (1991) Dual relationships in psychotherapy. *Ethics and Behavior*, 1: 21–34.

Prilleltensky, I. and Nelson, G. B. (2005) *Community Psychology: In Pursuit of Liberation and Well-being*. Basingstoke: Palgrave Macmillan.

Prochaska, J. O. and DiClemente, C. C. (2005) The transtheoretical approach. In J. C. Norcross and M. R. Goldfried (eds) *Handbook of Psychotherapy Integration*, 2nd edn. New York: Oxford University Press.

Prochaska, J. O., Norcross, J. C. and DiClemente, C. C. (1994) *Changing for Good*. New York: William Morrow.

Prouty, G. (2000) Pre-therapy and the pre-expressive self. In T. Merry (ed.) *The BAPCA Reader*. Hay-on-Wye: PCCS Books.

Prouty, G., Van Werde, D. and Portner, M. (2002) *Pre-therapy: Reaching Contact-impaired Clients*. Hay-on-Wye: PCCS Books.

Purton, C. (2005) *Person-centred Therapy: A Focusing-oriented Approach*. London: Sage.

Reeves, A., Bowl, R., Wheeler, S. and Guthrie, E. (2004) The hardest words: exploring the dialogue of suicide in the counselling process – a discourse analysis. *Counselling and Psychotherapy Research*, 4: 62–71.

Reid, M. (ed.) (2004) *Counselling in Different Settings: The Reality of Practice*. London: Palgrave.

Rennie, D. L. (1994) Clients' deference in psychotherapy. *Journal of Counseling Psychology*, 41: 427–37.

Rennie, D. L. (1998) *Person-centred Counselling: An Experiential Approach*. London: Sage.

Rodriguez, M. A., Quiroga, S. S. and Bauer, H. H. (1996) Breaking the silence: battered women's perspectives on medical care. *Archives of Family Medicine*, 5: 153–8.

Rogers, C. R. (1961) *On Becoming a Person*. London: Constable.

Rogers, N. (2000) *The Creative Connection: Expressive Arts as Healing*. Ross-on-Wye: PCCS Books.

Romme, M. and Escher, S. (2000) *Making Sense of Voices: A Guide for Mental Health Professionals Working with Voice Hearers*. London: Mind Publications.

Ronan, K. R. and Kazantis, N. (2006) The use of between-session (homework) activities in psychotherapy. *Journal of Psychotherapy Integration*, 16: 254–9.

Ronnestad, M. H. and Skovholt, T. M. (2001) Learning arena for professional development: retrospective accounts of senior psychotherapists. *Professional Psychology: Research and Practice*, 32: 181–7.

Russell, R. L. (2004) Curative factors in underlying structures of therapeutic discourse: toward a discourse analysis of common factors. Paper presented at the Society for Psychotherapy Research International Conference, Rome, June 2004.

Sabat, S. R. (2001) *The Experience of Alzheimer's Disease: Life Through a Tangled Veil*. Oxford: Blackwell.

Safran, J. D. (1993) Breaches in the therapeutic alliance: an arena for negotiating authentic relatedness. *Psychotherapy*, 30: 11–24.

Safran, J. D. and Muran, J. C. (2000) Resolving therapeutic alliance ruptures: diversity and integration. *In Session: Psychotherapy in Practice*, 56: 233–43.

Scheel, M. J., Seaman, S., Roach, K., Mullin, T. and Mahoney, K. B. (1999) Client implementation of therapist recommendations predicted by client perception of fit, difficulty of implementation, and therapist influence. *Journal of Counseling Psychology*, 46: 308–16.

Scheel, M. J., Hanson, W. E. and Razzhavaikina, T. I. (2004) The process of recommending homework in psychotherapy: a review of therapist delivery methods, client acceptability, and factors that affect compliance. *Psychotherapy: Theory, Research, Practice, Training*, 41: 38–55.

Schoenberg, M. and Shiloh, S. (2002) Hospitalized patients' views on in-ward psychological counseling. *Patient Education and Counseling*, 48: 123–9.

Schut, H. A., Stroebe, M. S., Van den Bout, J. and de Keijser, J. (1997) Interventions for the bereaved: gender differences in the efficacy of two counselling programmes. *British Journal of Clinical Psychology*, 36: 63–72.

Schut, M. and Stroebe, M. (2005) Interventions to enhance adaptation to bereavement. *Journal of Palliative Medicine*, 8: 140–7.

Scott, M. J. and Stradling, S. G. (2006) *Counselling for Post-traumatic Stress Disorder*, 3rd edn. London: Sage.

Seiser, L. and Wastell, C. (2002) *Interventions and Techniques*. Buckingham: Open University Press.

Sennett, R. (1998) *Corrosion of Character: The Personal Consequences of Work in the New Capitalism*. New York: Norton.

Shoaib, K. and Peel, J. (2003) Kashmiri women's perceptions of their emotional and psychological needs, and access to counselling. *Counselling and Psychotherapy Research*, 3: 87–94.

Silove, D. and Manicavasagar, V. (1997) *Overcoming Panic: A Self-help Guide using Cognitive Behavioural Techniques*. London: Constable & Robinson.

Silverstone, L. (1997) *Art Therapy: The Person-centred Way*, 2nd edn. London: Jessica Kingsley.

Skovholt, T. M. and Jennings, L. (2004) *Master Therapists: Exploring Expertise in Therapy and Counseling*. New York: Allyn & Bacon.

Stadler, H. A. (1986) Making hard choices: clarifying controversial ethical issues. *Counseling and Human Development*, 19: 1–10.

Stein, T., Frankel, R. M. and Krupat, E. (2005) Enhancing clinician communication skills in a large healthcare organization: a longtitudinal case study. *Patient Education and Counseling*, 58: 4–12.

Stewart, I. and Joines, V. (1987) *TA Today: A New Introduction to Transactional Analysis*. Nottingham: Lifespace Publishing.

Stokes, A. (2001) Settings. In S. Aldridge and S. Rigby (eds) *Counselling Skills in Context*. London: Hodder & Stoughton.

Stroebe, M. S. and Schut, H. W. (1999) The dual process model of coping with bereavement: rationale and description. *Death Studies*, 23: 197–224.

Stroebe, W., Schut, H. and Stroebe, M. (2005) Grief work, disclosure and counselling: do they help the bereaved? *Clinical Psychology Review*, 25: 395–414.

Sugarman, L. (2003) Life transitions. In R. Woolfe, W. Dryden and S. Strawbridge (eds) *Handbook of Counselling Psychology*, 2nd edn. London: Sage.

Sugarman, L. (2004) *Counselling and the Life Course*. London: Sage.

Syme, G. (2003) *Dual Relationships in Counselling and Psychotherapy*. London: Sage.

Talmon, S. (1990) *Single Session Therapy: Maximizing the Effect of the First (and often only) Therapeutic Encounter*. San Franciso: Jossey-Bass.

Tolan, J. (2003) *Skills in Person-centred Counselling and Therapy*. London: Sage.

Trower, P. (1988) *Cognitive-behavioural Counselling in Action*. London: Sage.

Trower, P., Bryant, B. and Argyle, M. (1978) *Social Skills and Mental Health*. London: Methuen.

Twentyman, C. T. and McFall, R. M. (1975) Behavioral training of social skills in shy males. *Journal of Consulting and Clinical Psychology*, 43: 384–95.

Vanaerschot, G. (1993) Empathy as releasing several micro-processes in the client. In D. Brazier (ed.) *Beyond Carl Rogers*. London: Constable.

Walter, T. (1999) *On Bereavement: The Culture of Grief*. Buckingham: Open University Press.

Warren, B. (ed.) (1993) *Using the Creative Arts in Therapy*, 2nd edn. London: Routledge.

Weaks, D. (2002) Unlocking the secrets of 'good' supervision. *Counselling and Psychotherapy Research*, 2: 33–9.

Weaks, D., McLeod, J. and Wilkinson, H. (2006) Dementia. *Therapy Today*, 17: 12–15.

Weiser, J. (1999) *PhotoTherapy Techniques: Exploring the Secrets of Personal Snapshots and Family Albums*, 2nd edn. Vancouver, BC: PhotoTherapy Centre Press.

White, M. and Epston, D. (1990) *Narrative Means to Therapeutic Ends*. New York: Norton.

Wiener, D. (2001) *Beyond Talk Therapy: Using Movement and Expressive Technique in Clinical Practice*. Washington, DC: American Psychological Association.

Williams, G. (1984) The genesis of chronic illness: narrative re-construction. *Sociology of Health and Illness*, 6: 175–200.

Williams, M. (1997) *Cry of Pain: Understanding Suicide and Self-harm*. London: Penguin.

Willi, J. (1999) *Ecological Psychotherapy: Developing by Shaping the Personal Niche*. Seattle, WA: Hogreve & Huber.

Wills, F. (1997) *Cognitive Therapy*. London: Sage.

Winslade, J. M. (2005) Utilising discursive positioning in counselling. *British Journal of Guidance and Counselling*, 33: 351–64.

Worden, W. (2001) *Grief Counselling and Grief Therapy: A Handbook for the Mental Health Practitioner*. London: Brunner-Routledge.

Yalom, I. (2002) *The Gift of Therapy: Reflections on Being a Therapist*. London: Piatkus.

Index

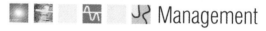